The Muslim Empires of the Ottomans, Safavids, and Mughals

Between 1453 and 1526 Muslims founded three major states in the Mediterranean, Iran, and South Asia: respectively the Ottoman, Safavid, and Mughal empires. By the early seventeenth century their descendants controlled territories that encompassed much of the Muslim world, stretching from the Balkans and North Africa to the Bay of Bengal and including a combined population of between 130 and 160 million people. This book is the first comparative study of the politics, religion, and culture of these three empires between 1300 and 1923. At the heart of the analysis is Islam, and how it influenced the political and military structures, the economy, language, literature, and religious traditions of these great empires. This original and sophisticated study provides an antidote to a common simplistic view of Muslim societies by illustrating the complexity, humanity, and vitality of these empires, empires that cannot be reduced simply to religious doctrine.

STEPHEN F. DALE is a Professor in the Department of History at Ohio State University. His previous publications include *Indian Merchants and Eurasian Trade 1600–1750* (Cambridge, 1994) and *The Garden of the Eight Paradises: Babur and the Culture of Empire in Central Asia, Afghanistan and India 1483–1530* (2004).

D1554324

This dynamic new series publishes books on the milestones in Asian history, those that have come to define particular periods or to mark turning points in the political, cultural, and social evolution of the region. The books in this series are intended as introductions for students to be used in the classroom. They are written by scholars whose credentials are well established in their particular fields and who have, in many cases, taught the subject across a number of years.

Books in the Series

The Muslim Empires of the Ottomans, Safavids, and Mughals

Stephen Frederic Dale

Ohio State University

CAMBRIDGE
UNIVERSITY PRESS

CAMBRIDGE
UNIVERSITY PRESS

32 Avenue of the Americas, New York NY 10013-2473, USA

Cambridge University Press is part of the University of Cambridge.

It furthers the University's mission by disseminating knowledge in the pursuit of
education, learning, and research at the highest international levels of excellence.

www.cambridge.org
Information on this title: www.cambridge.org/9780521691420

© Cambridge University Press 2010

First published 2010
7th printing 2013

A catalog record for this publication is available from the British Library.

ISBN 978-0-521-87095-5 Hardback
ISBN 978-0-521-69142-0 Paperback

For Roderic Maurice Kauai Dale
husband, father, brother, scientist, gentleman

Contents

Illustrations

Maps

Preface

Marigold Acland of Cambridge University Press commissioned this book and, like dozens of other scholars, I deeply appreciate both her encouragement and her sympathetic interest in and sophisticated knowledge of Islamic studies. The book was written during a wonderful leave year funded by a research fellowship from the National Endowment of the Humanities in Washington, DC, supported by matching funds from the Ohio State University.

I have benefited from the work of so many scholars in so many disciplines that it is impossible to credit them all. My intellectual debts will be obvious from the footnotes and bibliography, but beyond those citations, I want to particularly acknowledge Cornell Fleischer, who introduced me to both Turkish and Ottoman history; my own colleagues in Ottoman studies, Carter Findley and Jane Hathaway; Gülru Necipoğlu for her cultural studies of Ottoman architectural history; and Suraiya Faroqhi for her many works on Ottoman social history. Hamid Algar introduced me to Persian and modern Iranian history and John Masson Smith Jr. taught me the use of documents and coins for pre-modern Iranian and Middle Eastern history. In addition I am particularly indebted to Rudi Matthee for his publications on the Safavids and to Paul Losensky for his revealing studies of Persian poetry of the Safavid and Mughal eras. I first studied Indian history with Eugene F. Irschick, and began my studies of Mughal history with the work of the late John Richards. I have also benefited from the work of Muzaffar Alam and an entire galaxy of Indian historians who have produced seminal scholarship on the Mughal period, especially Tapan Raychaudhuri, Irfan Habib, Athar Ali, and the scholar of Indo-Persian literature, Abdu'l Ghani. Amina Okada's studies of Mughal art have also shaped the way in which I look at the paintings of the imperial atelier.

Three scholars took the time to read and critique this book in manuscript form, and they will recognize that many of their valuable suggestions are integrated into the final text. They are Catharine Asher, the historian of Mughal architectural history; Gene Garthwaite, a specialist on the Bakhtiyari nomads and the history of modern Iran; and Ruby Lal, who is known for her study of women in early Mughal history. The book is substantially better for their help.

My thanks go to three institutions for permission to quote from copyright material. They are: Princeton University Press, for Cornell H. Fleischer, *Bureaucrat and Intellectual in the Ottoman Empire: The Historian Mustafa Ali (1541–1600)* (1986); the University of Washington Press, for a book whose rights they now own, namely *Ottoman Lyric Poetry*, ed. and trans. Walter G. Andrews, Najaat Black, and Mehmet Kalpakli (Austin: University of Texas Press, 1997); and Mazda Press, for Paul E. Losensky, *Welcoming Fighani: Imitation and Poetic Individuality in the Safavid-Mughal Ghazal* (Costa Mesa, CA: Mazda, 1998).

I have dedicated this book to my late brother, Roderic M. K. Dale.

Languages and transliteration

Languages

Three principal languages were used in the Ottoman, Safavid, and Mughal empires. These were: first, the Semitic language Arabic, the native language of ethnic Arabs as well as religious and scientific language of the Islamic world; secondly, the Indo-European language Persian, the native language of ethnic Iranians, the lingua franca of educated Muslims in Anatolia, Central Asia, and northern and central India, and the prestigious literary language of Muslims in all three empires; thirdly, Turkish, one of a larger family of some thirty-four related languages, sometimes labeled, controversially, as Altaic languages. All three languages were written in the Arabic script, but the use of this script for Persian led to the creation of new letters to reflect Persian pronunciation. This script was particularly ill suited to Turkic languages, including Ottoman, so that some letters in Ottoman or other Turkic dialects have different values from those they have in Persian or Arabic.

Transliteration

Generally Arabic, Persian, and Turkish words have been spelled in accordance with the system used by the *International Journal of Middle East Studies*. However, some exceptions have been made for commonly accepted usages, such as "Mughal" for "Mughul," "Abu'l Fazl," the name of the Mughal minister, instead of "Abu'l-Fadl," and a few others. Such usages partly reflect customary pronunciations, and the pronunciation of all three languages, belonging as they do to three major language families, is distinctly different. To take just one simple example, the common name for a Muslim religious judge is usually written, reflecting its original Arabic pronunciation, as *qadi*. In Turkish, as will be seen, it is usually written, in the Latin script adopted in the Turkish Republic, as *kadi*, while in Persian the word is often written, as it is pronounced, *qazi*. And in both

Turkish and Persian the "a" of *qadi* is sounded differently than in Arabic. Speakers of each language have even modified the pronunciation of religious terminology. Readers familiar with one or more of these languages will supply their own pronunciations. Others need not be concerned, as it is the meaning of the terminology, as explained in the text or listed in the Glossary, which is most important.

Introduction

Between 1453 and 1526 Muslims founded three major states in the Mediterranean, Iran, and South Asia: respectively the Ottoman, Safavid, and Mughal empires. By the early seventeenth century their descendants controlled territories that encompassed much of the Muslim world, stretching from the Balkans and North Africa to the Bay of Bengal and including a combined population of between 130 and 160 million people. By that time also members of these dynasties had demonstrated their palpable self-confidence by constructing many of the fortresses, mosques, bazaars, and tombs that still stand as emblems of their military strength, wealth, sovereign pride, religious commitment, and aesthetic sophistication. Their record of stunning architectural achievement climaxed when in 1643 the Mughal emperor Shah Jahan completed the last exceptional building of this Muslim imperial era, the Taj Mahal.[1] Muslims and non-Muslims alike look back to the history of these states as collectively representing the last great moment of Muslim sovereignty. It is a world that Muslims lost in the eighteenth, nineteenth, and twentieth centuries. Many twenty-first-century Muslims are still profoundly saddened when they contemplate this imperial past and compare it with the community's loss of power, wealth, influence, and cultural splendor in the contemporary world.

These empires are significant because of what they represented and achieved, and because their complexity reminds us that Muslim civilization, like the predominantly Christian European civilization, cannot be equated solely with rigid, narrowly doctrinal interpretations of the faith. In the memoirs and monuments of kings, in the lyrics of poets, in the luminous paintings of artists, a world is revealed in the history and culture of these empires that is scarcely to be imagined by contemporary Middle Eastern Muslims or by Western observers familiar only with the

---

[1] Begun in 1632, the tomb complex was largely completed in 1643, but work on its decoration continued until 1647/48. Ebba Koch, *The Complete Taj Mahal* (New York: Thames and Hudson, 2006), 97–100.

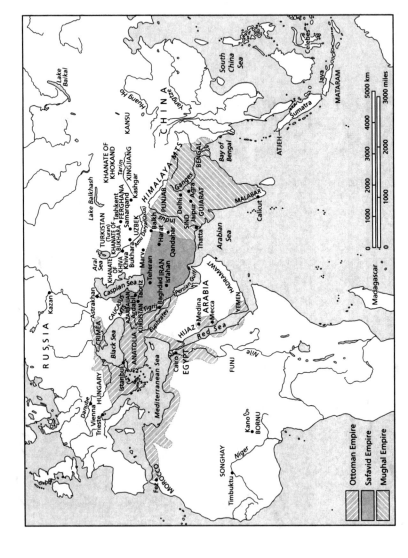

Map 1. The Muslim Empires in 1700

crabbed views of narrow-minded clerics or the simplistic distortions of their own popular media.

The Ottoman, Safavid, and Mughal empires are also important as a group because they, like the diverse but related states of Western Europe, comprised an imperial cultural zone within the broader Islamic civilization, which included parts of Southeast Asia and sub-Saharan Africa. Muslims in these contiguous empires jointly inherited political, religious, literary, and artistic traditions, and their shared inheritance was reinforced by the circulation of individuals along well-established and protected trade routes linking Istanbul with Isfahan and Delhi.[2] Merchants, poets, artists, scholars, religious vagabonds, military advisors, and philosophers all moved with relative ease along these caravan routes and across political boundaries.

While the history of these empires illumines a shared, complex culture, it also serves as a reminder that Muslim empires were not just Muslim but also empires. This means several things. First, Islam played an important but not always a dominant role in their policies, institutions, and court culture. The Ottoman, Safavid, and Mughal states are characterized here as Muslim empires because they were ruled by Muslim dynasties, whose individual monarchs embraced Muhammad's revelation and, to varying degrees, observed the tenets of the Islamic faith.[3] They patronized Islamic religious and social institutions, driven by either genuine piety or enlightened self-interest or by differing combinations of these motives. In this they were no different from rulers in Europe or in Asia; they were complex and distinct individuals, not stereotypes of twenty-first-century religious debates.

Some monarchs were especially pious and attempted to impose their vision of an imagined Quranic society on their subjects, but Ottomans, Safavids, and Mughals were also, like contemporary European Christian monarchs, dynastic rulers, whose first and last concern was the security, prosperity, and longevity of their lineages. Most members of these dynasties followed policies and established institutions primarily in order to perpetuate dynastic rule rather than to please God or their religious classes, although many felt formal piety and religious patronage to be inseparably linked to political survival. This rankled with some of their subjects, especially clerics, many of whom believed and sometimes openly asserted that

---

[2] An important article that notes these empires' analogous political institutions and common commercial traditions, while carefully delineating their shared religious knowledge, is Francis Robinson's, "Ottomans–Safavids–Mughals: Shared Knowledge and Connective Systems," *Journal of Islamic Studies* 8, No. 2 (1997), 151–84.

[3] Iqtidar Alam Khan dissents from this characterization of the Mughals and prefers to characterize their state as "Indian" rather than "Muslim": "State in Mughal India: Re-Examining the Myths of a Counter-Vision," *Social Scientist* 29, No. 1/2 (January–February 2001), 16–45.

imperial administrative codes were incompatible with religious law derived from the Quran and the traditions of the Prophet Muhammad.[4]

Many of these men or their advisors were also acutely conscious of pre-Islamic Iranian, Roman, and Turco-Mongol imperial traditions that bequeathed legitimizing concepts and prestigious precedents for the administration of diverse populations in far-flung territories. Thus, members of all three dynasties invoked pre-Islamic imperial Iranian nomenclature such as *shah, padishah* or *shahanshah*, as well as manipulating ideas of kingship derived from the pre-Islamic Iranian dynasty, the Sasanians (226–651 CE). Ottomans also reveled in the title *Kaysar* or *Caesar* after they occupied Constantinople (between 330 and 1453 CE the capital of the Byzantine or Eastern Roman Empire), and it is difficult to overestimate the influence that the possession of the city had on the Ottomans' sense of themselves as heirs to a grand imperial tradition, now possessed by Turkish Muslims. Descent from the Central Asian rulers, Chinggis Qan and Temür, legitimized the Mughals, and originally Central Asian Turkic traditions comprised a common heritage of rulers in all three empires. Most Ottoman, Safavid, and Mughal monarchs also patronized common literary and artistic cultures that were at least partly secular, and which especially pious individuals sometimes criticized for that reason.

The word "empire" also implies in this case, as in other periods and civilizations, that these Muslim monarchs ruled extensive territories with diverse populations. In the case of these empires this diversity involved different ethnicities, social groups, and religious communities: most prominently Turks, Iranians, Indians, and Arabs; agriculturalists, landed elites, nomads, clerics, merchants, and urban artisans, and Muslims and Christians of various ethnicities, social identities, and professions as well as Jews, Indians of many religious persuasions, and Zoroastrians, who might be Iranian or Indian.

The question of religious identity was especially important in states where rulers were Muslims who patronized Muslim clerics, whom the Mughal emperor, Jahangir (r. 1605–27), referred to as the "army of prayer."[5] There were both internal doctrinal differences within the Islamic world and also large non-Muslim populations in each of these states. Within the Islamic world and in these three empires, doctrinal and/or sectarian differences sometimes coincided with political, ethnic, or social divisions. The most

---

[4] See especially Cornell H. Fleischer's discussion of "Muslim and Ottoman" in his seminal work *Bureaucrat and Intellectual in the Ottoman Empire: The Historian Mustafa Âli (1541–1600)* (Princeton University Press, 1986), 253–72.

[5] Jahangir, *Tūzuk-i-Jahângîrî* or *Memoirs of Jahângîr*, trans. Alexander Rogers and ed. Henry Beveridge (New Delhi: Munshiram Manoharlal, repr. 1978), 10.

obvious instance was the distinction between Sunnis and Shi'as, which had both theological and political dimensions, as was illustrated by the hostility between the Sunni Ottomans and the Shi'i Safavids of Iran. There was also a divide within both Sunni and Shi'i communities between government-sanctioned or approved, emotionally restrained orthodoxy and popular, sometimes ecstatic or even socially disruptive millenarian beliefs of different social groups within the population.

Apart from Muslim doctrinal and sectarian divisions, all three empires also included substantial and diverse non-Muslim populations, whose presence Muslim rulers tolerated or welcomed for a number of practical and sometimes personal reasons. As a Eurasian state, the Ottoman Empire included a Christian population of various denominations, and it also welcomed Jews expelled by the intolerant Catholic monarchs of Christian Spain. Prior to its conquest of Egypt, the Empire was numerically more Christian than Muslim. Iran also contained substantial Christian minorities, as well as Hindus, Zoroastrians, and Jews, and the Mughals always ruled over a predominantly non-Muslim population, composed primarily of Hindus, but which also included other religious communities too numerous to mention. Members of the non-Muslim communities participated in the imperial rule of all three Muslim dynasties in a variety of important political and economic roles, as imperial aristocrats, as slaves, as influential wives, or as merchants.

The Ottoman, Safavid, and Mughal states, here designated as Muslim empires, have also been characterized in several other ways, some more useful than others. Three of the most common labels, also meant to be explanatory categories, are "patrimonial-bureaucratic," "gunpowder" and "early modern." "Patrimonial-bureaucratic" is the most useful of these, because it describes a real and important functional aspect of all three states at various times in their histories. All three dynasties, that is, operated as governments that involved both elements of Max Weber's idealized categories of personal and impersonal or bureaucratic rule.[6] The Ottomans notably evolved from a patrimonial state early in their history into a centralized, highly bureaucratic slave empire after conquering Constantinople. The Safavid and Mughal dynasties displayed both characteristics during their histories, with the Safavids the least bureaucratic and centralized, while the Mughals occupied a middle position on Weber's theoretical spectrum, possessing an elaborate bureaucracy, but always retaining a high degree of personal rule.

---

[6] Based on Max Weber's distinction but elaborated for the Muslim imperial case by Stephen P. Blake, "The Patrimonial-Bureaucratic Empire of the Mughals," *Journal of Asian Studies* 39, No. 1 (November 1979), 77–94.

As for "gunpowder" and "early modern," terms which might be seen as two sides of the same Western European coin,[7] neither term is easily applicable to all three empires, nor does it explain much about the nature of these states or the organization of their societies. Firearms, both artillery and guns, were a critical factor in Ottoman victories over Europeans and non-Europeans alike, but they did not play a significant role in the establishment of the Safavid or Mughal states, although members of these Iranian and Indian dynasties successfully employed them to varying degrees in later campaigns. The suggestive idea that firearms triggered fundamental changes in the organization of a particular Muslim empire is often alluded to but rarely demonstrated in a systematic fashion, and has not yet been applied to these three states. The "gunpowder empire" label is particularly questionable for the Safavids, who never really warmed to the use of heavy artillery.

The term "early modern" is even more problematic, for it involves tortured debates over the criteria of modernity at any given moment and is often evoked in a casual fashion rather than being rigorously employed to explain the nature of states. Many of the factors cited to illustrate "early" modernity – long-distance Asian or Eurasian trade, commercial capitalism, centralization, or rationality – can also be found in earlier empires, whether Roman, pre-Islamic Iranian or Mongol.[8] "Early modern" is a particularly difficult term to deploy as a concept to categorize or explain more than six centuries of Ottoman rule. Were the Ottomans "early modern" before they captured Constantinople in 1453 or during their sixteenth-century "golden age" or in 1800?

More important than controversial labels is the issue of the rise and fall of empires. Ibn Khaldun (d. 1406), the Greco-Islamic philosophical historian, was the most important Muslim theorist of dynastic states, utilizing an analytical method he derived primarily from Aristotle's logical writings known collectively as the *Organon*.[9] Ibn Khaldun was preoccupied with the problem of explaining the cyclical history of the dynasties of

---

[7] William H. McNeill summarized this concept in his pamphlet, *The Age of Gunpowder Empires 1450–1800* (Washington D.C.: American Historical Association, 1989). For one of the more stimulating discussions of "early modern" history as a definable period see Joseph F. Fletcher, "Integrative History: Parallels and Interconnections in the Early Modern Period 1500–1800," in Beatrice Manz, ed., *Studies on Chinese and Islamic Central Asia: Collected Articles of Joseph Fletcher* (Aldershot: Variorum, 1995), 1–35.

[8] See especially Jack Goldstone, "The Problem of the Early Modern World," *Journal of the Economic and Social History of the Orient* 41, No. 3 (1998), 249–84, and Peter Van Der Veer, "The Global History of Modernity," *Journal of the Economic and Social History of the Orient* 41, No. 3 (1998), 285–94.

[9] In his remarkable work *The Muqaddimah*, Ibn Khaldun offers an analytical methodology for historical study and, using that methodology, proposes an explanation for the chaotic, cyclic history of tribal dynasties in North Africa and Spain. See *The Muqaddimah*, trans. and ed. Franz Rosenthal (Princeton University Press, 1980), 3 vols. See also Muhsin

nomadic origin that ruled North Africa and Spain in his era. Yet his dismissal of the significance of transient political and military events in understanding historical change, and his conviction that historical change could only be understood by studying underlying social, psychological and political factors, raise fundamental questions about the fate of the Ottoman, Safavid, and Mughal empires. In the present book, the chapters devoted to political history focus on individual rulers as a stylistic device to introduce important lineaments of complex dynastic histories in a limited number of pages. This emphasis is not meant to suggest that Ottoman, Safavid, or Mughal monarchs were autonomous individuals who always controlled their own destiny and that of their empires. Individual rulers' intelligence and dynamism were often critical in establishing and shaping the character of empires. Yet not only was Ibn Khaldun prescient in understanding that the social and political environment and psychology of later members of a dynasty inevitably differed from that of their ancestors: in addition, he realised that both founders of empires and their descendants were subject to a variety of social, political, and economic forces beyond their control.

This is a short history of culturally related and commercially linked imperial entities from their foundation, through the height of their power, economic influence and artistic creativity and then to their dissolution. It focuses on monarchs and the aristocratic elite – men whose distinct subculture exhibited the same seemingly dissonant elements as typified their Italian near-contemporaries, the Medici, or the ruling classes of many other societies: ruthless brutality, self-indulgence, and aesthetic sophistication.[10] It necessarily ignores or gives short shrift to a variety of topics, most particularly the daily life of non-aristocratic urban and rural Muslim families, their religious rituals and social life, and their relatively short lives, truncated by poverty, disease, and war. Women and members of non-Muslim communities also receive relatively little attention, although both exerted formidable influence in their societies. Royal women are particularly visible in the histories of these dynasties for their political influence, both inside and beyond the confines of the *haram*, especially as wealthy patrons of religious and charitable institutions. Many of these women, particularly Safavid and Mughal royalty, were also well

Mahdi, *Ibn Khaldun's Philosophy of History* (London: George Allen and Unwin, 1957) and Stephen Frederic Dale, "Ibn Khaldun, the Last Greek and First Annaliste Historian," *International Journal of Middle East Studies* 38 (2006), 431–51.

[10] One of a Muslim ruler's most explicit assertions that indulgence was a perquisite of kingship is included in the memoir of the eleventh-century Berber Amir of Granada, Ibn Buluggin, who wrote, rhetorically, when defending his indulgence of young boys at court, "is not kingship or wealth intended for enjoyment and adornment?" *The Tibyân*, ed. and trans. Amin T. Tibi (Leiden: Brill: 1986), 192.

educated and wrote religious treatises or poetry. Members of non-Muslim communities also receive relatively little attention, except for their critical commercial functions in all three states and their administrative, political, and military role in the Mughal Empire, where some Hindus became imperial aristocrats.[11] Finally, limitations of space have made it impossible to do justice to the full range of architecture in these empires or to discuss gardens. The architectural focus here is on mosques and tombs, omitting any sustained discussion of fortresses, palaces, bazaars, or even, in the Mughal case, new cities. And gardens, which had such social and cultural importance in the royal and aristocratic life of all three empires, are only mentioned in passing.

The sources for these and other subjects also vary tremendously. Ottoman records of their elaborate, centralized bureaucracy have been preserved in Istanbul, a city last besieged and plundered in 1453, whereas most Safavid and Mughal administrative documents were destroyed during the political turmoil, recurring warfare, and destruction which occurred in the eighteenth and nineteenth centuries. Similarly, many more local court records survived the disintegration of the Ottoman state than have been preserved in Iran and India; in the latter case the semi-tropical climate is partly responsible for their disintegration. Such legal documents have preserved the voices not only of women but also of otherwise unknown farmers and merchants. The Mughals, in contrast, produced an especially rich autobiographical and historical literature, which offers unusual insight into individual character and motivation of both men and women, while in Iran, the religious debates of Shi'i scholars generated an extensive corpus of essays and tracts that illumine the country's clerical attitudes and its organization. The following chapters inevitably reflect the nature of the extant sources available for the study of each empire.

A community of outstanding scholars in Turkey, Iran, India, and the West have used both imperial and local records, travel accounts and

---

[11]   Three important studies of Ottoman, Iranian, and Mughal women are: Leslie Peirce, *The Imperial Haram: Women and Sovereignty in the Ottoman Empire* (New York: Oxford University Press, 1993); Guity Nashat and Lois Beck, *Women in Iran from the Rise of Islam to 1800* (Urbana, Illinois: University of Illinois Press, 2003); and Ruby Lal, *Domesticity and Power in the Early Mughal World* (Cambridge University Press, 2005). Religious minorities in each of these states are discussed in Suraiya N. Faroqhi, ed., *The Cambridge History of Islam*, III, *The Later Ottoman Empire 1603–1839* (Cambridge University Press, 2006); Aptin Khanbaghi, *The Fire, the Stone and the Cross: Minority Religions in Medieval and Early Modern Iran* (London: I.B. Tauris, 2006), and Father Pierre du Jarric, S.J., *Akbar and the Jesuits: An Account of the Jesuit Missions to the Court of Akbar* (London: Routledge, 1926). See also Suad Joseph *et al.*, *The Encyclopaedia of Women in Islamic Cultures* (Leiden: Brill, 2003–6).

memoirs, religious treatises, poetry, and art to produce the articles and books which constitute the intellectual basis for this synthesis. Cited in footnotes throughout this volume, they individually represent guides for future study, though any such study should begin with an examination of contributions to two outstanding encyclopedias available for students of Islamic history and the history of these particular empires: *The Encyclopaedia of Islam* and *The Encyclopaedia Iranica*. *The Encyclopaedia of Islam* contains articles on all aspects of Islamic faith, society, and history, and it is particularly strong on Ottoman history, while the still incomplete *Encyclopaedia Iranica* is a superb source, not only for pre-Islamic and Islamic Iran, but also for Indo-Persian history, including the Mughal Empire. The forthcoming multi-volume *The New Cambridge History of Islam* (2010) also contains a wealth of chronological and thematic essays on these empires and broader Islamic civilization.

1 India, Iran, and Anatolia from the tenth to the sixteenth century

Introduction

Founders of the Ottoman, Safavid, and Mughal empires established their states in territories long characterized by political fragmentation, religious distinctions, the flowering of Greco-Islamic philosophy, the pervasive influence of Iranian administrative traditions and cultural norms, and Turco-Mongol military dominance. It is impossible to comprehend either the continuity or the novelty of these three empires without both being aware of these legacies and also understanding how they affected the histories of northern India, Iran, and Anatolia in the centuries prior to the founding of the Ottoman state in the early fourteenth century and the Safavid and Mughal states two centuries later.

The decline and eventual destruction of the 'Abbasid Caliphate (750–1258) was the first of two fundamental, interrelated changes that altered the political landscape of these contiguous regions between the tenth and sixteenth centuries.[1] In the eighth century, Muslim rulers governed a vast multi-ethnic, religiously diverse empire stretching from Spain to Central Asia; by the tenth century 'Abbasid Caliphs had lost control of Baghdad, their capital, as well as more distant Muslim-ruled territories. While the 'Abbasids retained their status as the legitimate leaders of the Sunni Muslim world, in the mid-tenth century the Buyids (r. 945–1055), a Shi'i dynasty from northern Iran, occupied Baghdad and its adjacent territories, while independent Muslim dynasts, usually known as sultans, controlled most of the former provinces of the Caliphate.[2]

---

[1] Ira Lapidus provides a comprehensive political and religious history of the Islamic world in *A History of Islamic Societies* (Cambridge University Press, 2nd edn. 2002).

[2] By the early tenth century this process was far enough advanced to stimulate Muslim scholars to produce political theories rationalizing the decline of the Caliphate and justifying the rule of independent Muslim sultans. One such individual, al-Mawardi (d. 1052) argued for the necessity of what already existed in the persons of Ghaznavid sultans of Afghanistan and Iran and other regional Muslim rulers. See Erwin J. Rosenthal, *Political Thought in Medieval Islam* (Cambridge University Press, 1968), 27–37 and 243, n. 62, where al-Mawardi is quoted as codifying the process by which Caliphs legitimized rulers like Mahmud of Ghazna by formally investing them with authority.

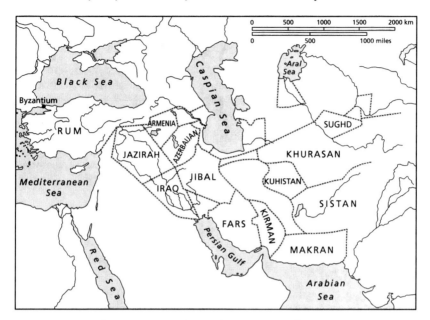

Map 2. The eastern provinces of the 'Abbasid Caliphate

This political fragmentation is the second major political fact of the era. Sultans, an evocative term derived from the Arabic root signifying power, derived their authority solely from military prowess, lacking the legitimacy of the Caliphs as the hereditary political leaders of the Muslim *umma* or community. Nonetheless, the sanctity and prestige of the Caliphs' titular Islamic sovereignty prompted most of these regional sultans to seek legitimacy by portraying themselves as agents of the 'Abbasids, petitioning for investiture by the reigning Caliph and demonstrating their loyalty and commitment to the greater Islamic cause by including his name on their coins. As self-proclaimed servants of the Caliphs, sultans usually characterized their wars against non-Muslims in ideological terms, either as *ghazas*, heroic warfare on the Muslim frontiers, or as *jihads*, strivings or campaigns to expand the *dar al-Islam*, the zone of Muslim sovereignty. In Anatolia, Iran, and India most of these independent local rulers were Turks, although Iranians and Afghans also formed dynasties in these regions.

During these centuries the Islamic world was also characterized by religious complexity: two major sectarian divisions of Sunnis and Shi'as, doctrinal differences within both Sunni and Shi'i communities, and distinctly different attitudes toward salvation and the relative importance of orthodox practice and individual piety. Sunnis comprised the majority of the Muslim population and the 'Abbasid Caliphs were Sunnis, as were most regional rulers. Sunnis ("traditionalists" in Arabic) recognized the legitimacy of the first four Caliphs, the "rightly guided" political successors to the Prophet Muhammad, and regarded these men and their successors – the Umayyad Caliphs of Damascus (661–750) and the 'Abbasid Caliphs of Baghdad – as guardians of the political integrity of the Muslim world. In Sunni Muslim eyes *khalifa*s or caliphs were ordinary mortals and emphatically not individuals who possessed unique religious status or divinely inspired insight. Sunni worshipers usually adhered to one of four Islamic legal schools – sometimes the source of sectarian tension, but these differences paled in comparison with the distinction between Sunnis and Shi'as.[3]

Shi'as were found in the Yemen, Lebanon, Iraq, and Iran and controlled some territories, most notably Egypt, where the militantly Shi'i Fatimid dynasty had held sway since the late tenth century CE and ruled until 1171. Fatimid sultans, like other Shi'as, did not recognize the legitimacy of the first three Caliphs, the 'Abbasids, or other Sunni rulers, since they held that only descendants of 'Ali, the Prophet Muhammad's first cousin and son-in-law and the fourth "rightly guided" Caliph, could be authentic leaders of the Muslim *umma*. Shi'as' belief in the sole legitimacy of 'Ali and his descendents, known as Imams, reflected their belief that 'Ali's bloodline inherited the unique ability to interpret the esoteric meaning of God's final revelation, the Quran. The most important issue dividing Shi'i Muslims was the question of the number of legitimate Imams, with most Shi'as eventually agreeing there were twelve, while Isma'ilis, such as the Fatimids, asserted there were only seven.[4]

Between the 'Abbasid collapse and the rise of the Ottoman, Safavid, and Mughal empires, a popular form of Islam, Sufism, spread throughout the Sunni and Shi'i Islamic world and profoundly influenced Ottoman, Safavid, and Mughal societies.[5] Supposedly named after the *suf*, a woolen shift worn by some of its early ascetic practitioners, Sufis taught a form of Islamic "protestantism." It was protestant in the sense that Sufis deemphasized traditional public worship in *masjid*s or mosques in favor of individual study with a religious teacher, a *pir* or *shaikh*, who could guide

---

[3] Noel J. Coulson surveys Islamic legal history in *A History of Islamic Law* (Edinburgh University Press, repr. 2006).

[4] Farhad Daftary discusses the most important medieval Isma'ili societies in Egypt, Syria, and Iran in *Ismailis in Medieval Muslim Societies* (London: I. B. Tauris, 2005).

[5] Of the many introductions to Sufism see William Chittick, *Sufism* (Oxford: One World Publications, 2000); Carl Ernst, *Teachings of Sufism* (Boston: Shambhala Publications, 1999); and Annemarie Schimmel, *Mystical Dimensions of Islam* (Chapel Hill: The University of North Carolina Press, 1975).

or inspire in them a passionate love for God, leading to spiritual union and personal salvation. This reciprocal love – of mankind for God and God for mankind – was the signature trait of Sufi worship. Many *pirs* or *shaikh*s offered their disciples a deeply satisfying piety they did not experience in mosque services, and Sufis' religiosity can be understood from their poems, which represent some of the most beautiful verses in the Islamic world. As many Sufis intended these poems to be sung, they collectively represent a kind of Muslim hymnal. Two of the most important Sufis, whose ideas and writings influenced Muslims in Anatolia, Iran, and India, were the Andalusian Muhammad Ibn al-'Arabi (1165–1240), generally known just as Ibn 'Arabi, and the Iranian Jalal al-Din Muhammad Rumi (1207–73). Ibn 'Arabi, also known as *al-shaikh al-akbar*, "the greatest master," was influential for his belief that God is the sole reality, summarized in the phrase *wahdat al-wujud*, "the unity of being," while Rumi was and is best known for his exquisite Persian-language devotional poetry.[6]

Some members of the clerical class – the theologians, mosque personnel, religious teachers and religious judges, collectively known as the *'ulama*, those 'learned' in Islamic knowledge and practice – were Sufis themselves. Many *'ulama*, however, viewed Sufism with distaste or even explicitly condemned it as un-Islamic, either because of the extraordinary veneration Sufis often showed to their teachers, which seemed to critics a form of polytheism, or simply because they used music in their devotions, which most *'ulama* held to be explicitly condemned in the Quran. In fact, the practice of individual Sufi orders ranged from conservative, restrained silent prayer to ecstatic, emotional song and dance. Yet despite orthodox criticism of various aspects of Sufism, this form of devotion spread rapidly throughout the Islamic world in the form of independent spiritual lineages or orders, many of whose leaders had close personal relationships with Muslim monarchs; it also exerted a powerful social and even political influence among both the rural and the urban Muslim populations. Sometimes, as in the Safavid case, these spiritual lineages evolved into political dynasties.

If many Muslim clerics were suspicious of or openly hostile to Sufism, most *'ulama* were also deeply opposed to philosophy that might, as in Christian Europe, implicitly or explicitly challenge the assumptions of revealed religion. Many Greek, Indian, and Iranian philosophical and scientific texts had been translated into Arabic during the reigns of the 'Abbasid Caliphs al-Mansur (r. 754–75), Harun al-Rashid (r. 786–809)

---

[6] For introductions to both men see William C. Chittick, *Ibn Arabi Heir to the Prophets* (Oxford: One World Publications, 2007) and Franklin Lewis, *Rumi Past and Present, East and West* (Oxford: One World Publications, 2005).

and al-Mansur's grandson, al-Ma'mun (r. 813–33). While medical and astronomical texts were often favored for their practical uses, many works of Plato, Aristotle, Galen, and others also were translated and Barmakids (Iranian ministers serving the 'Abbasids) were particularly influential in this effort.

Iranians had previously been exposed to Greek philosophy, especially after Christians closed the Platonic academy in Athens, prompting many Greek thinkers to migrate to Iran; and Iranian intellectuals also became the intellectual leaders in transmitting and advancing Greek philosophical thought.[7] Nearly all the principal intellectual lights of pre-Mongol Greco-Islamic philosophical and scientific thought were Iranians, and Iranians also used this intellectual inheritance in the Safavid period to create a sophisticated Shi'i theology. The principal exception to this Iranian dominance was the Spanish Muslim scholar Ibn Rushd (d. 1198), whose summaries of Aristotle's works were studied by the philosophical historian Ibn Khaldun.

Philosophy was only one aspect of Iranian influence that shaped the art, culture, and thought of the Islamic world in general and that of the Ottomans, Safavids, and Mughals in particular. In the first century following the death of the Prophet Muhammad, Islam had been overwhelmingly an Arab and Arabic-language enterprise, but in different ways Iranians and Turks began to play important roles in the Islamic world following the "revolution" that brought the 'Abbasids to power in 750. Iranian Muslims, such as the Barmakids, who were legatees of the sophisticated pre-Islamic Sasanian empire (226–651), became a conspicuous presence as highly trained administrators at the 'Abbasid court after the 'Abbasids moved the Muslim capital from Damascus to Baghdad, the latter city being located in a region of historic Iranian imperial control and cultural presence. Later Iranians performed this critical bureaucratic function for many regional Turkic dynasties. Then, as the 'Abbasid Caliphs' power atrophied in the late ninth and tenth centuries, some Iranian families established independent dynasties.

One of the most influential of these early Perso-Islamic dynasties was the Samanids of Bukhara in Mawarannahr, the region of Central Asia known in Western sources as Transoxiana. The dynasty was founded by an Iranian Muslim land-owning family, whose members first served as governors under the 'Abbasid Caliphs during the early ninth century; by 892 they had become fully independent rulers. Their rule initiated a

---

[7] For a summary of the evolution of Greco-Islamic philosophical thought see Majid Fakhry, *A History of Islamic Philosophy* (New York: Columbia University Press, 3rd edn. 2004), chapters 1 and 2.

period in Mawarannahr and Iran memorably characterized as the "Persian intermezzo," a period preceding the Turkic and Mongol invasions of Iran, during which there was a renaissance of Iranian culture produced by Muslims and expressed in "new Persian," that is Persian written in the Arabic script.[8] Prominent local Iranians, administrators, scholarly families, and Iranian poets and painters developed a new Perso-Islamic culture, and from the tenth to the sixteenth century Iranians and their cultural surrogates produced an influential corpus of political and historical literature, verse, art, and religious and scientific treatises that constituted fundamental legacies for Ottomans, Safavids, and Mughals.[9] It is difficult to exaggerate the degree of Iranian prestige and influence in all aspects of intellectual and cultural life among Indian, Central Asian, and Ottoman Muslims. Even Mehmet II, the Ottoman conqueror of Constantinople, "showed his marked predilection for the Persian language and literature, and in general for the Persian spirit. ... His preference for Persians, whom he distinguished with important government posts and who to the end were his favored associates at court, naturally aroused envy and dissatisfaction among native Turks."[10]

At virtually the same time that Iranians began reasserting themselves as Persian Muslims, Turks emerged as a third ethnic and linguistic presence in the Islamic world. As with Iranian influence in cultural and intellectual life, it is difficult to overstate the military and political importance of Turks in Muslim territories from the tenth century onward, for they ruled much of Anatolia, Iran, and India for centuries. In the view of the late sixteenth-century Ottoman bureaucrat and historian Mustafa Âli, "Turks and Tatars [Mongols]" dominated the third phase of world history, following the demise of the 'Abbasid Caliphate. Âli writes about this epoch:

> Herein is comprised the tale of the Tatar people,
> And all that concerns the affairs of the Oghuz,
> The Tîmûrid dynasty and the Cengizid house.
> Those sharp-headed plunderers
> Have all been described in this volume,

[8] "Persian Intermezzo" is a term coined by the Russian émigré scholar Vladimir Minorsky. See "La domination des Dailamites," Publications de la Société des Etudes Iraniennes, no. 3 (Paris, 1932), 21.

[9] The multi-volume *Cambridge History of Iran* discusses all aspects of pre-Islamic and Islamic Iranian history but, for the Safavid dynasty and its important Timurid predecessors see Peter Jackson and Laurence Lockhart, *The Cambridge History of Iran*, vol. 6, *The Timurid and Safavid Periods* (Cambridge University Press, 1986). For a concise survey of pre-Islamic and Islamic Iranian history see Gene R. Garthwaite, *The Persians* (Oxford: Blackwell, 2005).

[10] Franz Babinger, *Mehmed the Conqueror and His Time*, trans. Ralph Manheim, ed. William C. Hickman (Bollingen University Press, 1978), 472.

> From the start of the story to its end;
> From this garden, like a moist blossom,
> Bloomed those praiseworthy ones who are the Ottoman House.[11]

As Ottomans they developed Ottoman Turkish into the third literary language of Middle Eastern Muslims after Arabic and new Persian.

Central Asian Turks had been absorbed into the Islamic world following the Muslim conquest of Mawarannahr in the eighth century, and many Turks converted to Islam over the next two centuries, but it was not until the later 'Abbasid period that they became a significant presence in the central Islamic lands. Turks entered the Islamic world in two ways: as military slaves and as pastoral nomads. As early as the ninth century Turkic slaves became a significant Muslim military force, when the future 'Abbasid Caliph al-Mu'tasim (r. 833–42) founded a corps of approximately 3,000 Turkish slaves in Baghdad, hoping they would form the nucleus of a loyal, disciplined army to complement and partly supplant the tribally organized and habitually unreliable Arab tribal forces, which had led the Arab-Muslim conquests. In later centuries Turkic slaves, known as either *ghulams* or *mamluks*, were frequently trained to perform the same function for local dynasties, whose rulers sought to organize a dependable army, loyal solely to the reigning sultan. Yet in every case where they were employed, such slaves eventually became a threat to the dynasties that trained them, and by the late tenth century military slaves of the Iranian Samanids established the earliest Muslim "slave" sultanate in the eastern Afghan city of Ghazna, using the city as a base for the Muslim conquest of north India.[12]

Simultaneously with the founding of the Ghaznavid state, Turkic nomads began migrating into the Middle East from Mawarannahr in large numbers as partly Islamized Turkic pastoralists. These tribes, comprising a sprawling, loosely knit confederation of semi-Islamized Oghuz Turks, began making inroads into Ghaznavid territories in northeastern Iran and quickly overwhelmed the Sultanate's defenses. During the late tenth and early eleventh century they poured on to the Iranian plateau, nominally led by one of their dominant tribes, the Saljuqs. Within a century Saljuq-led Oghuz tribes established a state in Iran, and descendants of these tribes were not only precursors of the Safavid state but provided the principal military forces of the Safavid dynasty. Some Oghuz tribes also began raiding the Byzantine borderlands as early as the tenth century, and in 1071 a Saljuq-led Oghuz light cavalry army defeated the Byzantine Emperor Romanus IV Diogenes. Afterwards,

---

[11] Quoted by Fleischer, *Bureaucrat and Intellectual*, 278.
[12] For an extensive discussion of this critical slave institution in Islamic Iran, India, and the Ottoman Empire see Halil Inalcık, "Ghulâm," *Encyclopaedia of Islam*, II, Brill Online.

Oghuz Turks began settling in large numbers in Anatolia, where one of their families eventually founded the Ottoman Empire.[13]

Mongols also invaded, ravaged, and ruled parts of Iran and Anatolia in the thirteenth and fourteenth centuries, but it was the Turks – first Turkic slaves, then the Oghuz tribesmen, and later, in the fourteenth and fifteenth centuries, the Turk Temür and his descendants known as Timurids – who ultimately had the most profound and lasting political influence in Iran, Anatolia, and India. If Iranians were important in the pre-imperial era for their administrative and cultural influence, various Turkic lineages consti- tuted the dominant military and political elite in Anatolia, Iran, and India in the pre-imperial era and later. Turks, or in the Safavid case a partly Turkic dynasty, ruled Iran from the tenth century until 1921, Anatolia from the twelfth century to the present, and northern India beginning in the late tenth century and continuing intermittently until 1526, after which Turks, in the form of Timurids but commonly known in India as Mughals, ruled the north Indian heartland for a further two hundred years.[14]

The Ghaznavids and the origins of Muslim rule in India

The Ghaznavid dynasty (*c.* 998–1040) represents the earliest example of a Turkic sultanate whose Muslim rulers patronized Sunni Islam and Persianate culture. Its rulers, who originated as *ghulams* or military slaves, established a state covering parts of Mawarannahr, Iran, and India.[15] They were also responsible for the establishment of Muslim rule in north- western India, five centuries before the founding of the Mughal Empire.

Mahmud, the founder of the Ghaznavid state, began his life as a Turkic *ghulam* serving the Perso-Islamic Samanid dynasty of Bukhara. As rulers in Bukhara, the Sunni Samanids straddled the boundary of the Iranian and Turkic worlds in Mawarannahr, where they obtained Turks as captives in military campaigns or purchased them in local slave markets. Their ability to control and tax these slave markets also gave them a substantial income. Samanid rulers converted these Turks to Sunni Islam, taught them their own language, Persian, and trained them as soldiers. Like the later

---

[13] John Andrew Boyle, *The Cambridge History of Iran*, V, *The Saljuq and Mongol Periods* (Cambridge University Press, 1968). See Karen Barkey, *Empire of Difference: The Ottomans in Comparative Perspective* (Cambridge University Press, 2008), for a well- annotated examination of the Ottoman Empire as an empire.

[14] "Mughal" or more accurately "Mughul" is the Persian word for Mongol. Babur, the founder of the Mughal Empire was descended from Temür on his father's side and from Chinggis Qan through his mother. The Indian dynasty is thus often and more accurately labeled, "Timurid-Mughal."

[15] The definitive history of the dynasty is by Clifford Edmund Bosworth, *The Ghaznavids: Their Empire in Afghanistan and Eastern Iran, 994–1040* (Edinburgh University Press, 1963).

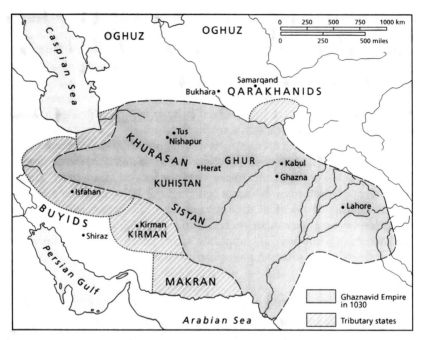

Map 3. The Ghaznavid Empire in 1030

Ottoman slave troops, the Janissaries, Samanid *ghulams* soon became a powerful, semi-autonomous faction within the state.

In 962 Alptegin, one of the Samanid Turkic slave commanders, a Muslim but known by his typically Turkic heroic name meaning "bold champion," supported the losing candidate in a Samanid succession struggle, and then fled with his troops to the distant Samanid outpost of Ghazna, a half-day's march south-west of Kabul. At first he and his officers constituted a petty, *ad hoc* oligarchy of Turkic slave soldiers, but in 997 when Subuktegin, one of Alptegin's successors, died, he founded a dynasty by bequeathing power to his two sons. One of them, Mahmud, became the sole Ghaznavid ruler by 998, and he personally exemplified most of the trends of this period in the nominal 'Abbasid territories to the east of Baghdad. Contemporaries recognized him and his descendants as sultans, a title later Ghaznavid rulers used on their coins. Not only had these military slaves founded a dynasty, but the fact that the new ruler's name, Mahmud, was Arabic and Islamic also illustrates the importance of the Ghaznavids' Islamic identity to a dynasty whose members possessed little legitimacy beyond their military prowess.

While in political terms Mahmud (r. 998–1030) presided over what became a highly centralized Turkic military despotism, he regarded himself in cultural terms as a Perso-Islamic heir to the Samanids.[16] After a Turkic nomadic confederation, the Qarakhanids, overran Mawarannahr and occupied the Samanid capital of Bukhara in 999, Mahmud focused his territorial ambitions on the agrarian and urban centers of northeastern and central Iran. He exploited the wealth of nearby India to fund his Iranian conquests by carrying out a series of plundering expeditions in the subcontinent in the late tenth and early eleventh century, ravaging the Punjab and, late in his life, penetrating as far as Kannauj in the western Gangetic valley. Even though Mahmud never exhibited a desire to do more than loot India, by the end of his life he had established a Ghaznavid garrison in the Punjabi city of Lahore, the first major Muslim settlement in north India.

Mahmud and his *ghulam* companions were professional warriors and conquerors, but they were also Muslims. Therefore Mahmud legitimized his conquests by presenting himself as a devoted Sunni Muslim servant of the 'Abbasid Caliph. He depicted himself as a *ghazi*, a Muslim frontier warrior, for his plundering expeditions in India against Hindu cities or temples, such as the famous Hindu temple at Somnath in Gujerat.[17] Mahmud also justified attacks on Buyid territories in Iran and Iraq by citing these Iranians' Shi'i faith and his own support for the Sunni 'Abbasid Caliph, whom the Buyids then controlled

Mahmud sought legitimacy not only as a devoted Sunni Muslim ruler, but also through his patronage of prestigious Iranian intellectuals, whether poets or other scholars. He had grown up in the culturally Persian Samanid world, and used Persian in his administration. Patronage of Iranians, whether poets or scientists, was an instinctual way for a Muslim ruler in a region long part of the Persian cultural sphere to demonstrate his civilized credentials. Mahmud, despite his dynasty's plebeian origins and the frigid isolation of his capital city, managed to coerce or attract to his court two of the most important Iranian scholars of his age: the scientist al-Biruni (973–1048) and the poet Firdausi (*c.* 940–1020).

Al-Biruni was an Iranian from Mawarannahr, who was one of the three or four most important scientists in the pre-industrial Muslim world. Like his contemporary, the Iranian philosopher and physician Ibn Sina (*c.* 980–1037), the slightly later mathematician and poet 'Umar Khayyam (1048–1123), and the thirteenth-century Iranian Shi'i theologian and scientist al-Tusi (1201–74), al-Biruni was a Greco-Islamic scholar whose conception of and approach to science was derived from

[16] Mahmud in Arabic means "praised" or "laudable." By taking an Arabic name, Mahmud emphasized his Islamic rather than his Turkic identity.

[17] Regarding Somnath and the various stories regarding Mahmud's expeditions, see Romila Thapar, *Somanatha* (London and New York: Verso, 2005).

Aristotle's natural philosophy.[18] He wrote more than a hundred treatises, some in Persian but most in Arabic, the first scientific language of Muslims, on subjects ranging from astronomy to mineralogy. Once, while resident in the Punjab, al-Biruni used trigonometric functions to estimate accurately the circumference of the earth. As a result of long stays in India, where he learned Sanskrit, al-Biruni wrote the single most accurate and sympathetic portrait of India and its Brahmanical, upper-caste culture that was available before the nineteenth century.[19]

His literary contemporary, the poet Firdausi, was an equally important individual, for his Persian-language poem, the *Shah-nama* or "Book (*nama*) of Kings (*shah*)," had an incalculably profound impact on the Persianate world, which then included Mawarannahr, Iran, Afghanistan, and the Punjab.[20] Firdausi was a native of Sabzawar in the region of northeastern Iran known as Khurasan, and studied in the nearby town of Nishapur, later the home of 'Umar Khayyam. His verse epic, which was based on pre-Islamic Persian language Sasanian written sources and oral traditions, relates the battles, personal conflicts, and infatuations of pre-Islamic Iranian monarchs, some legendary, some verifiably historical. The *Shah-nama* almost immediately became the revered cultural memory of the Iranian peoples and the model for later verse tales of monarchs, heroic and otherwise, in Mawarannahr, Iran, India, and Anatolia. Iranian names from the *Shah-nama* appear in later dynastic lists throughout these regions as legitimizing titles, and later writers commonly mined the text for aphorisms, whose cultural authority was second only to that of the Quran.

Subsequent Ghaznavids also patronized Iranian literati. These included the influential Sufi poet Sana'i Ghazanavi (1045–1131), the court panegyrist Mas'ud-i Sa'd Salman (1046–c.1121), and the historian Bayhaqi (995–1077), whose history of the later Ghaznavids was influenced by, among others, the Greek physician and philosopher Galen.[21]

---

[18] His full name was Abu Rayhan al-Biruni. Ibn Sina, known generally as Abu Ali Sina, is famous in the West (primarily for his medical text) as Avicenna. 'Umar Khayyam, or Ghiyas al-Din Abu'l Fath 'Umar ibn Ibrahim Khayyam Nishaburi, a mathematician, became famous in nineteenth-century England from Edward Fitzgerald's renditions of his four-line poems known as "rubaiyat." Nasir al-Din Tusi was a Shi'i polymath, who wrote treatises on Greco-Islamic science and Shi'i theology, and practiced astronomy under the patronage of the Mongol rulers of Iran.

[19] Ainslee Embree has edited an abridged version of this massive treatise. See Muhammad ibn Ahmad Biruni, *Tārikh al-Hind*, ed. Ainslee Embree (New York: Norton, 1971).

[20] An excellent recent translation is Dick Davis's *Shahnameh: The Persian Book of Kings* (New York: Viking Penguin, 2006). The poet's given name was Abu'l Qasim Mansur Tusi. "Firdausi" was a pen-name, in Persian, "firdaus" means garden or vineyard.

[21] J. T. P. de Bruijn analyzes Ghaznavi's work in *Of Piety and Poetry: The Interaction of Religion and Literature in the Life and Works of Hakîm Sanâ'i of Ghazna* (Leiden: Brill, 1983), while Salman's verse is discussed by Sunil Sharma, *Persian Poetry at the Indian Frontier: Mas'ud*

These latter three writers were Iranians and their work contributed to the increasing prestige of Perso-Islamic culture and, in the case of Salman (whose family emigrated from the Iranian town of Hamadan to Lahore in the Punjab), helped to establish Persian as a prestigious lingua franca in northwestern India. A further example of a major Persian-language writer who settled in Lahore in Ghaznavid times is the scholar Hujwiri, whose history of Sufis, the *Kashf al-Mahjub* (ca. 1120), represents the first extant Sufi treatise written in the Persian language.[22]

The increased presence of Iranian literati and religious scholars in Lahore is one sign of the degree to which Ghaznavid political fortunes deteriorated after the mid-eleventh century. Thus, although Mahmud still controlled territories stretching from southeastern Iran to the Punjab when he died in 1030, his hold on the rich, strategic Khurasan region of northeastern Iran was threatened by the inroads of Oghuz Turks, disparate bands of tribesmen many of whom were only nominally loyal to the leading Oghuz tribe, the Saljuqs. When Saljuq forces defeated a Ghaznavid army in 1040 it forced the Ghaznavids out of Khurasan and back on their Afghan and Indian possessions, and in 1163 the Saljuqs seized Ghazna itself, leaving the Ghaznavids with little more than the Punjab.[23] The later Ghaznavid monarchs' residence in Lahore attracted more Iranian intellectuals there who might previously have settled in Ghazna, and this date when Lahore became the capital of a weakened Ghaznavid dynasty marks the foundation of the first north Indian-based Muslim state.

It was, however, a state which indigenous Indian rulers initially identified as Turushka or Turkic, rather than Islamic. This was the Indian perception, despite the Ghaznavids' Muslim faith and multi-ethnic army, which by the end of Mahmud's reign may have included as many Iranians, Indians, and Afghans as Turks. The inscriptions in which the word *Turushka* appears offers a revealing hint at the dual identities of Ghaznavid rulers: one an obvious and proudly held ethnic and linguistic self-image, and the other a sincere faith but also a calculated legitimizing presentation made to the 'Abbasid Caliphs and the wider Islamic world.[24] No Indians, apparently,

---

Sa'd Salman of Lahore (New Delhi: Permanent Black, 2000). For Bayhaqi see the unpublished MA dissertation by Ranin Kazemi, "Morality and Idealism: Abu'l-Fazl Bayhaqi's Historical Thought in Tarikh-i Bayhaqi," Ohio State University, 2005.

[22] R. A. Nicolson, *The Kashf al-Mahjûb: The Oldest Persian Treatise on Sufism* (London: Luzac, 1976).

[23] See C. E. Bosworth, *The Later Ghaznavids. Splendour and Decay: The Dynasty in Afghanistan and Northern India 1040–1166* (Edinburgh University Press, 1977).

[24] Peter Jackson, *The Delhi Sultanate: A Political and Military History* (Cambridge University Press, 1999), 125 and 130. Jackson's work is the definitive political and military history of the succession of dynasties collectively known as the Delhi Sultanate.

believed they were being invaded by Iranians, despite the increasing numbers of Persian-language poets gathering in Lahore.

Ghaznavid rule in Lahore initiated a series of chronically unstable Muslim dynasties in north India, collectively known as the Delhi Sultanate, whose early rulers are known as the Slave Sultans of Delhi. The instability of these dynasties reflects their failure to establish the kind of charismatic, enduring legitimacy that later gave dynastic stability to the Ottomans, Safavids, and Mughals. The Delhi Sultans perpetuated the administrative and cultural traits of the Ghaznavid state as a centralized military despotism whose members used Persian as one of their principal administrative languages. These rulers patronized Persian-language literati, constructed mosques and other public buildings associated with Islamic piety and social welfare, and sought legitimacy from the 'Abbasid Caliphs, at least until the last Caliph was murdered by the Mongols in 1258. While the Ghaznavid dynasty's immediate successor and nemesis was an Iranian-Muslim dynasty (the Ghurids, who overran Lahore in 1186), it was another Turkic Muslim slave dynasty that firmly established Muslim power in the north Indian heartland at Delhi in 1206.

The "Slave Sultans" of Delhi

The Ghurid army was commanded by a Turkic *ghulam*, Aibak, an Ilbari Turk, and it was Aibak and his son-in-law Iltutmish (r. 1211–36), both generally known by their Turkic names, who firmly established Muslim power in the north Indian heartland. Iltutmish, who with his father built some of north India's first mosques, was formally recognized by the 'Abbasid Caliph al-Muntasir, who awarded the Turk the *laqab*, or honorary Muslim title, of Nasir Amir al-Mu'minin, the "Defender of the Commander of the Faithful."[25] Iltutmish arranged to have his children succeed him, thus founding the new dynasty, but, lacking any legitimacy beyond this distant caliphal recognition and an unstable kind of military camaraderie, his descendants were constantly threatened by shifting coalitions of Turkic and Afghan officers. These men first recognized and then deposed four of his successors before settling on a fifth descendant, who is known by a noticeably non-Turkic Arabic Muslim *laqab* of Nasir al-Din, the "Defender of Religion" (r. 1246–66).

Nasir al-Din briefly stabilized the regime between 1256 and 1266, and with the aid of his deputy and eventual murderer, Balban (r. 1266–87),

---

[25] Robert Hillenbrand, "Political Symbolism in Early Indo-Islamic Mosque Architecture: The Case of Ajmir," *Iran* 26 (1988), 105–17. The Ajmir mosque may have been built on the site of a Jain monastery.

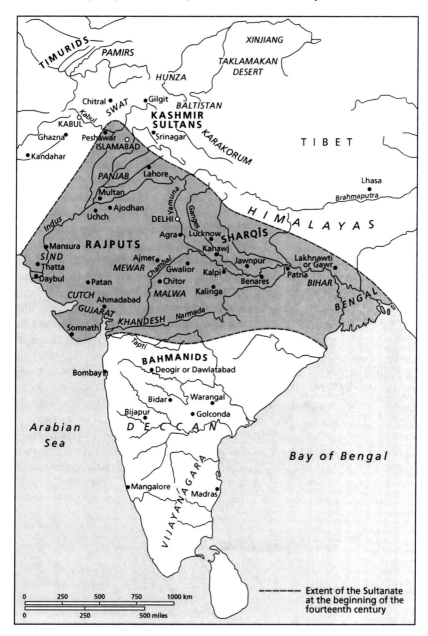

Map 4. The Delhi Sultanate in 1400

another *ghulam*, campaigned relentlessly to hold the Turkic Muslim bridgehead in north India against their most formidable Hindu opponents, various Rajput rajas, whose descendants would later offer fierce initial resistance to Mughal rule. Nasir al-Din and his *ghulam* Balban also successfully defended India's northwest frontier against the Mongols, who by then ruled Mawarannahr, Iran, and Afghanistan and periodically sent detachments into the subcontinent, raiding even as far as Delhi. However, despite its military success this first true Indo-Muslim dynasty succumbed to the factional infighting of Turkic officers and members of the Khalji family, who usurped control of the state and founded a new dynasty in 1290.[26]

By this time the rule of Turks in north India had persisted long enough to give them a form of collective legitimacy, for when the Khaljis overthrew the Ilbaris some of the Delhi population apparently resented the new rulers because they thought they were not Turks. In fact the Khaljis were probably Turks who had been long settled in Afghanistan, but the confusion about their identity accurately reflects the lack of verifiable information about this family and their supporters. Turks or Afghans, the Khaljis began their short-lived dynasty with the bloody infighting that marked the history of the Delhi Sultanate. The new sultan, Jalal al-Din Khalji, was murdered by his nephew, 'Ala al-Din; in 1296; the latter then blinded, imprisoned, or executed all of Jalal al-Din's male relatives. 'Ala al-Din's initial ferocity, while not qualitatively different from that of many previous Delhi Sultans, foreshadowed a military dictatorship of exceptional brutality, vitality, and military success. 'Ala al-Din successfully repulsed a series of threatening Chaghatai Mongol attacks in the late thirteenth and early fourteenth centuries, and extended Turkic Muslim paramountcy west into Rajasthan and Gujerat and south into the central Indian region known as the Deccan.[27] He also foreshadowed later Mughal policy toward Rajput chiefs by marrying the daughters of defeated Hindu rajas and allowing these men to rule as his tributary vassals.

Status of non-Muslim subjects

This seemingly conciliatory policy toward indigenous Hindu rulers, by a man known for his ferocity, reflected the reality of the thickly populated Indian countryside, replete with thousands of well-ensconced local rulers

---

[26] Jackson, *Delhi Sultanate*, 82–5.

[27] Chaghatai Mongols reached the environs of Delhi during his reign. Peter Jackson gives details of their later incursions in "The Mongols and the Delhi Sultanate in the Reign of Muhammad Tughluq (1325–51)," *Central Asiatic Journal* 19, nos. 1–2 (1975), 118–57.

of varying importance posing a formidable problem for Muslim conquerors who commanded relatively small numbers of Muslim troops. No South Asian government prior to the British Raj was capable of eradicating the many autonomous or independent rulers and effectively disarming the Indian countryside. Both Delhi Sultans and their Mughal successors had to make innumerable compromises in order to dominate north India, or at least to control the cities and the major transportation arteries and overawe rulers in the countryside. Predominantly Hindu India was never overrun and overwhelmed by masses of Muslims, something that did happen to the relatively small Greek Orthodox population of Anatolia, which had been experiencing waves of Oghuz Turkic migration since the Saljuqs defeated the Byzantine army in 1071.

Both the Delhi Sultanate and the later Mughal Empire represented military occupations. Compared with the Hindu population and that of other indigenous non-Muslim Indians, the combined total of Turkic, Afghan, and Iranian Muslims who invaded India or settled there during Ghaznavid or Sultanate rule comprised fairly small numbers of soldiers, bureaucrats, literati, *'ulama*, Sufis and merchants. The fourteenth century Indo-Persian historian and sometime courtier Zia al-Din Barani acknowledged this reality when he irritably complained in his unemployed, embittered old age about the number and prosperity of "idolators" (by his description, Hindus) living in Delhi – the capital, from his perspective, of a Muslim rather than a Turkic state.

Writing as a Muslim trained in the traditional religious sciences and in the belletristic knowledge of Islamic history and Persian literature known as *adab*, Barani criticized a number of aspects of Delhi society in a 1358/59 "mirror for princes" text. His critique included objections to bestowing offices on lowborn Muslims and to tolerance of philosophers, who were, he remarked in tones of pious orthodoxy, "enemies of correct religion and enemies of the Prophet." However, the number of Muslim philosophers on the streets of fourteenth-century Delhi undoubtedly paled in comparison with the population of prosperous Hindus, Barani's primary target. He complained that Delhi sultans taxed Hindus, but otherwise left them in peace – in his eyes, a policy that demonstrated their lack of commitment to Islam:

The desire for overthrowing infidels and knocking down Idolators and Polytheists does not fill the hearts of the Muslim kings (of India). ... Out of consideration for the fact that infidels and polytheists are payers of Tribute and protected persons (*zimmi*s) the infidels are honoured, distinguished, favoured and made eminent ... and in their Capital Delhi ... Muslim kings not only allow but are pleased with the fact that infidels, Polytheists, idol-worshippers and cow dung (*sargin*) worshippers build Houses like palaces, wear clothes of brocade and ride Arab horses

Caparisoned with gold and silver ornaments. ... They are called *rais* (great rulers), *ranas* (minor rulers), *thakurs* (warriors), *sahahs* (bankers), *mehtas* (clerks) and *pundits* (priests).[28]

Beyond revealing the continued existence of substantial Hindu rulers and indigenous warrior, commercial, and religious classes, Barani's complaint illustrates that the Delhi sultans were monarchs first and Muslims second when it came to realistic politics and taxation policy. Most Mughal, Ottoman, and even the fervently Shi'i Safavid rulers also preferred to tax their non-Muslim subjects rather than trying forcibly to convert or eradicate them – a ruinously expensive idea for Indo-Muslim monarchs especially, with their enormous non-Muslim populations. There was textual (that is Quranic) justification for this policy regarding Jews and Christians who were *dhimmis* (Persian: *zimmis*), "protected persons" and *ahl-i kitab*, "people of the book," that is, people with a revealed scripture in the Mosaic prophetic tradition. In India this category more often than not was extended, without concern for textual consistency, to Hindus, Buddhists, Jains, and other non-Muslims. Apart from simply sanctifying a realistic practice, the special tax levied on non-Muslims, known as *jizya*, brought in substantial sums to the Delhi Sultans and later rulers with substantial non-Muslim communities. This was particularly true of the Ottoman Empire, whose rulers Barani would also have found wanting as Muslims, but who badly needed the income realized from taxes on their substantial non-Muslim, predominantly Christian, religious communities.

Economy and administration

In addition to the income generated by taxing non-Muslims, engaging in commerce, and plundering wealthy Hindu principalities, land revenue provided most of the funds that were used to support the Delhi Sultans' army, the largest single state expense. As was true of so many pre-modern agrarian states, the sultans financed their military through a form of military feudalism, known in Muslim Iran, India, and Anatolia as the *iqta'* system.[29] *Iqta'*s were grants of agricultural land, or even whole provinces, whose revenue would be assigned to pay the expenses of Turkic or Afghan, Iranian, or other troops. Lacking administrative records from the period, it is impossible to say how the system actually

---

[28] Mohammed Habib, *The Political Theory of the Delhi Sultanate* (including a translation of Ziaud Din Barani's *Fatawa-i Jahandari* of c. 1358–9 AD) (Allahabad: Kitab Mahal, 1961), 48.

[29] "Military feudalism" refers here and later to the practice of granting theoretically temporary military fiefs to soldiers, bureaucrats, and others to support them in lieu of salaries. It is not meant to imply a contractual relationship as in European feudalism.

functioned or evolved over time. In theory, as in all such military-feudal systems, the reigning sultan controlled these grants or assignments and could transfer governors and officers at will from one district to another. In practice, energetic sultans such as 'Ala al-Din Khalji are said to have taken back the grants, collected the land revenue themselves, and paid troops in cash, but these reports may offer more insights into the centralizing ambitions of the rulers than the actual functioning of their financial administration. At the other extreme, less attentive or less powerful rulers allowed iqta'dars, the dars or holders of these grants, to evolve into autonomous tributaries or independent regional dynasts.

The Delhi Sultans administered a military occupation, whose territories they constantly endeavored to expand into wealthy regions on their borders. Beyond supporting the critical military institution, these men also sought to build the administrative infrastructure of the state as well as to support what the seventeenth-century Mughal emperor Jahangir later referred to in his memoirs as the "army of prayer." One of the ways they attempted to achieve these goals was to encourage the immigration into India of talented and prestigious foreign Muslims who could also be assumed to have no troublesome local ties. The itinerant Moroccan traveler Ibn Battuta (1304–68) described how enthusiastically one of 'Ala al-Din Khalji's successors, Muhammad bin Tughluq, welcomed such migrants in 1334 when they arrived at India's northwestern frontier border towns: "The king of India ... makes a practice of honouring strangers ... For he prefers them to the people of India."[30]

Foreigners flocked to India, then and later, partly because of the structural contrast between India's agricultural and mercantile wealth and the relative poverty of the adjacent Afghan, Iranian, and Central Asian regions. The devastating Mongol invasions and rapacious Mongol administration of these neighboring regions in the thirteenth and fourteenth centuries also drove many inhabitants to take refuge in India or Anatolia. Finally, the use of Persian by the Delhi Sultans encouraged Persian-speaking literati and religious classes from Iran, Afghanistan and Mawarannahr to market their literary talents or to find employment as administrators or religious officials, such as qadis – judges of the shari'a, Muslim religious law. Persian was not the sole language used by the Delhi Sultans. Apart from speaking Turkic dialects, they sometimes used Hinduvi, the precursor of Hindi, or other indigenous regional languages such as Bengali. Persian, nonetheless, steadily gained in popularity as the prestigious Muslim lingua franca of north India, setting the stage for its

---

[30] H. A. R. Gibb, *The Travels of Ibn Battuta: A.D. 1325–1354* (Cambridge University Press for the Hakluyt Society, 1971), 595 and 671.

flowering as the sole bureaucratic and aristocratic Indo-Muslim cultural language of the Mughal Empire.

Perso-Islamic culture

Perso-Islamic culture, the pre-Islamic and Islamic culture of Iran expressed in Persian, was firmly established among the urban, literate Muslim population of fourteenth-century Delhi, and is exemplified by two Indian Muslims, the Persian-speaking Sufi *pir* Nizam al-Din Auliya (1242–1335) and one of his disciples, the prolific Persian-language poet and musician Amir Khusrau Dihlavi (1253–1325). Nizam al-Din Auliya was a member of the Chishti Sufi order that had originated in Ghur, the isolated mountainous district just east of Herat, the region now in western Afghanistan that was home to the Ghurid destroyers of the Ghaznavid dynasty. Nizam al-Din, who spent much of his life in Delhi, exemplified the personalized version of Islam as a spiritually compelling, socially engaged faith, but not one whose representatives normally sought to convert the non-Muslim Indian population. In fact, Chishtis, despite their popular reputation for bridging the gap between Muslim and Hindu communities, did not actively proselytize, and some Chishtis accompanied the sultans' armies to legitimize campaigns when they attacked Hindu states. Nonetheless, within their own society the Chishtis tried to serve as moral exemplars and often functioned also as social and political critics. Chishti *pirs* routinely refused to serve as government-appointed *qadis*, believing that such legal appointments were inherently corrupting, although disciples of the order, such as Zia al-Din Barani, were not always so circumspect.

Nizam al-Din was typical of many other Sufi *pir*s in India and elsewhere, as he elevated the importance of Sufism over orthodox practice, the power of love over that of reason. His devotional practices paralleled those of the fourteenth-century *pirs* or *shaikhs* of the Safavid order in northwestern Iran, whose descendants founded the Safavid state in 1501.[31] "The 'ulama," he wrote, " are the partisans of reason; dervishes [Sufis], the partisans of love ... Prophets are equally strong in love or reason." Nizam al-Din and his *murid*s or disciples sought to generate intense emotional piety in their communal musical performances. "In

---

[31] See especially Kishwar Rizvi, "Transformations in Early Safavid Architecture: The Shrine of Shaykh Safi al-din Ishaq Ardebeli in Iran (1501–1629)," unpublished PhD dissertation, Department of Architecture, Massachusetts Institute of Technology, 2000. This dissertation is not limited to architecture but is partly a history of the Safavi Sufi order and a study of its *shaikhs'* ritual practices.

our practice of Qur'an recitation and listening to music," Nizam al-Din continued, "the devotee experiences a state of spiritual bliss, which may be manifest in celestial lights, mystical states, and physical effects."[32] Most orthodox *'ulama* condemned music as a means of worship as well as rejecting the poetry that Nizam al-Din also believed to possess a spiritual value. Nonetheless, the popularity of emotion-charged Sufi devotions survived such criticism. The *'urs* or birth commemoration that is still celebrated at Nizam al-Din's Delhi shrine in the twenty-first century features musical renditions of the mystical Persian verse of the important thirteenth-century Sufi Jalal al-Din Rumi, as well as that of the Delhi poet Amir Khusrau Dihlavi.[33]

Even more than Nizam al-Din Auliya, the panegyric and Sufi poet Amir Khusrau Dihlavi personifies the flowering of Perso-Islamic culture during the Delhi Sultanate.[34] The son of a Turkic father who had fled Mongol rule and an Indian-Muslim mother, Amir Khusrau was a native of India who composed an astonishing variety of inventive and accomplished panegyric, lyrical, narrative, and Sufi verse in Persian that made him famous throughout the Persianate world. He is to this day, even among the culturally chauvinistic Iranian literati, an acclaimed poet. His mystical *ghazal*s, or lyrical poems, which are sung at Nizam al-Din's Delhi shrine, typically exploit the imagery of profane love as a spiritual metaphor, as in the following lines from one of his *ghazal*s in which the beloved is God:

> O wondrous ecstatic eyes, o wondrous long locks,
> O wondrous wine worshipper, o wondrous mischievous sweetheart.
> As he draws the sword, I bow my head in
> prostration to be killed.
> O wondrous is his beneficence, o wondrous my submission.[35]

Amir Khusrau also wrote many panegyric poems praising both the Khaljis and their successors the Tughluqs, and in these poems he lauded his homeland, India, as a "paradise on earth" – made more so by these rulers – in contrast to the Persian province of Khurasan, where, unlike

---

[32] Bruce Lawrence, trans. and ed., *Nizam al-Din Awliya: Morals for the Heart* (New York: Paulist Press, 1992), 233 and 121.

[33] See among other sources Desidero Pinto, "The Mystery of the Nizamuddin Dargah: The Accounts of Pilgrims," in Christian W. Troll, ed., *Muslim Shrines in India* (Oxford University Press, Delhi, 1989), 112–24, and for an overview of Indian Sufism, Muhammad Ishaq Khan, "Sufism in Indian History," ibid., 275–91.

[34] Sunil Sharma has written an introduction to this important Indo-Persian poet: *Amir Khusrau: The Poet of Saints and Sufis* (Oxford: Oneworld, 2005). See also the outstanding literary biography by Muhammad Wahid Mirza, *The Life and Works of Amir Khusrau* (Delhi: Idarah-i Adabiyat-i Delli, repr. 1974).

[35] Translated by Regula Burkhardt Qureshi, Sufi *Music in India and Pakistan* (Cambridge University Press, 1986), 23–4.

India, there were extremes of both hot and cold. He was also a musician who performed with Hindu players, and he favorably compared Hindu pantheism to Islamic monotheism as well as praising Sanskrit as an elegant language equally as beautiful as Persian. In his case, perhaps, Chishti Sufism may have sensitized him to not only the beauty of his Indian homeland, the only land he knew, but also to the vitality of non-Muslim Indian culture.

The collapse of the Sultanate

Unlike Amir Khusrau's memorable verse, the Delhi Sultanate he praised so eloquently did not long survive. During the poet's lifetime it continued to suffer from fratricidal succession disputes and bloody usurpations. In 1320, for example, a Hindu convert to Islam murdered the last Khalji ruler, only to be deposed a few months later by yet another Turk, an officer in Khalji service, Ghiyas al-Din Tughluq (r. 1320–5). Ibn Battuta characterized Ghiyas's son and successor, Muhammad bin Tughluq, whom he met in Delhi, as a king "most addicted to the making of gifts and the shedding of blood." He illustrated his comment by describing the sultan's lavish presents to his favorites and the draconian punishments he visited on anyone who questioned his authority, including members of the 'ulama. Yet, while he sometimes tortured recalcitrant Muslim religious scholars, Muhammad bin Tughluq was also known for his ostentatious piety, including encouraging monumental religious architecture and enforcing orthodox Sunni practice. During his rule he even welcomed to Delhi a student of the conservative Arab theologian Ibn Taymiyya (1263–1328), a Quranic literalist and advocate of *jihad* whom twentieth-century Muslim fundamentalists revere.[36] Like earlier sultans he also sought caliphal investiture, but since the Mongols had murdered the last 'Abbasid Caliph in 1258, he sent a gift to the caliphal pretender in Egypt, who obligingly repaid him with a grant of authority.

   Ibn Battuta witnessed the brutality and splendor of Muhammad bin Tughluq's reign. He was impressed with the man, who in his early years was probably the most powerful ruler in the history of the Sultanate. His draconian rule included, however, an order in 1327 to move the capital – together with its commercial, religious, and administrative elite to Deogir or Daulatabad in the Deccan region of central India. The order caused enormous disruption and jeopardized his control over other regions of the subcontinent; more than a dozen serious revolts erupted during his reign.

---

[36] H. Laoust, "Ibn Taymiyya, Taki al-Din Ahmad," *Encyclopaedia of Islam* II, Brill Online.

Disenchantment with his rule and his rigid Sunni orthodoxy may have contributed to the decision by a group of Shi'i Muslims from the Deccan, the Bahmani, to proclaim the new Muslim Sultanate there. Its Shi'i rulers later established close relations with the Shi'i Safavids of Iran after the latter came to power in 1501, prompting many Iranian scholars to migrate to the Bahmani Sultanate in the sixteenth and seventeenth centuries. The establishment of the Bahmani Sultanate also began the development of a group of independent Muslim states in the Deccan, whose independence later challenged Mughal imperial ambitions in this region.

The remaining years of the Delhi Sultanate are memorable for their dismal history of constant military campaigns and repeated usurpations, unleavened by memorable writers or influential religious thinkers. The late fourteenth century might well be termed Muslim India's dark age. Tughluq progeny continued to reign in Delhi following Muhammad bin Tughluq's death, but none of them were capable of enforcing Delhi's authority, allowing many *iqtadar*s to attain the status of independent rulers. This period climaxed in the devastating 1398 invasion of India and sack of Delhi by Temür, the Turkic conqueror otherwise known in Persian as Timür-i leng, Temür the Lame, or in English, Tamerlane. When Temür appeared on the northwestern Indian horizon, the later Tughluqs were incapable of defending India's frontiers, in contrast to earlier sultans' success in repulsing the Mongols. Within a decade of Temür's precipitous withdrawal from India, the Delhi Sultans lost control of major provinces, including Gujerat in the west and Jaunpur in the central Ganges plain.

In the first half of the fifteenth century the Sultanate ceased to exist as a coherent state, and in 1451 an Afghan, Bahlul Ludi, the son of a Tughluq governor of the Punjab, seized power and established yet another ephemeral dynasty in Delhi, an unstable coalition of Afghan tribes. Afghan tribal infighting was as damaging to the nascent Ludhi state as military factions had been to the Sultanate, and disputes among Afghan tribes and clans gave one of Temür's descendants, Zahir al-Din Muhammad Babur, the opportunity to invade north India in 1526 and establish Timurid sovereignty in the subcontinent: the Mughal dynasty.

The Great Saljuqs of Iran: Turkic Muslim rule and Persian culture

Shortly after Mahmud of Ghazna began systematically plundering northern India, Oghuz tribes and clans spread southeastward from Mawarannahr towards Khurasan, the relatively well-watered and prosperous region that comprised territory now included in northeastern Iran and

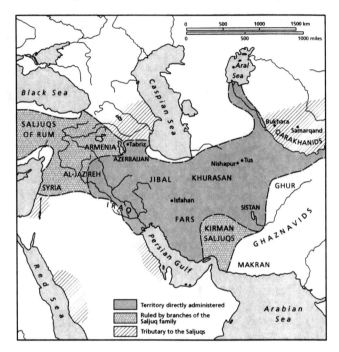

Map 5. The Great Saljuqs of Iran and the Saljuqs of Rum and Kirman in 1092

western Afghanistan. Initially many Oghuz had taken service with the Samanids in Bukhara and other sedentary dynasties as military auxiliaries, a recurring phenomenon of nomadic employment in Central Asian and Middle Eastern history. Gradually, however, their migration became a kind of inchoate invasion led but not controlled by the Saljuqs, one of the dominant Oghuz tribes.

In 1029 Mahmud of Ghazna tried to stem the tide of pastoral nomads in search of wealthy pasturage in Iran, and defeated a Saljuq-led contingent of Oghuz horsemen. His victory was, however, a pyrrhic one, for it had the effect of scattering various Oghuz clans throughout Khurasan and northern Iran. During the following decade Saljuqs first petitioned Ghaznavid rulers for permission for Oghuz nomads to graze their herds and flocks in Khurasan, even as largely independent Oghuz tribesmen spread further over the Iranian plateau. Like most nomadic peoples, they both ravaged agriculture with their animals and also plundered defenseless villages and towns. When Mahmud's son Mas'ud confronted an emboldened Saljuq-led Oghuz force in 1040, he lost the battle, and the Ghaznavids were left only with their Afghan and Indian possessions, while the Saljuqs and their allied Oghuz tribes migrated into Iran in even greater numbers. By the mid-eleventh century Oghuz tribesmen were pressing against Byzantium's eastern frontiers, and in 1055 the Saljuqs occupied Baghdad for the first time, where they were welcomed by the captive 'Abbasid Caliph, eager to free himself of Shi'i Buyid domination.[37]

When the Saljuqs defeated the Ghaznavids in 1040, they altered the history of India, Iran, and Anatolia in a number of fundamental ways. First of all they transformed the later Ghaznavids into a largely South Asian dynasty, rather than a Central Asian and Iranian one. Second, the victory had the effect of reinvigorating Sunni Islam in Iran and Anatolia at a time when the 'Abbasid Caliphs were hostages of the Shi'i Buyids and during years when the Isma'ili Shi'i Fatimids of Egypt were aggressively marketing their faith by sending out missionaries throughout the Islamic world. By the time they entered Iran most Oghuz seem to have become at least nominally Muslims and adherents of the Hanafi *madhhab* or school of Islamic law that prevailed in Mawarannahr, Afghanistan and Iran at this time.[38] While the Shafi'i school was also important in Iran, the Hanafi, Sunni variant of the Islamic faith became the dominant version in Iran, Anatolia and North India in these centuries and later the officially recognized school of the Ottoman Empire and Mughal India. Third, the influx of Oghuz tribesmen substantially increased the numbers of pastoral nomads in both Iran and Anatolia, with important long-term consequences for the military, economic, social, and political history of these two areas. Finally, the Saljuq conquests began the Turkification of Iran and Anatolia, causing a fundamental change in the ethnic composition of Iran, northern Syria, and Anatolia that was to continue and intensify during the Mongol invasions and occupation of Iran, Iraq, and eastern Anatolia in the thirteenth and fourteenth centuries.

The Saljuqs represent an alternative example to the Ghaznavids of how Central Asian Turks became Islamized and Persianized. In the early tenth century, when the Arab traveler Ibn Fadlan visited Oghuz camps in Mawarannahr, he found them to be uncouth barbarians, but by the time they entered Khurasan in the early tenth century their leaders at least had

---

[37] For a lucid, often witty survey of the history of the political and administrative history of Iran from the Ghaznavids to the collapse of Safavid rule, see David Morgan, *Medieval Persia* 1040–1797 (London: Longman, 1988).

[38] The geographic distribution of Muslim legal schools in the late tenth century is plotted on the map prepared by Heinz Halm and Angelika Schefter, "The Islamic Law Schools up to the end of the Samanid Dynasty," in *Tübinger Atlas des Vorderen Orients (TAVO)* (Wiesbaden: Dr. Ludwig Reichert Verlag, 1977), vol. VII, 7.

become Muslims.[39] In fact Saljuq leaders no longer identified themselves as Turkic *khans*, which they were socially and politically, but as Sunni Muslim rulers. When Tughril, the first Saljuq leader (r. 1038–63), entered Nishapur in 1038, two years before shattering the Ghaznavid army, he legitimized his occupation of this important Iranian city by having his Arabic (and therefore Islamic) *laqab* or title announced in the *khutba*, the Friday prayer, as Sultan al-Mu'azzam, "Exalted Ruler." He had previously been in contact with the captive 'Abbasid Caliph who now recognized him, as he earlier had the Ghaznavids, as a legitimate Muslim monarch. Later when Tughril entered Baghdad in 1055 the Caliph conferred an impressive list of honorific titles on him, glorifying the Turk's service to the 'Abbasid ruler, thus giving the Saljuq a far broader legitimacy in Islamic lands than he would have enjoyed as an Oghuz chieftain.

Tughril and his Saljuq kinsmen entered the Islamic world through the same Iranian cultural portal as the Ghaznavids. From the first, Saljuq rulers with their Turkic personal names used Persian as the principal language of their administration. It would be more accurate to say that they used Persian administrators to run their embryonic governments, as both Tughril and his son, Alp Arslan, were probably illiterate in any language. The individual who personified the Persian influence in Saljuq affairs was their famous, wealthy, and vastly influential minister who is known by his *laqab* as Nizam al-Mulk, the "Regulator of the State" (1018–92). An Iranian from Tus in Khurasan, whose father had served the Ghaznavids, Nizam al-Mulk worked for the same dynasty for a short time before joining the Saljuqs, and he became influential after joining Alp Arslan, sometime following the latter's appointment as governor of Khurasan in 1060. During the next thirty years he functioned as the de facto ruler of the Saljuq kingdom, which he modeled on its Ghaznavid predecessor.

Nizam al-Mulk and Saljuq administration

Nizam al-Mulk composed a treatise titled the *Siyasat-nama*, the "Book of Government," for the unlettered and inexperienced Saljuq sultans, Alp Arslan (r. 1063–73) and his successor, Malik Shah (r. 1073–92).[40] While instructing these men in the finer points of autocratic Iranian administration, Nizam al-Mulk played the same role for the Saljuqs as the Iranian

---

[39] Bosworth, *The Ghaznavids*, 216–18.
[40] Nizam al-Mulk, *The Book of Government or Rules for Kings: The Siyar al-Muluk or Siyâsat-nâma of Nizâm al-Mulk*, trans. Hubert Drake (London and Boston: Routledge and Keegan Paul, 1969), 102.

Jewish convert to Islam, Rashid al-Din, was to perform for the Mongol rulers of Iran in the late thirteenth century. In one famous passage Nizam al-Mulk pointedly advises the Saljuqs to conciliate their still largely uncivilized distant relatives and allies, despite the Oghuz tribesmen's disruptive behavior. His advice illuminates the difficulties that any tribal dynasty had when it attempted to transform itself into a sedentary, centralized state. The later Saljuqs, their Mongol and Ottoman successors and the Safavids also found it difficult to control tribal allies who prized their independence. Saljuq rulers never fully solved the problem, and the Safavids were only partly successful in doing so. Nizam al-Mulk observed about the Oghuz, all of whom, including the Saljuqs, were theoretically descended from a common ancestor:

Although the Turkmans have given rise to a certain amount of vexation, and they are very numerous, still they have a long-standing claim on the dynasty, because at its inception they served well and suffered much, and also they are attached by ties of kinship. ... When they are in continuous employment they will learn the use of arms and become trained in service. Then they will settle down with other people and cease to feel that aversion to settled life.[41]

Apart from his administrative role, Nizam al-Mulk is famous in Islamic history for vigorously condemning Shi'i Islam and strengthening the institutional basis of Sunni Islam, partly in response to Fatimid Egyptian Isma'ili missionary activities. He had reason to be concerned about militant Shi'as. He was eventually assassinated on the orders of a Fatimid agent in Iran, Hasan-i Sabbah, who in 1190 had seized the castle of Alamut near the Caspian Sea. Nizam al-Mulk was instrumental in founding a number of *madrasa*s or theological colleges in Khurasan, northern Iran, and Iraq in order to systemize Sunni Muslim religious training. The most famous of these colleges, known as *Nizamiyya*s, was consecrated in Baghdad in 1047.

Similar institutions had existed earlier in Iran and the Arab world, but they were greatly expanded with Saljuq patronage, and in later centuries, rulers in Anatolia, Iran, and Muslim India commonly built *madrasas* as part of the pious foundations they established in major cities to support not only religious colleges but also *masjids* and *hammams*, mosques and public baths, as well as public kitchens. The staff of most *madrasas* devoted themselves solely to religious subjects: studies of the Quran, *hadith* (reports of Muhammad's actions or sayings), Arabic grammar and *shari'a* or Islamic law. In some cases, however, particularly when rulers had broader interests, the colleges became centers of philosophical

[41] Nizam al-Mulk, *The Book of Government*, 41.

or scientific study. The governor of Samarqand during the first half of the fifteenth century, Ulugh Beg, a descendant of Temür, was one such individual whose interest in astronomy and mathematics led him to patronize a *madrasa* devoted to these subjects; indeed, with Ulugh Beg's support, Samarqand became the last important astronomical center in the pre-industrial Islamic world.

Sufis and theologians in Iran

Ironically, just at the time Nizam al-Mulk was giving orthodox Sunni Islam a strong institutional base, a free-spirited Sufi, Abu Sa'id ibn Abi'l Khair (967–1049), not only popularized an important Sufi institution, the *khangah*, the "chapter-house" or gathering place for Sufis, but also stimulated the popularity of Islamic mysticism that flourished outside of and criticized *madrasa* and *masjid*-centered education and worship.[42] A resident of Nishapur in Khurasan, Abu Sa'id did not found a *silsila* or spiritual lineage; but in the Persian-speaking world of Iran, Mawarannahr, Afghanistan, and northern India he came to personify the mystical tradition in which *pirs* or *shaikhs* strictly guided the devotions of their *murids* or spiritual disciples to enable them to achieve spiritual union with God. In the first known Sufi biography compiled by one of Abu Sa'id's disciples, he is portrayed as a man who, like Nizam al-Din Auliya in fourteenth-century Delhi, decried "intellectual" or rational knowledge – theology and Islamic law – in favor of ecstatic spiritual communion with God. Abu Sa'id preached a pantheistic doctrine that rejected the importance of the *hajj*, the Meccan pilgrimage, preferring instead an inner, spiritual journey.

Like some later Sufis, the Chishti Nizam al-Din Auliya in Delhi and Shaikh Safi, the founder of the Safavid Sufi order in northwestern Iran, Abu Sa'id used musical renditions of Persian devotional poetry to achieve the desired mystical state.[43] He also argued, favoring his own self-indulgent tastes, that asceticism was a proper discipline for a novice disciple but that a person like himself, who had achieved an advanced spiritual state, could indulge in sumptuous meals and take pleasure in the unrestrained dancing of his *murids*, activities that shocked neighboring members of the orthodox *'ulama*.[44] In fact, Abu Sa'id claimed he preached a doctrine that represented the eight-seventh of the Quran, that is, the mystical meaning of the Quran known only "by vision and not by hearsay," known to the heart and not to the mind – known, that is, to Sufis and not to theologians.[45]

---

[42] R. A. Nicolson, *Studies in Islamic Mysticism* (Cambridge University Press, repr. 1967), 2.
[43] Ibid., 23 and 29.   [44] Ibid., 29–37.   [45] Ibid., 59–60.

If Abu Sa'id's doctrines and practice outraged some *'ulama* in Khurasan, he exemplified aspects of the mystical tradition that became popular as well as socially and political influential in Iran, Mawarannahr, India, and Anatolia before and after the founding of the Ottoman, Safavid, and Mughal empires. One individual who made Sufism more broadly respectable by integrating mysticism into the mainstream of Islamic thought was Muhammad al-Ghazali (1058–1111), another Khurasani Iranian, one more example of the spiritual and philosophical dynamism of the Iranian population, and especially of the Khurasani Iranians, whose thinkers played Greece to the Ottomans' Rome as well as to the far less philosophically engaged Mughals.[46] As frequent references to important thinkers from Khurasan have shown, there was a group of influential philosophers, scientists, literati, theologians, and Sufis who came from Nishapur, Tus, Sabzawar, and other towns and villages in the region over the course of many centuries prior to the Mongol invasions. This "Khurasan cluster" illustrates how deeply rooted intellectual traditions can persist in one region, giving rise to important scholars and writers from one generation to the next.

A native of Tus, the home of Nizam al-Mulk, and also a long-time resident of Nishapur, the native city of his contemporary 'Umar Khayyam as well as Abu Sa'id a half-century earlier, al-Ghazali moved to Baghdad and was eventually chosen by Nizam al-Mulk to teach in the Saljuq minister's Nizamiyya *madrasa*. He is best known as the formidable theologian who, in his essay *Tahafut al-falasifa*, used Aristotelian logic to attack the *falsafa* or philosophy of Greco-Islamic intellectuals, the class of Muslim intellectuals decried by Zia al-Din Barani in Delhi. From this time forward, Muslim theologians commonly used Aristotle's syllogistic reasoning in their disputations. Later in life, though, al-Ghazali became disenchanted with theology – or more accurately with the materialism of the professional *'ulama* – and recognized restrained Sufi mysticism as a valid path to salvation. Unlike Abu Sa'id and other Sufis who dismissed the importance of communal prayer and other aspects of orthodox practice, al-Ghazali argued that such external expressions of faith and observance of the *shari'a*, the "straight path" of Islamic law, were essential aspects of a virtuous Islamic life. Al-Ghazali's theology became the accepted orthodoxy for most subsequent Sunni Muslim thinkers.[47]

---

[46] Majid Fakhry, "The Systematic Refutation of Neo-Platonism: Al-Ghazali," and "Synthesis and Sytematization – Al-Ghazali and Ibn 'Arabi," in his *A History of Islamic Philosophy*, 223–39 and 253–62.

[47] "The Ottoman ulema recognized him [al-Ghazali] as their master": Halil Inalcık, *The Ottoman Empire: The Classical Age 1300–1600* (London: Phoenix Press, repr. 1988), 175.

The Great Saljuqs: tribe and state

Al-Ghazali's theology, Abu Sa'id's Sufism and Nizam al-Mulk's *madrasas* exerted a profound and lasting influence on the Islamic societies that Tughril and his descendants conquered in Mawarannahr, Iran, Iraq, and, after 1071, Anatolia. Two dynasties emerged as the Oghuz overran these regions. The first, known as the Great Saljuqs, represented the Oghuz conquests in Mawarannahr, Iran, and Iraq, territories the dynasty dominated but did not always directly control, until the death of Malik Shah in 1092. Despite Nizam al-Mulk's attempt to transform the Saljuq family and their nominal Oghuz allies into something resembling a Ghaznavid centralized military despotism, the somewhat misleadingly titled Great Saljuqs never completed the transition from a Turkic tribal oligarchy to an Iranian imperial dynasty. The very fact that they never established a permanent capital reflects the persisting, semi-nomadic character of their enterprise.

Two problems bedeviled the dynasty: their tribal tradition of collective sovereignty and the sheer numbers of Oghuz tribesmen, whom the Saljuq family never effectively controlled. Collective sovereignty typified Central Asian pastoral nomadic dynasties such as the Saljuqs and later the Mongols. It meant two things in practice. Male members of the ruling family had communal rights to the conquered territories, and when the leader of the family died, while seniority often was preferred, each male member of the family had an equal right to contest the succession. The Great Saljuq sultans parceled out many of their conquests as semi-autonomous appanages, known (as they were later in Delhi) as *iqta*'s, to family members. These appanages always had the potential of becoming, as they so often did, the nuclei of miniature courts for ambitious princes. The early Saljuqs successfully established a kind of ad hoc primogeniture going from the childless Tughril to his nephew Alp Arslan and to Alp Arslan's son Malik Shah, so that they were able to establish a dynastic line, but uncles or brothers often contested the succession none the less, and after Malik Shah's death the claims of rival family lines tore the Great Saljuq state to pieces.

Despite the inherent problems of the Saljuq confederation, the first three rulers – Tughril, Alp Arslan, and Malik Shah – were able to establish a measure of control over the principal agricultural regions and major cities in western Mawarannahr, Khurasan, and Central Iran. One of the ways they did this was increasingly to rely on *ghulam* or slave troops instead of their habitually unreliable tribesmen: a reprise of earlier 'Abbasid policies. Malik Shah, whose very Arab-Persian name connotes a degree of imperial ambition in its meanings of "ownership" (*malik*) and "imperial rule" (*shah*), made a serious effort to realize Nizam al-Mulk's goal of transforming the Turkic Saljuq tribal oligarchy into a Perso-Islamic, Ghaznavid-style state. During the eleventh century at least, the Great Saljuq territories enjoyed a measure of prosperity that rulers themselves fostered with their construction of *caravansarais* along major trade routes.

While Saljuq cities, like those in other regions of the Islamic world, did not enjoy legal autonomy, major urban centers in Khurasan and Central Iran such as Herat, Nishapur, Tus, Isfahan, and Shiraz seem to have prospered, although they were sometimes plagued with outbursts of sectarian violence between Sunnis and Shi'as, or even among members of different Sunni legal schools. Nishapur particularly, the important Khurasan city of pre-Mongol times, functioned as the principal Saljuq mint town and major commercial emporium of this northeast Iranian region well into the late twelfth century – perhaps a contributing factor to its role as a native city to so many prominent Iranian intellectuals. Jews, Christians, and Zoroastrians also continued to live in relative peace under the Great Saljuqs, and members of these communities sometimes served in Saljuq administrations, as indeed did Shi'as. Christian communities gradually declined in the Saljuq era in Mawarannahr and Iran – to be virtually annihilated by Temür in the fourteenth century. Both Jews and Christians survived in larger numbers in Baghdad, but even there they always constituted small minorities, and their position never resembled that of the majority Hindu population in the Delhi Sultanate.

Less than three-quarters of a century after they had defeated the Ghaznavids, the "Great" Saljuq enterprise fragmented and dissolved into a chaos of competing family factions and Oghuz revolts. When Malik Shah died in 1092 CE various Turkic *atabegs* (a Turkic title meaning literally "father of a *beg*" or princely guardians) fought for provincial control, triggering a downward spiral of weakening central government and declining revenues.[48] By the early twelfth century Malik Shah's state, or more accurately Nizam al-Mulk's government, split into two major sections: the eastern territories of Mawarannahr together with Khurasan, and the western region of northern and western Iran and Iraq, and these sections were themselves plagued by internecine family conflicts. In 1153 an Oghuz uprising against Sanjar (d. 1157), the last effective Saljuq ruler of Mawarannahr and Khurasan, precipitated the final collapse of the

---

[48] The Turkic word commonly written "beg" is pronounced, as it is sometimes written, as "bey." In modern Turkish, the soft Turkish *g*, which elongates the sound of the preceding vowel, is written as *ğ*. The other unfamiliar Turkish letter and sound is the undotted i, written as ı and pronounced like the syllable "uh" in American English.

dynasty's authority in the east, ravaging the economy of this strategic region in the process. The Khwarazm Shahs then filled the vacuum in Mawarannahr, Khurasan, and central Iran for roughly three-quarters of a century. Based in Khwarazm, the fertile estuary of the Amu Darya River where it flows into the Aral Sea, the Khwarazm shahs began dynastic life as Turkic governors for the Saljuqs. In different circumstances the dynasty might have survived longer, but in 1219 the reigning monarch fell foul of Chinggis Qan and between 1219 and 1223 the Mongols invaded and destroyed the Khwarazm shah state and leveled the principal cities of Mawarannahr and Khurasan.

In the west, succession disputes among the sons of Muhammad ibn Malik Shah produced a state of perpetual civil war among contending clans within the Oghuz confederation. By the middle of the twelfth century Saljuq rule in the west evaporated in the chaos of competing family members and assertive local rulers including, remarkably, the 'Abbasid Caliphs, who used the opportunity to reassert their authority in Iraq during the final two decades of the century. Saljuq military dominance of Syria and Palestine had evaporated even earlier. Shortly after Malik Shah seized Aleppo in 1086 and appointed governors in Antioch and Jerusalem, Europeans from the First Crusade began attacking coastal fortresses and captured Antioch from its Turkic *ghulam* commander late in the eleventh century. In the following years violent quarrels between Saljuq princes and their *ghulam*s gave way to a patchwork of Fatimid, Crusader, and Turkic rulers in the Fertile Crescent, sometimes allied, sometimes at war with one another.[49] By 1123 the Great Saljuqs lost control of Syria, bequeathing as their legacy (as in Iran) a new Turkic ethnic element in the population.

The Saljuqs of Rum (Rome) and the Il-Khanid Mongols of Iran and Anatolia

In contrast to the Saljuq's chaotic, ephemeral rule in Syria, members of the Saljuq family, cousins of the Great Saljuq Malik Shah, founded the important Saljuq Sultanate of Rum at Konya in central Anatolia, not long after Alp Arslan defeated the Byzantine army at Manzikert (Malazgird) in 1071.[50] Even before the Saljuq victory, however, independent bands of

---

[49] An engaging autobiography offers intriguing insights into the reality of this warfare. See Phillip H. Hitti, trans., *An Arab-Syrian Gentleman and Warrior in the Period of the Crusades: Memoirs of Usamah Ibn Munqidh* (New York: Columbia University Press, 2000).

[50] For an Iranian Mongol historian's interesting take on Saljuq history see Rashîd al-Dîn ibn Tabîb, *The History of the Seljuq Turks from the Jâmi' al-tawârikh: An Il-Khanid Adaptation of the Saljûq-nâma of Zâhîr*, trans. Kenneth A. Luther and Clifford Edmund Bosworth (Richmond, UK: Curzon, 2001).

Oghuz tribesmen had raided Byzantine, that is, Eastern Roman, territories in Anatolia. Now in the eleventh century they reached the shores of the Aegean and the Sea of Marmara, the beginning of the Turkification of Asia Minor that culminated in the formation of the Ottoman state and, in 1453, the Ottoman conquest of Constantinople.

The embryonic Saljuq state at Konya initially represented but one of a number of Turkic *beğliks*, small Turkic principalities that emerged in central and western Anatolia as Byzantine defenses crumbled before the onslaught of Saljuq armies and Oghuz raiders. The Ottomans originated as one of these *beğliks*, but in the late eleventh and twelfth centuries the Saljuqs represented the most formidable Oghuz kingdom in Anatolia. They defeated a Byzantine counterattack on Konya in 1147 and in 1176 repulsed a Crusader army. With these victories the Saljuqs consolidated their power in Konya and effectively ended any semblance of Byzantine control over central and eastern Anatolia.

After defeating the Crusader army, the Saljuqs led a series of campaigns southward to reach the Mediterranean. Frederick Barbarossa's sack of Konya with another Crusader force in 1190 did not irreversibly damage Saljuq fortunes, and in 1207 they seized Atalya, putting them in touch with influential Venetian merchants. By 1214 they had also conquered Sinope on the Black Sea, enabling them to begin profiting from the lucrative sea-borne commerce linking Anatolia with the Crimea in the north, and with Alexandria in Egypt. Commerce in Turkic slaves sent from the Crimea to Syria and Egypt comprised part of this lucrative north–south trade: men who became military slaves and who, like other *ghulams* and *mamluks*, eventually rebelled against their masters and founded the Mamluk slave dynasty in Egypt (1250–1517).

The importance of the north–south commerce as a whole was reflected in the number of *caravansarais* the Saljuqs or their feudatories constructed – more than 200 by the end of the thirteenth century. Most of these *caravansarais* – secure, sometimes elaborately constructed halting posts for merchants' caravans – were built along north–south routes, many of them well-established Byzantine trade networks that linked the capital, Konya, with Black Sea and Mediterranean ports.[51] Wealth derived from profitable overland commerce provided much of the revenue that Saljuq rulers used to build impressive Muslim religious complexes and palaces in the early thirteenth century. They were aided in this by a peace treaty with Byzantium, which gave them four decades of peace on their western frontiers.

---

[51] D. E. Roxburgh, ed., *The Turks, A Journey of a Thousand Years*, (London: Royal Academy of Arts, 2005), 108–9.

The last independent Saljuqs of Rum had pre-Islamic Iranian names taken from Firdausi's *Shah-nama*, such as Kai Kaus I (r. 1211–20), Kai Kubad I (r. 1220–37), and Kai Khusrau II (r. 1237–46): one superficial sign that this branch of the Saljuq family was just as much part of Perso-Islamic culture as the Ghaznavids and their Great Saljuq relatives. Iranian influence can be seen in their administration and court life and in the religious and literary texts produced during the period of Saljuq rule, although Turkish would have been used for many purposes, most importantly in military affairs and in dealing with the population in the countryside, both agrarian and nomadic. At this time some of the leaders of the Turkic *begliks*, such as the Karamanids, used Turkish in their administration, and Arabic was a necessary skill for diplomatic relations with the Mamluks and lesser rulers in Syria, apart from its everyday use by religious scholars and scientists.[52] The Saljuqs of Rum also echoed their Iranian cousins in their support for Hanafi Sunni Islam in Anatolia. Whether or not elements of the Oghuz population retained traces of their Central Asian shamanist beliefs, in religious terms Saljuq Anatolia became an extension of the state-supported Sunni Islam that the Oghuz brought with them from Mawarannahr and had reinforced as they occupied Iran. The religious infrastructure of Sunni Islam in Anatolia was also strengthened as the Mongols drove Muslim scholars into Saljuq territory.

Sufism and popular Islam in Saljuq Anatolia

One of these refugees was Jalal al-Din Rumi (1207–75), who accompanied his father, an influential Iranian Sunni scholar, to Konya when the latter left Balkh in northern Afghanistan to escape the Mongols. Konya had earlier been home to the influential Andalusian Sufi Ibn 'Arabi, for a few years between 1205 and 1211. Jalal al-Din, who personifies one strain of Perso-Islamic religious influence in Anatolia, became a Sufi in 1240, although for several years afterward he continued to function as a public preacher and Sunni scholar. In 1244 he met a wandering mystic, Shams al-Din of Tabriz, whose ecstatic mysticism profoundly influenced Jalal al-Din's thought and led him to devote his life to an intensely devotional form of Sufism.[53] Rumi wrote what is probably the single most influential *diwan* or collection of Persian mystical verses, most of which, like other verses of later Sufi poets such as Amir Khusrau Dihlavi, were meant to be

---

[52] Mehmet Fuat Köprülü, *The Saljuqs of Anatolia: Their History and Culture According to Local Muslim Sources*, trans. and ed. Gary Leiser (Salt Lake City: University of Utah Press, 1992), 32.

[53] A. J. Arberry, *Classical Persian Literature* (London: George, Allen & Unwin, 1967), 222.

sung. He is especially remembered for the stately, twirling dance his disciples, the Mevlevis, performed to the lute as a means of stimulating the mental state that culminated in the annihilation of the self as it merged in spiritual union with the divine. As he wrote:

> Death's Angel Cries,
> When the lute is played
> Our hearts arise
> Living from the dead.
> These passions deep
> That were drowned and died
> Like fishes leap
> From the boiling tide.[54]

Rumi's "passions deep" were his love for God, the "divine beloved," whom he described in another poem.

> He comes, a Moon whose like the sky ne'er saw, awake or dreaming,
> Crowned with eternal flame no flood can lay.
> Lo, from the flagon of Thy love, Lord, my soul is swimming,
> And ruined all my body's house of clay.[55]

Rumi personified the aristocratic, urban Sunni face of Persian devotional practice, but the Turkic inhabitants of the countryside were prone to more inchoate if no less emotional piety.[56]

While Saljuq rulers are known to have supported restrained, urban, upper-class Sunni orders such as Jalal al-Din Rumi's, they feared and suppressed ecstatic, popular religious challenges that threatened their tenuous stability. One of the most serious socio-religious uprisings was the Baba'i revolt of 1240, in which Oghuz tribesmen responded to the extreme Shi'i doctrines of a Syrian Muslim named Baba Ishak, who preferred to be known as Rasul Allah, the Messenger of God. Illiterate Oghuz tribesmen did not usually debate theological fine points of Sunni and Shi'i Islam, but were often attracted to such charismatic religious figures, perhaps because they resembled familiar Central Asian *shaman*s.

---

[54] Ibid., 222.   [55] Ibid., 233.

[56] Mehmet Fuat Köprülü outlines the dichotomy between the urban and rural population in his 1922 work written in Ottoman Turkish, *Islam in Anatolia after the Turkish Invasion*, trans. and ed. Gary Leister (Salt Lake City: University of Utah Press, 1983), 11. Note that urban Turks, like the later Ottomans, distinguished between themselves and their country cousins. A thirteenth-century sultan in Konya referred to the urban Turks as "Rumis" and Turkic nomads as "turks," a word which when used as an adjective meant simple or rustic (Köprülü, *The Saljuqs of Anatolia*, 60). Zahir al-Din Muhammad Babur, the founder of the Mughal Empire, made a similar distinction between the sedentary population of villages and cities and the steppe inhabitants of Central Asia in the late fifteenth and early sixteenth century.

Baba Ishak's movement, which in social terms pitted impoverished nomads against relatively prosperous urban Muslims, seems to have anticipated in certain respects the confederation of Anatolian Turkic tribes that the Safavids inspired with their mixture of Sufi and Shi'i doctrines in the late fifteenth century. The parallels extend not only to the doctrines, leadership, and tribal followers of both movements, but also to their red turbans, which caused Safavid supporters to be known as Qizilbash, Turkish for "Redheads."

Saljuq rulers put down the Baba'i movement with great difficulty and the military help of "Frankish" mercenaries. Nonetheless it is generally believed to have survived in the later Bektashi Sufi order, whose founder, Haji Bektash, came to Anatolia, like so many other Sufis, from Khurasan, the locus not only of Iranian philosophy and science in the pre-Mongol era but of many popular Islamic sects as well. Haji Bektash arrived in Anatolia sometime in the thirteenth century and preached a doctrine similar in many respects to that of other Iranian Sufis; he was especially dismissive of orthodox practices.[57] His teachings did not, however, pose a threat to the Saljuqs, as his followers only slowly coalesced into an institutionalized order during the fourteenth century and did not become prominent for another two centuries.

The Bektashis, like their Baba'i predecessors, resembled the later Safavid order in certain respects. They preached a form of Shi'i Islam focused on 'Ali, the fourth Caliph and first Imam, and appealed particularly to the rural Oghuz population. They also wore a distinctive turban, with either four or twelve folds, the latter designed to commemorate the twelve Imams revered by the largest Shi'i community. They were nonetheless distinguished by their adoption of Christian elements, including monasteries and rituals such as communion. They also played a special role in Ottoman history as the exclusive Sufi order of the Ottoman slave troops, the Janissaries, most of whom in the early days of the empire had been Christians before they were drafted and converted to Islam. They had an even broader significance as a popular Sufi order in the Ottoman Empire, where in the seventeenth century they built thousands of the Sufi hospices known as *tekkes* or *khangahs*, and retained a devotional following estimated to have been 20 percent of the Ottoman Muslim population two centuries later.[58]

Just as the Saljuqs began enjoying their dominance of central and eastern Anatolia, they came under threat from Iran, where in 1194 the Khwarazm Shah had defeated the last of the Great Saljuqs, thus

---

[57] Köprülü, echoing the German scholar Goldziher, notes the similarity between Sufi movements and basic Shi'i beliefs: *Islam in Anatolia after the Turkish Invasion*, 64 n. 22.

[58] Inalcık, *The Ottoman Empire: The Classical Age*, 199.

extinguishing the dynasty. While these eastern Turkic rulers subsequently occupied most of the Iranian plateau, they were too preoccupied with Mawarannahr to attempt to extend their rule into Anatolia, especially after the Mongols arrived on their doorstep in 1219. The Mongols not only destroyed the Khwarazm Shahs' dynasty, but also altered the history of Iran and Saljuq Anatolia. Apart from driving refugees into Anatolia, the Mongol invasion had a major impact on the history of those regions and on the Islamic world at large, but much less so on north India, a refuge, like Anatolia, for Muslim refugees.

Chinggis Qan and the Il-Khanid Mongols of Iran

Mongols represented a completely different and vastly more destructive nomadic force than the Oghuz. Originating as raiders typical of a pastoral nomadic tribe, the Mongols under Chinggis Qan, or in Persian spelling Chingiz Khan, transformed the inter-tribal raid into an imperial principle sanctioned by the shamanistic deity Tengri, the overarching blue sky. Unlike the Oghuz who had preceded them, the Mongols were not acculturated to and respectful of either Islamic culture or the religious or ethical culture of any other civilization, and even more than the Oghuz, they were unfamiliar with and even hostile to cities. While their first series of raids into western Mawarannahr appear to have been a minor diversion from their goal of subjugating China, after a clash with the Khwarazm Shah the Mongols subjugated Mawarannahr and Khurasan with the destructive ferocity that characterized their warfare.

In the first wave of conquests that largely concluded in 1223, cities whose defenders refused to surrender were leveled and their inhabitants, apart from useful craftsmen, slaughtered. Great urban centers such as Samarqand in Mawarannahr, Balkh in northern Afghanistan, and Herat and Nishapur in Khurasan were destroyed, and the agrarian economy of Khurasan was at least temporarily ruined. It was in 1243, between this onslaught and the return of the Mongols in force in 1255–6, that a Mongol commander in northern Iran invaded Anatolia and defeated the Saljuqs; but unlike their earlier campaigns in Iran, in Anatolia the Mongols did not devastate Saljuq territories but were content to govern the region through Saljuq feudatories until 1277, when they took direct control of the state.

The first phase of the Mongol invasion devastated Iran, destroying the vitality of the Khurasanian cities that had been home to so many important scholars and scientists, as well as driving both urban Iranian and Oghuz refugees eastward into Anatolia. In ending the independence of the Saljuq sultanate, the invasion also gave more freedom for maneuver to many Turkic *begliks*, particularly those in western Anatolia which were located on the margins of Saljuq and Mongol power in Konya. The second phase of Mongol conquests, which were led by Hulagu Khan, one of Chinggis Qan's grandsons, had other but equally significant consequences. Hulagu first attacked and destroyed the Isma'ili Shi'i stronghold of Alamut in 1256 and then moved on to Baghdad to murder the last 'Abbasid Caliph, thus eliminating the symbolic political center of the Islamic world. After other campaigns in Syria, where the Mongols were finally repulsed in 1260 by the new slave dynasty of Egypt, the Mamluks, Hulagu and his successors settled down in northwestern Iran as a regional Mongol dynasty, the Il-Khans, contemporary with the Mongol dynasty of China, the Yüan, whose best-known ruler was Qubilai Khan.

The history of the Il-khans falls into two periods. At first, the Mongols conducted themselves not as typical rulers of a predominantly sedentary society but as plunderers, ravaging the Iranian urban and rural economy in what amounted to a sustained, decades-long tribal raid. In 1295, however, Ghazan Khan (r. 1295–1304) came to power as a recent Muslim convert and began the process of transforming the Mongols into a sedentary dynasty that relied for its income on systemized taxation rather than indiscriminate looting. Ghazan's principal minister was Rashid al-Din (1247–1318), who performed a function similar to that of Nizam al-Mulk with the Saljuqs – and to that of Yeh-lü Ch'u Ts'ai, the Chin advisor to the Yüan dynasty in China.[59] Once again an Iranian administrator helped to train nomads with little knowledge of or training in government administration. Ghazan Khan, his successor Uljaitu, and Rashid al-Din apparently were able to end the worst excesses of Mongol rule, but it is impossible to know how thoroughly their reform policies were implemented. And having converted to Islam, the Muslim Il-Khans began a religious persecution of Buddhists, Christians, and Jews that never occurred under their theologically laissez-faire, shamanist predecessors. Ultimately, however, neither Ghazan Khan nor his successors were able to transform the Il-Khans into a long-lived sedentary dynasty, and in 1336 these Mongols dissolved into the same kind of tribal internecine warfare as had destroyed the Saljuqs.

The positive legacies of Mongol rule in Iran were limited to individual scholarly achievements. Three Iranians, who enjoyed the benefits of Mongol employment, produced important works during this time. They included two historians, Rashid al-Din himself and Ata Malik Juvaini

---

[59] See Rashîd al-Dîn ibn Tabîb, *The Successors of Genghis Khan* (New York: Columbia University Press, 1971); Igor de Rachewiltz, "Personnel and Personalities in North China in the Early Mongol Period," *Journal of the Economic and Social History of the Orient* 9, no. 1-2 (November 1966), 88–104; Reuven Amitai Preiss and David Morgan, *The Mongol Empire and its Legacy* (Leiden: Brill, 1999); and Thomas T. Allsen, *Culture and Conquest in Mongol Eurasia* (Cambridge University Press, 2001).

(d. 1285), both of whose works were informed by their intimate knowledge of Mongol administration and, in Rashid al-Din's case, exceptionally detailed information about the entire Mongol Empire, including China. The third individual was Nasir al-Din Tusi (1201–74), the Shi'i theologian, scientist, and astronomer for whom Hulagu erected an observatory at Maragha, near the Mongol capital in Azerbaijan in northwestern Iran. Tusi was another Iranian scholar from Tus in Khurasan, who studied Shi'i thought as well as Greco-Islamic philosophy in Nishapur, just prior to the Mongol invasions. Later residing in Baghdad and at Alamut, he became a Shi'i emissary to the Mongols and eventually joined Hulagu's entourage. The single most prolific scholar of the age, his Shi'i theological works, which were informed by the Neoplatonic doctrines of his Khurasani predecessor Ibn Sina, were especially influential in Shi'i Safavid Iran.

The Mongols left in their destructive wake a series of ephemeral provincial dynasties in Iran that were incapable of resisting the next devastating Central Asian onslaught, the invasion of the Turco-Mongol Temür (d. 1405), who began ravaging Iranian lands in 1381 from his base in Samarqand, and in 1402, just three years before his death, stunned but did not destroy the nascent Ottoman state at the Battle of Ankara. Temür's successors ruled Mawarannahr and Iran during much of the fifteenth century, and, in contrast to their ancestor, patronized Perso-Islamic culture to the extent that the last fifteenth-century Timurid ruler, Sultan Husain Baiqara of Herat (r. 1469–1506), came to epitomize an Islamic golden age of art, literature, and historical writing that influenced all three Muslim empires. These Timurids, however, while great aesthetes, were politically inept, and in the second half of the century fought one another for control of Mawarannahr and Iran. As a result of their disunity the two other Muslim empires ultimately emerged alongside the revived Ottoman state that conquered Constantinople in 1453.

In Iran two new Oghuz semi-nomadic dynasties in the west filled the vacuum left by the declining Timurids. Memorably named the "Black Sheep" (Qara Quyunlu) and "White Sheep" (Aq Quyunlu), they demonstrated once again how difficult it was for tribal dynasties to make the successful transition to long-lived sedentary states, and by the late fifteenth century they were pushed aside by the Safavids, relatives of the Aq Quyunlu but a family whose leaders offered the unifying appeal of a charismatic Shi'i Sufi order to the Oghuz tribes of eastern Anatolia. Then, just three years after Shah Isma'il founded the Safavid state in Tabriz in 1501, Zahir al-Din Muhammad Babur emerged from the chaos of fratricidal late-Timurid politics in Mawarannahr to occupy Kabul and eventually use it as a base for his 1525–6 invasion of north India and the founding of the Mughal Empire.

2 The rise of Muslim empires

Turco-Mongol, Perso-Islamic states

The Ottoman, Safavid, and Mughal empires arose between the fourteenth and the sixteenth centuries. Identifying precise dates for the founding of each state is a matter of emphasis, and this is especially true in the case of the Ottomans, Sunni Muslims who had a considerable history as leaders of a minor Oghuz *beğlik* before they became fully independent as rulers of a state that threatened other *beğlik*s or the Byzantine Empire. Led by Osman (d. 1324), the Ottomans became independent of their Mongol overlords sometime around 1300 CE – a conveniently memorable date – but they might be seen to have achieved significant status only after defeating a Byzantine army near Iznik, just southeast of Constantinople, in 1302.[1] Based on the issue of coins, which (along with the proclamation of a ruler's name in the Friday prayers) was one of the two symbols of Muslim sovereignty, the Ottoman state became a fully self-conscious, independent state only in 1326, when Osman's son Orhan (r. 1324–62) issued coins with such legends as: "The great Sultan, Orhan son of Osman, God perpetuate."[2] Between then and the conquest of Constantinople in 1453, the Ottomans evolved through constant warfare to become rulers of a Eurasian sultanate, with their first Asian or Anatolian capital at Bursa in 1326 and the second, European or Balkan capital at Edirne in Thrace after 1402.

By the time of the Ottoman conquest of Constantinople, the partly Turkic, originally Sunni, Safavid family had become influential *pir*s of a Sufi order based in Ardebil in northwestern Iran. During the remainder of the fifteenth century they underwent two major changes. First, at some indeterminate date these Sunni Sufis became Shi'as and secondly, by the end of the century the order had also become militarized. In addition, the

---

[1] Halil Inalcık, "Osman Ghâzî's Siege of Nicea and the Battle of Bapheus," in *Essays in Ottoman History* (Istanbul: EREN, 1998), 55–84.

[2] Şevket Pamuk, *A Monetary History of the Ottoman Empire* (Cambridge University Press, 2000), 30.

48

Safavid order's leader in 1500, Isma'il (r. 1501–26), possessed a significant political lineage, as he was a matrilineal descendant of the dominant
dynasty in northwestern Iran and eastern Anatolia, the Aq Quyunlu or
"White Sheep" Turks. By 1500 Isma'il had successfully exploited the
spiritual appeal of a Sufi *pir* who preached a millenarian Shi'i ideology to
attract the support of Oghuz clans and tribes in eastern Anatolia and
northwestern Iran. In 1501 he captured Tabriz, the former Aq Quyunlu
capital city. This event marks the beginning of the Safavids as a dynasty in
Iran, and within a decade Isma'il conquered most of the Iranian plateau.

In that same year, 1501, Zahir al-Din Muhammad Babur (r. 1526–30),
a Sunni Muslim fifth-generation descendant of Temür, was expelled from
Temür's capital, Samarqand, by the Uzbeks. They represented a Mongol-
led but largely Turkic tribal confederation that had moved into
Mawarannahr from the steppe land to the west in the late fifteenth century. By 1501, Uzbeks were completing their conquest of Mawarannahr,
annihilating any descendants of Temür who challenged their supremacy
in the region. In 1504 Babur, as he is generally known, fled from
Mawarannahr as a hunted refugee to take control of the distant Timurid
outpost of Kabul, which he ruled for the next two decades. In 1525–6 he
used the city as a base to invade India and defeat the ruling Ludi Afghan
dynasty just north of the city of Delhi, and this date is generally cited as the
beginning of the Mughal Empire, in essence a Timurid renaissance in
Afghanistan and India.

Osman, Isma'il, and Babur, the founders of the Osmanlı, Safavi, and
South Asian Timuri states, were joint legatees of the Turco-Mongol,
Perso-Islamic political and cultural heritage of the preceding centuries.
All three men traced at least part of their lineage to earlier Turkic
commanders or rulers: Osman to the legendary Central Asian Oghuz
leader, Oghuz Khan, Isma'il to the Aq Quyunlu Turks, and Babur to
Temür. All three men spoke some form of what originally had been
Central Asian Turkish dialects as their native language, or, in Isma'il's
case, one of his native languages: Osman's Oghuz Turkish, Isma'il's
Azerbaijani or Azeri Turkish, and Babur's Turki or Chaghatai Turkish.
All three men led Turkic troops in their campaigns and conquests, supplemented in Ottoman forces by *ghulam*s, known in Turkish as *yeni cheri*,
"new men" or Janissaries, and complemented in Timurid armies by
substantial detachments of Mongols.

All three men were at least formally observant Muslims who were
strongly influenced by Sufism and, in the Safavid case, were Sufi *pir*s
themselves, and all three and their descendants faithfully patronized the
'ulama and Muslim religious institutions: *masjid*s, *madrasa*s, and also Sufi
shrines. As Muslim warriors and rulers, all three also depicted themselves

on their coinage as *ghazi*s, heroic warriors for the faith, after they had fought Christians, Hindus, or, in the Ottoman case, either Christians or heretical Iranian Shi'as. All three were literate, to varying degrees, in Persian, the prestigious lingua franca among Muslims in Iran, north India, and Anatolia. They were also familiar with Persian poetry, including Sufi verse and Persian-language histories, which they accepted as normative models of personal creativity, devotional expression, and dynastic glorification.

One implicit guide to these men's shared heritage was their regard for the dynastic legitimacy and cultural prestige of the Central Asian Timurids who ruled Mawarannahr between Temür's death in 1405 and the death of Sultan Husain Baiqara (r. 1467–1506) of Herat in 1506.[3] The Timurids, after all, had enjoyed undisputed dynastic prestige as descendants of the last great, if gratuitously brutal, Turco-Mongol conqueror Temür, who had overrun Iran in the 1380s, sacked Delhi in 1398, and defeated the Ottoman sultan Bayezid in 1402. More recently their descendants, and Husain Baiqara particularly, had established a standard of aristocratic literary and artistic culture and historical writing in Herat that the founders of these dynasties and most of their immediate descendants admired as the defining "golden age" of courtly Islamic culture.

Yet just as European states of the same period may be seen as variants of a common civilization, the Ottomans, Safavids, and Timurid Mughals were distinct in a number of significant ways. Most of all, they had distinct historical experiences in contrasting geographical and cultural settings; and the Safavids espoused Shi'i rather than Sunni Islam. An understanding of how members of each dynasty acquired legitimacy helps to highlight some of these differences. In the minds of the dynastic rulers, or in the words of their sycophantic historians, the nature of their legitimacy evolved over time. Initially, however, the Ottomans, who could not claim descent from a famous conqueror or renowned ruling dynasty, gradually accumulated a charisma of success, while the Safavids, and especially the founder Isma'il, possessed the charisma of religious sanctity, and the Mughals – as they so often reminded themselves – enjoyed the charisma of dynastic prestige.

---

[3] Ottoman and Safavid court historians longed for a Timurid connection to bolster their rulers' legitimacy, and shared a respect for Husain Baiqara's court. Fleischer discusses the Ottoman regard for Temür and steppe traditions in *Bureaucrat and Intellectual in the Ottoman Empire*, 276 and 283–92. Sholeh A. Quinn describes how Safavid historians struggled to link the dynasty with Temür and the Timurids in her article "Notes on Timurid Legitimacy in Three Safavid Chronicles," *Iranian Studies* 31, No. 2 (Spring 1998), 149–58.

Charisma and legitimacy

In the minds of some chroniclers and perhaps even the rulers themselves, the early Ottomans acquired legitimacy and possessed charisma because they were so successful for so many years in their struggles with other Oghuz *beğlik*s and even more so with the Byzantine Empire – which in the fourteenth century was a shell of its former self, but still an imperial dynasty that was not only an offshoot of the original Roman Empire but was itself the Eastern Roman Empire that had endured for more than a thousand years.[4] Osman's initial defeat of a Byzantine army in 1302 was an event of enormous significance in Ottoman eyes and in the eyes of the rest of the Muslim world, whose early leaders had dreamt of and attempted to conquer Byzantium. In the minds of many Muslims, particularly literate clerics, the Ottomans' military success also legitimized them as *ghazis*, heroic warriors on the frontiers of Islam. In other respects Ottoman legitimacy was extremely weak "from the standpoint of both Islamic and nomadic political tradition ... their success ... owed far more to efficiency than to ideology."[5] Some early Ottoman writers claimed, on no particular evidence, that the Ottomans were the legitimate successors of the Saljuqs, and in certain ethnic and religious respects they were; but this assertion represented merely a transparent ex post facto justification.[6] In contrast, the argument of some sixteenth-century chroniclers, that the Ottomans were legitimate simply because they had arisen so early and ruled for so long – for two and a half centuries when Mehmet II entered Constantinople – remained an important element in their self-identity throughout the history of the dynasty, and constituted an important rationale considering what is known about the psychology of political charisma.[7] This was so even after Ottoman sultans conquered first Constantinople and later Egypt and the holy cities of Mecca and Medina, thereby becoming not only Caesars and but also de facto Caliphs, the protectors of Islam and by extension, of the entire Muslim world.

The Safavids identified themselves as *ghazis* when they attacked Georgian Christians and other non-Muslims, but they also possessed a

---

[4] As Said Amir Arjomand observes when citing Max Weber's theory, "quintessentially, power engenders charisma and ... the continuous exercise of power is self-legitimatory." *The Shadow of God and the Hidden Imam* (Chicago: University of Chicago Press, 1984), 6.

[5] Fleischer, *Bureaucrat and Intellectual in the Ottoman Empire*, 276.

[6] See Colin Imber's concise description of how assertions of Ottoman legitimacy shifted to meet the needs of changing times in *The Ottoman Empire* (Basingstoke and New York: Palgrave Macmillan, 2002), 120–7.

[7] The psychology, that is, which Max Weber identified when he talked about just this phenomenon of acquiring charisma through success. See note 4 above.

far more potent and distinctive religious charisma. It was the kind that contained an intoxicating allure of prophecy, which was understood by the fourteenth-century philosophical Muslim historian Ibn Khaldun as the quality that could unite pastoral nomadic tribes in unusually cohesive and enduring alliances.[8] In contrast to the Ottomans, the Safavids had a very short dynastic history, although they could identify a spiritual lineage of considerable length. Originating as a landholding Sufi order in the chaotic aftermath of the Mongol invasions of Iran, Safavid *pirs* exploited their wealth and prestige to acquire additional substantial lands and influence in Ardebil, a small town located on the fertile Mughan steppe just south of the Caucasus Mountains and bordering on the medieval Christian kingdom of Georgia. At a time when Sunni and Shi'i boundaries were far less rigidly defined than they became in the seventeenth century, the Safavids gradually shed their earlier predominantly Sunni identity. They embraced an idiosyncratic Shi'i faith, which reflected a complex mix of Islamic, shamanist, Christian, and Iranian religious ideas that circulated in Iranian and Anatolian lands as Mongol rule disintegrated.

Unlike the Ottomans and Mughals, whose conquests were in their initial phase – relatively simple acts of dynastic imperialism – the Safavids evolved into an armed religious order whose legitimacy derived from their dual Sufi and Shi'i religious identities and only modestly, as far as can be determined, from Isma'il's matrilineal descent from the Aq Quyunlu. As Sufi *pirs* they exerted the same powerful, almost autocratic authority over their *murids* that characterized many devotional orders – and alienated so many orthodox *'ulama* – since their disciples saw the Safavids as infallible guides to salvation. In addition, Safavids also came to offer a millenarian appeal as Shi'i representatives of the Imams, in their eyes the only legitimate leaders of the Muslim community, the last of whom had long since disappeared into eschatological concealment to return in some unknown future moment, in a manner reminiscent of the second coming of Christ. The Safavids' dual religious identity exerted a powerful appeal among the untutored, not to say totally uneducated, Oghuz tribes of the northwest Iranian and eastern Anatolian countryside, some of whose ancestors had been attracted to Babism or to the Bektashis. It was exactly the kind of appeal that Ibn Khaldun theorized could cement an alliance of fractious tribes who would otherwise be plundering and killing one another. Precisely this type of appeal had enabled the Prophet Muhammad to unite the otherwise hostile tribes of Arabia in the seventh century.

[8] Ibn Khaldun, *The Muqaddimah*, I, 319–22.

In contrast with the Safavids and the later Ottomans, the Mughals made no pretence of possessing religious charisma, even though they, like their fellow Muslims, identified themselves as *ghazis* on their coinage and elsewhere after their military encounters with non-Muslims in India. Conceived of solely as an Indian or South Asian dynasty, the Mughals reigned as emperors only a little longer than the Safavids; but when Zahir al-Din Muhammad Babur led his armies into northwestern India in January 1526 he justified his invasion as a re-establishment of Timurid sovereignty that originally dated to Temür's destructive but brief invasion of 1398.[9] In his eyes and those of his descendants, Timurid descent justified and sanctified their rule, although they also frequently invoked Babur's matrilineal Mongol lineage in genealogical diagrams, court histories, and miniature paintings.

The Mughals, therefore, possessed the most prestigious lineage of all three Muslim dynasties, and Babur himself related how this lineage alone gave him the charisma that helped him to survive as he fled through the Afghan mountains in 1504, closely pursued by Uzbeks intent on executing this elusive Timurid refugee. In his telling of the incident, some twenty to thirty thousand Mongol followers of a Kipchak Turk named Khusrau Shah, who had previously controlled Qunduz in northeastern Afghanistan, defected to Babur for no apparent reason other than that he possessed a superb Turco-Mongol lineage. Babur at the time led a rag-tag band of approximately 240 men, women, and children. He had a history of military disasters, possessed few arms, controlled no territory, and had no prospect of a future kingdom. Only the life-saving power of legitimacy explains what Babur reported happening on an Afghan riverbank north of Kabul:

Great and small, good and bad, *begs* and their retainers, group by group with their family retainers and herds began coming from them [Khusrau Shah and his retinue] to us.

Between the midday and evening prayer the next day not one of those people remained in his [Khusrau Shah's] presence.[10]

With these troops Babur was able to overawe the ruler of Kabul, gradually resuscitate his own fortunes, and ultimately, two decades later, successfully invade north India.

---

[9] The Mughal Empire ceased to be an empire as such in 1739, but Mughal rulers resided in Delhi, first as regional monarchs and then as puppets, until 1857.

[10] Stephen F. Dale, *The Garden of the Eight Paradises: Bâbur and the Culture of Empire in Central Asia, Afghanistan and India* (1483–1530) (Leiden and Boston: Brill, 2004), 131.

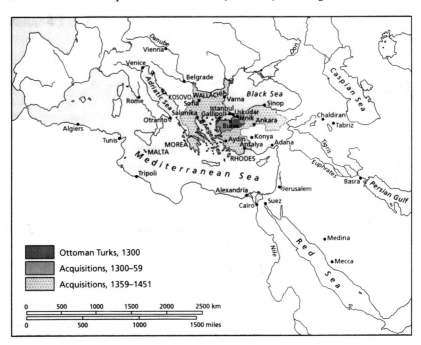

Map 6. The Ottoman Empire to 1451

The Ottomans: Turks and *Ghazis*

The Ottomans began political life as one of the Anatolian *beğlik*s, descended from Oghuz chieftans, which arose following the Oghuz migration into and invasion of Byzantine Anatolia. They never forgot their Turkic origins or kinship with Turks in the countryside, even when later Ottomans and their aristocratic followers in Istanbul developed a sophisticated court culture that led them to ridicule such "Turks" as rustic, provincial country folk. Members of the Ottoman elite later commonly used the word "turk" as a synonym for the Persian and Indo-European word *rusta'i*, the Latinate *rustic*, which is precisely the way the Mughal founder Babur also employed the term – not as an ethnic label but a social category – when he discussed the *sahra-nishin* or nomadic population of the Central Asian and Afghan countryside.

Despite this social snobbery, so typical of urban sophisticates in all ages, the Ottomans' sense of themselves as Turks was sustained throughout their history, to emerge in a new form in the 1920s. In 1923 Mustafa Kemal founded an explicitly Turkish nation-state with its capital at Ankara, in the Turkic heartland, rather than cosmopolitan Istanbul, and in 1935 assumed the title Atatürk, "Father of the Turks." Muslim Turks continued to be seen as a loyal core of what became, even before the conquest of Constantinople in 1453, a multi-ethnic empire. After the Ottomans conquered large swathes of Balkan territory, Turks were settled there in an attempt to consolidate Ottoman control of this largely Christian, culturally European territory. Ottoman sultans and the civil, military, and religious elite also spoke and wrote an elaborate, partly Persianized, baroque Turkic dialect known as Ottoman. Yet it was grammatically a Turkic language, not Persian and certainly not Arabic.

If this sense of Turkishness endured through seven centuries, so did an original aspect of the public face of Ottoman legitimacy, the concept of the *ghazi*. Kemal Atatürk was not simply the "Father of the Turks," he was also known, until 1935 at least, as Kemal Atatürk Ghazi, the warrior who, as the Ottomans had done centuries earlier, defeated Europeans – in his case the British, French, and Greeks during and following the First World War. The cultural memory of the *ghazi* ideal has survived in many forms in modern Turkish culture, including recently naming an American-style football team the "Ghazi Warriors."[11] Halil Inalcık, the enormously erudite and prolific doyen of Ottoman historical studies, has written, echoing the view of many others, that the Ottoman Empire was a "ghazi state owing its success mainly to its espousal of the role of the guardian of Islam."[12] Yet while Ottoman sultans often invoked the *ghazi* ideal and studiously patronized Hanafi Sunni Islam throughout the history of the dynasty, ostentatiously proclaiming their devotion in the great mosque complexes of the empire, the ideal served more as a legitimizing ideology than as an organizing principle of the state.[13]

The seventeenth-century Ottoman soldier and peripatetic traveler Evliya Chelebi offers an example of the gritty and, in his telling, comic reality of the *ghaza* when he describes how, in the aftermath of a battle in Hungary in 1661, he went to relieve himself and was attacked by an "infidel soldier" who jumped on him, knocking him back into his own "filth," following which he stabbed the man and cut off his head, thus avoiding becoming a "shitty martyr." Chelebi reports that afterwards "I was soaked in blood as well as in shit, and I had to laugh, seeing that I had

[11] Mark St. Amant, *New York Times* (3 June 2007), p. 9. The Boğaziçi or Bosphorus team is called "The Sultans."
[12] Halil Inalcık, "Islam in the Ottoman Empire," in his *Essays in Ottoman History*, 234.
[13] In an influential essay, the Austrian historian Paul Wittek argued that the history of the Ottoman Empire could be interpreted as a *ghazi* phenomenon, and that once the *ghaza* stalled in seventeenth-century Europe, the Empire inevitably declined. See *The Rise of the Ottoman Empire* (London: School of Oriental and African Studies, 1938). Cemal Kafadar recently analyzed and revised Wittek's thesis in his book *Between Two Worlds: The Construction of the Ottoman State* (Berkeley: University of California Press, 1995). Colin Imber is a recent historian who, while discussing the *ghazi* as a legitimizing device, does not mention Wittek's thesis that the concept offers a key to the history of the Ottoman Empire. See his *The Ottoman Empire*, 120–1.

become the shitty gazi."[14] His matter-of-fact account, without a touch of religious emotion, may be only a single anecdote, but probably reflects how many Ottomans used the term, not tinged with religious fanaticism but as part of the common vocabulary that distinguished friend from foe. Safavids when they fought Georgian Christians, or Mughals when they fought Hindus, also depicted themselves as *ghazis* or, when they died, as *shahids* or martyrs. Ottoman conquests represented old-fashioned dynastic imperialism, as is made perfectly clear in engagingly ingenuous inscriptions on some imperial mosques in Istanbul which explain how religious architecture helped to prolong dynastic longevity.[15]

Christians and Jews in Ottoman lands

The true organizing principal of the Ottoman state was loyalty to the Ottoman dynasty, whose profession was, like that of other members of the Turco-Mongol military class, conquest. No Ottomans, sultans or conquerors, are known to have been as openly frank as the Mughal founder Babur, who in his Turki-language autobiography explains that he left Kabul for India to satisfy his *mulkgirliq*, his "kingdom-seizing" or imperial ambitions. Nonetheless the Ottomans, like the Mughals, were primarily motivated by the desire to conquer wealthy territories. They were not excessively concerned, as was the Safavid Shah Isma'il, with Islamic doctrinal or sectarian uniformity, though as their conflicts with the Safavids became more intense, Ottomans increasingly emphasized their own devotion to Sunni Islam. However, their Sunni commitment never led them to Shah Isma'il's extremes.

The Iranian ruler took an obscene delight in torturing Sunni dissenters, burning some alive, as part of his effort to establish Shi'i religious uniformity. Mughals, practicing Sunnis, were the least preoccupied with Islamic theology, and always employed both Sunnis and Shi'is as well as Hindus in the upper levels of the imperial hierarchy. Whatever their attitudes to Islamic sectarian divisions, Ottomans and most rulers in all three dynasties generally tolerated non-Muslim communities. Ottoman rulers were particularly known for their system, in which they treated non-Muslims – Jews and Christians – as autonomous self-governing communities of tax-paying *dhimmis*, whose communities were known as *millats*. Muslim ideologues, such as the Indian Sultanate historian Barani, might wish Muslim rulers to act more like clerics than sultans and forcibly

---

[14] Robert Dankoff, *An Ottoman Mentality: The World of Evliya Çelebi* (Leiden and Boston: Brill, 2004), 143–4.
[15] See below, Chapter 7.

convert non-Muslims to Islam, but Ottoman rulers subjugated the 'ulama to their imperial interests throughout the history of the dynasty.

Nonetheless, despite the Ottomans' pragmatic tolerance, non-Muslims were seen and expected to act as second-class citizens, which was what Barani had yearned for in fourteenth-century Delhi. Jews and Christians were required to wear distinctive clothing, and they were forbidden to ride horses or build new synagogues or churches – the latter the kind of restriction that Mughals sometimes enforced against the construction of new Hindu temples in India. Ottoman sultans periodically issued edicts in which they tried to revive languishing restrictions on prosperous Jews and Christians, such as Murad IV's pronouncement of 1631, which cited both religious and imperial law, *shari'a* and *kanun*, as the legal basis for discrimination:

> According to the religious requisites based on Sharia and *kanun*, infidels are not to mount a horse, wear a sable fur, fur caps, European silk velvet, and satin. Infidel women are not to go about in the Muslim style and manner or dress and wear "Paris" overcoats. Thus they are expected to be treated with contempt, made submissive and humbled in their clothes. For some time, however, these rules have been neglected. ... infidels and Jews go about the market place on horseback and wear sable fur and sumptuous garments.
>
> When infidels encounter Muslims in the market place they do not get off the pavement and they and their women have become the possessors of more pomp and circumstance than the people of Islam.[16]

Early Ottomans: Oghuz, military slaves, and the 'ulama

Owing to its beginnings in an obscure principality on the outer, western fringes of the Saljuq state, early Ottoman history is not well documented; the first official histories were written more than a century after Osman's defeat of the Byzantines in 1302. This fact of composition is the principal reason why the authors of these works – or the authors of the court history of any ruler – should not be taken at face value when they depict a dynasty's early history in flattering political or religious terms. Men with religious training, such as the Indian Muslim Barani, are particularly untrustworthy as interpreters of rulers' motives, especially when they wrote long after the fact.[17] In the reign of Osman Beğ, he and his followers, like members of other *beğlik*s, functioned as a semi-rural predatory confederation composed largely, but not exclusively, of a

---

[16] Quoted by Barkey, *Empire of Difference*, 120–1.
[17] All students of pre-modern Muslim historical writing should read Peter Hardy's *Historians of Medieval India* (London: Luzac, 1966) for its warnings about the profound biases of fourteenth-century Indo-Persian historiography – warnings which are equally valid for Safavid and Ottoman historiography.

seemingly inexhaustible supply of Oghuz Turks from the east, first as allies of the Saljuqs and later as refugees fleeing the Mongols. Whether or not Osman and his successors were exceptionally clever tacticians and strategists in their early raids, they were fortunate to be situated in northwestern Anatolia, far from the center of Il-Khanid Mongol power in Iranian Azerbaijan and close to the prosperous agrarian regions and trading centers around Constantinople. Whatever Osman's actual relations with the last Saljuqs, his son Orhan (r. 1324–62) began minting coins in 1326 as a declaration of sovereignty and also proclaimed himself sultan. His son Murad I (r. 1362–89) began using the Saljuq title "Exalted Sultan" previously held by Tughril of the Great Saljuqs, while Murad's son, Bayezid I (r. 1389–1402), the unhappy victim of Temür's victory at Ankara, took matters one titular step further and declared himself, in the absence of Saljuq power, Sultan of Rum.

The military structure and economic basis of the Ottoman *beğlik* resembled the Saljuq system in general outline. Turkic cavalrymen (known as *sipahis*) comprised the majority of Osman's troops and those of his successors as late as the sixteenth century. The sultans supported these troops with the same general type of military feudalism that the Safavids and Mughals later employed, granting them theoretically temporary grants of agricultural land and/or small towns similar to *iqta's*, but known both as *dirliks* (livings) or *timars* (funds to support cavalry). As in the case of the Great Saljuqs, slave troops, originally just a palace guard, grew in numbers and importance as units of these men proved reliable and loyal, and the Ottomans, far more than their Saljuq predecessors, increasingly came to rely on their *ghulams* or *mamluks*, their "Janissaries."

After the conquest most Janissary regiments were barracked in Constantinople, where in the early sixteenth century they totaled about 10,000 highly disciplined infantry troops. This number is relatively small in comparison with the numbers of *sipahi* cavalry in 1525, when 10,000 horsemen were based in Europe and 17,000 in Anatolia, but the Janissaries were effective far beyond their numbers. They were superior to any European foot soldiers at the time. The fact that many were garrisoned at the heart of the empire, in Constantinople, meant they also could exert considerable political influence. Eventually the Janisssaries, like the slave troops of the Samanids, evolved from a military asset into a political liability, sometimes dethroning or even murdering sultans, a problem that the reigning Ottoman sultan finally resolved in 1826 when he used newly formed European-style regiments to massacre the remnants of this once elite force.[18]

---

[18] The figures are taken from Imber, *The Ottoman Empire*, 207 and 209.

Slaves were commonly employed in Islamic societies as troops and for a variety of domestic purposes, but the Ottomans were unusual in that they systematized the use of slaves not only in military units but to serve in their bureaucracy. After 1453 the Ottoman regime became in many respects a slave state. Initially Ottoman sultans had simply claimed a share of Christians taken in battle, enslaved and converted them, trained them as Janissaries, or brought them into the royal household. By the late fourteenth and early fifteenth centuries, however, the need for greater numbers of slaves prompted Ottomans to create the *devshirme* system, which in theory mandated that one young boy in every forty households in Christian villages within imperial territories would be taken as a slave and either trained for service in the palace or, more commonly, sent to be enrolled as a Janissary.

Gradually some of these boys matured and became ministers and even viziers, the sultan's principal ministers. During the fourteenth century Ottoman sultans generally appointed free-born Muslims, usually Turks, as viziers. After 1453 this ceased to happen, and by the reign of Süleyman the Magnificent (r. 1520–66) nearly all the viziers had originated as Christian peasant boys taken in the *devshirme* draft. As viziers, they wielded enormous power, whether on campaigns or within the palace, but when they lost the favor of the sultan they were often executed without warning – and certainly without trial – even though many of them had married into the reigning sultan's family.

Janissaries and "slave" viziers were members of the Ottoman elite, known as the *askeri*, literally soldiers, the military class. This class, which also included *sipahi* cavalrymen and free-born Ottoman-speaking bureaucratic officials, was functionally similar in some ways to the military-bureaucrat personnel of the Mughal Empire, who were known as *mansabdars*, those who held (*dar*) imperially granted ranks or offices (*mansabs*). In both cases these officials were exempt from taxation and formed a self-conscious imperial elite, speaking the court dialect (respectively Ottoman or Persian) and, in theory at least, observing well-known norms of behavior and etiquette.[19] In both cases this elite formed a privileged class, distinct in Ottoman parlance from the *re'âyâ*, the tax-paying class of peasants, artisans and merchants, who were often known in Timurid-Mughal terminology simply as the *'amm*, the "vulgar" or common people.[20] The two elite classes also differed from one another in fundamental ways.

---

[19] For the Timurid-Mughal case see Rosalind O'Hanlon, "Manliness and Imperial Service in Mughal North India," *Journal of the Economic and Social History of the Orient* 42, No. 1 (1999), 47–93.

[20] The common Arabic-Persian phrase is: *khass u 'amm* or "nobles and plebeians."

The Ottoman *askeri* class included the *'ulama,* and indeed, in the pre-conquest Ottoman state the principal *qadis* or religious judges were known as *kadi askers* or "army judges," a reflection of the highly militarized nature of Ottoman rule. The framework of what was to become an Ottoman clerical bureaucracy composed of learned clerics, trained in Hanafi Sunni *madrasas* and known collectively as the *'ilmiye* class, was in place by 1453. Sultan Orhon founded the first Ottoman *madrasa* in Iznik in the early fourteenth century; later institutions were built in the capital, Bursa.[21] Ottoman sultans gradually subordinated their *'ulama* to their imperial authority, and the lack of independence of the *'ilmiye* class made it easier for Atatürk in the 1920s to treat the Ottoman clerics of his day as little more than the religious bureaucracy they became in the Turkish Republic.

There were major differences between the Ottoman slave state of the fifteenth century, with its bureaucratized religious class, and both the Safavid and the Mughal administrations. In contrast to the Ottomans, both the Safavids and the Mughals initially relied on free-born Muslims (and also, in the Indian case, Hindus) rather than slaves to serve the dynasty. This continued to be true throughout Mughal history, but in the seventeenth century the Safavids created their own slave bureaucracy, although it was never as elaborate as the Ottoman example. Safavid and Mughal reliance on influential free-born commanders and ministers – by necessity, in the sixteenth-century Safavid case – probably explains some of the noticeable lack of imperial discipline among their troops and officials. This may have been one of the reasons why early Safavid and Mughal rulers did not, like the Ottomans of the fifteenth and sixteenth centuries, regularly slaughter their own officials. There were also striking differences between the situation of the Ottoman *'ulama* and those of Safavid Iran and Mughal India. The Safavids systematically created an Iranian Shi'i clergy which, by the last years of the dynasty, had become an autonomous and politically influential religious institution, some of whose individuals invoked Shi'i theology to challenge the legitimacy of Safavid shahs. Mughal rulers, in contrast, were far more laissez-faire in religious matters, offering traditional patronage to their *'ulama,* while neither subordinating them to the state nor encouraging their development as a state institution.

Ottoman conquests

Ottoman rulers began developing their distinctive slave and clerical institutions in the late fourteenth century, the period in which they emerged as

---

[21] Imber, *The Ottoman Empire*, 226–7.

the superior *beğlik* among several neighboring Turkic lineages in western Anatolia. Their proximity to Byzantine lands and the Bosphorus enabled them to expand across the straits, distinguishing them from their Turkic rivals and giving them access to rich, thickly populated agricultural lands in the Balkans. First, by exploiting a succession dispute in the neighboring *beğlik* of Kayseri in 1345 they gained territory along the Dardanelles, a base they used seven years later to send troops to Gallipoli in alliance with a claimant to the Byzantine throne. A year later Orhan seized the opportunity of a Byzantine succession struggle to marry one of the emperor's daughters. In 1352, with the Byzantines still at war, he received permission to send troops to the Gallipoli peninsula, and shortly afterwards he was able to occupy the main Gallipoli fortress, the foundation of Ottoman power in Europe.

His son Murad consolidated Ottoman power in Anatolia, gaining control over rich trade routes leading to the Ottoman capital at Bursa, and he followed these successes by successful campaigns in Europe to capture Adrianople (Edirne) in 1369, opening the way into Bulgaria. By 1385 Ottoman armies campaigning against fractious European opponents had occupied Sofia and reached the Albanian coast. Four years later, following other victories in Anatolia, Murad defeated Serbian and Bosnian armies at the now famous battle of Kosovo. Despite suffering occasional setbacks Ottoman armies pressed deeper into Europe and the new sultan, Bayezid, reached the River Danube in 1395 and annexed the kingdom of Bulgaria. In 1398 Bayezid returned to Anatolia to formally annex Sivas in Central Anatolia, as well as to seize valuable territories along the Black Sea coast. Among other benefits, these Anatolian conquests gave the Ottomans control over old Saljuq administrative and educational centers. Two years later, however, the new Central Asian conqueror, Temür, appeared in Anatolia, threatening the existence of the Ottoman state.

Temür and the Ottoman interregnum

Two years after sacking Delhi, Temür led a large nomadic army composed of Central Asian Turks and Mongols into Anatolia, first plundering Sivas before moving south to occupy Damascus, where he met Ibn Khaldun, whose cyclical theory of North African and Iberian history later became popular among thoughtful Ottoman intellectuals trying to understand the trajectory of Ottoman fortunes.[22] Returning north, he

---

[22] Cornell Fleischer, "Royal Authority, Dynastic Cyclism and 'Ibn Khaldunism'" in Sixteenth Century Ottoman Letters," in Bruce Lawrence, ed., *Ibn Khaldun and Islamic Ideology* (Leiden: Brill, 1984), 198–220.

offered protection from the Ottomans to four formerly independent Oghuz *begliks*, who fought with him against Bayezid at Ankara in 1402. Temür's crushing defeat of the Ottoman army and capture of Bayezid himself was an important moment in Ottoman history. First and foremost, it taught Ottomans to rely increasingly on their Janissary forces, for during the clash many *sipahis* and tribal contingents deserted to Temür, while Janissaries remained loyal to the Sultan.

Temür's policies after the Ankara battle were also important, because despite his resounding victory – after which he carried Bayezid about in an iron cage for the remaining months of the latter's life – he acted as he had done in Delhi four years earlier. Temür, that is, did not try to occupy Anatolia or integrate Ottoman dominions into a centrally administered empire, but quickly withdrew to conduct other campaigns. He merely claimed a kind of suzerainty over Bayezid's sons, among whom he divided Ottoman territories in Anatolia. In 1403 Temür, already a relatively old man, left Anatolia to return to Samarqand and prepare for the conquest of China. His partition of Anatolia precipitated a civil war among Bayezid's sons and (temporarily at least) restored the independence of many small Anatolian Oghuz families. Nonetheless Temür left intact an Ottoman dynasty with its ambitions, knowledge, European provinces, and military and administrative institutions, albeit in a distracted and reduced condition.

By 1423 the nineteen-year-old sultan, Murad II, who had been crowned in 1421 through the intervention of Janissaries and members of the *'ulama*, repossessed most of the Ottomans' Anatolian territories and began a series of European campaigns against Hungary and Venice to secure their Balkan territories. He campaigned relentlessly in Europe for the next two decades, demonstrating the continued superiority of the Ottoman military over European armies, and returned to Anatolia only in 1444 to make peace with the last major independent Oghuz *beglik* of Karaman, as well as to placate Temür's son Shah Rukh, who still dominated Khurasan and central Iran from his capital at Herat. In that same year Murad crossed back into Europe to defeat a formidable Hungarian army, thus decisively consolidating Ottoman control of the Balkans and in effect sealing the fate of what remained of the Byzantine Empire, now reduced to the isolated city-state of Constantinople. At Murad's death in 1451 the Ottomans were poised to realize the Muslim community's dream of conquering the great imperial city, which his son Mehmet II accomplished after a siege of fifty-four days from May to June, 1453, having battered the city walls with the powerful cannon which had long since become a critically important arm of the formidable Ottoman military.

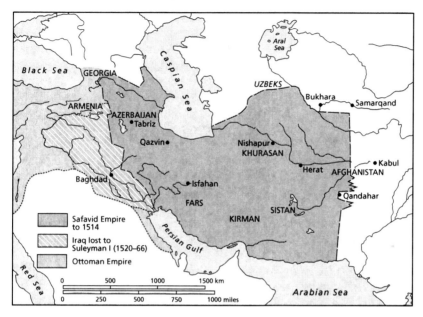

Map 7. The Safavid Empire to 1514; Iraq was later lost to Süleyman I, (1520–66)

The Safavids

When Mehmet II occupied Constantinople in 1453, the political and religious lineages that combined to produce the Safavid dynasty were just emerging as influential actors in eastern Anatolia and northwestern Iran. These were the Aq Quyunlu or "White Sheep" Turks and the Safavid Sufi *pirs* of Ardebil. In 1453 neither the Aq Quyunlu (1378–1502) nor the Safavids had acquired substantial political or religious influence in these regions. At that time two other dynasties dominated most of the Iranian plateau, the contiguous territories of Iraq and Anatolia and Mawarannahr: the Qara Quyunlu (1378–1469) or "Black Sheep" Turks based in Tabriz, near the old Mongol capital at Sultaniye and the Timurids in Herat and Samarqand.

In the 1450s, however, the Aq Quyunlu gradually displaced the Qara Quyunlu as the dominant power in the west. Between 1453, when Uzun Hasan (r. 1453–78) came to power as leader of his clan, and the end of the dynasty in 1502, the White Sheep constituted a formidable power in eastern Anatolia, Iraq, and northwestern Iran. Both the Qara and the Aq Quyunlu represented yet another chapter in the continued Turkic tribal domination of Iran and Anatolia, a domination which had begun with the

Saljuq migrations (or invasion) in the tenth century and revived after the collapse of Mongol rule in 1336.

Like so many Anatolian *begliks*, both the Black and White Sheep dynasties began life as loosely organized pastoral nomadic bands of raiders. By the middle of the fourteenth century the leading clans of what was later to emerge as the Aq Quyunlu tribal confederation were settled in the Diyarbekir region of eastern Anatolia and in Armenia, driven there, probably, by the Mongol invasion. Subsequently they were forced to submit to Temür and joined with him to defeat Bayezid at the Battle of Ankara in 1402, receiving as their reward the entire Diyarbekir region to rule as Temür's vassals. During the early fourteenth century the Aq Quyunlu ruler Qara 'Usman (r. 1403–35) began transforming his largely nomadic tribal confederation into a partly sedentarized *beglik* with a Perso-Islamic administration, in essence attempting to repeat the evolutionary process of the Saljuqs under Nizam al-Mulk's direction or that of the Il-Khanid Mongols with Rashid al-Din.

Qara 'Usman became sufficiently powerful to threaten the territories of the Timurids and the Ottomans. He himself retained important elements of his nomadic heritage, not the least his conviction that settlement of his tribal followers threatened "sovereignty, Turkishness and liberty."[23] Like Chinggis Qan, who made similar warnings about the socially disruptive and corrupting influence of city life upon Mongols, Qara 'Usman cited a traditional body of unwritten laws, the *yasaq*, in the course of giving advice to his sons.[24] He also reminded them and his followers to respect the legitimizing force of Oghuz traditions, roughly at the same time as the reigning Ottoman sultan, Murad II, was emphasizing his own dynasty's Central Asian Oghuz heritage as a way to reassert Ottoman authority in the wake of Temür's victory.[25]

As an Oghuz confederation, the Aq Quyunlu followed the same inheritance and political tradition as the Saljuqs, the early Ottomans, and the Mughals, so Qara 'Usman's death precipitated a civil war among his sons. Not until 1453 did Uzun Hasan emerge triumphant from this struggle; in 1466 he defeated the Qara Quyunlu and reigned as the leader of the now ascendant Aq Quyunlu until 1478.[26] During his reign he conquered

---

[23] John E. Woods, *The Aqquyunlu: Clan, Confederation, Empire* (Minneapolis and Chicago: Biblioteca Islamica, 1876), p. 67.

[24] David O. Morgan discusses the question of the nature of the Mongol *yasa* with special reference to the Mongols of Il-Khanid Iran in his article "The Great Yasa of Chingiz Khan and Mongol Law in the IlKhanate," *Bulletin of the School of Oriental and African Studies* 49 (1986), 163–76.

[25] Imber, *The Ottoman Empire*, 122–3.

[26] For an interesting study of Aq Quyunlu administration taken from primary sources see Vladimir Minorsky, "The Aq Quyunlu and Land Reforms," *Bulletin of the School of Oriental and African Studies* 17, No. 3 (1955), 449–62.

territory in Georgia, Kurdistan in eastern Anatolia, and northwestern and central Iran, displacing the severely weakened Timurids from most of their Iranian possessions west of Herat. Prior to his defeat by the Ottomans in 1473, he transformed the Aq Quyunlu confederation into a major Perso-Islamic principality, attracting the attention of the Timurid Persian-language poet Jami (d. 1492), who from Herat proclaimed Uzun Hasan the "Sultan of the Ghazis" for his exploits against the Georgian Christians.

Uzun Hasan, like most of his Oghuz predecessors and contemporaries, was a Sunni Muslim who assiduously patronized Muslim religious institutions and Sufi orders to broaden his own legitimacy. By this time the Safavids constituted one of the most influential Sufi orders within his dominions, and Uzun Hasan not only married his sister to Junaid, the Safavid *pir* until his death in 1460 CE, but also married one of his daughters to Junaid's son Haidar, the leader of the Safavid order until his death in 1488.

Safavids and Sufis in post-Mongol Iran

The Safavid order had been founded by Shaikh Safi-al Din (1252–1334), a member of an important landed family near Ardebil, during the chaotic period that witnessed the rapid spread of these mystical lineages in both Iran and Anatolia.[27] In the roughly two and a half centuries between the establishment of the Il-Khanid Mongols in Iran and the foundation of the Safavid dynasty in 1501, Sufism gained popular influence throughout this broad territory, organized as distinctly individual orders with institutional bases in the *khangah*, the Sufi hospice or chapter house pioneered by the Khurasanian Abu Sa'yid ibn Abi'l Khair. A number of these orders preached messianic doctrines, as did, for example, the Nurbakhshiyya, whose founder declared he was the *mahdi*, the individual who would restore justice and true religion to the Islamic world.[28] This was an idea that was strongly developed by and usually associated with Muslims who revered the *ahl al-bayt*, members of the Prophet Muhammad's family; and even more so with Shi'as, for whom the doctrine of the hidden Imam was central to their belief and expectation of being freed from oppressive Sunni rule.

[27] For a summary of the history of the Safavid shrine town see X. de Planhol, "Ardebil," in Ehsan Yarshater, ed., *Encyclopaedia Iranica*, II (London and New York: Routledge and Keegan Paul, 1987), 357–61.

[28] Shahzad Bashir, "After the Messiah: The Nurbakhshiyya in Late Timurid and Early Safavid Times," in Andrew J. Newman, ed., *Society and Culture in the Early Modern Middle East* (Leiden: Brill, 2003), 295–314.

Pilgrimages to the shrines of revered Sufi *pirs* became widespread during these centuries, when these men often served as the most influential representatives of Islam among the general populace. Some Sufis, such as the Chishtis of Afghanistan and India, preached withdrawal from a corrupting world, but others, such as the Naqshbandiyya, an order whose *pirs* were closely allied with Timurid rulers, actively preached a restrained mystical doctrine, engaged in politics, and even intermarried with the ruling elite. Sufis exerted considerable influence at the Il-Khanid court in the late thirteenth century, and Il-Khanid Mongols, Muslims since the conversion of Ghazan Khan, who inherited the state in 1295, patronized the Safavid shrine at Ardabil in the early fourteenth century, leading to an expansion of the order's economic base and religious influence. Indeed, during the late or Muslim Il-Khanid period, Shaikh Safi steadily acquired more agricultural and commercial land.[29] Most of the Iranian orders prior to Safavid times were Sunni, although some such as the Nurbakhshiyya initially disclaimed any sectarian identity. Some *pirs* were Shi'a, however, and in an era when distinctions between Sunnis and Shi'as were often blurred, some Sunnis, especially those with a powerful reverence for 'Ali and the Prophet Muhammad's family, became Shi'as.

Before the Safavids became rulers of Iran, there were instances in Iran where Shi'i Sufis battled for political power. The ephemeral Sarbadar dynasty of Sabzawar in fourteenth-century Khurasan is the best-documented example of an alliance between a Sufi *pir* and a local political leader that culminated in the establishment of a radical Shi'i state. Beginning in the late 1330s, when the Il-Khanid Mongol regime was disintegrating, the dynasty began life as a wealthy Khurasanian landowner's tax revolt against Mongol rulers. The picaresque dynastic name, which in Persian means "head on the gallows," supposedly originated when the founder proclaimed that he and his followers would either expel their oppressors or end with their "heads on the gallows."

In 1340 the original leaders of the revolt seized Nishapur, defeating the forces of the Mongol Taghaytimur two years later. Then, in order to attract support from the substantial population of Shi'i Muslims living in Sabzawar, the Sarbadar leader, Mas'ud, a Sunni, enlisted the support of one Shaikh Hasan, a Shi'i Sufi living in the city. Shaikh Hasan, who had earlier built up an armed following of artisans and tradesmen, responded

---

[29] See, among other discussions of this relationship, Kishwar Rizvi, "Transformations in Early Safavid Architecture: The Shrine of Shaykh Safi al-Din Ishaq Ardebili," unpublished PhD dissertation, (Department of Architecture, Massachusetts Institute of Technology, 2000), 35–44 and Fariba Zarinebaf-Shahr, "Economic Activities of Safavid Women in the Shrine-City of Ardabil," *Iranian Studies* 31, No. 2 (Spring 1998), 253.

to the Sarbadar appeal and tried to impose his Shi'i faith on nearby Sunnis, while encouraging expectations of the imminent appearance of the *mahdi*. One measure that Mas'ud and his clerical ally took to legitimize their rule was to invite a Shi'i theologian from the long-established Shi'i theological center of Jabal 'Amil in Lebanon, a precedent for the influx of Jabal 'Amil Shi'i clerics that occurred in Safavid times.[30] In Sabzawar, however, tensions among the coalition of Sunni political leaders and Shi'i religious extremists caused violent conflicts, including assassinations. The entire movement imploded around 1380, when a revolt broke out in the city directed against radical Shi'i *pirs*, who had established an ideologically rigid Shi'i government in Sabzawar three years earlier.[31]

The Safavids succeeded where the Sarbadar landowners and Shi'i clerics failed, at least partly because they combined both political and religious lines in themselves. It seems to have been Junaid who began to transform the Safavid order into a militant religio-political movement. It was Junaid who married Uzun Hasan Aq Quyunlu's sister and it was he who conducted missionary activities among Oghuz tribes in Azerbaijan and fought *ghazas* against Christians in the Caucasus. Junaid's religious beliefs are not well known, but his son Haidar, who continued his father's military activities, was evidently a Shi'a to some degree, even though he was raised in the Sunni Aq Quyunlu court and was married to one of Uzun Hasan's daughters.

Perhaps because of his dual religious and political lineages, he was perceived to be a threat by Uzun Hasan's son and successor, Yakub. After Haidar died fighting in the Caucasus, Yakub imprisoned Haidar's two sons in distant Fars province, where the Aq Quyunlu later killed one of them. The second, Isma'il, survived and escaped to take refuge in northern Iran, a Shi'i area since Buyid times, where he lived with a minor Shi'i ruler. He eventually emerged as a young man, to rally his family's tribal supporters and contest the Aq Quyunlu throne. Yet, unlike his Aq Quyunlu kin, Isma'il gathered support not merely by claiming Aq Quyunlu descent, but through the dissemination of a powerful Shi'i messianic ideology delivered by a man who was an hereditary Sufi *pir*.

Shah Isma'il and Safavid ideology

Shah Isma'il appealed to his largely illiterate Turkic tribal followers in verse, which is remarkable for its ideological complexity, if not for its

---

[30] Rula Jurdi Abisaab, "The Ulama of Jabal 'Amil in Safavid Iran, 1501–1736: Marginality, Migration and Social Change," *Iranian Studies* 27, Nos. 1–4 (1994), 114.

[31] This summary is taken from John Masson Smith Jr.'s book *The History of the Sarbadar Dynasty and Its Sources* (The Hague: Mouton, 1970).

literary quality.[32] Written in a Turkic dialect similar to modern Azeri Turkish, which, along with Persian, was probably a language he knew from birth or as a very young man, Isma'il appealed to the tribes and probably also the urban proletariat of eastern Anatolia and northern and northwestern Iran. These included the Afshar and Qajar tribes, whose descendants became ruling dynasties in Iran in post-Safavid times. In the poems Isma'il praises 'Ali over Muhammad and claims descent from 'Ali through 'Ali's son, Husain, and Muhammad's daughter, Fatima. While giving his pen name as Khata'i or "sinner," he assumes Muhammad's title, the "Seal of the Prophets," as well as the status of the Shi'i Imam, who in his words, has now appeared on earth as mankind's "perfect guide." In one of his many verses he presents himself in his dual religious role as both a Shi'a and a Sufi, beginning the poem with the Safavid battle cry of "Allah, Allah." Yet Isma'il also both connects himself to the Old Testament prophets and alludes to his family's *ghazi* tradition against Christians:

> O fighters in the path of God, say: Allah, Allah! I am the faith of the
> Shah ['Ali].
> Come to meet (me), prostrate yourself (*sijda*). I am the faith of the Shah.
> In flying I am a parakeet, I am the leader of a mighty army, a companion
> of Sufis.
> Whenever you sow me, I will grow; whenever you call me,
> I will come up. I shall catch the Sufis by the hand.
> I was on the gibbet with Mansur; with Abraham in the fire and with
> Moses on Sinai.
> Come from the eve, celebrate the New Year [*Nau Ruz*], join the King.
> With discernment come to know the King. O ghazis prostrate yourselves.
> I wear a red crown, my charger is grey, I (lead a) mighty army.
> I have the virtues of the Prophet Joseph (i.e. I am beautiful).
> I am Khata'i, my charger is sorrel; my words are sweeter
> than sugar, I have the essence of Murtada 'Ali. I am the faith of
> the Shah.[33]

Isma'il's legitimizing propaganda reflected the extraordinarily variegated and unstructured religious environment of his audience, the predominantly Turkic-speaking Oghuz tribes of eastern Anatolia and northwestern Iran. Isma'il espoused an intoxicating brew of Shi'i concepts and messianic claims, which Shi'i theologians, residents of more settled environments such as the Jabal 'Amil region of Lebanon, often labeled as

[32] See Charles Melville, ed., *Safavid Persia: The History and Politics of an Islamic Society* (London and New York. I.B. Tauris, 1996), for a collection of useful essays on both early and later Safavid history.

[33] Vladimir Minorsky, "The Poetry of Shah Isma'il I," *Bulletin of the School of Oriental and African Studies* 10, No. 4 (1942), 1025a–1026a, 1032a and 1042a.

ghuluww, unorthodox or extremist. Isma'il also demanded obedience, even *sijda* or prostration – a demand for semi-divine respect abhorrent to most Sunni Muslims but appropriate for Sufi *pirs* and Shi'i Imams. Using his Shi'i and Sufi appeal and indiscriminately linking himself to any religious or political tradition that might evoke a sympathetic murmur in his untutored audience, Isma'il created a charismatic authority that drew Oghuz tribes to his banner and produced a tribal military coalition in the service of a theocratic dynasty. His tribal followers were hereafter known as the Qizilbash, Turkic for "redheads," a name given to them because they wore a distinctive turban with a red baton and twelve folds that symbolized the Imams of Twelver Shi'ism. Isma'il also solidified his relations with these tribes by marrying his sisters to tribal leaders, just as early Ottoman sultans had also married women of Turkic and Christian lineages to consolidate their embryonic state, and similar intermarriages between Safavids and Qizilbash continued throughout the sixteenth century, complicating tribal loyalties with dynastic matrilineal ties.[34]

Shi'i Islam in Safavid Iran

Isma'il's commitment to Shi'i Islam became apparent after he and his followers seized Tabriz from his Aq Quyunlu relatives in 1501, beginning a decade during which they conquered most of the Iranian plateau. Almost immediately he began the process of spreading and institutionalizing Shi'ism in a country whose population had been mostly Sunni, although (as we have seen in the cases of the Buyids and Sarbadars), there were substantial numbers of Shi'as in northern Iran and Khurasan well before the Safavid victories. Early in his reign Isma'il followed the Sarbadar precedent by inviting Twelver Shi'i theologians from established clerical families in Jabal 'Amil in Lebanon to come to Iran and build up a Shi'i *'ulama* establishment that had not existed in Iran prior to this time. 'Ali al-Karaki al-'Amili (*c.* 1466–1534) was the most influential of these early Shi'i émigrés. He first settled in Najaf in Iraq around 1504, and beginning in 1504–5 he visited the Safavid court several times during Isma'il's reign and that of his son, Tahmasp, initiating a family network of Shi'i theologians who served the Safavids throughout the sixteenth and seventeenth centuries.[35]

---

[34] Maria Szuppe, "Kinship Ties between the Safavids and the Qizilbash Amirs in Late Sixteenth-Century Iran: A Case Study of the Political Career of Members of the Sharafaldin Oghli Tekelu Family," in Melville, ed., *Safavid Persia,* (1996), 79–104.

[35] See especially Abisaab, "The Ulama of Jabal 'Amil," 108–9, and Rosemary Stanfield Johnson, "Sunni Survival in Safavid Iran: Anti-Sunni Activities during the Reign of Shah Tahmasp I," *Iranian Studies* 27, No. 1/4 (1994), 125.

In other verses Isma'il broadened his appeal to include pre-Islamic Iranian monarchs of the *Shah-nama*, as well as Alexander (a hero well known to Muslims under the name of Iskandar), and wrote: "I am Faridun, Khusrau, Jamshid, and Zohak. I am Zal's son [Rustam] and Alexander." Indeed, when Isma'il captured Tabriz in 1501 he proclaimed himself in pre-Islamic Iranian political terms as Padishah-i Iran. In using the Persian term "Padishah," to describe his status in "Iran," he was repeating pre-Islamic Iranian political and geographical/political terminology that had only recently been revived by the Il-Khanid Mongols and used also by the Aq Quyunlu. His invocation of these terms suggests he thought of himself as a political heir of his matrilineal relatives, the Aq Quyunlu. The ancient term "Iran" had fallen out of use following the Arab-Muslim invasions and had not been used by the Caliphs, or their successors, the Samanids, or the many Turkic dynasties that succeeded them. A final irony of Isma'il's use of the term "Iran," or in one of his poems the phrase *mulk-i 'Ajam*, the "state" or "kingdom of Iran," is that even though Tabriz, Azerbaijan, and Mesopotamia represented provinces of the pre-Islamic Shahanshahs, the "kings of Kings" of Iran, there is no evidence that Isma'il imagined himself to be reconstituting a new Iranian empire; rather he planned to establish a messianic Shi'i state on Aq Quyunlu foundations.

Within the decade following his capture of Tabriz in 1501, Isma'il occupied the geographic center of the pre-Islamic Achaemenid and Sasanian Iranian empires. He did so, though, with Oghuz tribes whose knowledge of the *Shah-nama* and the glories of pre-Islamic Iranian kingship was almost certainly limited to inchoate oral traditions. Isma'il was reconstituting the Aq Quyunlu state in these conquests, and like that of the Aq Quyunlu, the ultimate focus of his ambitions was eastern Anatolia, where his father and grandfather and he himself had proselytized among the Turks. After he returned to Anatolia and began winning over more of the Oghuz tribes, he so frightened the Ottomans with his seductive propaganda that the reigning Ottoman emperor Selim (r. 1512–20) marched east, carrying a religious proclamation that Isma'il was a heretic. In 1514 Selim destroyed the Safavid army at Chaldiran in Azerbaijan, psychologically shattering Isma'il's confidence and charisma at the same time. This and subsequent Ottoman victories prevented the Safavids from controlling even eastern Anatolia and forced them back onto the Iranian plateau and boundaries that nearly approximate the modern borders of the Shi'i Islamic Republic of Iran.

The Mughals

Just as Isma'il emerged from hiding in northern Iran to rally his tribal supporters and challenge his Aq Quyunlu relatives, the last Central Asian

Timurids were losing control of Temür's former homelands in and around his capital city, Samarqand. Following Temür's death in 1405, the Timurid world of Mawarannahr and Iran suffered its first taste of the dynastic succession struggle so typical of Turkic dynasties, with their traditions of shared sovereignty. During the first half of the fifteenth century Temür's son Shah Rukh, ruling Iran from Herat, and the latter's son Ulugh Beg, governing Mawarannahr from Samarqand as his father's largely autonomous deputy, held Temür's core dominions together. Temür had not bequeathed a sense of shared mission or joint governance to his descendants, however; instead he left each with a conviction that as a Timurid he had a legitimate right to rule. In the latter half of the fifteenth century the proliferation of Timurids seeking to claim their ancestor's authority led to the formation of autonomous, warring city-states and a fragmentation of both Mawarannahr's and also Iran's modest resources.[36] Cultural flowering was an unintended offshoot of this fragmentation, as Timurid princes competed for cultural legitimacy by patronizing an impressive florescence of traditional Perso-Islamic culture as well as an evolving body of Turki or Chaghatai Turkish literature that Ottoman writers came to revere. Nonetheless the Timurids' inability to cooperate with one another left these *mirzas*, as Temür's offspring were known, vulnerable to the ambition of the Uzbeks in Mawarannahr and the Qara and Aq Quyunlu confederations in Iran.

The founder of the Mughal Empire, Zahir al-Din Muhammad Babur (1483–1530), was one of the Timurids who before his twelfth birthday was thrown into the maelstrom of competing Timurid lineages and Uzbek expansion in Mawarannahr.[37] After twice seizing but only briefly occupying Samarqand, he finally fled from Mawarannahr as Uzbeks eliminated most of the Timurid and Chaghatai Mongol relatives who stood in their way. Seizing the impoverished outpost of Kabul as a refuge in 1504, he spent most of the next seven years trying to restore his fortunes in Mawarannahr, first by defending the last Timurid outpost of Herat against Uzbek attacks and then, when that city fell in 1507, avoiding being overrun by the Uzbeks after they took Qandahar in Central Afghanistan and threatened to move on Kabul. Babur's fortunes

[36] For the Timurids of Mawarannahr see Beatrice Forbes Manz, *Power, Politics and Religion in Timurid Iran* (Cambridge University Press, 2007), Maria E. Subtelny, *Timurids in Transition* (Leiden: Brill, 2007) and for the Timurids' impressive artistic patronage, Thomas W. Lentz and Glenn D. Lowry, *Temür and the Princely Vision: Persian Art and Culture in the Fifteenth Century* (Los Angeles and Washington: Los Angeles County Museum of Art and the Arthur M. Sackler Gallery, 1989).

[37] Babur's remarkable autobiography, translated by Wheeler M. Thackston, is available in an inexpensive paper edition, *The Baburnama* (New York: Modern Library, 2002).

improved when Shah Isma'il Safavi completed his conquest of the Iranian plateau in 1510 with an attack on the Uzbeks, during which he killed the Uzbek chief, Shaibaq or in Persian, Shibani Khan. Then with the aid of Safavid troops Babur returned to Mawarannahr to seize Samarqand for the third time in 1511, before suffering another defeat from disciplined Uzbek tribal cavalry and fleeing once again to Afghanistan.[38]

Babur's Conquest of north India

Babur's third loss of Temür's ancestral capital demonstrated his military weakness in the face of Uzbek expansion, and sometime after 1514 he abandoned his revanchist ambitions and decided to revive his family's fortunes in India. He had earlier sent plundering expeditions to the Indus in the manner of other Central Asian invaders of the subcontinent, but by 1519 he evidently decided upon a full-scale invasion because, as he openly wrote in his memoirs, it was the only valuable territory available where an ambitious Timurid could establish a new empire. Kabul and the surrounding region were beautiful, but far too poor. In 1519 he unmistakably announced his intentions when he named his newly born son Hind-al, "the taking or conquest of India," and began a series of probing attacks against the Ludi Afghans that led to the occupation of Lahore in 1520. He legitimized his actions by claiming sovereign rights stemming from Temür's 1398 campaign. His long-term intentions were further broadcast when he ordered his men not to plunder and alienate the wealthy inhabitants of Punjabi villages he overran in the 1520s but to tax them.

After securing his northern and western Afghan flanks, he marched out of Kabul in December 1525, and in April 1526 defeated the Ludis in a pitched battle at Panipat, north of Delhi. According to his daughter Gulbadan Begim, Babur commanded only 8,000 battle-ready troops when he defeated the Afghan force, which he estimated, in the self-serving manner of autobiographers, at over 100,000 men.[39] By the evidence of his detailed narrative, the only extant description of the clash and one of the few eyewitness accounts of a major battle in the early history of these three Muslim empires, he won by combining defensive tactics recommended by his Ottoman military advisors with traditional Central Asian cavalry maneuvers carried out by Mongol detachments. Thus he fortified his center in Ottoman fashion with chain-linked carts protecting his matchlock men, artillery and

---

[38] For a study of Babur's career, autobiography, and poetry see Dale, *The Garden of the Eight Paradises*.

[39] Gulbadan Begim, *The History of Humâyûn* (*Humâyûn-nâma*) (Delhi: Idarah-i Adabiyât-i Delhi, repr. 1972), f. 9b, p. 12.

cavalry reserves, while sending swift Mongol mounted archers to outflank and envelop the enemy who had been lured into the center of the battlefield. This was not primarily a gunpowder victory, for Babur himself reports that his new artillery pieces fired only a "few shots." Firearms may have contributed to his triumph by helping to defend his center, but Mongol flanking attacks won the battle, as they had so many times before in Central Asia.

Babur's victory is the clearest case possible of dynastic imperialism, unleavened with any self-serving suggestions of religious sanctity. In his rich, remarkably frank but still self-congratulatory autobiography, a classic of Turki or Chaghatai Turkish prose, he offers the best insight into the inherited ambition and pecuniary motives of a pre-modern conqueror, an openly aggressive, unapologetic member of a warrior class whose profession was conquest and rule. Babur conquered India simply because he had lost the hope of establishing an empire in Mawarannahr or anywhere else, and so he turned his *mulkgirliq*, his "kingdom-seizing" ambitions, to India, where the perpetual factional disputes of its Afghan rulers offered him an opportunity. In his autobiography he also realistically depicts the hesitations, misgivings, accidents, and disasters that marked his early career, and then finally conveys the excitement of a great victory and his undisguised pleasure at becoming the Timurid who rescued his relatives and restored the dynasty's fortunes. Ironically he was victorious in a country whose climate, topography, and society he despised.

Unlike Mehmet II, the Conqueror, who was thrilled to have conquered imperial Constantinople and pleased to govern from there, and even Isma'il, who from secondary evidence seems to have been happy with Tabriz, Babur found only one thing appealing about India: its wealth, although he was intrigued by its exotic flora and fauna. He begins his catalog of criticisms of north India with an implicit denunciation of the socially isolating consequences of Hindu caste social life, which could not tolerate "convivial society" or "social intercourse" across caste lines. Babur then goes on to reveal the intensity of his culture shock and homesickness:

The people of Hindustan have no beauty; they have no convivial society, no social intercourse, no character or genius, no urbanity, no nobility or chivalry. In the skilled arts and sciences there is no regularity, proportionality, straightness or rectangularity. There are no good horses, no good dogs, no grapes, no muskmelons or first-rate fruits, no ice or cold water, no good bread or cooked food in the bazaars, no hammams, no madrasas, no candles, no torches, or candlesticks.[40]

Babur also implies that after subduing northwestern India and the Gangetic valley, he planned to rule "Hindustan" from Kabul: a city,

---

[40] Dale, *The Garden of the Eight Paradises*, 369.

however, poor, whose climate allowed one to sleep under blankets, as he wistfully notes in one passage. His death from disease in 1530 prevented him from rejoining many of his closest companions, whose horror at India's climate and environment led them to flee India for Kabul shortly after Babur's initial victories there.

Thanks to Babur's slightly more than four years of rule following his victory at Panipat, he was able to bequeath to his son Humayun the idea of a new Timurid empire, but one that in 1530 consisted of little more than a superficially pacified countryside. It was, in fact, a series of occupied fortresses and cities stretching from Kabul to Lahore, southwards to Delhi and Agra, and then southeast into the western Ganges valley, with most of the countryside occupied by independent Hindu and Afghan rulers and lesser lineages. In the few years that elapsed between his defeat of the Ludis and his death, Babur had nonetheless begun to assemble the human infrastructure for what was during his lifetime a small Afghan–north Indian Timurid kingdom.

The Mughal Empire in 1530

In a north India long ruled by Muslim dynasties, Babur inherited an established Hanafi Sunni *'ulama* with established *madrasas* – despite Babur's complaint – as well as a number of flourishing Sufi orders, most notably the Chishti. Then, almost immediately after Babur had reported his victory to relatives, allies, and even enemies in Afghanistan, Iran, and Mawarannahr, new Muslims began arriving in the subcontinent. They included Timurid and Chaghatai Mongol relatives, soldiers, and administrators from Mawarannahr and Khurasan, Persian-language historians, musicians, and artists from Herat, and Naqshbandi Sufis, the Timurid's spiritual allies, from Samarqand and other cities in Mawarannahr. Using the Ludis' Persian-language administrative and taxation records, Babur first established a provisional division of territories into temporary military fiefs or appanages administered by Timurid and Chaghatai officers known as *wajhdars*, but similar in general intent to the *iqta'* grants of his predecessors, the Delhi Sultans.

Although no documents have survived from this Indian period of his life, it is safe to surmise that Babur based his taxation, as well as his legal or juridical administration, on the Hanafi Sunni models he knew from Mawarannahr, and which he summarized himself in a work he wrote in Kabul, during a period when he was studying Islamic law with a Muslim scholar there.[41] He was familiar, after all, with the *Hidaya*, a monumental

---

[41] For a brief outline of Babur's Indian government see Dale, *The Garden of the Eight Paradises*, 404–10.

Map 8. The Mughal Empire in 1530

compendium of Hanafi Sunni law compiled by the twelfth-century
Central Asian scholar al-Marghinani, a text that British judges later used
as their principal reference for Muslim law in British India.[42] The Hanafi

---

[42] The works of al-Marghinani (d. 1197), who came from a line of well-known Hanafi Sunni
scholars native to Marghinan, a town near Babur's homeland in the Ferghana valley, east-
southeast of Tashkent, are described by W. Heffening, "al-Marghînânî," *Encyclopaedia of
Islam*, II, Brill Online.

legal school of Sunni Islam remained the norm in the Mughal Empire, although neither Babur nor any of his successors imitated Ottoman practice, whereby the sultans themselves presided over a religious hierarchy that enforced Hanafi Sunni norms.

Babur's political arrangements are also evidence of his continued adherence to Timurid or Turco-Mongol inheritance or succession norms of shared sovereignty. During his lifetime he governed his territories as two distinct units, the "Afghan" lands of northern and central Afghanistan and Kabul, and Hindustan. He and two of his three sons ruled all the Afghan lands except Kabul, which Babur declared to be *khalisa* or crown land. In assigning his two older sons to rule different parts of Afghanistan he was creating a typical Timurid appanage system, and in a letter to Humayun written while in India, Babur said that he had always assigned six parts to him, the eldest, and five parts to his younger brother. The assumption of shared sovereignty came back to haunt Humayun, who, after he succeeded his father in 1530, governed for only a decade before being forced from India by resurgent Afghan forces. He was bedeviled by the actions of his three brothers, who drifted in and out of cooperation with him as he tried to pacify northern India. The youngest, Hind-al, even proclaimed his own sovereignty in 1538 by having the *khutba*, the Friday prayer, read in his name. In addition, two descendants of Sultan Husain Baiqara, the prestigious Timurid ruler of Herat until his death in 1506, flouted Humayun's authority from the beginning of his reign, despite having earlier been given sanctuary in India by Babur.

Lacking the support of his brothers and other Timurids, Humayun fled from India after losing two battles to Afghans, and after having been refused sanctuary by his two other brothers who controlled Kabul and Qandahar, he eventually sought refuge with Shah Isma'il's son and successor, Shah Tahmasp I, in 1544. Received by Tahmasp not as a refugee but as the Mughal *padishah* – another demonstration of the life-saving power of dynastic legitimacy – Humayun bought the Iranian monarch's help with a huge diamond (possibly the *kuh-i nur*, the diamond now part of the British crown jewels), bags of rubies, and possibly a vague promise to embrace Shi'i Islam. With Iranian troops Humayun returned to Afghanistan and began the decade-long process of reclaiming Timurid possessions there and in India; finally, in 1555, he won a decisive battle against Afghan forces. Ever the unlucky monarch, however, he died accidentally the following year in a fall down the stone steps of his library while rushing to respond to the call to prayer. It was left to his son Akbar (r. 1556–1605) to transform the tentatively restored Timurid Indian kingdom into the imposing empire of vast wealth and unchallenged power that awed Europeans in the seventeenth century.

3   The legitimacy of monarchs and
       the institutions of empires

Introduction

Following the emergence of the Ottoman, Safavid, and Mughal dynasties, there was a subsequent ruler in each ruling lineage who transformed the nature of his state. In the fifteenth and sixteenth centuries these were the Ottoman Fatih Mehmet, that is Mehmet II, the Conqueror (1444–81); the Safavid Shah 'Abbas I (1588–1629); and the Mughal Akbar (1556–1605). Each of them exhibited an adaptive personality and personal dynamism that enabled him to mold the state he inherited into a distinctly different and more formidable imperial entity. They did not play precisely analogous roles, since their dynasties had distinct histories and characteristics. In 1444 Mehmet II inherited a powerful and expansionist Anatolian and Balkan sultanate with established military, political, and religious institutions. Yet by his conquest of Constantinople and subsequent policies he substantially altered the Ottomans' self-perceptions as well as the character of the Ottoman state. By the time of his death the Ottoman Sultanate had become a dominant, highly centralized slave empire whose ruler possessed hitherto unequalled autocratic power. In contrast, Shah 'Abbas at age sixteen in 1588 inherited a fragile Safavid regime with a questionable future. During the sixteenth century Isma'il's original religious charisma had atrophied in the face of his defeat at Chaldiran in 1514 and subsequent inertia, and his successors had proved incapable either of solving the intractable internecine conflicts and independent power of the Qizilbash or of decisively defeating their Ottoman and Uzbek enemies. Shah 'Abbas nonetheless transformed every aspect of the Safavid state and left it for the first time an economically viable and formidable Iranian empire whose military defeated Ottoman armies and recaptured Iraq. Akbar played a similarly transformative role in India to that of Shah 'Abbas I in Iran. Coming to the throne at age twelve in 1556, he initially reigned over, but did not rule, a modest, insecure north Indian state that his father, Humayun, had recovered from his Afghan enemies just a year earlier. By his conquests and institutional innovations he bequeathed to his successors a stable, populous empire, whose wealth dwarfed that of his Safavid and Ottoman contemporaries.

The new legitimacies

The degree to which these men altered the states they inherited can partly be measured by the way in which each redefined his dynasty's legitimacy and authority. By his conquest of Constantinople, Mehmet II instantly transformed a sultanate whose rulers had gained legitimacy by their victories – and victories as *ghazi*s – into an empire that overshadowed the Mamluk Sultanate of Egypt, hitherto the most prestigious state in the Islamic world. Constantinople, the former capital of the Eastern Roman or Byzantine Empire, had been an imperial capital and an imperial Christian city. As the Ottoman capital it not only overshadowed Cairo, but also dwarfed the historic, strategic, and symbolic importance of the successive Safavid capital cities of Tabriz, Qazvin, and Isfahan or the Mughal cities of Agra, Fathepur Sikri, Lahore, and Delhi. The contrast between the status of Constantinople as the Ottomans' sole capital and the several Safavid capitals and multiple Mughal residences in itself highlights the relative importance of these cities for each dynasty. In dynastic terms the Ottoman conquest of Constantinople represented the ultimate success of the Ottomans as military leaders of a *ghazi* enterprise. It conferred powerful new charisma and authority on the sultan, far more powerful even than Mustapha Kemal earned when he defeated British, French, and Greek forces in defense of a new Turkish nation after the First World War.

Mehmet II declared himself to be the new *Kaysar* or Caesar, the possessor of the imperial Roman capital, and he referred to Constantinople in Persian as *takhtgah*, the place, *gah*, of the throne, *takht*, and in Arabic as *dar al-saltana*, the "Abode of the Sultan."[1] It remained the imperial seat, the sultans' abode, and the site of successive Ottoman palaces, including the later Top Kapı Sarai, until 1923. Possession of the city, though, also meant that Mehmet became the military leader of the Muslim world, the supreme *ghazi*, whose conquest, the work of God, had been foretold by Mehmet's Sufi *pir*, Aq Şemseddin, a follower of the important Neoplatonic Islamic philosopher al-Suhrawardi (d. 1191), whose works influenced seventeenth-century Iranian intellectuals.[2] Muslims, after all, who believed that the conquest of the city they described as "Islambol," the city of Islam was pre-destined, had first sent an Arab-Muslim army against

---

[1] Colin Imber points out that Ottoman rulers did not publicize their imperial Roman title widely until the sixteenth century: *The Ottoman Empire*, 125.

[2] See Fakhry, *A History of Islamic Philosophy*, 302–14, and Chapter 6 below.

it in 650.[3] Abu Ayyub al-Ansari, one of the Prophet Muhammad's
"Companions," who died during a later attack on Constantinople in 668,
became the patron saint of the Ottoman city.[4] Immediately after the conquest Mehmet symbolically transformed Constantinople into an "Islambol"
by converting the principal churches into mosques. Constantine's great
cathedral became the Aya Sofia, the normative model for later Ottoman
imperial religious architecture.

The legitimacy and authority of the Safavi Shah 'Abbas and the Mughal
Akbar also changed significantly from that of their predecessors, Isma'il
and Babur, although in both cases their charisma grew slowly over time,
rather than, as in Mehmet's case, changing at one climactic moment. Still,
in the case of Shah 'Abbas, nothing could be more complete than his
evolution from the sixteen-year-old pawn of a Qizilbash tribe to the most
powerful shah of the Safavid dynasty. It was his Shamlu *atabeğ*, his
Qizilbash guardian, who placed him on the throne at Qazvin, then the
Safavid capital, in 1587, an act which itself dramatized the degree to which
the original Safavid charisma had deteriorated to the equivocal prestige of
a weak ruling house. During the course of his long reign, however, Shah
'Abbas transformed himself from a pawn of Qizilbash kingmakers to a
successful general and centralizing Iranian monarch whose entire, brilliant career was given over to concentrating power in his own hands.

Shah 'Abbas carefully nurtured both his Sufi and his Twelver Shi'i credentials through endowments and patronage of the Ardebil shrine and other
Shi'i monuments, but he subordinated these elements to a traditional Iranian
imperial identity.[5] The terms Safavid historians used to characterize him
when they described his building activities in his new capital, Isfahan, indi-
cate how Safavid legitimacy had evolved from Isma'il's charismatic Shi'i
millenarianism to a more traditional Iranian imperial autocracy. Of the four
historians who discuss the construction of the new capital only one, the
sometime court astrologer Jalal al-Din Muhammad, Munajjim-i Yazdi,
refers to him in Shi'i terminology as "The Dog of 'Ali's Threshold," and

---

[3] Inalcık, "Istanbul: an Islamic City," in Inalcık, *Essays in Ottoman History*, 249–50. Eckart
Ehlers and Thomas Krafft discuss what the term "Islamic city" has meant to various
scholars in "Islamic Cities in India? Theoretical Concepts and the Case of
Shâhjahânâbâd/Old Delhi," in Ehlers and Krafft, eds., *Shâhjahânâbâd/Old Delhi
Tradition and Colonial Change* (Delhi: Manohar, repr. 2003), 11–27. Cities in Shi'i countries such as Iran have some idiosyncratic architectural elements dedicated to the Imams
and to Husain: *Imamzadihs* and *husainiyyihs*. See Masoud Kheirabadi, *Iranian Cities:
Formation and Development* (Austin: University of Texas Press, 1991), 68–75.
[4] Inalcık, "Istanbul: An Islamic City," 252.
[5] Robert D. McChesney, "Waqf and Public Policy: The Waqfs of Shah 'Abbas, 1011–1023/
1602–1614," *Asian and African Studies* 15 (1981), 165–90. See especially the subsection
titled "Ideological and Political Implications of Waqf Grants," 182–6.

mentions that the shops in the new square were made *waqf*, a religious endowment "on behalf of the infallible [Shi'i] imams." The other historians allude to Isfahan, as Ottoman chroniclers labelled Constantinople, as the *dar al-Saltana*, the abode of the ruler, but also describe Shah 'Abbas himself in traditionally exalted pre-Islamic Iranian imperial rhetorical terms, both as one who possessed *farr*, the divine essence of Sasanian Iranian monarchs, and as the "Shadow of God" and the "*Padishah* of the World."[6]

Akbar underwent a similar legitimizing transformation during his rule. He evolved from a twelve-year-old Timurid prince supervised by his own *atabeğ*, the Qara Quyunlu Turk Bairam Khan, to the triumphant status of a dominant South Asian emperor, himself a *padishah* in reality rather than in aspiration, as Babur had been when he assumed this title while ruling uneasily in Kabul in 1506. Akbar at least began with the advantage of his Turco-Mongol, that is Timurid-Chingizid, genealogy, which he had court historians and artists repeatedly publicize in the relative calm of his later years. At that time in the late sixteenth century, his boon companion and court historian, Abu'l Fazl 'Allami, like the nearly contemporary Safavid historians of Isfahan, proclaimed that Akbar himself possessed or radiated the pre-Islamic Iranian divine essence, the *farr*. By then Akbar, like Shah 'Abbas, had not only acquired his own charisma of success through relentlessly successful campaigning, but had also broadened his legitimacy in two other related ways.

First, he integrated the Rajputs, the dominant north Indian Hindu warrior class, into the empire through intermarriage, imperial appointments, and concessions to Hindu sensibilities. Secondly, Akbar sought to define himself not just as a Timurid or as a Muslim ruler but more broadly as an Indian monarch by publicizing his non-sectarian piety, shaped partly by a profound interest in Hinduism and such other Indian religious traditions as Buddhism and Jainism. He eventually set himself above the *'ulama* as the *sultan-i 'adil*, the just sultan who possessed the right of *ijtihad* or Quranic interpretation, reserved in Safavid Iran to the *'ulama*. He asserted that Mughals should rule according to the fundamental principle of *sulh-i kull*, "peace with all," and act as the "refuge of all the people." His ideas may not have been broadly influential or even well understood in the sixteenth century – and they deeply offended some *'ulama*. They ensured, however, that he would enjoy a charismatic status among twentieth and twenty-first-century Indian and Western intellectuals.[7]

---

[6] R. D. McChesney "Four Sources on Shah 'Abbas's Building of Isfahan," *Muqarnas* 5 (1988), 109, 111, 112.

[7] Reflecting her own spiritual sympathy with Sufism and unusual knowledge of South Asian Islam, Annemarie Schimmel sensitively and concisely describes Akbar's religious experiments in *The Empire of the Great Mughals*, trans. Corinne Attwood (London: Reaktion Books, 2004), 35–8.

Mehmet II: from sultanate to empire

Enthroned by his father at age twelve in 1444 to avoid a succession dispute, Mehmet II was briefly set aside because later in that year he proved incapable of coping with a revolt by members of the Hurufi sect in the Ottoman capital, Edirne, and the threat of a Crusader army attacking across the Danube.[8] By the time he took full control of the Ottoman state in 1451, he was married to the daughter of the Ottomans' Turkic allies in Anatolia, the Dhu'l Kadirids – one of the last Ottoman marriages with another royal family. (In later years Ottoman rulers were, with some important exceptions, the children of concubines). Mehmet had gained military experience by serving with his father in two major Balkan campaigns, in 1448 and 1450. His decision to attack Constantinople seems to have been the inevitable culmination of the history of Ottoman expansion that had left the Byzantine capital impoverished and surrounded on the landward side, but Mehmet also had immediate motives for attacking the city. He responded to the advice of one of his ministerial factions that he could consolidate his power by conquering the city, and by doing so would also put an end to the challenge of his cousin Orhon, then residing within the Byzantine capital. Having secured peace agreements with Venice and Hungary to protect his European sea and land flanks, Mehmet enlisted the technical aid of an Hungarian armorer to construct powerful siege artillery that battered and ultimately breached the formidable city walls that some of his advisors had argued were impregnable.[9] He took the city after a two-month siege on June 29th, 1453; Orhon, who fought on the Byzantine side with approximately 8,000 defenders, was captured and executed shortly after the city fell.

Mehmet in Europe and Asia

Mehmet II "is the true founder of the classical Ottoman Empire, establishing its territorial, ideological and economic bases."[10] In his conquests – Istanbul and subsequently the Balkans, Anatolia, and Mesopotamia – his administrative innovations, economic centralization, and organization of

---

[8] The standard biography is Franz Babinger's *Mehmed the Conqueror and His Time*, ed. William C. Hickman, trans. Ralph Manheim (Princeton: Bollingen Press, 1978).

[9] Ottomans developed artillery that surpassed that of any other Muslim state, as became evident when Ottoman gunners became advisors in Mughal India and elsewhere. See especially the recent important study by Gábor Ágoston, *Guns for the Sultan: Military Power and the Weapons Industry in the Ottoman Empire* (Cambridge University Press, 2005).

[10] The conclusion of Halil Inalcık, in his article "Mehemmed II," *Encyclopaedia of Islam*, II, Brill Online. My summary of Mehmet's achievements is based primarily on Inalcık's work in this article and elsewhere.

religious teaching, he originated or systematized the fundamental institutions of the empire. First of all, as a relentless military commander throughout the thirty years of his reign, he extended Ottoman conquests in Europe and in Asia. In Europe, even while occasionally suffering defeats at the hands of the Venetians and Hungarians, he campaigned repeatedly and successfully in the Balkans and against Venice for more than twenty-five years. In 1479, after forcing the Venetians to make peace, Mehmet began what appears to have been a plan to follow his conquest of Constantinople with that of Italy and more particularly Rome, the logical final goal of Ottoman expansion after Constantinople. His forces actually occupied the southern Italian town of Otranto in 1480. In the east, his success in gaining complete control of the straits was followed by the Ottoman conquest in 1461 of Trebizond, the last substantial Greek kingdom on the Black Sea. Subsequently he turned his attention to eastern Anatolia, where Uzun Hasan, formally allied with the Venetians since 1464, had transformed the Aq Quyunlu into a formidable anti-Ottoman power. Mehmet's victory over Uzun Hasan's army in 1473 not only confirmed the superiority of firearms over nomadic cavalry but also established indisputable Ottoman dominance in central and eastern Anatolia. In southeastern Anatolia it also brought them into direct conflict with the Mamluks, the slave dynasty of Egypt, whose agriculturally rich Nile delta and commercially valuable Red Sea and Arabian Sea trade attracted the expansionist ambitions of his successor, Selim.

The apparatus of empire

In the midst of nearly continuous campaigns, Mehmet, like Akbar in India and Shah 'Abbas in Iran, presided over a systemization and consolidation of government. Using an ethnic variety of administrators – Persians, Arabs, Greeks, and Italians, among others – and his own 'ulama, he promulgated two secular or imperial administrative legal codes, the famous Kanunnames that dealt with state organization, criminal law, and the relationship between the state, its military class, and the tax-paying agriculturalists. Distinct from the shari'a, Islamic law, the Kanunnames were primarily administrative and tax codes, sections of which carefully specified the duties and/or taxes that the peasantry owed to the sipahis. The agrarian regulations were based on the sultans' claim to possess all of the empire's land. In issuing the Kanunnames he was formally codifying the common practice of the independent sultans who had arisen in the Islamic world as the power of the 'Abbasid Caliphs waned. He was more immediately continuing a practice of the Il-Khans, the Mongol rulers of Iran, for whom the term yasa (later, yasakname) meant a body of administrative customs or laws. The Aq Quyunlu ruler, Uzun

Hasan, had issued similar *yasakname*s or *kanunname*s in his territories, which Mehmet and his immediate successors retained.

Like some Delhi Sultans, Mehmet II was ostentatiously pious, but like them too, he brooked no interference from the *'ulama* when it came to matters of state. "Autocratic principle, which made the sultan's person the one and only source of authority and legitimation and claimed it as the foundation of both state and society, found its full expression under Mehemmed II."[11] The measures he took to organize the empire reflect both his systematizing mind and also the powerful charismatic stature his conquest gave him to enforce a high degree of centralized control over the political and economic life of the state. These included the reduction of many indigenous aristocratic families to the status of *timar* holders – or their replacement by slave officials; the systematic appointment of converted Christian slaves, rather than members of the *'ulama*, to the position of Grand Vizier; cancellation of questionable or corrupt *waqf* or religious endowment grants and resumption of *waqf* properties; issuance of regulations for systematizing and regulating the urban economy included in the *Kanunname*s; state ownership of all rice-growing lands; periodic issuance and debasement of the standard silver coin, the *akçe* to economically benefit the state; and, with the help of the great astronomer of Timurid Samarqand, 'Ali b. Muhammad al-Kushdi (d. 1474), who became a professor of sciences in the Aya Sophia, the organization of the *'ulama* hierarchy and its religious instruction.[12] His ideological justification included the inherent authority of the dynasty, his status as the Muslim world's pre-eminent *ghazi*, and the classic Sasanian and now Muslim ideal of the just ruler, who governed on behalf of *yoksullar* (Turkish), literally those who "possessed nothing," that is, the poor and powerless.

Non-Muslim subjects

One of Mehmet's significant acts that had long-term implications for the empire and the modern Middle East was his continuation of the earlier Muslim practice of recognizing the integrity of non-Muslim subject communities and granting capitulary privileges to foreigners – in his case, Genoese merchants. Immediately following the conquest Mehmet issued an *ahd-name* or "imperial covenant," in which he guaranteed the autonomy

---

[11] Inalcık, "Mehemmed II."

[12] Regarding the appointment of *kul*s or slaves to the highest administrative posts and particularly to the position of Grand Vezir see Theoharis Stavrides, *The Sultan of Vezirs: The Life and Times of the Ottoman Grand Vezir Mahmud Pasha Angelović (1453–1474)* (Leiden: Brill, 2001), 55 and 68.

and commercial privileges of foreign, non-Muslim merchant settlements as well as the safety and autonomy of indigenous, non-Muslim populations and the commercial privileges of the merchants. The indigenous communities included Orthodox but not Latin Christians, Armenians, and Jews, all of whom were recognized as *ahl al-kitab*, ""People of the Book," or *ahl al-dhimma*, "protected people." In political terms they were *millats*, communities of certain "peoples" or "creeds." Ottoman policy later attracted Jews expelled from Catholic Spain and guaranteed the preservation of both Jewish and Christian communities.

Both pragmatic measures eventually came to haunt the weakened Ottoman state of the eighteenth and nineteenth centuries, as Europeans exploited the "capitulations" and began agitating for the rights of Christian minorities. The Armenian Christians' position in particular became an issue in nineteenth and early twentieth-century European and Ottoman politics, and culminated in the Armenian massacres, which are officially denied by Republican Turkey. The concept of a *millat* as an autonomous religious community, also became an issue in British First World War negotiations with Hussain, the Sharif of Mecca, regarding the Jewish settlements in Palestine.[13] That is, were *millat*s religious communities – or nations?

This Quranically sanctioned practice demonstrates that the *ghaza* ideal applied to non-Muslim states and did not imply an annihilation of non-Muslim communities within Muslim-controlled territories. Mehmet's recognition of a protected but still subordinate status for non-Muslims followed a practice that dated from Muhammad's lifetime, as did the custom of differential taxation for these communities. In the Prophetic period, as under the Umayyad and 'Abbasid Caliphates, newly conquered non-Muslim populations, including at that time Zoroastrians as well as Jews and Christians, were protected but required to pay a separate poll tax known as the *jizya*. While the use of this term varied considerably in early periods, by the 'Abbasid era it was generally levied as a tax on individual free male subjects, but exempted foreigners who did not permanently reside in Muslim-controlled lands. While the Safavids observed the same fundamental principles when dealing with their Christian and Jewish minorities, the situation of the large Hindu majority in Muslim India was much more problematic. As will be seen, in the Mughal Empire the imposition or suspension of *jizya* became a touchstone of imperial cultural attitudes and a contentious issue during Mughal rule and later in the communal debates of Indian nationalist politics in the late nineteenth

---

[13] Known as the Hussein-McMahon Correspondence. George Antonius published this correspondence in *The Arab Awakening* (Philadelphia: J. B. Lippincott, 1939).

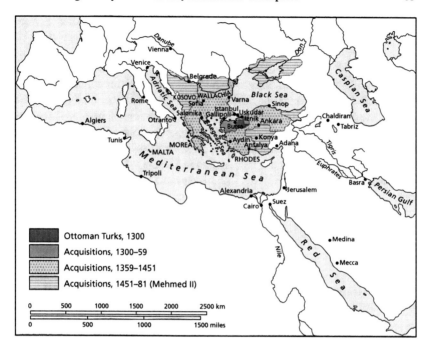

Map 9. The Ottoman Empire in 1481

and twentieth centuries. In the Ottoman case *jizya*, which represented the largest single source of central government income in the sixteenth century, did not generate major controversy at the time, or in subsequent historiography.[14] The contrasting history of this practice reflects the fact that Mughal India included substantial territories of autonomous Hindu rulers, whereas in Ottoman lands, most Christians had been effectively subordinated to the state.

Bayezid II and imperial retrenchment

Mehmet II extended and consolidated Ottoman territorial control over two of the three central regions of the mature empire: the Balkans and Anatolia. The immediate aftermath of Mehmet's remarkable reign was a period of reaction and retrenchment during the rule of Bayezid II (1481–1512). With Bayezid the exhausting whirlwind of conquests and ruthless expansion of

---

[14] Linda Darling, *Revenue-Raising and Legitimacy: Tax Collection and Finance Administration in the Ottoman Empire 1550–1660* (Leiden: Brill, 1996).

state power was sharply curtailed. His relatively peaceful policies were partly a result of his hatred for his father and partly, a response to strained finances – wars financed by currency devaluation and an exhausted military.[15] Indeed, he had been brought to power by a powerful coalition of disaffected *'ulama* and notables who had lost power under Mehmet and the Janissaries, exhausted by the former sultan's constant campaigns.[16] The *waqf*s resumed by Mehmet, for example, were returned to their previous clerical administrators. Despite contemporary complaints about his lack of aggressiveness, Bayezid consolidated Ottoman power, and undertook or ordered several military campaigns against targets which his son and successor Selim later conquered. The perennial conflict with Venice was resumed, but more important were the campaigns against the Mamluks, whose Syrian territories abutted Ottoman-controlled lands in southeastern Anatolia, and those against the Safavids and their ideological fellow travellers in Anatolia.

Between 1485 and 1490 Ottoman and Mamluk armies fought a series of what amounted to border wars in the ill-defined marchlands of the Taurus Mountains, with neither side bent on extensive territorial conquests. A far more serious challenge to Ottoman power arose in far eastern Anatolia at the end of the century, when Shah Isma'il Safavi emerged from hiding to overthrow his Aq Quyunlu relatives. Recruiting most of his supporters from among the Turkic tribes in Azerbaijan and the Erzincan region of Anatolia, Isma'il posed a far more serious threat to the Ottomans than his Aq Quyunlu predecessors, because he carried out aggressive missionary activity among tribesmen who had previously shown themselves susceptible to millenarian religious appeals, such as the Baba'i insurrection against the Saljuqs. Apart from exiling Safavid supporters to Greece, the now aged Bayezid did little to challenge the Safavids directly between 1501 and 1510, the decade in which Isma'il conquered most of the Iranian plateau. In 1511, however, the serious nature of the Safavid threat forced him to act.

In that year a Turk who had served Shah Isma'il's grandfather, Shaikh Haidar, led a millenarian revolt in southwestern Anatolia based on Shah Isma'il's ideology.[17] This Shah Kulu, the "Slave of the Shah" (Isma'il), may have claimed divine inspiration for himself, but whether or not he or his followers actually did so, he led an anti-Ottoman campaign conducted as a religious war, as is clear from the report that he burnt the corpse of the captured Ottoman governor of Anatolia, a treatment Isma'il had meted

---

[15] See Imber's summary of Bayezid's reign in *The Ottoman Empire*, 37–4.
[16] Inalcık, *The Ottoman Empire*, 30.
[17] Imber, *The Ottoman Empire*, 37–44.

out to non-Shi'i opponents/heretics.[18] However, the military leaders of the uprising were *sipahis*, who had, they claimed, been fraudulently deprived of their landholdings. Within a few months, in the spring of 1511, Shah Kulu even threatened the former Ottoman capital and commercial center of Bursa before an Ottoman army finally defeated and killed him. The threat, nonetheless, was sufficient justification for Bayezid's son Selim (r. 1512–20) to revolt and depose his aged father and to begin a new period of Ottoman military dynamism with the 1514 defeat of Shah Isma'il Safavi. This expansionist era culminated with the reign of Süleyman (r. 1520–66), generally known in the West as the Magnificent.

Safavids: from Qizilbash confederacy to Iranian empire

After Shah Isma'il's first decade of conquest between 1501 and 1511, the Safavids suffered their catastrophic defeat at Chaldiran in 1514, and for more than three-quarters of a century afterwards, they struggled to survive internal conflicts and foreign threats to their rule while trying to impose Shi'i Islam in their territories as the sole confessional version of the faith. During these years, the Safavids did not possess a reliable military force independent of the Qizilbash tribal oligarchy. The dynasty's lack of coercive power meant that the Safavid state of the sixteenth century was more of an aspiration than a political reality. In addition, both Ottomans and Uzbeks repeatedly attacked Safavid territories in the west and northeast, and after the reestablishment of Mughal rule in India in 1556, Safavid shahs also had to contend with Indian competition for control of Qandahar and valuable trade routes through Afghanistan. Throughout this period the powerful Qizilbash tribes limited Safavid attempts to centralize their control of the Iranian plateau, while threatening the dominance and even the survival of the dynasty. At the same time the Safavids continued their efforts to eradicate Sunni Islam and institutionalize Shi'ism as the orthodox faith of their state.

The Safavids survived as a dynasty because of their latent charisma, even though Isma'il's appeal had been badly compromised by his defeat in 1514. Externally they retained their independence due to their comparative poverty and relative isolation, far from the centers of Ottoman and

---

[18] The Safavids may sometimes have practiced cannibalism before or after roasting the bodies of their enemies. If true, it seems likely this practice reflects the religious claims of Shah Isma'il, which defined him and his descendants' opponents not only as enemies but also as heretics. See Shahzad Bashir, "Shah Isma'il and the Qizilbash: Cannibalism in the Religious History of Early Safavid Iran," *History of Religions*, 45 No. 3 (2006), 234–56.

Mughal power. Iran's economy did not rival that of Egypt or of north India, wealthy regions coveted, respectively, by the Ottomans and Mughals. The lines of communication from Istanbul and Agra or Delhi to the Iranian plateau also gave pause to Ottomans and Mughals alike. The Safavid state only began to prosper after Shah 'Abbas took the throne in 1588 and partly succeeded in doing in one reign what the Ottomans had taken a century and a half to accomplish. He transformed Safavid legitimacy and the dynasty's military system, centralized authority, developed the state's economic base, and reconquered strategic and economically valuable territory from the Ottomans.

Tribe and state in early Safavid Iran

The fundamental political problem of the Safavid state was its structure as a Turkic tribal confederation. It exhibited many of the same weaknesses as the Saljuq, Il-Khanid Mongol, Ludhi Afghan, early Ottoman, and Aq Quyunlu regimes, even if Shah Isma'il differed from the founders of those dynasties in his ability to convince followers of his semi-divine authority. Tribal confederations were notoriously unstable, as tribes had a corporate existence or autonomy, as well as economic interests and military ambitions, distinct from and antagonistic to one another and a centralized state. 'Abbasid Caliphs had tried to solve this problem by turning away from the Arab *muqatila* tribes, the basis of the early Islamic conquests, to Turkic slave troops, and the Ottomans increasingly did the same, especially after their defeat at the Battle of Ankara, by relying on their own slave troops, the Janissaries. In the fifteenth century, Safavid rulers slowly developed their own slave forces, a trend that culminated in the expansion of this policy by Shah 'Abbas.

When Tahmasp inherited Isma'il's throne in 1524 at age ten he was especially vulnerable to the contentious ambitions of Qizilbash tribal factionalism, because of the typical Turkic custom of assigning *atabeğ*s or guardians to supervise young princes, leaving him under the control of first one tribe and then another. Shah Tahmasp in his memoirs bitterly complains about the chaos caused by inter-tribal rivalries, and well he might, for his first quarter century on the throne was plagued by the internecine wars of several Qizilbash tribes. "For years," he writes, "I was forced patiently to watch the bloodshed between the tribes and I tried to see what was the will of God in these events."[19] Safavid legitimacy apparently ensured his survival as at least a nominal monarch in his early years, as he was passed like a dynastic trophy from one feuding

---

[19] *Tazkirah-i Shah Tahmasb*, ed. Imralah Safari (Tehran, 1984), Introduction, p. 3.

Qizilbash chieftain to another, but throughout his "reign" members of different Qizilbash tribes dominated the military and political offices both at the center and in the provinces. Evidently in response to the Qizilbash threat, Tahmasp appointed many Tajiks or Iranians as administrators, in the tradition of Nizam al-Mulk under the Saljuqs. By the middle of the sixteenth century some Iranians had intermarried with the Safavid royal family, but they did not act as *atabeğ*s, nor did they usually command substantial military forces of their own. Tahmasp also continued Isma'il's policy of building up a *ghulam* force from captured Georgians, and began marrying Georgian and Circassian women, thus breaking with the earlier Safavid tradition of marrying wives solely from important Qizilbash tribes.

The Qizilbash infighting known in Iranian history as the First Civil War ended in 1536 with the victory of the Ustajlu Qizilbash, who strengthened their authority throughout the remainder of Shah Tahmasp's reign. What is probably most remarkable about this period, and the remainder of Tahmasp's reign until his death in 1576, was his ability to survive the murderous, chaotic conflicts within Iran while enduring Uzbek and Ottoman assaults on or conquests of some of the Safavids' most economically valuable territory: Khurasan and Iraq. The Ustajlu and Tahmasp still presided over what amounted to a decentralized tribal coalition whose members treated their huge *iqta'* grants as personal fiefs. The weakness of the Safavid regime during and after the years of the civil war was demonstrated by the ease with which Uzbeks and Ottomans violated the tentatively established boundaries of the Safavid state.

The Uzbeks attacked Khurasan five times between 1524 and 1540, penetrating as far as Rayy, ten miles south of present-day Tehran, in 1534. While Uzbek incursions resembled plundering expeditions rather than territorial conquests, the Ottomans represented a much more profound threat. Between 1532 and 1535 they seized Tabriz, Isma'il's capital, and Kurdistan, occupied Baghdad and Arab Iraq, and took control of the Shi'i shrine cities of Najaf and Karbala. Two more successful Ottoman invasions of northwestern Iran in 1546 and 1553 concluded with a formal treaty in 1555 recognizing Ottoman sovereignty over Mesopotamia, including Baghdad and Kurdistan. As an illustration of Ottoman Sunni commitment, the treaty required the Safavids to terminate the practice of ritual cursing of the first three Caliphs – a demand the Ottomans made again in their 1590 treaty with their defeated Iranian enemies. While the 1555 treaty left the Safavids with Tabriz, they nonetheless decided to move their capital southeast to Qazvin to avoid future Ottoman incursions.

Tahmasp and the spread of Shi'i Islam

Shah Tahmasp is notable not only for surviving half a century in the face of extraordinary internal and external threats, but for furthering the spread of Shi'i Islam. A devout man himself, who became ostentatiously pious and ascetic by the 1540s, he led by his own example by making pilgrimages to the shrine of one of the Shi'i Imams, Imam Riza, at Mashhad in Khurasan; patronizing Ashura ceremonies celebrating the martyrdom of 'Ali's son Husain at Karbala; restoring Shi'i shrines and mosques; and commissioning a Shi'i-biased *Shah-nama*. In 1533 Tahmasp appointed his father's favorite Shi'i theologian, 'Ali Karaki al-'Amili, to be the "seal of the *mujtahids*" and final interpreter of the Quran, and the *na'ib al-Imam* the Deputy of the Twelfth Imam, both titles that publicized 'Ali Karaki's supreme authority over religious affairs in Safavid dominions. The latter title of *na'ib al-Imam* anticipated the religious claims that some of Ayatollah Khomeini's followers made for him after the 1979 Iranian revolution.

In the year before his death 'Ali Karaki asserted his exceptional authority by ordering the appointment of a prayer leader in every town to instruct people in Shi'i Islam, and even altered the land tax. In 1563 his grandson, previously the *Shaikh al-Islam* at the original Safavid shrine complex at Ardebil, was appointed to the same position at the new Safavid capital, Qazvin. Later Shi'i scholars from Jabal 'Amil became especially prominent as a small but interconnected and influential kinship network of scholars in Safavid Iran, although the largest number came to Iran in the late sixteenth and early seventeenth centuries. Relatively unimportant in their homeland, where they faced persecution first from Mamluk and subsequently from Ottoman authorities, several lineages migrated to seek their fortunes in Safavid Iran, where they were welcomed as a class of thinkers who could articulate a systematized Twelver Shi'i theology in Safavid territories.[20] These theologians emphasized the activist role of legal scholars who practiced *ijtihad*, rational interpretation, in developing the Shi'i canon, initiating an Iranian rationalist Shi'i tradition that flowered in seventeenth-century Iran.

While this institutional structure was developing, Shah Tahmasp continued Shah Isma'il's policies designed to force the inhabitants of Iran to convert to Shi'ism. When he took Tabriz in 1501, Isma'il is said to have demanded that his subjects abandon Sunni Islam and publicly demonstrate their commitment by ritually cursing the first three Caliphs. Under Tahmasp, the *Tabarra'* or ritual cursing of these Caliphs was ordered to

---

[20] Andrew J. Newman, *Safavid Iran, Rebirth of a Persian Empire* (London and New York: I. B. Tauris, 2006), 36–8.

take place in mosques and public places throughout Iran and was enforced, to some degree, by roving bands of religious inspectors. The Shah even developed a longer list of ninety individuals to be publicly denounced. These included the great Sunni Caliph Harun al-Rashid and the Herati Persian-language poet and Naqshbandi Sufi 'Abd al-Rahman Jami.[21] The condemnation of Jami was consistent with and probably a continuation of earlier Safavid persecution of the steadfastly Sunni and politically activist Naqshbandi order, several of whose Iranian *khalifa*s were imprisoned and tortured or executed by the regime.[22]

During the sixteenth century the Shi'i culture of Safavid Iran also began to take hold at the local level, popularized by verse laments for Husain, the Prophet's grandson killed at Karbala, and increasingly elaborate Ashura rituals held on the anniversary of Husain's death in the month of Muharram. The Italian aristocrat Pietro della Valle witnessed these intensely emotional observances when he visited Iran in 1617:

The ceremonies with which they celebrate the *asciur* [Ashura] and lament this death [of Husain] are as follows. They all live in a state of dejection; they all dress sadly, and many wear black, which otherwise they rarely put on; no one shaves head or beard; no one takes a bath; and they all abstain, not only from what is thought sinful, but also from every kind of enjoyment. ... Also, where people circulate in the square, toward noon every day one of their mullahs preaches about Hussein, recounting his praises and his death ... and he [the mulla] sits on a slightly raised seat, encircled by an audience of men and women ... and from time to time he shows some painted figures illustrating what he is recounting; and, in brief, in every way he endeavours as much as he can to move the onlookers to tears ... and the preachings are accompanied by the moans and groans of the hearers, and particularly of the women, who beat their breasts and make piteous gestures.[23]

The second civil war and the rise of Shah 'Abbas

Shah Tahmasp's death in 1576 precipitated a second Safavid civil war during which Qizilbash and personal factions initially placed Tahmasp's son Isma'il II on the throne. However, his death a year later from an opium overdose led to the enthronement of Isma'il's half-blind older brother Khudabanda, then already forty-six years old. Each of these

---

[21] Ibid., 130.

[22] Hamid Algar, "Nakshbandiyya," *Encyclopaedia of Islam*, II, Brill Online, 2.

[23] Pietro della Valle, *The Pilgrim: The Journeys of Pietro della Valle*, trans. and abridged George Bull (London: The Folio Society, 1989), 144–5. For an evocative, beautifully written twentieth-century description of the 'Ashura laments in southern Iraq see Elizabeth Warnock Fernea, *Guests of the Sheik: An Ethnography of an Iraqi Village* (New York: Doubleday, repr. 1989).

coronations was followed by the murder of male and sometimes even female relatives and their Qizilbash supporters, and the political scheming and vicious infighting continued virtually uninterrupted through Khudabanda's short reign from 1576 to 1587. As after Shah Isma'il's death, the political chaos encouraged the Safavids' enemies. The Uzbeks unsuccessfully attacked Mashhad in Khurasan, and the Ottoman Sultan Murad III (1574–95) launched a series of devastating assaults in the west, beginning in 1578 and continuing through the early years of Khudabanda's successor, 'Abbas. The fall of Tabriz in 1585 climaxed a series of territorial losses in Azerbaijan, Georgia, Kurdistan, and Luristan.

Throughout this period Qizilbash chiefs continued to dominate both central and provincial military and political positions, amidst constantly shifting alliances among the tribes. Tajiks, especially Iranian Sayyids, descendants of the Prophet, staffed most of the middle and lower-level administrative posts, even when they were practicing Sunnis, illustrating the still lagging Shi'i orthodoxy in Iran. One such individual was Mirza Makhdum Sharifi (d. 1587), who had acted as chief judge in Fars before becoming an important official in Qazvin, then the capital, during Isma'il II's reign.[24] Both Isma'il II and Khudabanda continued to contract marriage alliances with important Qizilbash and Tajik families. Georgian and Circassian slaves also gained increasing influence throughout this chaotic era, alerting observers to the increasingly important role of *ghulam* elements in the Safavid state that had been growing since the reign of Shah Tahmasp.

When Shah 'Abbas I (r. 1588–1629), second son of Khudabanda, deposed his father and inherited the Safavid throne in 1587–8 at age eighteen in the midst of the second Qizilbash civil war, he reigned but did not rule over the territory of Iran. Qizilbash chiefs not only dominated the capital, Qazvin, but also the provinces. The Safavid state still represented an unstable tribal confederation and even Shah 'Abbas's claim to be the legitimate *pir* of the Safavid Sufi order was challenged by supporters of the still-living Khudabanda. Yet by the time he died in 1629 'Abbas had transformed the militarily prostrate, economically weak, and faction-ridden Safavid regime. While scholars have long since dismissed the idea that he created a new Safavid state *ex nihilo*, 'Abbas was the pivotal figure who not only transformed the Safavid state from a fragile tribal oligarchy to an Iranian empire but also presided over its sole military, political, and architectural "golden age."

At age eighteen Shah 'Abbas was at least able to assert his authority more quickly than Tahmasp at age ten, and he and the dominant Ustajlu

---

[24] Newman, *Safavid Iran*, 46.

Qizilbash tribal faction moved against other tribal groups and Sufis who challenged his authority. His Qizilbash opponents included the Qajars, who were to form the last Turkic tribal dynasty in Iranian history between 1796 and 1925, and who now, along with other Qizilbash tribes, supported competing Safavid princes. The continued political disarray encouraged both the Uzbeks and the Ottomans to persist in their anti-Safavid campaigns in the northeast and northwest. It was not until Shah 'Abbas signed another humiliating treaty with the Ottomans in 1590 that he and the Ustajlus had the opportunity to move against some of the regime's most formidable internal opponents, thus effectively concluding the second Qizilbash civil war. While struggling with external enemies, dissident Qizilbash tribes and Safavid family members, Shah 'Abbas simultaneously had to cope with Sufis who challenged one of the critical bases of the Safavids' legitimacy, their status as Sufi *pirs*.

He took what came to be typically ruthless measures to ensure both his status as *pir* of the Safavid order and the supremacy of that order over other Sufis. Indeed, Shah 'Abbas is known for the gratuitous cruelty he practiced against his opponents as he gradually developed autocratic power. Safavid *murids* or Sufi disciples who supported any of his family rivals were executed, and in 1593 he staged at court what can only be described as a Shakespearean tableau to eliminate the subversive ideological threat from the Nuqtavis, a sect whose doctrines included belief in reincarnation and a cyclical theory of time. The latter idea served to advance an Iranian ethnic or cultural agenda, since the Nuqtavis held that the 8,000-year cycle, which included the Safavid dynasty, was the Persian epoch, in which Gilan and Mazandaran in northern Iran ranked above Mecca and Medina. Shah 'Abbas's own flirtation with the Nuqtavis evaporated when the contemporary leader of the order predicted that in 1593 a Nuqtavi might seize the Safavid throne. In the following year Shah 'Abbas enthroned one of the Nuqtavis for three days in a bizarre mock coronation, before executing him by firing squad.[25] This was followed by mass arrests of Nuqtavi followers, with Shah 'Abbas personally beheading a leading poet of the order.[26]

Shah 'Abbas and the Safavid renaissance

If true, Shah 'Abbas's novel method of executing the Nuqtavi leader reflected the Safavid ruler's greater use of firearms, which he introduced

---

[25] For an alternative version of this entire episode see Charles Melville, "New Light on the Reign of Shah 'Abbas: Volume III of the *Afzal al-Tavarikh*," in Newman, ed., *Society and Culture in the Early Modern Middle East*, 83–4.

[26] Hamid Algar, "Nuktawiyya," *Encyclopaedia of Islam* II, Brill Online.

as part of his reorganization of the Safavid army. In order to deal with both internal and external threats Shah 'Abbas developed a new standing force of *ghulams*, systematizing what Shah Tahmasp had already begun during his long reign. In doing so he paralleled earlier Ottoman policies of demoting unreliable *sipahis* in favor of Janissaries. While Qizilbash tribal forces continued to constitute the majority of Safavid troops, they gradually became relatively less powerful during his reign, as *ghulams* were not only organized into a standing army with important regiments of musketeers, but also, as in the Ottoman case, became increasingly numerous and influential as generals and administrators. To finance the new military units Shah 'Abbas raised additional income by bringing more provinces under direct state control.

As part of his tireless effort to increase the power of the state, 'Abbas also implemented measures to improve the finances of the regime through the encouragement of trade, both within Iran and with the outside world.[27] Apart from simply protecting roads and building *caravansarais* and bazaars – standard measures in the other Islamic empires – 'Abbas forcibly uprooted the important Armenian mercantile community of Julfa in eastern Anatolia and resettled them in his new capital, Isfahan, in a suburb known as New Julfa, where as a critically important, semi-autonomous group of merchants they were protected in exchange for their commercial skills. Trade in silk became, in effect, a government-organized and government-supervised monopoly presided over by the Armenians, a Christian minority whose merchants could utilize their pre-existing international network that stretched from Asia to Europe. Silk cloth represented then, as it had for centuries, Iran's most important source of hard currency, and 'Abbas carefully encouraged the production of silk in the Caspian Sea littoral province of Mazandaran, which also became one of the dynasty's centrally administered provinces.

Shah 'Abbas's forced resettlement of Armenians in Isfahan was part of his grand scheme to enrich and embellish the city, which he had made his capital sometime in the 1590s. Safely located on a river in central Iran, far from Ottoman and Uzbek forces and close to the historic centers of pre-Islamic Iranian empires in Fars province, Isfahan became the principal focus of Shah 'Abbas' architectural projects. These included the institutionalization of the Shi'i religious establishment. His buildings, which inspired later Iranians to say – and Europeans to echo – *Isfahan nisf-i jahan*, "Isfahan is half the world," included the Chahar Bagh or "Four Garden Avenue," the beautiful Khwaju stone bridge over the Zayindah

---

[27] Rudi Matthee, *The Politics of Trade in Safavid Iran: Silk for Silver 1600–1730* (Cambridge University Press, 1999).

River, and most of all the *Maidan-i Naqsh-i Jahan*, the "Square of the World's Image." A Venetian traveler, the nobleman Ambrosio Bembo, who had Italian bases for comparison, praised the square during a visit in July 1673. " "This maydan," he wrote, "is the King's square ... For its size and beauty it surpasses many of the most beautiful in Europe."[28]

The *Maidan*, which immediately became the focus of the city's commercial and religious life, was surrounded by bazaars, and included two important *masjids*: the exquisite Shaikh Lutf Allah *masjid* with a single beige dome and no minarets and the massive, imperial-scale *Masjid-i Shah*, the Shah's Mosque. The latter included two *madrasas*, two of several such institutions that graduated orthodox Twelver Shi'i clergy for a ruler whose inscriptions on these buildings emphasized his continuing role as the supporter of the faith of the Twelve Imams, even while he increasingly stressed his imperial Iranian status. 'Abbas was also publicly attentive to his Sufi religious heritage, making repeated visits to the family shrine at Ardebil to remind Muslims of his role as *pir* of the Safavid order and celebrating Sufi ceremonies at the 'Ali Qapu palace that 'Abbas constructed on the Maidan opposite the Shaikh Lutf Allah *masjid*. The second-story veranda of the palace also enabled the Shah to watch military reviews or polo matches in the Maidan below.

Isfahan unmistakably symbolized Shah 'Abbas' remarkable achievements in reconstructing the Safavid state, assembling a new army, vastly expanding its economy, and elevating himself to be an imperial Iranian ruler rather than a creature of the Qizilbash. The tribes still retained great influence, but the Safavids largely ceased to be a later theocratic variant of the Aq Quyunlu. The Qizilbash were now balanced by several elements: new army units armed with firearms, increasingly important Tajik and *ghulam* officials, a growing Shi'i clerical class, and a vital Armenian mercantile community. Presiding over these groups was a man who was not only powerful enough but sufficiently insightful to popularize *nauruz*, the pre-Islamic Iranian festival celebrating the spring equinox which, despite clerical influence, remains the single most popular festival in twenty-first-century Shi'i Iran.

By the end of Shah 'Abbas' reign in 1629 not only did historians use traditional pre-Islamic terminology to portray him as an imperial Iranian ruler, but the Safavid state had also become in a certain limited sense a culturally Iranian or Persian state as well as a religious entity. Persian was the language of the administration. The *Shah-nama* was its single most important literary and historical text. Its ruler encouraged the celebration

---

[28] Anthony Welch, "Safavi Iran as Seen through Venetian Eyes," in Newman, ed., *Society and Culture in the Early Modern Middle East*, 106.

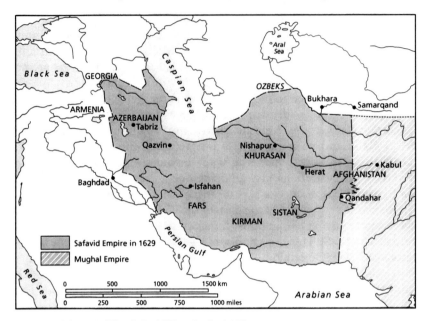

Map 10. The Safavid Empire in 1629

of a Zoroastrian festival, *nauruz*, and his territories encompassed the historic heartlands of the pre-Islamic Achaemenid and Sasanian empires of Fars and Khurasan. The dynasty still publicized its original religious legitimacy from its Shi'i and Sufi origins, and most of its historians reflected their royal patrons' wish to be genealogically connected to the twelve Shi'i Imams – and not to pre-Islamic Iranian rulers. Nonetheless, some writers also supplied the Safavids with a tenuous connection with Temür as a way of legitimizing the dynasty as an imperial lineage, although in this case a Turkic rather than Iranian one: a fictitious connection also devoutly desired by some Ottoman writers, who also suffered from lineage envy of their Mughal contemporaries.[29]

Akbar and the Mughal Empire

Court historians writing for the Mughals never had to search for ways to bolster their patrons' self-image as legitimate monarchs. Mughal rulers' patrilineal Timurid and matrilineal Chingizid genealogies were the envy of their contemporaries, as these blood lines demonstrated their descent from the two greatest Central Asian conquerors. However, these lineages,

[29] Fleischer, *Bureaucrat and Intellectual*, 273–314.

which impressed Central Asian and Iranian populations, did not have a
calming effect on ambitious monarchs in South Asia, where Mongols and
Temür had plundered but never ruled. Nor did it dampen the dynastic
ambitions of other Timurids. Before Babur died in Agra in 1530, he had
succeeded in defeating his most threatening Muslim Afghan and Hindu
Rajput enemies, but the Mughal state represented little more than a
military occupation of northwestern and northern Indian cities and fortresses rather than a broadly acknowledged sovereignty. In addition,
Babur had bequeathed to his descendants a typical Turco-Mongol joint
inheritance and succession system similar to that of the Saljuqs, where
each male relative usually was assigned an appanage to govern and rea-
sonably believed he had the right to rule. This contributed to the difficulties that left Babur's son, Humayun, a stateless refugee who took fifteen
years to recover his Indian throne.

Akbar's conquests and the Rajput nobility

Humayun's son Akbar, who succeeded to what was little more than a
north Indian city-state, was twelve years old when his father died. He had
spent a tumultuous youth, first as a refugee with his father and then as his
uncle's captive in Kabul. He was illiterate, or largely so, throughout his
life, but nonetheless is known for his inquisitive intelligence and, like
Mehmet, his systematizing mind. Akbar was dominated by his guardian,
Bairam Khan, for the first four years of his reign. During this period and
for nearly a decade after Akbar dismissed Bairam Khan in 1560, Mughal
armies were preoccupied with reasserting their control over the core of
Babur's nascent empire in the Punjab, the Delhi–Agra axis, the western
Ganges valley, and eastern Rajasthan. Akbar directed the later campaigns
with the care, organization, and determination that marked his entire
reign. His victory against the formidable Rajput desert fortress of Chitor
in 1567 was particularly notable for the use of siege artillery to breach the
walls and for Akbar's subsequent slaughter of an estimated 30,000 members of the garrison. His effective use of artillery signaled a new Mughal
gunpowder military era, which featured sieges more often than open-field
cavalry battles. Akbar's slaughter of the garrison also signaled his ferocious determination to subjugate major north Indian rulers who resisted
his Timurid ambitions.

During this same decade in the 1560s Akbar also dealt successfully with a
revolt of Uzbek nobles who had joined the Mughal enterprise, and with
more threatening challenges from two Timurids who claimed legitimacy.
The latter were, first, a descendant of Sultan Husain Baiqara of Herat, and
secondly, Akbar's half-brother Mirza Hakim, who, however, remained the

ruler of Kabul after Akbar expelled him from the Punjab. As a Timurid descendant of Babur, Mirza Hakim remained the greatest threat to Akbar's reign, and in 1579 he allied himself with a group of Afghans and disaffected Mughal officers in a serious rebellion, made more threatening by some members of the 'ulama who gave it religious sanction because they had been alienated by Akbar's religious experiments. Akbar responded to this threat with a rapid march to Kabul where he finally deposed his brother, thus finally eliminating any serious rival to his dynastic legitimacy.

Akbar was as pivotal a figure as Shah 'Abbas Safavi in reclaiming and expanding an empire, although his circumstances, personality, and religious interests were profoundly different. Like Shah 'Abbas I, his Ottoman predecessor Mehmet II, and Akbar's Ottoman contemporary, Süleyman, Akbar personally commanded armies throughout his reign. He rarely suffered a serious defeat as he went about subjugating Afghans in the Gangetic valley, Rajput rajas in the desert regions west of Agra, and established Indo-Muslim rulers such as the sultans of Gujerat (1572) and Ahmednagar (1599) in the Deccan. He was still campaigning in 1602, three years before his death.

One of the principal reasons for Akbar's triumphs was his success in coopting Hindu lineages to serve his empire. Formidable Rajput chiefs were the most important of these men. Even before his conquest of Chitor, Akbar had begun integrating Rajputs into his military system. Following a visit to a Chishti Sufi at Sikri, the site of his ancestor Babur's epic victory over the Rajputs in 1527, Akbar the emperor married a Rajput princess, who was offered to him by a minor Rajput chief eager for help against a local Mughal governor.[30] Akbar then enrolled the girl's father, brother, and nephew in Mughal service, the first of many Rajputs who served the empire – all the more willingly, apparently, because Akbar's Hindu wives were allowed to remain Hindus and to practice their devotional rituals within the imperial *haram*.

This marriage and Rajput recruitment were probably the events that led Akbar, two years later, to abolish the pilgrimage tax on Hindus and issue regulations allowing Hindus to repair their temples and forbidding the conversion of non-Muslim captives to Islam – a contrast with Ottoman and Safavid enslavement and conversion practices. After the slaughter of Rajputs at Chitor, Akbar invited or coerced other Rajputs to join the imperial service, and such men as his Rajput general Man Singh served

---

[30] P. M. Currie has written a well-illustrated history of the Chishti shrine at nearby Ajmir, which was a pilgrimage site during the Sultanate and attained special importance during the Mughal era: *The Shrine and Cult of Mu'in al-din Chishti of Ajmer* (Delhi: Oxford University Press, 1989).

Map 11. The Mughal Empire in 1605

him brilliantly as he expanded and consolidated his control over the north Indian region known as Hindustan. Despite the military slave institutions of the Ghaznavids and their successors in the Delhi Sultanate, Mughal rulers never established their own *ghulam* forces. Not only were Man Singh and other Rajput chiefs allowed to remain Hindus, but Akbar also permitted them to retain their historic territories as a special category of military fiefs, unlike most Muslim nobles whose *iqta'* or *timar*-like lands were periodically reassigned to prevent them from developing autonomous territorial power. By 1580 forty Rajput chiefs held high ranks and major responsibilities in Akbar's state.

The imperial system

Akbar's systematizing mind, like those of Mehmet and 'Abbas, is evident throughout his reign and was documented by his amanuensis and companion Abu'l Fazl 'Allami, who wrote a history of his reign which included a detailed gazetteer titled the *A'in-i Akbari* or *Institutes of Akbar*. While Akbar's regulations, which Abu'l Fazl describes, are not characterized as *kanuns* (Ottoman imperial regulations), they deal with an encyclopedic range of administrative subjects outside the subject matter of Islamic law. However, this ruler's single most important measure was the institutionalization of a system of military feudalism that resembled earlier eastern Islamic practices and those of the early Ottomans. Babur and his Mughal descendants were intimately familiar with the *iqta'* and *soyurghal* land grants used to support troops in Central Asia and Iran. Akbar introduced a similar type of institution to finance the army that was the basis of Mughal rule. It was formally launched in 1574–5, and while, like most complex administrative systems, the system was subject to abuse, it served the empire well for nearly a century and a half.

Akbar and his successors retained substantial amounts of demesne or crown land known as *khalisa*, but much of the remaining territory was parceled out to support troops. These assignments were known as *jagirs*, literally "holding places," and most imperial officers, known as *mansabdar*s (men who "held rank"), were given these temporary grants – temporarily "held" not owned – to support military contingents. They resembled the *iqta'* grants of the Saljuqs, or those of the Safavids to Qizilbash tribes, only in outline, for under Akbar and his successors, officers were not allowed to remain permanently in one *jagir*, but were rotated from one to another. This system required accurate land-revenue estimates, which in turn necessitated land surveys in order to make assignments that generated sufficient funds to support the number of troops commanded by each officer. These features necessarily generated an enormous financial bureaucracy. The principal exceptions to this system of surveys, assessments, and rotation were the Rajputs, whose historic territories were simply classified as *watan* or "homeland" *jagirs*. In essence, after Akbar defeated or intimidated Rajput chiefs, they were allowed to retain their autonomy if they served the regime as *mansabdar*s.

Experiments with truth

While Akbar's conquests and systematizing administrative instincts resembled those of his contemporaries in certain respects, his evolving spiritual interests and manipulation of Islamic concepts for his idiosyncratic imperial ideology set him apart. To the extent that he was deeply attached to Sufi beliefs and revered particular *pirs*, he resembled his father and grandfather as well as other men of his age in Istanbul and Isfahan. Akbar particularly revered and patronized Chishti *shaikhs*, spiritual descendants of the individuals who exercised so much influence over such men as Amir Khusrau Dihlavi in fourteenth-century Delhi. During Akbar's reign Naqshbandis, some of whose representatives had entered India in Babur's day – and retreated back to Kabul with Humayun – were more prominent as *mansabdars* than as the pious representatives of the influential Indian order they were to become in the seventeenth century. Akbar's Sufism, however, is not a sufficient explanation for his spirituality and latitudinarian religious interests. These may have been due more immediately to his first Hindu marriage and the incorporation of Rajput Hindus into his regime, and to his knowledge of Zoroastrian doctrine and possible exposure to Jainism, Buddhism, and Portuguese-mediated Roman Catholic Christianity following his conquest of Gujerat. Since he left no autobiography, it is only possible to speculate about the ways in which his personal religiosity and early exposure to other faiths mixed with imperial interests to shape his religious policies.

His devotion to the Chishti order was evidently the first reason why in 1571 he built a new and still perfectly preserved red sandstone city nearby at Sikri, about thirty-four kilometers from Agra. However, Sufism, and especially Chishti Sufism, does not explain why in 1575 Akbar began holding religious debates at Fatehpur Sikri. Beginning with Muslims, Akbar subsequently invited Jains, Zoroastrians, and, in 1580, Christians to participate in theological debates, setting himself apart from any of his predecessors or contemporaries in the Ottoman Empire or Safavid Iran. In retrospect, these fascinating debates, unique in any culture at this time, appear to have served a political purpose as well as a personal religious quest, for in 1579 Akbar proclaimed himself to be the final arbiter in religious matters, overriding intolerant, fractious *'ulama* by insisting he had the right of *ijtihad*, interpretation of Islamic law. His contemporary, Shah Tahmasp, had granted this authority to 'Ali Karaki and the Shi'i *'ulama*.

In the imperial decree promulgating Akbar's authority, he is also described as *imam-i 'adil*, the "just Imam," normally a Shi'i title, as well as the "just sultan," the inherited Sasanian ideal. Shaikh Mubarak, Akbar's ideological spokesman, also suggested at this time that Akbar embodied *farr*, the pre-Islamic Iranian concept of a divinely bestowed charismatic essence, the idea Abu'l Fazl later incorporated into his monumental history, the *Akbar Nama*. Akbar was seemingly influenced by a number of Zoroastrian ideas, including fire worship – actually an Indo-European practice found in Hindu ritual involving sacrifices to Agni, the god of fire.

However various religious streams came together in Akbar's mind, the 1579 decree was probably issued to anticipate the first Islamic millennium in 1591–2, a date that prompted millenarian expectations throughout the Muslim world. This was the period of the Nuqtavi episode in Safavid Iran. One of the men who sat on the committee that approved Akbar's claims was Mir Sharif Amuli, a Nuqtavi refugee from Iran, one of many Nuqtavis, including several poets, who eventually fled Iran for the far more tolerant environment of the Mughal court. Mir Sharif Amuli may have directly supplied Akbar and his loyalists with some of their more radical glorifications of Akbar's person, although Abu'l Fazl 'Allami himself is known to have corresponded with Nuqtavis. At least one Nuqtavi refugee in India, Mir Sayyid Ahmad Kashi, was influential enough to persuade Akbar to write to Shah 'Abbas urging him to practice religious tolerance.[31] In any case, two years later, in 1581, Akbar further shocked a number of conservative *'ulama*, some of whom had been deeply offended by the emperor's eclectic religious tastes and practices, by initiating an imperial cult known as the *din-i ilahi* or *tauhid-i ilahi*, the "faith of God" or the "divine unity," in which he enrolled a number of disciples who pledged to him the kind of absolute devotion that Sufi *pir*s, including Nizam al-Din Awliya in fourteenth-century Delhi, demanded of their disciples.

Akbar's tolerance seemed to please his Hindu and other non-Muslim subjects, but his more quixotic "experiments with [religious] truth" (to borrow the title of Gandhi's spiritual autobiography), or, in other words, his search for a unique type of spiritual authority to complement dynastic legitimacy, were not taken up by his successors. Even one of his Rajput officers refused to enroll in his personal cult. His assertion that he enjoyed a unique spiritual status also triggered a conservative Muslim reaction, and one of his critics was the Naqshbandi Sufi *Shaikh* Ahmad Sirhindi, the disciple of a Naqshbandi *pir* who arrived in Delhi in 1602. It was Sirhindi who founded a vigorous South Asian version of the conservative Naqshbandi order, whose disciples influenced later Islamic thought in India and also helped to popularize the order in Ottoman territories.[32] Sirhindi and his Naqshbandi Sufi disciples helped to fuel a conservative,

---

[31] Algar, "Nuktawiyya."
[32] Yohanan Friedmann, *Shaykh Ahmad Sirhindi: An Outline of his Thought and a Study of his Image in the Eyes of Posterity* (Montreal: McGill Institute of Islamic Studies, 1971).

Shari'a-based orthodox resurgence among north Indian Muslims in the seventeenth century. As a Sufi order, they were an ideological and political world apart from Nuqtavis in Iran, the Bektashis in the Ottoman Empire, or even the Chishtis in India.

In other respects, though, Akbar's reign was as formative and enduring as his administrative measures. He adopted the Iranian solar calendar for administrative purposes and formally instituted Persian as the language of administration, thus definitively turning away from Babur's Turki, which atrophied as a spoken language among the Mughal elite. Akbar also actively recruited Persian-speaking Iranians, many of them Shi'as, to fill positions at court, swelling the numbers of Iranian literati and administrators, who left their relatively impoverished and politically chaotic homeland for the wealth and relative stability of late sixteenth-century Mughal India. Akbar also consciously set about creating a Mughal dynastic mystique through his building projects and court histories.

Building of his new capital at Sikri (1571–84) was preceded by the construction of a monumental tomb-garden for his father, Humayun, ordered by Humayun's wife, Hamida Banu Begim, but undoubtedly approved by Akbar, the first of several garden tomb structures that set Mughal funerary tastes apart from those of their Ottoman and Safavid contemporaries. Combining both Timurid and Indic design elements, it dwarfed Temür's Gur-i Amir tomb in Samarqand. Akbar also linked himself with his Timurid past through his artistic and literary patronage. Babur's *Vaqa'i'* was translated from Turki into Persian and illustrated with Persian-style paintings from Akbar's atelier, and individuals who knew Babur were encouraged to write their memoirs, producing one of the most remarkable woman's autobiographies of the time, by Babur's daughter Gulbadan Begim.[33]

Other texts echoed Akbar's religious and cultural ambitions as well as his sensitivity to Indian culture. One, the *Tarikh-i alfi*, the history of the first Islamic millennium, may have represented Akbar's historic and artistic footnote to his religious innovations, while illustrated versions of such classic Persian-language poetic works as Nizami's and Amir Khusrau Dihlavi's *Khamsa*s reiterated his commitment to Persian as the high cultural language of the Mughal court. The production of a Hindu text, the *Harivamsa*, advertised Akbar's interest in Hindu culture, which he had manifested as early as 1562 when he forced Miyan Tansen, the most celebrated Hindu musician and singer of his day, to leave the court of his Rajput patron and reside at Akbar's court until his death in 1586. Tansen's

---

[33] Gulbadan Begim, *The History of Humâyûn.*

drupad form of singing was based on the *raga* tradition of classical Indian music, and Tansen himself was an individual who moved in the devotional religious movements of both Hinduism (*bhakti*) and Islam (Sufism), very much like the celebrated fourteenth-century Muslim poet and musician, Amir Khusrau Dihlavi. Both men personified a syncretic strain in Indo-Muslim aristocratic artistic culture that was largely absent from the Ottoman and Safavid Empires.

It was a culture whose religious tolerance Akbar's successor, Jahangir, described approvingly at the time of his accession in 1605; but in doing so he seems to have been referring more to the state religion, Islam, for he does not allude to the Ottoman *millat* system or Shah 'Abbas's pragmatic protection of non-Muslim religious communities.[34] He writes:

The professors of various faiths had room in the broad expanse of his incomparable sway. This was different from the practices in other realms, for in Persia there is room for Shias only, and in Turkey ... and Tûrân [Mawarannahr] there is room for Sunnis only. As in the wide expanse of divine compassion there is room for all classes and followers of all creeds ... there was room for the professors of opposite religions, and for beliefs good and bad ... Sunnis and Shias met in one mosque, and Franks and Jews in one church, and observed their own forms of worship.[35]

Jahangir's observation was, in turn, confirmed when Pietro della Valle described the Indian society he saw during his visit to the principal Mughal port of Surat in 1623. Della Valle's account seems to confirm the public knowledge of Akbar and Jahangir's religious tolerance (or, in the *'ulama*'s eyes, deviance) and it serves as a useful reminder of the limited nature of Mughal sovereignty when he remarks that the "Mohammedans ... seem to possess somewhat more of authority" in India:

Its population is partly gentile [Hindus and other non-Muslims] and partly Mohammedan, and if I am not mistaken the gentiles are the more numerous; however they live all intermingled and peaceably among themselves, because the Great Mogul to whom Gujerat is now subject (having its own king in other times), although he is a Mohammedan (but not a pure one, they say) makes no difference in his states between the one people and the other. And in his court and armies, and even among the men at the highest level, both have equal place. It is true that

---

[34] Della Valle, for example, remarks about Shah 'Abbas's Iran: "Something that comes to mind now is that in Persia all foreign peoples, whether by country or by belief, live and are able to live through ancient custom and privilege, in their own way under their own laws." Della Valle, *The Pilgrim*, 130.

[35] *Memoirs of Jahângîr*, I, 37, and n. 1 regarding this translation. See also Gregory C. Kozlowski's comment on Mughal religious "heterogeneity" in his article "Imperial Authority, Benefactions and Endowments (Awqaf) in Mughal India," *Journal of the Economic and Social History of the Orient* 38, No. 3 (1995), 362–3.

the Mohammedans, as the masters (especially those of the Mongolian race, which today is dominant in these parts), seem to possess somewhat more of authority.[36]

In religious and cultural terms Akbar's and Jahangir's reigns constituted a brief dynastic moment in time. Akbar's eclecticism and Jahangir's tolerance set Mughal India apart from other contemporary empires, Muslim and non-Muslim, and the Mughal emperors' lack of demand for ideological conformity distinguished their reigns from most others in premodern world history.

---

[36] Della Valle, *The Pilgrim*, 211.

4   The economies around 1600

Introduction

Imperial, warrior dynasties generally had three principal economic goals: to acquire sufficient wealth to allow the ruling class to have, in the words of the Mughal historian of Shah Jahan's era, " a civilized and comfortable life"; to acquire sufficient wealth to fund further conquests and the acquisition of additional resources; and to acquire sufficient wealth to fund grandiose building projects that would glorify the dynasty and legitimize it in the eyes of its subjects and posterity. Apart from plunder, often but not always a lucrative activity, most pre-industrial dynasties had access to three principal sources of wealth: taxes on agriculture, commodity production, and commerce. The economies of the Ottoman, Safavid, and Mughal Empires were structurally identical, and the economic policies of their rulers fundamentally similar. They were also linked with one another through the exchange of commodities and the circulation of merchants.

All three empires were predominantly agrarian states whose rulers derived the bulk of their income from taxes on agriculture, and the size of their populations and economies depended primarily on the agricultural potential of their territories. After agriculture, taxes on commerce constituted a secondary but nonetheless vital source of income, which might come from transit trade, such as the valuable commerce in Indian spices funneled through the Red Sea to Cairo, or from the production and export of manufactured commodities, such as cloth, whether Iranian and Ottoman silk or Indian cotton. In the case of the Ottomans, the *jizya*, the special tax on major communities of non-Muslim subjects, also represented a significant source of income. The rulers of all three dynasties inherited and generally followed similar economic policies to enrich themselves and their states, although the Safavids' relative poverty caused at least one Iranian ruler, Shah 'Abbas I, to take a more activist role in the economy than his royal contemporaries. In general Ottoman, Safavid, and Mughal rulers protected, while systematically exploiting their peasantry, encouraged but did not usually control manufactures and took every measure possible to increase the flow of taxable commerce.

A topographical map of Ottoman, Safavid, and Mughal territories offers valuable insights into the population density, settlement patterns, and agricultural productivity of these empires. After 1517 the Ottoman Empire consisted of three principal regions: Anatolia and Mesopotamia; Rumelia or the European provinces; and Syria, Egypt, and the Hijaz. The Ottomans lost Baghdad and part of Mesopotamia in the early sixteenth century but regained these territories later. Of these, Anatolia had major river systems only in Mesopotamia and was otherwise predominantly dry and thinly populated, except for Baghdad and Basra and cities along the Aegean and Black Sea coasts. Rumelia – the Balkan peninsula and adjacent European territories – was far better watered and more densely settled, and constituted the richest region of the empire. Egypt possessed ample water for irrigated agriculture along the Nile – sufficient, as in Mesopotamia, to have sustained ancient civilizations – and Cairo was, in addition to Aleppo and Constantinople itself, a valuable, taxable emporium for Indian Ocean and Mediterranean commerce. In 1600 the total Ottoman population is estimated to have been about twenty-two million.[1]

During the brief periods when they controlled Baghdad and its hinterlands, the Safavids too benefited from the productivity of this fertile region, but otherwise they ruled over a thinly settled, desiccated plateau of mountains and salt deserts, with major river systems located only in the northwestern and southeastern frontier zones. The three richest areas in an otherwise unproductive Iranian landscape were Azerbaijan in the northwest, Khurasan in the northeast, and Fars province in central Iran; the latter two provinces had constituted the major urban and cultural centers of the great pre-Islamic Iranian empires, the Achaemenid and Sasanian, both of whose rulers also controlled Mesopotamia. Iran also benefited from the overland trade networks that connected India, Central Asia, and China with the Middle East. Ten million people are estimated to have been living within Iranian territories when the Safavids controlled Baghdad and Mesopotamia during the reign of Shah 'Abbas I.[2]

In contrast to Iran, the Mughals controlled a south Asian fertile crescent that extended from the mouth of the Indus River, northeast to the rich, well-watered, densely populated lands of the Punjab, and then down

---

[1] Halil Inalcık and Donald Quataert (eds.), *An Economic and Social History of the Ottoman Empire 1300–1914* (Cambridge University Press, 1994), 29: the authors cite Barkan's estimate of 30–35 million, which they consider to be greatly exaggerated.

[2] Elsewhere I have given estimates of the Safavid population at the time the dynasty controlled Baghdad and parts of Iraq. See Stephen F. Dale, *Indian Merchants and Eurasian Trade 1600–1750* (Cambridge University Press, 1994), 18–19.

the even richer Ganges Valley to the Bay of Bengal. The Indus valley resembled Mesopotamia and Egypt as an agriculturally rich site of ancient south Asian civilization, while the Ganges constituted the productive core and population center of later north Indian empires. Indian ports in Bengal, southwest India, and Gujerat were emporia for sea-borne trade between China, Southeast Asia, and the Middle East, as well as sites for the export of Indian raw materials and manufactured products. Estimates of the population of Mughal territories in 1600, prior to the dynasty's conquest of the Deccan and the southeast coast of the subcontinent, range from 100 to 145 million people.[3]

Muslim economic policies and the prestige of trade

Ottoman, Safavid, and Mughal rulers generally followed similar economic policies that were the norm throughout the Islamic world, except that the poverty of Safavid Iran persuaded Shah 'Abbas I to promote economic development and restrict some forms of economic activity far more actively and aggressively than his contemporaries. Muslim writers on economic topics usually included their opinions in texts known as "Mirrors for Princes," or as *nasihat namas*, literally "letters of advice." Usually these treatises advocated, first of all, protecting and exploiting the peasantry, since these princes, like most pre-industrial rulers, relied on agriculturalists as the economic foundation of their states. Rulers and their ministers generally did so, except in the case of the Oghuz and the Mongols in their early years – pastoral nomadic rulers or plunderers, who had to be taught by ethnic Iranian ministers such as Nizam al-Mulk and Rashid al-Din that merely ravaging the countryside, instead of carefully taxing the peasantry, destroyed the economic basis for sustained rule. It is estimated that 80 percent of the Iranian and 90 percent of the Indian population was employed in agricultural or related activities.

In Muslim states the ruler's self-interested compassion for the peasantry or merchants was often presented as part of the duties of the "just sultan," the well-known, pre-Islamic Iranian ideal of the ruler as one who technically owned all the agricultural land in any particular country, but was nonetheless committed to protect its occupants from danger or exploitation. Until economic practice caught up with liberal theory in the nineteenth century, Ottoman rulers and officials, for example,

---

[3] Shireen Moosvi gives the highest estimate of 14.5 crores, or 145 million people, for the Indian population in 1601. See her article "The Silver Influx, Money Supply, Prices and Revenue Extraction in Mughal India," *Journal of the Economic and Social History of the Orient* 30, No. 1 (1987), 82.

idealized and tried to ensure the survival of the family farm (what they described as the *çift hane* system, a peasant household with one pair of oxen) by forbidding its subdivision or alienation – partly because that made it much easier to collect agrarian taxes from this socio-economic unit. In doing so they were closely following Byzantine precedents.

Mughal rulers and officials took much the same line as Ottomans, as was exemplified by their idealized view of the responsibilities of revenue collectors – who, as Akbar's minister, Abu'l Fazl wrote, were expected to aid the cultivator while representing the interest of the ruler. The revenue collector, he wrote,

Should be a friend of the agriculturalists ... He should consider himself the representative of the lord paramount ... He should assist the needy husbandman with advances of money and recover them gradually ... He should ascertain the extent of the soil in cultivation and weigh each several portion in the scales of personal observation and be acquainted with its quality. The agricultural value of the land varies in different districts and certain soils are adapted to certain crops. He should deal differently with each agriculturalist and take his case into consideration.[4]

Part of this official's duties, observed Abu'l Fazl, was to see that the cultivator brought wasteland under cultivation, thereby increasing the revenue of the empire.

After agriculture most Muslim authors devoted their attention to commerce, advising monarchs to create an infrastructure of roads, bridges, and *caravansarais* and to protect travelers and merchants. A typical example of this literature is the late Safavid-era treatise of a religious scholar, Mulla Muhammad Baqir Sabzawari, entitled the *Rawzat al-anwar-i 'Abbasi*, in which the author urges rulers to be benevolent and just to merchants.[5] Ottoman, Safavid, and Mughal monarchs all followed this advice, though it would be more accurate to say that they invested in infrastructure, persuaded or coerced their nobles to do the same, and the literati then abstracted their policies in their advice treatises. Ottoman, Safavid, and Mughal rulers protected caravan routes and built *caravansarais* that ultimately connected all three empires with a relatively safe system for commercial travelers.

Ottomans perpetuated the elaborate Saljuq *caravansarai* system with these elaborate, fortified commercial staging posts built about thirty

---

[4] Abû'l Fazl 'Allâmî, *The A'in-i Akbari*, trans. H. Blochmann, ed. D. C. Phillott (New Delhi: Crown Publications, 1988), 3 vols., II, 46.

[5] Cited by Rudi Matthee in his article "Merchants in Safavid Iran: Participants and Perceptions," *Journal of Early Modern History* 4, No. 3–4 (2000), 254. The author wrote during the reign of Shah 'Abbas II in the middle of the seventeenth century.

kilometers apart and linking the major commercial nodes of their territories.[6] Shah 'Abbas I is perhaps best known among his contemporaries for the *caravansarais* constructed during his reign, but the Timurid Mughals shared his concern for this important institution. Travelers often commented on these networks, which Babur began in India in 1528 and Akbar systematically developed in the late sixteenth century. As his historian Abu'l Fazl noted of Akbar, "The gracious sovereign cast an eye upon the comfort of travellers and ordered that in the serais on the high roads, refuges and kitchens should be established."[7] By the early seventeenth century, *caravansarais* extended along the length of the Grand Trunk Road linking Agra and Delhi with the Punjab and continued over the mountains of central Afghanistan to Balkh in the far north. Two English travelers described some of these between Agra and Lahore in 1615, reporting that: "Every five or six coss, there are serais built by the king or some great man, which add greatly to the beauty of the road, [and] are very convenient for the accommodation of travellers, and serve to perpetuate the memory of their founders."[8]

The *waqf* institution

In legal terms the *caravansarais* were *waqfs*, charitable or religious endowments, whereby Muslim public institutions such as *masjids*, Sufi *khangahs*, *hammams* or public baths and kitchens, cemeteries, and public fountains were supported by income from agricultural land, water mills or, in cities, the rent from shops. *Waqfs* were one of the single most important institutions in pre-modern Muslim societies. They expressed piety, preserved memory, supported public institutions, generated commercial incomes, and protected family property.[9]

In Istanbul, for example, these endowments supported the Aya Sofia and other great mosques and the associated institutions of imperial *kulliye* complexes, partly with confiscated Byzantine property. In India they paid

---

[6] See above, Chapter I, and for its photographs and summary of Saljuq trade routes, "The Caravan Route: The Anatolian Staging Posts," in Stierlin, *Turkey from the Selçuks to the Ottomans* (Cologne: Taschen, 1998), 55–75.

[7] AN, III, 1236.

[8] Richard Steel and John Crowther, "Journey of Richard Steel and John Crowther, from Ajmeer in India to Isfahan in Persia, in the years 1615 and 1616," in Robert Kerr, ed., *A General Collection of Voyages and Travels* (Edinburgh: Blackwood, 1824), 208. For descriptions of specific Indian *caravansarais* see Ebba Koch, *Mughal Architecture: An Outline of its History and Development, 1526–1858* (Munich: Prestel, 1991), 66–8.

[9] One of the best introductions to the significance and function of *waqf* endowments in a particular city is the book by Haim Gerber on seventeenth-century Bursa, *Economy and Society in an Ottoman City: Bursa, 1600–1700* (Jerusalem: The Hebrew University, 1988).

for the maintenance of the Taj Mahal, but were less common than in Safavid or Ottoman dominions. In commercial terms the most important *waqfs* in Istanbul, Isfahan, and Delhi included the shops of bazaar complexes, which both served as commercial centers in their respective empires and provided income to support the general spiritual and material welfare of the urban populace.[10] The Bedestan in Istanbul, the shops of the Maidan-i Shah in Isfahan, and the Chandni Chowk complex in Delhi all served these functions. Shops surrounding mosques would, more often than not, be included in a *waqf* grant dedicated to support the mosque, its personnel, and associated educational institutions. Surplus *waqf* cash might be used to generate additional income through loans, and thus these endowments sometimes became an informal banking system, often offering rates below the level of the *sarrafs* or moneylenders in bazaars.[11]

Waqfs were also commonly used in all Muslim societies as a legal device to ensure that property, which would otherwise be divided among children, could be retained intact by the family with one of them acting as a *mutawalli* or custodian. In this case pious intent was often expressed as protection of poor children over the generations. Sometimes the founders even ignored Islamic inheritance laws by stipulating that daughters should get the same shares as sons.[12] The former type of pious or public endowment was known as *waqf ayri* and the latter as *waqf ahli*.[13] In actual practice the distinction between these types was often blurred. Families frequently benefited even from public *waqfs* by stipulating in the deed that their members and descendants should be appointed as *mutawallis*.[14] *Mutawallis* were important individuals who could, if they so chose, misappropriate funds from public endowments or grow rich by investing funds from family endowments in land or commerce.

Waqfs were especially prominent in Ottoman society, both in Anatolia and in Egypt, where their alienation of wealth often became an issue of imperial concern, as it did to Mehmet II.

---

[10] For an introduction to this aspect see Gabriel Baer, "The Waqf as a Prop for the Social System (Sixteenth to Twentieth Centuries)," *Islamic Law and Society* 4 No. 3 (1997), 264–97, and Miriam Hoexter, "Waqf Studies in the Twentieth Century: the State of the Art," *Journal of the Economic and Social History of the Orient* 41, No. 4 (1998), 474–95.

[11] See especially Murat Çizakça, "Cash Waqfs of Bursa, 1555–1823," *Journal of the Economic and Social History of the Orient* 38, No. 2, 313–54.

[12] R. Peters *et al.*, "Wakf (A.) *Encyclopaedia of Islam* II, Brill Online, Part 12.

[13] Suraiya Faroqhi gives fascinating financial details of agricultural land used to support a Sufi hospice in her article "*Vakif* Administration in Sixteenth century Konya. The Zaviye of Sadreddin-i Konevi," *Journal of the Economic and Social History of the Orient* 17, No. 2 (May 1974), 145–72. She also shows how this land both supported the hospice and also provided income for the local *timar* holder.

[14] For multiple examples of such use see Baer, "The Waqf As a Prop for the Social System," 264–97.

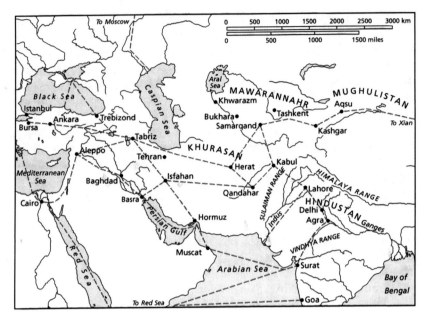

Map 12. Trade routes

To grasp the ubiquitous character of the Ottoman foundations, one may say that the three most striking traits of the Ottoman *wakf* were its widespread vertical and horizontal use throughout all socio-economic strata of society; its capacity to adapt to individual, group and state needs within Islamic as well as within Christian and Jewish communities and, finally, its longevity – not only of the institution itself but also of the abundant individual *wakf*s, whether founded in the Ottoman period or founded during Ayyûbid or Mamlûk times.[15]

Merchants and commerce

Apart from protecting the peasantry and financing infrastructure, Muslim monarchs were explicitly instructed to respect, protect, and encourage merchants. In one Ottoman treatise the author urged his readers to

Look with favour on the merchants in the land; always care for them; let no one harass them; let no one order them about; for through their trading the land becomes prosperous, and by their wares cheapness abounds in the world; through them, the excellent fame of the sultan is carried to surrounding lands, and by them the wealth within the land is increased.[16]

[15] Peters *et al.*, "Wakf" Section IV, "In the Ottoman Empire."
[16] Inalcık, "Capital Formation in the Ottoman Empire," *Journal of Economic History* 39, No. 1 (March 1969), 97–8.

Muslim elites in these empires were undoubtedly happy to follow such advice, as many of them had merchant trading partners: a common custom known to their Mongol predecessors, who formed partnerships known as *ortaqs*.[17] In India during Akbar's day, Mughal nobles were known to employ members of Hindu commercial castes as financial and commercial managers and, as the French Huguenot Jean Chardin testified, Safavid kings and nobles also employed merchant partners.[18] Chardin then went on to observe about the status of merchants in Muslim countries, distinguishing between prestigious long-distance traders and shopkeepers.

The name of Merchant, is a Name much respected in the *East*, and is not allowed to Shop-keepers or Dealers in trifling Goods, nor to those who trade not in foreign countries ... In the Indies the Laws are still more favourable to Traders, for tho' they are much more numerous than in *Persia*, they are nevertheless more set by. The Reason of this additional respect is, because in the *East* Traders are Sacred Persons, who are never molested even in time of War; and are allowed a free Passage, they and their Effects, through the Middle of Armies: 'Tis on their account especially that the Roads are so safe all over Asia, especially in *Persia*.[19]

The Ottomans

Ottomans, like their neighbors to the east in Iran and India, ruled over a predominantly rural population of agriculturalists and, particularly in Anatolia, numbers of pastoral nomads. Throughout the history of the empire, the peasantry provided the bulk of the state's income. Initially these taxes, relatively light ones, were collected by *sipahis*, but during the sixteenth century, as taxes increased to finance almost continuous warfare, Ottomans gradually shifted to tax-farming, and in 1695 they established the *malikhane* system, which granted fixed taxes and substantial privileges to large tax-farmers – a settlement that contributed to the subsequent increased power of provincial notables, known as *ayyan*s. Of the three distinct regions that composed the empire by the early sixteenth century – Anatolia, Egypt and Syria, and Rumelia – the European

---

[17] Thomas T. Allsen, "Mongolian Princes and their Merchant Partners," *Asia Major*, 3rd series II/2 (1989), 83–125.

[18] Al-Badâonî, 'Abdul-l Qâdir Ibn-i-Mulûk Shâh, *Muntakhabu-T-Tawarikh*, trans. George S. A. Ranking, introduction by Brahmadeva Prasad Ambashthya (Patna: Academica Asiatica, repr. 1973), II, 65 and Sir John (Jean) Chardin, *Travels in Persia 1673–1677* (Mineola, New York: Dover Books, repr. 1988), 279. See also Satish Chandra, "Commercial Activities of the Mughal Emperors during the Seventeenth Century," in Satish Chandra, ed., *Essays in Medieval Indian Economic History* (New Delhi: Munshiram Manoharlal, 1987), 163–9.

[19] Chardin, *Travels in Persia*, 279–80.

province of Rumelia was the most productive. In 1475 67 percent of the Ottoman state's total revenue came from this region, although this figure included not only agrarian taxes, but also special taxes on the large Christian population, tolls and customs in Istanbul and elsewhere, mint charges, and the critical gold and silver mines in Serbia and Bosnia, as well as a variety of other smaller sources of income, such as bathhouses. However, in 1475 the Ottomans had not yet conquered Egypt and Syria, which in the sixteenth century constituted the empire's second most lucrative region. Anatolia, the Ottomans' original home, was the third at this time, and 45 percent of its income was derived from copper mines. In the late fifteenth century nearly 8 percent of total Ottoman income came from the *jizya* tax on non-Muslim, predominantly Christian households, and this money usually flowed directly into the treasury. In 1527, following the Syrian and Egyptian conquests, Rumelia accounted for slightly less than 40 percent, Egypt about 25 percent, Anatolia just under 25 percent, and Aleppo and Damascus or Syria, just under 10 percent of total Ottoman revenues.[20]

The Silk trade and the Ottoman economy

In Istanbul and many Ottoman provinces a significant proportion of the state's income came from taxes on commerce, in fact customs revenues were the principal source of hard cash for the Ottoman treasury in later times.[21] In the provinces this was especially true of Yemen and Egypt, where large sums were derived from the Indian transit trade, while Aleppo in Syria was a major entrepôt for goods flowing north and south between Rumelia and Anatolia and Egypt, the Hijaz, and Yemen. Silk, however, represented the single most important commodity traded in Ottoman and well as Safavid lands and the principal source of foreign capital for both states. Silk had been manufactured in Iran since the seventh century CE, after being introduced there from Khotan in Chinese Turkestan, the modern Xinjiang Province. It was produced in most provinces of Iran prior to the Safavid period, with some of the finest cloth being produced not on the Iranian plateau proper, but within the Iranian cultural zone at Marv. As a result of the Mongol invasions Iranian silk producers came into direct contact with Chinese products, and early Iranian geometrical designs gave way to the Chinese motifs commonly found on later Iranian silk garments.[22]

---

[20] Inalcık and Quataert, *An Economic and Social History of the Ottoman Empire*, 55 and 82.
[21] Inalcık, "Imtiyâzât," *Encyclopaedia of Islam* II, Brill Online.
[22] D. Thompson, "Silk Textiles in Iran," in "Abrişam, Silk," *Encyclopaedia Iranica*, www. iraniuca.com/newsite, pp. 9–15.

The Mongol invasions badly disrupted the production of Iranian silk cloth, but it recovered quickly, and by 1300 Iran became the principal supplier of raw silk to the Ottoman Empire, where it was sold to European merchants. Tabriz, near Sultaniye, the Il-Khanid Mongol capital in Azerbaijan, developed into one of the Middle East's great emporia after the Mongol conquests, largely because of its role in the Iranian silk trade. Iranian silk produced in Mawarannahr, the Caspian littoral and other centers was shipped through Tabriz and into Ottoman territories, where it furnished the Ottomans with a major source of income. Much of the silk was then shipped to Bursa in western Anatolia, the first Ottoman capital. Some of the Ottoman campaigns in Anatolia in the fourteenth century were conducted to gain control over the silk-road routes there, and when Selim I occupied Tabriz in 1514, following the Battle of Chaldiran, the Ottomans temporarily gained control over the entire route from Iran to the Mediterranean. In 1617 the Ottomans went to war against the Safavids because the latter had failed to export the amount of silk that had been agreed in a 1613 treaty, thus threatening Ottoman revenues![23]

Well before this, in the fourteenth century, Bursa became one of the world's centers of the silk trade and silk industry. Its role both as an entrepôt for the silk trade between Asia and Europe and also as a center for processing Iranian silk thread contributed to its continued importance after the conquest of Constantinople.[24] Bursa was the primary production center of Ottoman silk cloth and the terminus for silk caravans in the fifteenth and sixteenth centuries, although by the later seventeenth century most Iranian silk came to Izmir, further south.[25] Iranian Muslim merchants initially dominated the trade between Iran and Bursa. Most came from the northern Iranian silk-producing centers, and they sometimes settled in Bursa and occasionally even traveled to Italy. Some Armenians also participated in the trade at this time, but in the late sixteenth century they gained control over it as agents of the dynamic Iranian ruler Shah 'Abbas I. The operation of the Bursa silk market can be seen with a personalized vividness in the records of the Florentine Giovanni di Francesco Maringhi. Maringhi made regular trips between Florence and Bursa to purchase silk, selling woolen cloth there to cover

---

[23] Murat Çizakça, "A Short History of the Bursa Silk Industry," *Journal of the Economic and Social History of the Orient* 23, No. 1–2 (April 1980), 146.

[24] Ibid., 142–3.

[25] For Bursa's economy and commerce in the fifteenth and sixteenth century see Halil Inalcık, Bursa I: "Asir Sanayi ve Ticaret Tarihine Dair Vesikalar," in Inalcık, *Osmanlı Imparatoruğlu* (Istanbul: EREN, repr. 1996), 203–58.

his expenses.[26] Florentines had been selling their wool in Byzantine dominions before the Ottoman conquests. After 1520 Europeans began paying for a significant percentage of their exports with South American silver, but much of this currency was then shipped to Iran to pay for silk imports and/or directly to India via Basra and the Persian Gulf to purchase cotton.

Thus, while the Ottoman Empire had a balance of payments surplus with Europe in this period, it always had a balance of payments deficit with Iran and India. Even though the Indian trade is less well known, the imbalance led one Ottoman observer to complain. "An invasion of Indian fabrics was so alarming that even an official annalist of the empire, Naima, complained of the drain of bullion from the empire, saying 'so much cash treasury goes for Indian merchandise that ... the world's wealth accumulates in India.'"[27]

Ottoman devaluation

Prior to the conquest, early Ottoman coinage was minted in Bursa and Edirne. The principal coin for commerce was the silver akçe, after the Turkish ak or "white," and during the first half of the fifteenth century the Ottomans obtained silver from newly captured mines in the Balkans.[28] Beginning in the late fifteenth century, however, the Ottomans also began minting some gold coins, first using Italian and Egyptian currency and then, following the conquest of Egypt, using gold from Egypt and the Sudan. Copper, which was also found in Ottoman-held territories, was used for local transactions as early as the mid-fourteenth century. The akçe remained relatively stable for the first century and a half of Ottoman rule, but was debased six times or 30 percent during Mehmet II's reign in order to build up funds in the treasury to meet the increasing military and other expenses of his highly centralized state. After Mehmet's reign Ottoman agricultural and commercial revenues were usually not sufficient to cover the state's ever-increasing military and bureaucratic expenses, and the problem became critical in the late sixteenth century following Süleyman's relentless (if militarily successful) campaigns. Nonetheless, prices remained relatively constant from the end of Mehmet's reign until the late sixteenth century. The greatest change in

---

[26] Inalcık and Quataert, "Bursa and the Silk Trade," in *An Economic and Social History of the Ottoman Empire*, 227, 234–6.

[27] See Halil Inalcık, "The India Trade," in Inalcık and Quataert, *An Economic and Social History of the Ottoman Empire*, 354–5.

[28] John F. Richards, *The Mughal Empire* (Cambridge University Press, 1994), 179.

Ottoman currency – and prices – occurred in 1585–6, when the *akçe* was radically debased by 44 percent during a time of rising expenses and deficits, initiating a period of monetary instability that culminated with the complete disappearance of the coin from circulation between 1640 and 1650 and its replacement by various European coins.[29] Debasement caused profound problems, not the least of which were the financial strains it put on salaried Janissary regiments, who because they were well trained, armed, and based in Constantinople could intimidate sultans or their ministers. Janissaries, however, were only the most powerful and potentially troublesome part of Ottoman society that experienced dramatic inflation caused by these devaluations.

The steep inflation or price revolution that occurred in the Ottoman Empire during the last quarter of the sixteenth century has often been attributed to the influx of European silver into Ottoman lands to pay for Iranian silk and Indian spices re-exported from Istanbul, Bursa, Alexandria, and other cities. Yet this argument seems to ignore a number of basic factors, including the quantity theory of money, the relative lack of inflation in Mughal territories and the spice kingdoms of the southwest Indian coast where far larger sums arrived and remained, and the more likely cause of Ottoman inflation, the repeated devaluations of its currency. The theory that European silver caused Ottoman inflation assumes not only that the money remained in Ottoman territories but also that the volume of transactions remained constant. Yet substantial amounts of European silver left the country to pay for Iranian silk, and the population of the empire increased during the sixteenth century, although it declined in the seventeenth century, especially in its European provinces.[30] At the same time enormous volumes of silver were entering India: perhaps as much as one-third of all the silver entering Europe between 1600 and 1750 ultimately reached India, with 124 tons arriving there between 1588 and 1602. Yet inflation in Mughal India was never a major economic issue and is estimated to have been no more than 0.3 percent a year.[31] Finally, continued debasements of the *akçe* from the late fifteenth century represent the most obvious cause of Ottoman inflation, with a major debasement in 1585–86 constituting a "turning point" in Ottoman economic

---

[29] Pamuk, *A Monetary History of the Ottoman Empire*, Chapter 8, "Debasement and Disintegration." *Ak* in Arabic/Persian spelling is *Aq*, as in Aq Quyunlu, the "White Sheep."

[30] See Shireen Moosvi's careful analysis of monetary theory and the Indian case in "The Silver Influx," 81–3.

[31] Ibid., 79 and 94 and Najaf Haidar, "Precious Metal Flows and Currency Circulation in the Mughal Empire," *Journal of the Economic and Social History of the Orient* 39, No. 3 (1996), 323.

history.[32] This debasement was undoubtedly related to the major budgetary shortfall that the Ottomans experienced in 1581, and deficits continued until the late seventeenth century, after which the *malikhane* farming system led to a major increase in government funds.[33]

The Safavids

Throughout most of their history the Safavids controlled the territory coextensive with the modern state of Iran, plus the areas of northwestern Afghanistan regarded as part of the broad region of Khurasan, Balkh, and nearby parts of the northern Afghan region known as Badakhshan, and sections of Georgia, Armenia, and Azerbaijan. Thus apart from its Transcaucasian and Caspian provinces, most Safavid territory was located on the Iranian plateau, a region characterized in modern geographical terms as an interior basin, an "arid zone with green islets ... a parched country" in which "the religious and traditional value of water ... has been magnified in Zoroastrianism" and symbolized by the association of paradise with irrigated gardens.[34] Even in the twenty-first century a traveller to Iran immediately notices how most cities and villages are located along the fringes of the mountains, where water runoff supports agriculture and urban settlement, contrasted with vast stretches of thinly inhabited landscape in the center, where the northern and southern salt deserts, the Dasht-i Kavir and the Dasht-i Lut, make agriculture all but impossible.

During much of the sixteenth century Safavid Iran also suffered from its political impotence and loss of valuable territory to the Ottomans. From Isma'il's defeat at Chaldiran in 1514 until Shah 'Abbas reconstituted the Safavid state at the end of the century, the Safavid economy was in a precarious condition. During Tahmasp's reign Uzbek depredations in Khurasan, and Ottoman attacks leading to the occupation of Tabriz and the loss of Baghdad and Iraq by 1534, meant the temporary or permanent loss of two of the most productive regions of Shah Isma'il's nascent

---

[32] Şevkat Pamuk, "Money in the Ottoman Empire, 1326–1914," in Inalcık and Quataert, eds., *An Economic and Social History of the Ottoman Empire*, 947–81. See also Pamuk's questioning of the inflationary effects of European currency imports in his *A Monetary History of the Ottoman Empire*; see especially Chapter 7, "The Price Revolution of the Near East Revisited," and his article "The Price Revolution in the Ottoman Empire Reconsidered," *International Journal of Middle East Studies* 33, No. 1 (February 2001), 69–89.

[33] Darling, *Revenue Raising and Legitimacy*, 239.

[34] J. Behnan, "Population," *The Cambridge History of Iran*, I, *The Land*, 470–1; Elizabeth B. Moynihan, *Paradise as a Garden: in Persia and Mughal India* (New York: Braziller, 1979).

empire. During most of the sixteenth century the state of Safavid finances was reflected in general by the irregular, decentralized nature of Iran's monetary system, and more particularly by Tahmasp's repeated depreciation of the silver currency. The Shahi silver coin, for example, weighed 9.22 grams during Shah Isma'il's reign and 2.30 grams when 'Abbas I came to power. By the sixteenth century Iran had no substantial silver deposits and, like India, depended on trade to generate specie for its coins. The silk trade provided most of this currency.

As with so many other aspects of the Safavid administration, Shah 'Abbas I reformed the currency, as well as eliminating anachronistic legends in use since Mongol days and replaced them with a suitably Shi'i declaration. Shah 'Abbas also reinstated a prohibition against currency exports to India, which Tahmasp had tried earlier, and some Indians were executed for violating the ban. He needed the money for his wars, but the Iranian silver shortage was more than a reflection of a short-term military need: it was a structural problem, even more severe than that of the Ottomans, of an impoverished territory. Shah 'Abbas I's successors continued debasing the Iranian coinage, even though they rarely engaged in protracted military campaigns. By the time the last Safavid ruler was crowned in 1694, the state's financial situation was critical, although this was due in no small measure to the incompetence of the regime. However, the shortage of silver coinage primarily affected long-distance trade, especially that with India, as most internal business was conducted with copper coinage. Gold coins were scarcely used at all, except as presentation medals.[35]

Traditionally much village agriculture in Iran depended on distinctive underground irrigation channels known as qanats, which led underground streams from mountain slopes to the surface through tunnels dug by sinking a series of shafts following outward from the foothills.[36] These ingenious irrigation channels required considerable labor and constant maintenance and were therefore vulnerable to marauding armies that swept through Iran with depressing regularity. And even when well maintained they could support only a modest population, a fact noticed by such European travelers in Safavid times as the well-informed, Persian-speaking Jean Chardin, who lived in Iran for prolonged periods between 1664 and 1677. Iran, he observed, was

---

[35] Willem Floor, "The Monetary System," in Floor, *The Economy of Safavid Persia* (Wiesbaden: Reichert Verlag, 2000), 65–85.

[36] Peter Beaumont, "Âb ["Water"]," *Encyclopaedia Iranica*, ed. Ehsan Yarshater, I (London: Routledge & Keegan Paul, 1985), 27–39.

Dry, barren, mountainous, and but thinly inhabited. I speak in general, the twelfth Part is not inhabited, nor cultivated; and after you have pass'd any great Towns about two Leagues, you will never meet a Mansion-house nor people in twenty leagues more. The *Western* side above all the rest is most defective, and wants to be peopl'd and, nothing is to be met there almost, but large and spacious deserts. This barrenness proceeds from no other Cause than the scarcity of Water, there is a want of it in most parts of the whole Kingdom.[37]

Agriculturalists also had to compete with pastoral nomadic tribes for scarce resources: a particular problem between the tenth and sixteenth centuries as first Saljuq and then Mongol tribes swept through Khurasan to occupy large swathes of territory, where their animals often destroyed cultivated fields and irrigation systems.

Like its Ottoman and Mughal neighbors to the west and east, Safavid Iran was overwhelmingly rural. Even at the height of the empire, under Shah 'Abbas I, urban residents probably comprised no more than 15 percent of the total population, with fully 5 percent concentrated in Isfahan, which the well-traveled Jean Chardin knew well and described as "the most beautiful town in the whole orient."[38] The Frenchman believed the city to have been as populous as London, which would have given it 600–700,000 inhabitants in the second half of the seventeenth century. At that time its population included Muslims, Armenian Christians, Hindus, Jews, and Zoroastrians, which reflected the major religious communities in the country as a whole. Armenians and Hindus, the two most important mercantile communities in Isfahan, may have numbered as many as 30,000 and 10,000 respectively in Chardin's time. Only the original Safavid capital of Tabriz is likely to have had more than 100,000 inhabitants in the seventeenth century. Two groups comprised the rural population: sedentary agriculturalists with their associated artisans, merchants, and clerics, and pastoral nomads. The first probably amounted to about 60 percent of the total and the latter 20 to 30 percent. Many pastoral nomads would have been Qizilbash or Oghuz tribesmen, who were concentrated in Azerbaijan and Mazandaran, with the Iranian Lurs and Bakhtiyari in the Central Zagros and the Turkic Qashqai further south near Shiraz.

The income of the Safavid state reflected the modest resources of its territory as well as Armenian and Hindu dominance of its foreign trade. The country was not even self-sufficient in some of the most basic food-stuffs. Rice, sugar, and spices were imported in large amounts from India, which also supplied Iran with indigo and with Mughal India's most

---

[37] Chardin, *Travels in Persia*, 128.
[38] Quoted by J. Sourdel-Thomine in "Isfahân," *Encyclopaedia of Islam*, II, Brill Online, 11.

valuable export commodity, cotton cloth, some of which was consumed locally while substantial quantities were transhipped to Ottoman territories.[39] Goods from India came by both land and sea, depending on political conditions. Spices also reached Iran from India, although most came from the southwest or Malabar Coast or Southeast Asia, rather than from Mughal territories. Iran exported only a small amount of goods to India: almonds, the prized cooking additive asafoetida, melons, and some horses. A significant number of Iranian literati and bureaucrats also went to India to find work, but it is not known how much of their income they remitted to families left behind in Iran. Iran, therefore, had a perennial balance of payments deficit with India, which was compensated for by the streams of currency.[40]

Iranian silk, Shah 'Abbas, and Iranian "mercantilism"

As regards Ottoman lands, on the other hand, silk exports gave Iran an economic advantage. Silk, much of it silk thread, represented Iran's principal and most valuable export, with most of it exported by caravans overland to Ottoman territories. This trade was critical to both Iran and the Ottomans. Its sales gave Iran a balance of payments surplus with the Ottomans and the precious metals it lacked for its coinage, substantial quantities of which passed through Iran on their way to India. Ottoman transit duties in turn produced large revenues each year. Both dynasties, therefore, had a vested interest in the vitality of this trade, which was sometimes allowed to continue even during open warfare between the two states. The 1614 Ottoman–Safavid treaty mentioned above stipulated that Iran would send thirty-two tons of silk a year to Ottoman territories.[41] In 1660 Ralph du Mans memorably summarized the monetary relationship between the Ottomans, Safavids, and Mughals that still existed at that time:

Persia is like a big caravansarai which has only two doors, one toward the side of Turkey by which silver from the West enters [in the form of] piastres which come from the New World to Spain, from there to France ... [and] leaving France through Marseilles, they enter into Turkey, from where they arrive here [Iran], where one recasts them into abbasis ... Some carry their piastres until the Indies...

---

[39] Floor, *The Economy of Safavid Persia*, 156; Willem Floor and Patrick Clawson, "Safavid Iran's search for Silver and Gold," *International Journal of Middle East Studies* 32 (2000), 345–68; Halil Inalcık, "Osmanlı Pamuklu Pazarı, Hindistan ve Ingiltere," in *Osmanlı Imparatoruğlu*, 259–317.

[40] See among numerous other sources Floor and Clawson, "Safavid Iran's Search for Silver and Gold," 345–68.

[41] Ibid., 346 and 356.

The other door of exit is Bandar Abbas ... for going to the Indies, to Surat, where all silver of the world unloads, and from there as fallen in an abyss, it does not re-emerge.[42]

Ottoman silver did not, it should be emphasized, pay only for Iranian silk, but also for Indian spices and cotton cloth, some of which came overland through Iran, though they were also carried by ship to Basra in southern Iraq, or to Cairo and Alexandria via the Red Sea.

Lacking population, natural resources, and valuable export manufactures other than silk cloth, attentive Iranian monarchs such as Shah 'Abbas I not only followed typical policies of Muslim rulers, but also actively intervened in economic activities to a greater degree than any of their Ottoman or Safavid contemporaries. First of all, Shah 'Abbas I was probably better known than any of his contemporaries for establishing the conditions and infrastructure to encourage commerce. He was known at the time for the care he took to protect merchants. As two Englishmen observed when crossing from Indian to Iranian territories in 1615, "Merchants are used with much favour, lest they should make complaints to the king, who will have the merchants kindly treated."[43] 'Abbas supplemented his solicitous treatment of merchants with the enforcement of security that Iskandar Beg Munshi discussed in his section "On Shah 'Abbas' Justice, Concern for Security of Roads, and Concern for the Welfare of his Subjects":

The greater part of governing is the preservation of stability within the kingdom and security on the roads. Prior to the accession of Shah 'Abbas, this peace and security had disappeared in Iran, and it had become extremely difficult for people to travel about the country. As soon as he came to the throne Shah 'Abbas turned his attention to this problem. He called for the principal highway robbers to be identified in each province and he then set about eliminating this class of people ... With security restored to the roads, merchants and tradesmen travelled to and from the Safavid empire."[44]

Rahdars, a corps of highway police, enforced a level of security during Shah 'Abbas's reign that many Europeans felt surpassed that of both the Ottoman and the Mughal territories.[45] Security was, in turn supplemented by a vastly enhanced system of bridges, *caravansarais*, and occasionally new roads, such as the *sang farash* or metaled highway across a

---

[42] Quoted by Haidar, "Precious Metal Flows and Currency Circulation in the Mughal Empire," 307.

[43] Steele and Crowther, *Journey*, 214.

[44] Eskander Beg Monshi, *History of Shah 'Abbas the Great (Târîk-e 'âlamârâ-ye 'Abbâsî)*, trans. Roger Savory (Boulder, CO: Westview Press, 1978), 3 vols., II, 523.

[45] Dale, *Indian Merchants and Eurasian Trade*, 39.

swampy stretch of land north of his new capital at Isfahan that "at a single stroke ... made Isfahan the centre of Iranian internal trade."[46] *Caravansarais* were not just protected lodgings for traveling merchants. They could also develop into agricultural market towns with their own covered bazaars.[47] Isfahan itself, Chardin testified, possessed 1,802 *caravansarais*, and surrounding the great maidan in the center of the city there were hundreds of shops that collectively constituted the Safavid equivalent of the Bedestan in Istanbul.[48]

While court historians were habitually prone to encomium and exaggeration, Iskandar Beg Munshi properly credits Shah 'Abbas I with systematically developing and directing the Iranian economy to a degree that far exceeded the situation in the more prosperous Ottoman and Mughal empires. Among the other steps he took toward his overall goal of maximizing royal power, he tried to develop the Iranian cotton industry, cultivate Bengal rice, and cultivate indigo to reduce the reliance on Indian imports; and in 1618 he, like Shah Tahmasp before him, banned the export of gold and silver to prevent the constant outflow of coinage from Safavid territories.[49] Taken together his economic policies have sometimes been described as a kind of Iranian mercantilism – albeit without the theory.[50]

Whatever the validity of that characterization, 'Abbas's most important economic measures involved his single-minded development of the silk trade, Iran's most important source of foreign exchange. To this end the Shah took two major steps. He converted the silk-producing provinces of Gilan and Mazandaran in northern Iran into *khassa*, demesne or crown land, after which state treasury officials were in charge of purchasing silk and oversaw its transport to Isfahan. Second, in 1605 he brutally resettled the Armenian merchant community of Julfa in eastern Anatolia to Isfahan, where he created a new suburb for them south of the Zayandih Rud, the river that ran from west to east through the city. This community, which had earlier been granted special privileges by the Aq Quyunlu, were forcibly enlisted as the principal brokers and traders in Iranian silk because they were highly sophisticated merchants, who possessed a commercial network of tightly knit family firms that extended from India through the Ottoman Empire to Venice and Holland in the early sixteenth century.

[46] Bert Fragner, "Social and Economic Affairs," in *The Cambridge History of Iran*, VI, *The Timurid and Safavid Periods*, 527.
[47] Kheirabadi, *Iranian Cities*.   [48] Sourdel-Thomine, "Isfahân," 11.
[49] Matthee, *The Politics of Trade in Safavid Iran*, 63–9.   [50] Ibid., 69–74.

Armenians and Hindus in Iranian commerce

Shah 'Abbas granted the Armenians of New Julfa, Isfahan, autonomy and the status of a privileged community, whose rights were protected by the queen mother.[51] New Julfa itself was made demesne land. Armenians were not equal partners in the Safavid state, and were occasionally threatened with forced conversion to Islam, but they retained their religion and protected status through the late twentieth century because of their commercial importance to Safavid, Qajar, and Pahlavi regimes. The New Julfa Armenians not only became the principal brokers for the Shah's silk but also performed a variety of commercial and diplomatic missions for the Shah. Armenians also acted as court financiers. While they traded with the expanding Romanov Russian empire – trade which expanded substantially in the late seventeenth century – their most important role in Iranian commerce and Safavid state finances was their virtual monopoly of the Iranian silk trade with the Ottoman Empire and the Mediterranean. As Chardin observed, when succinctly analyzing the foreign trade of all three Muslim empires:

Wherefore in *Turkey*, the Christians [Armenians] and *Jews* carry on the main foreign trade; And in Persia the *Christians* [Armenians] and the Indian Gentiles [Hindus and Jains]. As to the Persians they trade with their own Countrymen, one Province with another, and most of them Trade with *Indians*. The Armenians alone manage the whole [Iranian] European trade.[52]

It was during Shah 'Abbas's reign and later that the number of Armenian communities in Italy and Holland began to grow rapidly.[53] While Shah 'Abbas's successors loosened Safavid state control over the silk trade, the Armenians adapted to the changes, and even as the Safavid state began to deteriorate in the late seventeenth century, many Armenian merchants continued to prosper. However, by 1700 the inept Safavid regime, whose last rulers were as concerned with religious purity as with economic viability, no longer offered the New Julfan Armenians the same degree of protection or privileges they had enjoyed earlier.[54]

If Armenians dominated trade with the west, Hindu Indians controlled most Indo-Iranian commerce. Iranian merchants also traveled to India and exported Indian goods to their homeland, but in Shah 'Abbas's day and in later decades Hindu merchants dominated this trade. It has been said of

---

[51] Rudi Matthee discusses not only Armenians but also other Iranian merchants in the Safavid period in "Merchants in Safavid Iran: Participants and Perceptions," *The Journal of Early Modern History* 4, No. 3–4 (2000), 233–68.
[52] Chardin, *Travels in Persia*, 280–1.
[53] Matthee, *The Politics of Trade in Safavid Iran*, 84–92.   [54] Ibid., 205–6.

Hindu merchants operating in Iran that the "presence and proliferation of Indian 'moneychangers' in several major Iranian cities" is "an astonishing and unexplained episode of Iranian economic history."[55] Yet it is not at all difficult to understand the presence of an Indian mercantile diaspora in seventeenth-century Iran that an Indian merchant estimated to number 10,000 in 1647 – "10,000 Indians who live in Iran without leaving."[56]

Economically these Indians represented the regionally dominant Indian economy, whose reach extended from Southeast Asia to the Mediterranean. In social terms most of the Indian expatriates constituted one segment of the complex, highly differentiated Hindu caste system, which had developed specialized, endogamous castes in pre-Christian centuries. Marwaris, a subcaste of Hindu merchants from Rajasthan who, along with their Jain competitors, grew wealthy during the Mughal era by furnishing credit for Muslim land revenue collections, are probably the best known of these merchants. Some of them, known in sources as *banians*, sold goods and lent money in the Persian Gulf port of Bandar 'Abbas. However, most of the 10,000 Indians whom Chardin estimated resided in Isfahan in 1670 belonged to the prominent Khatri caste group, whose members were native to the Punjab and northwestern India.

Khatris had probably been traveling from the Punjab since the days of the Sultanate curmudgeon Zia al-Din Barani, whose denunciation of the Hindu dominance of the Indo-Muslim economy would have been appropriate for the Mughal period as well. Khatris would have found it easy to join caravans that had traversed the Khyber and other Indo-Afghan passes since ancient times. During Babur's two-decade-long residence in Kabul, he estimated that 20,000 merchants came from India to Kabul each year. Some of these merchants traveled north to Bukhara, Samarqand and then east to the Ferghanah valley and beyond, to Xinjiang or Chinese Turkestan. During Shah 'Abbas's reign, however, probably the majority of them continued on westwards to the larger market in Iran, where they established branches of family firms in the Armenian or Italian manner. Some eventually sent their representatives to the Russians' newly conquered Caspian Sea port of Astrakhan, and from there a few continued on to Moscow where they resided in the Kitae Gorod or "Chinese Town" suburb. In Iran, Khatris both sold cloth and various other Indian goods in bazaars, such as Isfahan's Maidan-i Shah, and lent money to merchants in the cash-starved Iranian economy. In the early eighteenth century the

[55] Mehdi Keyvani, *Artisans and Guild Life in the Later Iranian Period* (Berlin: Klaus Schwartz, 1982), 228.
[56] K. A. Antonova *et al.*, *Russko-Indiiskie Otnosheniia v XVII Veke: Sbornik Dokumentov* (Moscow: Nauka, 1958), no. 33, 1647, 85.

Englishman Edward Pettus, who served the East India Company in Isfahan, complained about Indian aggressive marketing techniques. Using *banian* as a general term for all non–Muslim Indians, he wrote:

> The bannians, the Cheif [*sic*] Marchantes who vende Linene of India, of all sorts and prices, which this Countrye cannot bee without, except the people should goe naked ... they vende most of the linene they bring to Spahan after a most base peddlinge, and unmarchante like manner ... carrying it up and down on their shoulders [in] the Bazar.[57]

Later in the century Chardin criticized Indians for their moneylending and wrote a stereotyped characterization of the Khatris that reminds readers of European Christian portrayals of Jews, particularly ironic considering Chardin was a Huguenot who had taken refuge in England. He pictured the Khatris as a nefarious class of usurious moneylenders who drained Iran of its precious metals by repatriating their ill-gotten gains to India.[58] His was an ethnic explanation for a fundamental economic imbalance between the two regions.

Mughal India

Ottomans, Safavids, and European observers may have exaggerated the flow of precious metals from their economy to India. It is certain, however, that even without data to quantify the exact volumes of monetary flows among these states, their conclusions about the commercial relationship between the empires were generally accurate. As has been seen, European silver flowed to India from both Ottoman and Safavid territories as well as directly on European ships to Surat, the principal Mughal port on the Arabian Sea. In a region with no substantial deposits of silver, these imports provided the basis for the heavy silver coins that became the principal currency of large-scale trade in Akbar's time. Abandoning the Timurid coin known as the *tanka-i shahrukhi*, which had been used in Mawarannahr, India, and Iran, Akbar began coining nearly pure silver rupees that weighed 11.6 grams, although, as in Ottoman and Safavid territories, copper continued to be used for many local transactions. The silver rupee retained most of its value under Akbar's successors owing to the strength of the Mughal economy relative to both Muslim and European states, for horses

---

[57] R. W. Ferrier, "An English View of Persian Trade in 1618: Reports from the Merchants Edward Pettus and Thomas Barker," *Journal of the Social and Economic History of the Orient* 19, No. 2 (1976), 192.

[58] Cited in Vladimir Minorsky, ed. and trans., *Tadhkirat al-Muluk: A Manual of Safavid Administration c. 1137/1725* (Cambridge University Press for the E. J. W. Gibb Memorial Series, repr. 1980), 19.

represented the only major important import into Mughal territories in north India. Most of these mounts came from Mawarannahr, whose people, like those in Ottoman territories and Iran, purchased large quantities of Indian textiles, indigo, and sugar that probably also left India with a positive balance of payments vis-à-vis Central Asia.

The size of the Mughal economy can be understood first of all as a factor of the kingdom's breadth and agricultural fertility. The Indian subcontinent has one of the largest acreages of arable land in the world. Mughal territories supported a population whose numbers in 1600 were rivaled only by Ming China. Twenty years earlier the Mughal historian and administrator Nizam al-Din Ahmad had written to praise his patron Akbar by observing:

In a description of the countries ruled over by the servants of His Majesty [Akbar], let it not remain concealed, that the length of the country, which is to-day in the possession of this powerful State, from Hindu Koh on the borders of Badakshan [northern Afghanistan] to the country of Orissa, which is on the further side of Bengal, from west to east is one thousand and two hundred *Akbar Shahi karohs* by the Ilahi yard measure ... and its breadth from Kashmir to the hills of Bardah, which are at the extreme limit of the country of Sorath and Gujrat, is eight hundred *karoh*s *ilahi* ... At present there are three thousand and two hundred towns; and one or two or five hundred or a thousand villages appertain to each of these towns ... Out of these there are one hundred and twenty great cities, which are now well populated and flourishing.[59]

Or, as John Chardin remarked in the course of making his comparison between Iran and India; the "Indies ... is a Country very Rich, Fruitful and Prosperous," adding, however, that India, like Iran and the Ottoman Empire, would have had greater population and prosperity had it not been for the "Arbitrary Government" of all three empires.[60]

By 1600 the Mughals controlled most of India's fertile crescent. The large population of these territories generated a substantial and diverse agricultural and manufacturing economy that made India a regional economic giant and a net exporter of goods throughout most recorded history until the time of the industrial revolution.[61] The subcontinent was largely self-sufficient in food; Hindu and Jain merchants from the Punjab and Gujerat exported foodstuffs such as sugar, rice, and saffron, as well as

---

[59] Khwaja Nizam al-Din Ahmad, *The Tabaqat-i-Akbari*, trans. Brajendranath De, ed. Baini Prashad (Calcutta: Asiatic Society of Bengal, 1937), 811. *The Akbar Shahi karoh*s represented about 2.5 miles. See Irfan Habib, *An Atlas of the Mughal Empire* (Delhi: Oxford University Press, 1982), xiii.

[60] Chardin, *Travels in Persia*, 129.

[61] For agriculture see Irfan Habib, "The System of Agricultural Production: Mughal India," *The Cambridge Economic History of India*, I, 217.

indigo and, later in the seventeenth century, tobacco. Most of the Mughal trade in agricultural products was with Iran and Uzbek Central Asia. In terms of food, Indians generally imported such specialty items as asafoe-tida and gum resin, but the Mughal elite probably drove the trade for the largest and most valuable imports – dried fruits and melons from Iran and Central Asia. They coveted fruits similar to those of their homelands, and once in the seventeenth century, when Mughal authorities believed that unfriendly Safavid officials had banned the export of a particularly fine variety of melon from Kariz in Khurasan, Shah Jahan is reported to have banned Iranian caravans from entering his realm.[62]

Mughal exports: cotton cloth

The Mughals enjoyed an unmistakable advantage over Safavid Iran and the Ottoman Empire when it came to exports of Indian cotton cloth. As is true of most other items in the commercial exchanges among these three empires, there are no statistics to document the actual level of trade. Nonetheless, there is persuasive anecdotal evidence in Roman, Middle Eastern, Iranian, Central Asian, Southeast Asian, and Chinese sources for the sale of Indian cotton goods in those areas from ancient times to the British colonial period. During the sixteenth century "the export of Indian cotton fabrics to the Middle East and Europe reached unprecedented levels."[63] Cotton was grown in all three empires, but demand for Indian cotton goods in Iran and Ottoman dominions, including Egypt, seems never to have lessened until the industrial revolution reversed the balance of trade between Europe and the rest of the world.

Writing about his visit to the modest west Indian port of "Bharuch" (Broach), near Surat, in 1623, the Italian nobleman Pietro della Valle observed:

There is a substantial trade in fine cotton cloth, made in greater quantity there than elsewhere, and distributed not only throughout Asia, but as far as Europe. ... So you may well be able to infer what riches come forth from this single little city, which, as regards compass and buildings, is not greater than Siena of Tuscany. ... And you may also be able to infer what sum the customs duties produce for the prince.[64]

Writing a generation later, Jean Chardin explained why Indian cloth continued to sell in Iran, even after Shah 'Abbas had tried to stimulate

---

[62] Quoted in Dale, *Indian Merchants and Eurasian Trade*, 22.
[63] Inalcık, "The India Trade," in Inalcık and Quataert, *An Economic and Social History of the Ottoman Empire*, 354.
[64] Della Valle, *The Pilgrim*, 218.

the production of Iranian cotton. Writing about conditions in the early 1670s, Chardin observed of Iran that "The *Persians* do not understand to make cloth, [although] they make very fine and very light Felt Tufts," and he succinctly summed up the comparative advantage of low Indian costs:

They make *Calico cloth* very reasonable, but they make none fine, because they have it cheaper out of the *Indies* than they can make it [and] ... they understand also the painting of Linnen, but not so well as the *Indians*, because they buy in the Indies the finest painted Linnen so cheap, that they would get nothing by improving themselves in that manufacture.[65]

Prices for Indian cloth were also competitive with indigenous Ottoman manufactured products, but unlike the situation in Iran, where Hindus and Jains represented the most numerous and influential Indian merchants, Indo-Muslim merchants seem to have been the principal Indians who traded in Ottoman dominions.[66]

Indian commercial culture

If low costs gave Indian merchants one competitive advantage over Iran, the thoughtful Jean Chardin believed that Hindu – or Jain – culture gave them another, because they were not constrained by religious prohibitions on profit or usury. He noted that some Iranian merchants traveled to India, but still argued that Iranians had "not a Genius naturally bent on Traffick."[67] He reasoned that because Islam forbade usury, pious Muslims restricted their trading activities. Thus, instead of loaning money themselves, Iranians would buy houses, bazaars, and *caravansarai*s.[68] Chardin painted the differences between Indian and Iranian merchants in shades of grey rather than black and white, for, as he himself pointed out, Muslims – both Iranians and others – had many ways of concealing interest payments, often by simply omitting mention of interest from contracts, a practice permitted by Hanafi law.[69] He observed that some Muslims were more than willing to lend money at usurious rates, despite Islamic prescriptions against *riba*. Nevertheless, prohibitions on usury may have discouraged many Muslim merchants in Iran and elsewhere from reinvesting profits in commerce or engaging in moneylending. In modern times at least, mid-level merchants in major bazaars often exhibit social conservatism and great piety, including

---

[65] Chardin, *Travels in Persia*, 278–9.
[66] Inalcık and Quataert, *An Economic and Social History of the Ottoman Empire*, 524.
[67] Chardin, *Travels in Persia*, 195.
[68] Ibid., 195; see also Floor, *The Economy of Safavid Persia*, 93.
[69] Coulson, *A History of Islamic Law*, 100.

undertaking group pilgrimages.[70] Chardin certainly believed Iranian merchants could not envisage (or, as Muslims, did not feel comfortable) investing their funds more profitably – a point recently made about the investment habits of Ottoman officials.[71]

Marwaris or Khatris, on the other hand, were not open to criticism for financial practices that might have earned their Muslim contemporaries public censure. Not only were these Hindus and Jains free from such religious injunctions, but Marwaris in particular practiced a type of commercial piety which featured reverence shown to the tools of their trade as household incarnations of Hindu deities: pens, ink, and, most of all, account books.[72] Neither the Huguenots nor the profit-hungry Karimi merchants of Egypt ever made such an explicit connection between their professions and their faith. The ability of Indians to use capital from trade for moneylending enabled them to become bankers in an Iranian society that possessed no formal banking institutions. Indians are known to have lent money to Iranian merchants in most major Iranian cities. Despite Chardin's condemnation of Indian moneylenders, he as much as anyone knew what an Indo-British officer, Henry Pottinger, observed about Hindus in Herat in 1810. Pottinger reported that the community of approximately 600 Indians in the city in Iranian Khurasan was respected and protected by authorities because they "alone possess capital."[73] At least some part of this capital would, of course, have been repatriated from Iran to India, thus swelling the stream of silver already at flood stage from the sale of cloth and other Indian products.

Economic integration and European trade

By 1600 Ottoman, Safavid, and Mughal rulers had pacified an immense territory extending from the gates of Vienna to the Bay of Bengal, including Egypt and north Africa. Their governments were relatively stable and also successful in extracting revenue from the agrarian population and stimulating domestic manufacturing and trade. While it is impossible to measure the exact degree to which the prosperity of the countryside and the level of commercial exchanges increased compared to the previous centuries, the

---

[70] Anecdotal evidence based on conversations in Istanbul and Isfahan in the 1970s and 1980s.

[71] Chardin, *Travels in Persia*, 195, and Suraiya Faroqhi, *Towns and Townsmen in Ottoman Anatolia: Trade, Crafts and Food Production in an Urban Setting 1520–1650* (Cambridge University Press, 1984), 46.

[72] D. K. Taknet, *Industrial Entrepreneurship of the Shekawati Marwaris* (Jaipur: Taknet, 1986), 163 and accompanying photograph.

[73] Henry Pottinger, *Travels in Beeloochistan and Sinde* (London: Longman, 1816), 415.

monumental architecture produced under Süleyman, Shah 'Abbas, and Akbar alone testifies to the ability of these monarchs to extract revenue from the peasantry and merchants and benefit from the productivity of their artisans. The lack of economic statistics notwithstanding, what Tapan Raychaudhuri and H. R. Roemer have written respectively about India and Iran under Shah 'Abbas I can also be cautiously applied to Iran's Ottoman neighbors. First, writing about late sixteenth-century Mughal India, Raychaudhuri concludes:

If the Mughuls were ruthless in their expropriation of surplus, their rule beyond doubt brought a high level of peace and security. From the 1570's – by which time Akbar had consolidated his empire – for more than a hundred years the greater part of India enjoyed such freedom from war and anarchy as it had not known for centuries. ... The economy of the empire derived direct benefits from this altered state of peace and security. Substantial increases in trade, both inland and foreign, were rendered possible by this development. It would perhaps be an exaggeration to say that the Mughul age saw the emergence of an integrated national market. Still, the commercial ties which bound together different parts of the empire, had no precedents.[74]

Echoing these sentiments, Roemer has written of Iran in the age of Shah 'Abbas that:

At the end of the 10th/16th century Shah 'Abbas had mastered the crises which had shaken his country at the time of his accession ... After security had been restored in the country 'Abbas turned his attention to establishing an effective administration. In the development of transport routes, which he pursued with energy, particularly noteworthy is the network of caravansaries he created ... These and other measures invigorated trade and industry so that the broad masses of the population also found that their standard of living was at first improved and ultimately reached a level never known up to that time.[75]

It is possible to paraphrase Raychaudhuri's comments on Mughal India and apply them to all three empires so that they read "It would perhaps be an exaggeration to say that the Ottoman–Safavid–Mughal age realized an integrated regional market, but the commercial ties that now bound these empires together had no precedents." When political and administrative decline threatened these markets, as in the early eighteenth century when the Safavids suddenly collapsed, commerce suffered and prosperity declined.[76]

---

[74] T. Raychaudhuri, "The State and the Economy: The Mughal Empire," in *The Cambridge Economic History of India*, I, 184.

[75] Roemer, "The Safavid Period," in *The Cambridge History of Iran*, VI, 269.

[76] See Muzaffar Alam's discussion of the deterioration of the prosperity of Khatri merchants in the Punjab as a result of disturbances in Iran in *The Crises of Empire in Mughal North India: Awadh and the Punjab 1707–1748* (Delhi: Oxford University Press, 1986), 181–3.

Yet, while "celebrating" this economic integration, it is also important to recall that at that particular moment in time, in 1600, Mughal India and Safavid Iran were both entering their most prosperous years under Akbar and Shah 'Abbas, while the Ottoman Empire was experiencing a profound monetary and fiscal crisis, exacerbated by a decline in central authority and revolts in Anatolia. While Iranian prosperity was closely tied to Shah 'Abbas I and began to decline under his successors, the Mughals continued to prosper throughout most of the seventeenth century, even as the Ottoman Empire was experiencing its most difficult period.

Ottoman troubles were caused by a number of interrelated problems. First, as the Ottomans increasingly came to rely on Janissary troops and artillery to ensure their victories, their expenses rose dramatically in comparison with early Ottoman armies that primarily utilized *sipahi* cavalry supported through *timar* grants. Secondly, and partly because of this, the prolonged if successful Ottoman campaigns in the second half of the sixteenth century drained the treasury. Thirdly, the new conquests in Hapsburg and Iranian territories and the subsequent defense of these territories cost more money than the new lands produced in plunder and taxation. Imperialism, quite simply, ceased to be profitable. The fourth problem was the monetary solution of devaluation, which may have solved deficits in the short term, but ultimately weakened the entire economy. Finally, there is the question of the impact of European, especially Portuguese, Dutch, and English, commerce, which became a factor for the Ottoman Empire in the second half of the sixteenth century, and for Iran and India from the early seventeenth century.

All of the Muslim empires controlled territories that had been for millennia linked to the surrounding areas by a web of commercial connections, and none of the economies of these empires were structurally changed initially by the emergence of Western European maritime states and the activities of their officials and merchants. The ultimate decline of these states was not primarily due to the effect of European economic expansion. In general, the Eurasian Ottoman Empire suffered the most negative effects from the political and economic expansion of Western Europe, while Safavid Iran and, even more, Mughal India benefited from the arrival of European merchants at their ports, at least initially.

European political and economic development affected the Ottoman economy in a number of ways. First, new economic changes in Europe, independent of newly aggressive merchants, affected Ottoman exports, most notably the lucrative Bursa silk industry, which in the middle of the sixteenth century supplied one and a half million *akçe*s a year in tax revenue to the Ottoman government.[77] As first Italian and later French silk cloth production developed, the demand for Ottoman cloth declined while the need for silk thread increased.

Second, the appearance of Portuguese, and later British and Dutch, ships in the Indian Ocean affected the Ottoman economy in two ways: it reduced revenues and caused Ottomans to spend funds in Indian Ocean naval campaigns. The initial Portuguese attempt to monopolize Indian Ocean trade reduced the flow of taxable commodities through the Red Sea to Cairo, which the Ottomans had conquered in 1517. While this trade recovered in the second part of the century, Portuguese actions not only reduced customs receipts, but also provoked the Ottomans to solve the Portuguese problem by attacking the Portuguese base at Diu in Gujerat, not far from the pre-eminent Mughal port of Surat.[78] The Ottomans enjoyed an unexpected benefit from this expedition in that it led them to occupy Yemen and benefit from the profitable coffee trade, but by 1625 a new European competitor, the Dutch, all but monopolized the Indian Ocean spice trade, leading to a collapse of the market in Egypt.[79]

Thirdly, the greatest European impact on the Ottoman economy came much later and in two ways. In the eighteenth and nineteenth centuries the empire lost territory and valuable tax revenues, first through Russian expansion, secondly through the increased power of the *ayyan* (the empire's provincial notables), most notably Muhammad 'Ali in Egypt, and then from nationalist movements in the Balkans. Finally, in the nineteenth century, as industrial production rose in Europe, Ottoman industry, particularly cotton, declined, although silk production in Bursa and elsewhere experienced a revival late in the century.

In contrast to the Ottoman experience, both Safavid Iran and Mughal India benefited from European commerce, and both states either collapsed, or in the Mughal case, declined so early and to such an extent that they were not substantially affected by European military aggression or later industrial production.[80] Portuguese aggression in the Indian Ocean region – at Hurmuz in the Persian Gulf or along the west Indian coast – was disruptive, but overall Europeans, especially the Dutch and British, opened new markets for Iranian silk and Indian cloth production. Portuguese aggression at the center of the Indian spice trade, along the

---

[77] Çizakça, *A Short History of the Ottoman Silk Industry*, 146.
[78] See Giancarlo Casale, "The Ottoman Administration of the Spice Trade in the Sixteenth-Century Red Sea and Persian Gulf," *Journal of the Economic and Social History of the Orient* 49, No. 2 (2006), 170–98.
[79] See especially Inalcık, "The India Trade."
[80] Newman, though, cites Iranian economic difficulties caused by shifts in regional and international trade: *Safavid Iran*, 95.

southwestern Indian or Malabar coast, occurred outside Mughal territory. European commerce in the Persian Gulf not only brought additional, badly needed silver into the currency-starved kingdom, but also to some degree freed Iran from its dependence on the overland trade through Ottoman territory.

As has been described, European trade with India poured huge sums of European silver into the country, contributing to the dramatically increased monetization of a region that had no silver deposits of its own. European, Middle Eastern, and Southeast Asian commerce continued to provide money for the Mughal treasury even as the empire began to unravel with ever-increasing speed during the first four decades of the eighteenth century. This undoubtedly contributed to the continuing solvency of the empire, which even after a half-century of war during the Emperor Aurangzib's reign (1658–1707) possessed a substantial reserve in its treasury. European imperialism, in the form of British and French wars in the Karnatak in the far southeast between 1740 to 1766 and British intervention in and subsequent occupation of Bengal after 1757, occurred well after the Mughal Empire had ceased to exist as an empire, leaving in its wake the Kingdom of Delhi and a bewildering congeries of provincial states.

5   Imperial cultures

Introduction

In the Ottoman, Safavid, and Mughal empires rulers and their aristocratic elites patronized the major monuments and cultural activities that served simultaneously as emblems of their common civilization and as signs of their idiosyncratic regional cultures. Ottoman, Safavid, and Mughal rulers exhibited their membership in a common civilization when they built similar royal and religious architectural complexes in Bursa, Edirne, and Istanbul, Qazvin and Isfahan, and Agra and Delhi. These ensembles included the fortress or palace, the Friday or "cathedral" mosque, the bazaar, and often royal tombs; symbols, respectively, of sovereignty, religious affiliation, commercial interests, and dynastic prestige. Most of these men also applauded and rewarded poets who produced panegyric verse in their honor, as well as appreciating and writing lyrical poems that reflected a widely shared literary sensibility. With a few exceptions these monarchs supported elaborate imperial ateliers, whose artists produced brilliantly colorful paintings. Yet Ottoman, Safavid, and Mughal architects also designed stylistically unique buildings, while poets, whose literary culture was broadly shared across political boundaries, gradually came to adapt their verse to the peculiar linguistic and cultural circumstances of each empire, and miniature painters shaped a common artistic heritage to reflect the tastes and priorities of each court and society.

Architecture

Ottoman, Safavid, and Mughal architecture was functionally similar but stylistically distinct. Members of all three dynasties built on a grand scale in their capital cities and constructed similar architectural complexes that included four major types of buildings: dynastic or imperial structures – fortresses, palaces, and tombs – religious buildings – *masjids* and associated buildings such as *maktabs* or religious schools and *madrasas*, and sometimes Sufi *khangahs* – charitable institutions associated with Muslim

135

piety – hospitals, public kitchens, and fountains – and commercial complexes – bazaars and *caravansarais*, which simultaneously fulfilled economic and religious functions. The commercial properties were usually held by and provided revenue for religious and charitable institutions as *waqfs* or pious endowments.[1] Members of these dynasties and their elite imitators erected these various buildings to demonstrate their piety and religious affiliation and to proclaim their grandeur as Muslim rulers: motives that contemporary observers openly recognized when they observed, as did the Arab historian Ibn Khaldun, that "The monuments of a given dynasty are proportionate to its original power."[2] His opinion was echoed and frankly embellished by the sixteenth-century Ottoman historian and official Mustafa Ali, who wrote in his 1586–87 book of etiquette:

To build masjids and mosques in the well-developed and prosperous seat of government and likewise to construct convents or madrasas in a famous capital are not pious deeds performed to acquire merit in God's sight. Every wise and intelligent man knows that these are pious deeds performed in order to accomplish being a leader and to make a good reputation.[3]

Ottoman, Safavid, and Mughal fortresses and palaces served as sanctuaries, administrative centers, and pleasure gardens for their imperial families and immediate servants. The Topkapı Palace in Istanbul, the 'Ali Qapu and the Chihil Sutun palaces in Isfahan, and the Agra fort and Shahjahanabad complex in Delhi were distinctive complexes of architecture that reflected certain aspects of their individual dynasty's imperial court culture.[4] Within the imposing old Byzantine walls, the Topkapı palace was structured as a segmented and physically claustrophobic series of audience halls and other structures, which from the late sixteenth century onward housed a reclusive sultan, his immediate family and servants, and the eunuchs and women of the *haram*. The Safavids' 'Ali Qapu palace had its own private family quarters and *haram*, but its external opening onto the great *Maidan* or square built by Shah 'Abbas I served as the palace whose rulers, and Shah 'Abbas I himself more than any others, presided over a more informal court. Indeed, Shah 'Abbas, unique among his own dynasty as well as Ottoman and Mughal rulers,

---

[1] See above, Chapter 4, for a discussion of this institution.

[2] Ibn Khaldun, *The Muqaddimah*, I, 356.

[3] Quoted by Gülru Necipoğlu, "The Sülemaniye Complex in Istanbul: An Interpretation," *Muqarnas* 3 (1985), 99. The translation should read "masjids or mosques."

[4] The Topkapı palace in Istanbul served as the official royal residence between 1465 and 1863, but from the late seventeenth century Ottoman rulers increasingly chose to live in new residences along the Bosphorus. Safavid and Mughal buildings are briefly discussed below.

sometimes conducted himself publicly more like a bourgeois president as he walked about and chatted with Isfahani residents in the royal square and the streets of his capital. The Mughals' massive fortresses, first Agra and later Delhi's Red Fort, were structures whose court life represented a kind of middle way between the Ottoman and Safavid courts, at least during the reign of Shah Jahan, the builder of the Taj Mahal. These Indian fortress-palaces housed a more highly structured – and physically more splendid – court than the Safavids', but one whose ruler was far more visible and actively involved in everyday life than any Ottoman sultan after the reign of Süleyman the Magnificent.[5]

Close to the fortresses, palaces, and bazaars in Ottoman, Safavid, and Mughal capital cities, rulers and members of their families constructed the buildings which, far more than the fortresses themselves, symbolized the religious identity, power, wealth, and sophisticated aesthetics of these dynasties. These were the *masjids* and tombs that constituted the ostentatious imperial monuments of Ottoman, Safavid, and Mughal rulers: public displays of piety and power intended both for their subjects and for posterity that were to reach the height of magnificence under Süleyman, Shah 'Abbas I, and Shah Jahan. A study of these important buildings involves both a description of architectural styles and an analysis of their cultural significance. At the outset, though, it should be recognized that the common feature of otherwise distinct Ottoman, Safavid, and Mughal imperial architecture was the dome. This was the most imposing and distinctive feature of Islamic religious and funerary architecture in these empires, a characteristic feature of their mosques and tombs well before they became a dramatic aspect of Renaissance Christian buildings.[6]

One of the earliest surviving such domes was the massive fourteenth-century structure that housed the tomb of the Mongol ruler of Iran, Uljaitu, near Tabriz. They had become commonplace in the Timurid era, and, as has been said in comparisons of contemporary Christian and Islamic architecture, "The career of the [Iranian] architect Qavam al-Din of Shiraz (1410–1438) coincides with that of Brunelleschi. While all of Florence stood amazed in 1436 as the last courses of the great

---

[5] Gülrü Necipoğlu has written a stimulating comparison of these three courts. See "Framing the Gaze in Ottoman, Safavid and Mughal Palaces," *Ars Orientalis* 23 (1993), 303–42.

[6] The dome was not used in much of the pre-modern Islamic architecture of the Indian Ocean coastal region sometimes known as "monsoon Asia," where mosques and tombs used indigenous non-Muslim designs. For one southwest Indian example of such buildings see "Islamic Monuments of Calicut," in Mehrdad Shokoohy, "Architecture of the Sultanate of Ma'bar in Madura and Other Muslim Monuments in South India," *Journal of the Royal Asiatic Society* 3rd Series, I, Pt. I (April 1991), 75–92.

cathedral dome (42 meters) fell into place, had he been there he would not have marveled at this. His predecessors had been employing similar techniques for almost a century."[7]

Ottoman religious architecture

Saljuqs constructed the first mosques in Anatolia, and in most cases they adopted local stone construction and enclosed their buildings against the severe Anatolian winters, in contrast to the open structures the Safavids sometimes constructed in Iran and those which Mughals regularly built in India. Surviving thirteenth-century Saljuq structures are relatively simple, one-story buildings, featuring a minaret at the right-hand corner and enclosing a series of barrel vaults, rather than a large open central space. Frequently, small cylindrical, conical, or octagonal mausoleums known as *türbes* were built nearby to house the remains of and to commemorate royal or aristocratic individuals. One such structure, constructed at Niğde in 1223, is also distinguished by three shallow ribbed domes of the type found in such profusion in later Ottoman mosques. The Saljuqs are also known for their construction of *madrasas*, some of which were built by or attributed to the formidable Iranian minister of the early Saljuqs, Nizam al-Mulk, as part of his and his masters' attempt to institutionalize Sunni Islam in Iran and Anatolia. Many of these ambitious and still imposing structures have survived, some of them distinguished by the open *iwans* or barrel vaults associated with Iranian architecture, such as the Saljuq-era *madrasa* in Isfahan. These *iwans* are another feature of Saljuq architecture that is visible in certain types of Ottoman mosques.[8]

Like the Ottoman dynasty, so too Ottoman architectural history began long before the appearance of the Safavids and the Mughals, and continued to evolve well after those two dynasties had disappeared.[9] Ottoman religious or pious architecture is far more distinctly regional than its poetry and painting, both of which derived directly from Perso-Islamic literary and artistic traditions. By the time the Safavid and Mughal dynasties were founded, Ottoman religious architecture had already developed from the relatively simple mosques of Orhan (r. 1326–60) at Iznik to the more

---

[7] Lisa Golombek and Donald Wilber, *The Timurid Architecture of Iran and Turan* (Princeton University Press, 1988), I, xxi.

[8] Henri Stierlin, "The Monuments of the Turkish Sultans during the Thirteenth and Fourteenth Centuries," in *Turkey from the Selçuks to the Ottomans*, 23–75.

[9] An early eighteenth-century Ottoman scholar recorded detailed descriptions of the most important Istanbul mosques still standing in his day. The author also noted later additions to the interior and exterior of the buildings. See Howard Crane, *The Garden of Mosques: Hafiz Hüseyin Al-Ayvansarayi's Guide to the Muslim Monuments of Ottoman Istanbul* (Leiden: Brill 2000).

ambitious structures erected in the early Ottoman capitals at Bursa and
Edirne. In those two early capital cities Ottomans often constructed not
only mosques but what became a typical *kulliye* complex of structures that
usually also included *madrasas*, libraries, *hammam*s or public baths, kitchens, and even hospitals, as well as the commercial structures that were part
of the *waqf* endowment of the religious and adjacent charitable buildings.
A distinctive feature of many of these early Ottoman, Anatolian *kulliye*
complexes were the attached Sufi *khangahs* or *tekkes*, whose presence
reflected the crucial influence of Sufis in the Islamization of Anatolia in
the Saljuq and pre-conquest Ottoman era. Fewer such Sufi buildings were
attached to the great imperial Istanbul mosques of the post-conquest era,
as sultans increasingly emphasized a kind of establishment Hanafi Sunni
orthodoxy. This is especially true of Süleyman the Magnificent's reign in
the mid-sixteenth century. During the reigns of his two immediate successors, however, Sufism regained some of its public presence, particularly due to the influence at court of the Halveti order.[10]

The dominant early type of Ottoman mosque construction, which
continued throughout Ottoman history, is the simple "domed-square"
structure, that is, a square base supporting a large semi-circular dome,
with a columned front porch and a single minaret – many of these, like
those of Saljuq mosques, at the right-hand corner of the building. While
there are Saljuq examples of single "domed-square" constructions, this
idea may be generally attributable to a long Middle Eastern tradition
extending from ancient Mesopotamia and continuing through Sasanian,
Armenian, and Byzantine times. "It constituted the focal point of the
centrally planned Greek-cross church and domed basilica."[11] Ottoman
rulers constructed such buildings at Iznik, where the Green Mosque of
1344 is distinguished by a minaret decorated with blue-green tiles provided by Iranians from Tabriz, who also provided tiles for the later
Ottoman decoration on the Dome of the Rock in Jerusalem.[12] A mature

---

[10] For a study of Sufi *khangahs*, especially important institutions in rural Anatolia during the
Ottoman rise to power, although less so later in imperial Istanbul, see Ethel Sara Wolper,
Cities and Saints: Sufism and the Transformation of Urban Space in Medieval Anatolia
(University Park, PA: Pennsylvania State University Press, 2003) and M. Baha Tanman,
"Ottoman Architecture and the Sufi Orders," in Ahmed Yaşar Ocak, ed., *Sufism and Sufis
in Ottoman Society* (Ankara: Atatürk Kültür, 2005), 317–83. Gülru Necipoğlu discusses the
shifting influence of Sufism at court in *The Age of Sinan Architectural Culture in the Ottoman
Empire* (Princeton University Press, 2005), 28–9 and 54–5.

[11] Aptullah Kuran, *The Mosque in Early Ottoman Architecture* (Chicago: University of
Chicago Press, 1968), 27.

[12] Sheila S. Blair and Jonathan Bloom, *The Art and Architecture of Islam 1250–1800* (New
Haven and London: Yale University Press, 1994), 220: "a tile on the north porch painted
in blue, turquoise and black on a white background is signed 'Abdallah of Tabriz' and
dated 959/1551…"

example of this style is the mosque of Firuz Ağa in Istanbul (1490), with a perfectly square interior and a minaret placed on the left side of the building. A variant of this simple type of early mosque was the so-called *iwan* (or in Turkish, *eyvan*) mosque, which adapted the barrel vaults of Saljuq *madrasas* to provide side-rooms or halls opening out from a common central hallway.[13] The earliest of these building types, such as the Bursa mosque of Orhan Ghazi, also date to the first half of the fifteenth century, and many such structures originally had no minarets, although often imperial-style minarets were added in the eighteenth or nineteenth century.[14] Some of the early fifteenth-century examples, such as the Yeşil Cami, the "Green Mosque" in Bursa (1412–19), have gateways and windows framed in marble with turquoise ceramic tiles. Both these early types are "one-unit" mosques, because in the more elaborate *iwan* type the space is fragmented, and worshipers in the side halls cannot see the *mihrab*, the wall niche indicating the direction of Mecca.[15]

The multi-domed or multi-unit mosque, often designated as the *ulucami*, the Friday or "cathedral" mosque, is the third major Ottoman type, and while the earliest examples antedate the imperial era, the most famous buildings were constructed after the conquest, such as the Şehzade mosque designed by the pre-eminent Ottoman architect Sinan in 1543. The earliest of these structures, such as the *ulucami* in Bursa (1399), has multiple domes whose vertical supports divide up the space, so that only worshipers in the central aisle have an unobstructed view of the *mihrab*, and the interior has a distinctive Saljuq "light-well," not found in later structures. Later multi-dome mosques, such as Sultan Bayezid II's mosque at Amasya (1486), are distinguished by two or more equal-sized domes placed either beside or following each other, opening up a large, unobstructed central space for worshipers. This latter mosque is also distinguished by its two minarets, which are placed on either side of this symmetrical structure, a distinguishing feature of royal Ottoman mosques.

Bayezid II's mosque in his *kulliye* complex in Edirne (1484–8), the Ottomans' Rumelian or Balkan capital, also has two minarets placed symmetrically on the left and right side of the mosque, which was designed by

---

[13] Aptullah Kuran discusses both these early types in *The Mosque in Early Ottoman Architecture*, Chapters 1 and 2. For a drawing of a square Ottoman *madrasa* with an *iwan* on each side see Behçet Ünsal, *Turkish Islamic Architecture in Saljuq and Ottoman Times 1071–1923* (London and New York: St Martins Press, 1973), 39. The earliest known examples of what Ünsal calls the "horasan [Khurasan] house plan, with a courtyard and four *eyvans* [*iwans*]" were built in Ghazna in the eleventh century and this plan "served also as the prototype for the pavilions and main buildings of the palaces," ibid., 57.

[14] Kuran, *The Mosque in Early Ottoman Architecture*, "The Eyvan Mosque," 71–136.

[15] Ibid., 138.

Hayrettin, one of the two outstanding architects of the imperial era. Bayezid, who later invited both Leonardo da Vinci and Michelangelo to design a bridge over the Golden Horn, commissioned one of the most elaborate *kulliye* complexes in Edirne, which included not only a mosque, but also a complex aligned with the mosque comprising a hospital and mental asylum, a medical school, a kitchen and bakery, and a *madrasa* with a library. However, the mosque in this *kulliye*, which has been described as the "first masterpiece of Ottoman art," is itself an elaborate version of the "domed-square" structure, with a single but massive dome twenty-three meters in diameter. Perhaps the finest building in the entire complex, though, is the aesthetically pleasing mental hospital, with its central dome surrounded by twelve small domes, although this building is entered through an asymmetrical portico. Indeed, the complex as a whole is not symmetrically arranged.

Hayrettin's second great building for Bayezid was also the second great structure of the imperial age in Istanbul. Mehmet II commissioned the first, the "Fatih" or "Conqueror" *kulliye* complex in Istanbul with a *madrasa*, *caravansarai*, and library as well as a *türbe* or tomb behind the

Fig. 1. Aya Sophia, Istanbul (the Byzantine Hagia Sophia), constructed between 532 and 537, converted to a mosque by Mehmet the Conqueror; two of the minarets were designed by the architect Sinan.

prayer hall. Designed by a Christian architect and built between 1463 and 1471, the complex broke with the earlier *kulliye* tradition in which the various buildings were not arranged according to an obvious, much less a symmetrical, pattern. Destroyed by an earthquake in 1767, the complex is known only from excavations and contemporary drawings, but it was symmetrically designed and, not surprisingly, influenced by the example of the Hagia Sophia, an influence that becomes a dominant theme in later Ottoman imperial mosques.

The mosque of the Fatih *kulliye* is the first known "multi-domed" imperial structure, having a large central dome of twenty-six meters and one semi-dome above the *mihrab*. Hayrettin's later mosque for Bayezid in Istanbul, which he began in 1501, borrowed both from the Fatih mosque and the Hagia Sophia. This structure is "rigorously symmetrical," with two minarets and a central dome and two semi-domes in back and front. While Hayrettin designed one further mosque for Selim I in 1522, in that building he reverted to the simple "domed-square" plan of his Edirne structure. The great series of Ottoman mosques patronized by Süleyman the Magnificent and designed by the pre-eminent Ottoman architect Sinan were all "multi-domed" structures, directly modeled on the Hagia Sophia (Aya Sophia).

Safavids

Whereas the Safavids came to power only in 1501 with Shah Isma'il's capture of Tabriz, a distinctly Perso-Islamic architectural style, which culminated in Shah 'Abbas I's magnificent complex of buildings in Isfahan, was already well developed. The geographical dividing line between the distinctive Anatolian buildings of the Saljuqs and Ottomans and those of the Persian cultural sphere ran roughly north to south from Tabriz to southeastern Mesopotamia. Iranian influence not only predominated within the present-day territories of the Iranian nation-state, but also extended deep into western Central Asia and included Afghanistan and the northern Indian region Muslims knew as Hindustan. Indeed, the *iwan*, one of the distinctive features of Iranian architecture – and the one element adopted for so many Saljuq *madrasas* and early Ottoman mosques – can be traced to the monumental, thirty-six-meter high arch of the sixth-century CE Sasanian palace in Ctesiphon in southeastern Mesopotamia, just south of Baghdad. However, the most obvious and well-known precursor of the Iranian style that featured the typical Iranian four-*iwan* mosque and *madrasa* design is the restored Friday mosque in Isfahan, built in the late eleventh century and modified in subsequent years, one of whose domes was originally designed to hold the tomb of the Saljuq ruler Malik Shah (d. 1092). Apart from the characteristic four *iwan*s, three of which feature the elaborate *muqarnas* or honeycombs (three-dimensional geometric forms within the *iwan*), the entire structure, including all of the multiple bays, is covered with blue, yellow, white, and green tile work in geometric or foliate designs added during the Timurid period.[16]

A symptomatic Iranian building from the Il-Khanid or Mongol period of Iranian history is the tomb of the Muslim Mongol Sultan Uljaitu (r. 1304–16), the second of the Muslim Mongol rulers of Iran. Uljaitu's tomb at Sultaniya, his new capital south of Tabriz, typifies Mongol and later Temür's monumental structures, as its internal dome of 24.5 meters rises to 48 meters above the floor. The exterior of the dome is covered with typically Iranian blue tiles. The only surviving structure of a *kulliye*-like complex that included a mosque, hospice, hospital, and other buildings, Uljaitu's tomb might be regarded as the first known major Twelver Shi'i structure in Iran, as Uljaitu had converted to Shi'i Islam. Yet even if the tomb is seen in this light, its octagonal design was not peculiar to Shi'as, although the earliest known domed octagonal structure in Iran dates to 999, the end of the period of Shi'i Buyid control of northern Iran and the Caliphate.[17] While the early Safavids used this design, the octagon was also employed by the Tugluqs of the Delhi Sultanate, the Ottomans in their modest *türbes*, and, most of all, by the Mughals in their tomb architecture.[18]

There are other Iranian buildings of the Mongol and post-Mongol period that can be recognized as precursors, in different ways, of the Safavid era. One of these is the portal of the congregational mosque at Yazd, in central Iran, which was begun in 1325. During Temür's reign and those of his descendants, the focus of Iranian architecture shifted to Samarqand, Bukhara, and Herat. Temür, whose taste for monumental structures exceeded even that of his Mongol predecessors, forcibly recruited architects and craftsmen from Iran, India, and elsewhere during his campaigns in those regions, and during the late fourteenth and early fifteenth century Iranian architects from Isfahan, Shiraz, and Tabriz transferred their building techniques to Central Asia and Khurasan. In architectural and artistic terms the Timurid period has been appropriately characterized as the "Persianization of Transoxiana."[19] It was during the

---

[16] Henri and Anne Stierlin, *Islamic Art and Architecture* (New York: Thames and Hudson, 2002), 20–1 and 212–21.

[17] Sheila S. Blair, "The Octagonal Pavilion at Natanz: A Reexamination of Early Islamic Architecture in Iran," *Muqarnas* 1 (1983), 69–94.

[18] The Stierlins argue Uljaitu's tomb was first conceived as a Shi'i reliquary (*Islamic Art and Architecture*, 50), but Blair and Bloom reject this idea as a "spurious tale" (*The Art and Architecture of Islam 1250–1800*, 8). For the use of what is usually called the "Baghdadi octagon" in India see especially Koch, *The Complete Taj Mahal*, 125.

[19] Stierlin and Stierlin, *Islamic Art and Architecture*, 60.

era of Temür's descendants, the Timurids, that standardized designs and architectural notation of the kind displayed in the late fifteenth-century Topkapı scroll seem to have been developed.[20] The Timurids, in particular, elevated the Islamic architectural preoccupation with geometry, which had been the hallmark of an architect's training since early Islamic times, into a central aesthetic principle. "What supplies the unifying force to Timurid architecture, then, is the geometrization of design, structure, ornament and space... A building must not only have a geometric skeleton, but in the final analysis it must look geometric."[21] Perhaps as part of this overriding concern with geometry, Timurid architects also seem to have developed the double-shelled dome, constructing a structurally useless interior shell to give a proportion to the inside of the building that would not exist otherwise because of the monumental height of the outer domes.

The first of Temür's major structures was the monumental mosque of Bibi Khanum begun in 1398, built according to the by now typical Iranian four-*iwan* pattern in baked brick with its domes and other surfaces also typically covered with multi-colored tiles. Set side by side, it is impossible to confuse the majestic stone, relatively unadorned Ottoman buildings with brilliantly colored Iranian brick mosques, tombs, and *madrasas* that stand out against the khaki-colored landscape of Iran and Central Asia. The aesthetics of these geometrically precise structures have inspired rapturous responses from Western observers, as in the following description of Timurid decoration:

The determination of this splendour-loving dynasty to give religious buildings a special grandeur and lustre led to rivalry, as to who could produce the most perfect work, the design that was most united while fully exploiting a variety of motifs, and a multiplicity of techniques including brick, glazed surfaces, mosaics, pierced screens and sculptured friezes. The designers unhesitatingly juxtaposed rigorous geometry, borders with repeating patterns, arabesques of twirling stems that spiral out across panels and into corners, and the blaze of gold that heightened the sacred character of the building and the splendours of paradise.[22]

Significant Timurid buildings were constructed throughout the fifteenth century, and it is important to reiterate that Ottomans, Safavids, and Mughals had an exaggerated regard for all aspects of Timurid culture, including its monumental buildings.[23] It is also useful to recall that

---

[20] Gülrü Necipoğlu, *The Topkapı Scroll: Geometry and Ornament in Islamic Architecture* (Santa Monica, CA: Getty Center for the History of Art and the Humanities, 1995).

[21] Golombek and Wilber, *The Timurid Architecture of Iran and Turan*, 216.

[22] Stierlin and Stierlin, *Islamic Art and Architecture*, 76.

[23] For an introduction to Timurid architectural influence in India see Koch, *Mughal Architecture*, 35–8.

Timurid architecture was Iranian architecture, both because Iranian architects are known to have designed many of the most important structures,
such as Temür's own tomb, and because Temür and his descendants
controlled central and eastern Iran throughout much of the fifteenth
century. This is evident in the second major Shi'i building in Iran: the
shrine of Imam Riza, the eighth Imam, in Mashhad, renovated by
Gauharshad, wife of the Timurid ruler of Herat, Shah Rukh. She also
added a congregational mosque designed by Qavam al-Din Shirazi and
constructed on the four-*iwan* plan, with a largely undecorated but luminescent turquoise dome over the *qibla* (the *iwan* placed in the direction of
Mecca) and typical Iranian glazed-tile decoration with fine calligraphy
surrounding the arch of each *iwan*. The Timurid prince and prolific poet
Baisunghar Mirza designed the calligraphy before the *iwan*.

The Timurids' rivals and successors, the Qara Quyunlu and Aq
Quyunlu Turks, who seized some of their important cities in northwestern
and central Iran during the mid and late fifteenth century, themselves
patronized the Timurid-Iranian style. Examples include the Blue Mosque
of the Qara Quyunlu dynasty at Tabriz (1465), with its luminescent
turquoise tiles, and Jahanshah Qara Quyunlu's Darb-i Imam, the shrine
of the two Shi'i imams, built in Isfahan in 1453–4, the third great
Shi'i structure in pre-Safavid Iran. It has beautiful polychrome tiles
and a bulbous green dome with interlacing floral decorations above two
layers of calligraphy on the drum supporting the dome, all features characteristic of later Safavid buildings. These later structures continued to
exemplify the earlier characteristics of Timurid buildings, especially in
their decorative elements. "The technique of ceramic mosaic soon
became widespread: entire *iwan*s and *pishtaqs* or porticoes, were covered
with floral motifs, as though permanently overgrown with flowering vines,
against which geometric designs and calligraphic inscriptions formed a
counterpoint."[24] The buildings dedicated to Shi'i imams also stand as a
reminder of the significant Shi'i strains in Iranian society before the
Safavids, a religious presence which is also known from the Buyid and
Sarbadar dynasties of previous centuries.

There is, therefore, a continuous Iranian architectural tradition from
the Great Saljuqs to the time of the Safavids, but few Safavid religious
buildings or tombs survive from the sixteenth century. Apart from the
impoverished state of the dynasty in the sixteenth century, the most
obvious reason for the lack of great cathedral mosques dating to this
period is the assertion of some Shi'i theologians that Friday prayers were

---

[24] Stierlin and Stierlin, *Islamic Art and Architecture*, 83.

inappropriate in the absence of the true Shi'i Imam. The earliest buildings that can be characterized as truly Safavid are the structures built at the shrine of Safi al-Din, the founder of the Safavi Sufi order at Ardebil, built between the fourteenth and sixteenth centuries.[25] While the tomb of Safi al-Din's eldest son seems to echo Il-Khanid Mongol designs, Safi al-Din's own tomb tower, a tall cylinder with a spherical, tile-covered dome and an octagonal interior, represents the late Timurid influence on early Safavid architecture. Another interesting building at the Ardebil complex is the *Chini-khanah* or China-house, an example of an octagonal structure with decoration that was found in Timurid buildings in Samarqand. *Chini-khanah*s were common to the eastern Islamic world as places where Chinese porcelain and other valuables were displayed or locked away.[26] Shah 'Abbas I's collection of Chinese export porcelain, now kept in Tehran, was originally housed here.

The next major Safavid architectural complex consisted of the buildings Shah Tahmasp had constructed in the dynasty's second capital at Qazvin. Shah Tahmasp's complex was laid out somewhat like Shah 'Abbas's later *Maidan* in Isfahan, with its open space and bazaar around the periphery,[27] although in Qazvin no *masjid* was built on the *maidan*, perhaps because there were already major mosques nearby. Shah Tahmasp may have modeled this complex on the *maidan* and the Hasht Bihisht palace Shah Isma'il inherited in Tabriz, when he captured that city from his Aq Quyunlu relatives in 1501. The only surviving building from this complex is the Chihil Sutun, or "Forty-Columned Palace," an odd name for a typical Timurid/Persian octagonal building, with alternating open and closed spaces around the periphery and an internal courtyard. The other major building dating to Shah Tahmasp's period, but not attributed to the Shah's patronage, is the tomb of Mullah Hasan-i Shirazi in Sultaniya, the old Il-Khanid Mongol capital. Designed to stand in the middle of a garden, a typical feature of later Timurid tomb architecture, it is also an octagonal or *Hasht Bihisht* structure, with a turquoise dome, resting on a drum with bands of geometric and kufic script invoking blessings on the "fourteen immortals": the twelve Shi'i Imams plus Muhammad and Fatima. Both of these buildings may be modeled on Timurid octagonal princely pavilions,[28]

---

[25] See the beautifully reproduced photographs of the complex in the article by Sussan Babaie in Jon Thompson and Sheila R. Canby, eds., *Hunt for Paradise: Court Arts of Safavid Iran 1501–1576* (New York: Asia Society, 2003), 28–9.

[26] Kishwar Rizvi, "Transformations in Early Safavid Architecture," 68–91.

[27] For these insights and much of what follows on the early Safavid period I am indebted to Sussan Babaie in Thompson and Canby, *Hunt for Paradise*, Chapter 2: "Building on the Past: the Shaping of Safavid Architecture."

[28] Ibid., 40 and 36.

although in the case of Mullah Shirazi's tomb, the nearby octagonal tomb of Uljaitu seems a more likely precursor.

Mughals

Unlike the impoverished and politically distracted Safavids of the sixteenth century, Akbar and the Mughal nobles decorated the north Indian landscape with a panoply of structures during his reign. However, unlike imperial Ottoman and Safavid buildings with their distinct but imposing mosques and elegant *madrasas*, the iconic Mughal buildings were tombs. These rulers' great mosques were huge enclosed outdoor spaces permitted by the Indian climate, buildings with imposing gates and beautiful domes over the *mihrab*, but nothing so monumental as the great Ottoman and Safavid religious buildings. Akbar constructed one of the earliest of these open-air *masjids* at his new city of Fatehpur Sikri, west of Agra.[29] During the latter half of the sixteenth century a unique Mughal style of octagonal tomb design developed, melding elements of pre-Mughal Islamic styles and Timurid and Indian elements, although it is not always possible to trace the precise source of influences on a particular building. Thus, the octagonal design of Uljaitu's tomb at Sultaniya also characterized the tombs of the Indo-Muslim ruler Sayyid Sultan Muhammad Shah (*c.* 1340s) and the massive structure in Bihar of Shir Shah Suri, the Afghan leader who defeated Humayun and forced him to flee India in 1540.[30]

Like Uljaitu's tomb, and the Dome of the Rock, the natural model for many octagonal Muslim tombs, early Indo-Muslim buildings featured colonnaded ambulatory arcades but also included *chatris*: small domed kiosks associated with Hindu architecture, but ultimately derived from medieval Islamic structures, as pre-Muslim Hindu architects did not employ domes in their buildings. Some subsidiary buildings at the Taj Mahal site also feature the octagonal design with ambulatory arcades. It seems more likely, however, that the octagonal structures of the Mughals, which represent a special type of *Hasht Bihisht* structure, were derived from late Timurid or early Safavid models, such as Shah Tahmasp's palace in Qazvin. Humayun may have seen some of these octagonal buildings during his visit to Iran to seek Shah Tahmasp's help in the 1540s. His father, Babur, describes one such "pleasure palace" in Herat, which he visited and

---

[29] An excellent introduction to Akbar's new city is Michael Brand and Glenn D. Lowrey, eds., *Fatehpur-Sikri* (Bombay: Marg, 1987). Catharine. B. Asher's work, *Architecture of Mughal India* (Cambridge University Press, 1992) is the most complete study of Mughal architecture available, and it includes both descriptions of buildings and analyses of their cultural significance.

[30] Blair and Bloom, *Art and Architecture of Islam*, 268.

Fig. 2. Humayun's tomb, Delhi, constructed between 1562 and 1570, the first garden tomb in Mughal India.

drank in one evening in December 1506. Humayun's tomb, generally regarded as the first truly Mughal building, was evidently inspired by the same ruler's wooden octagonal boat palace, which he constructed during his first decade of rule in India; but his tomb was actually designed by an Iranian architect, Sayyid Muhammad, son of Mirak-i Sayyid Ghiyas, who would have been familiar with Timurid-era and probably also Safavid Iranian examples. Both father and son had worked for Husain Baiqara in Herat and Babur in India; after Humayun returned to India, the son, Sayyid Muhammad, returned to work for Akbar.[31]

Babur was buried in an unpretentious, uncovered tomb – as was his descendant Aurangzib – but Humayun's tomb was an enormous, perfectly symmetrical structure that overshadowed any Ottoman or Safavid mausoleum. Ottoman *türbes*, for example, were extremely modest structures by comparison. The fact that *hadiths*, traditions or sayings attributed to the Prophet Muhammad, explicitly denounce elaborate funerary monuments as non-Islamic, suggesting a divine status for humans, did

---

[31] Ebba Koch, *Mughal Architecture* (Munich: Prestel, 1991), 44 and Koch, *The Complete Taj Mahal*, 27 and 85–6.

not inhibit most Mughal rulers. They were certainly aware of these strictures, but in their case dynastic (or for their nobles, aristocratic) pride trumped religious orthodoxy – with the exception of the last great Mughal ruler, Aurangzib (r. 1658–1707), whose genuine piety was respected by his successor, who built for him an uncovered, chaste marble tomb. The Mughals had, after all, the example of Temür's tomb in Samarqand and the many tombs of their Muslim predecessors in northern India as buildings they might admire and desire to emulate or surpass.

Humayun's tomb is a special monumental type of *Hasht Bihisht* structure set in a symmetrical *chahar bagh* or four-part garden, of the type Babur so lovingly describes in his memoirs as the late fifteenth-century Timurid ideal. Its architect, who was familiar with the Timurid architecture of Bukhara and Samarqand, associated the building with Temür's tomb in Samarqand; there seems little doubt that the structure's enormous size was meant to symbolize the Timurid renaissance in India.[32] It is a genuine Indo-Muslim, or Timurid renaissance, building in that its design echoes Timurid architecture while its decoration borrows from earlier Indian designs.

It is not a single octagon, but instead four irregular octagonal structures grouped around a central and perfectly octagonal tomb chamber. The chamber lies beneath a bulbous white marble dome that anticipates the dome of the Taj Mahal. On the roof surrounding the dome are four *chatris* such as those found on the tomb of the Afghan ruler Shir Shah at Sasaram. Inside the dome is another Timurid double shell, which, as in the case of Temür's Samarqand tomb, lends interior proportion to a dome that would otherwise be disproportionately high. The passion for symmetry extends even to the *jalis*, the typically Indian carved stone screens, here designed and exquisitely crafted as a series of interlaced octagons. The exterior of the building echoes some earlier Indian Muslim structures in its use of red sandstone, the building material so common in the Rajasthan desert that villagers there still use it in place of non-existent wood for fencing. White marble is used sparingly as an inlay throughout the exterior of the structure and on the gates through which it is approached, partly for false windows and partly just as decorative elements. There are no tile decorations of any kind and the only designs incised on the exterior are two six-pointed stars placed about each of the major *iwans*. Until the construction of the Taj Mahal, this was the pre-eminent Mughal imperial structure.

---

[32] Glenn D. Lowrey, 'Humayun's Tomb: Form, Function, and Meaning in Early Mughal Architecture," *Muqarnas* 4 (1987), 138 and 145.

Poetry and painting

Unlike the distinctive architectural styles that from earliest times clearly demonstrated that the three empires each had variant Muslim cultures, the other two principal aristocratic art forms, poetry and miniature painting, initially derived from the same Iranian source. Both arts gradually evolved into noticeably different styles, partly as a result of indigenous developments and partly in consequence of the impact of European art, which influenced Ottoman, Safavid, and Mughal societies at different times. These two arts were often intimately related, as classical Persian-language poetical works frequently formed the subjects for illustrations, which were included in many of the exquisite books produced during these centuries.

Poetry and painting were also, in social terms, distinct art forms, in that poetry was the most accessible art in these as in other pre-modern societies, requiring only literacy and knowledge of earlier verse. It was practiced and patronized not only by royalty and aristocracy, but more widely by many literate members of the population. Thus while many poets were employed by the court to provide panegyrics or chronograms for coronations, birthdays, military victories, and other royal occasions – or just for their literary skill – probably the majority were members of the scholarly or bureaucratic classes, for whom poetry, not prose, provided a means to express religious, erotic or scatological ideas, communicate with friends, or demonstrate their cultural sophistication. Painting, in contrast, was largely, although not exclusively, an expensive court undertaking, requiring ateliers of talented artists and years of painstaking labor to complete groups of images. Later in the histories of these dynasties merchants and literati also sometimes purchased art works, particularly more inexpensive single images, but most major painting was produced with imperial patronage.

The early poetry of the Islamic empires was rooted in Persian-language poetic tradition – the verse so often illumined by Iranian, Ottoman, and Indian artists as the arts of the book flourished in Timurid, Iranian, Ottoman, and Indian courts. During the "Persian intermezzo," the period between the collapse of the 'Abbasid Caliphate and the Mongol invasion, Iranian poets quickly established Persian literature as the prestigious "Great Tradition" of the eastern Islamic world, the territory stretching from Anatolia to Central Asia and India. Often patronized by ethnic Iranian dynasties such as the Samanids of Bukhara, or culturally Persian Turkic dynasties such as the Ghaznavids, two authors in particular, Firdausi and Nizami Ganjawi (1141–1203) produced Persian-language poems of compelling artistry that formed the prestigious, repeatedly imitated foundation of the New Persian literary tradition. Five other major authors subsequently consolidated this formidable canon: Sa'di (c. 1213–91) and Hafiz (c. 1320/ 25–1388/89) in Iran, Rumi (1207–73) in Anatolia, Amir Khusrau Dihlavi (1253–1325) in Delhi, and Jami (1414–92) in Herat, all poets whose writings provided the subject of illustrated texts in the three Islamic empires. In the thirteenth and fourteenth centuries the reality of the geographic reach of this literary lingua franca was personified by three of these later writers: Rumi in Anatolia, Hafiz in Iran, and Amir Khusrau Dihlavi in Delhi.

In Safavid Iran, where a large proportion and perhaps the majority of the urban and rural sedentary population comprised native Persian speakers, these authors of what came to be accepted as the classic Persian literary tradition constituted the literary core of Iranian cultural identity. Among Muslims in Mughal India, Persian letters constituted a vital tradition for Muslim elites in north India and the Deccan, men and women who continued to speak Persian in their daily life as well as using it as their principal administrative and literary language. North Indian Muslims had been using Persian since the twelfth century. By the early eighteenth century, however, Urdu – highly Persianized Hindi written in the Arabic script – displaced Persian as the popular literary language, and subsequently became the language of most Indian Muslim prose writers as well.

In the Ottoman Empire, where the supremacy of Ottoman Turkish as a state dialect and court literary language reflected the weight of the Anatolian Turkic population, the New Persian poetical tradition was revered, particularly in the earlier centuries when many rulers appreciated and sometimes composed Persian verse. Persian literary models continued to influence Ottoman writers well after the sixteenth century, even as fewer emigrants arrived from Iran, fewer Ottomans spoke Persian, and additional Arabic-speaking populations were added to the empire, diluting the influence of the Iranian tradition. Nonetheless, during the fifteenth through the early eighteenth century, "Irrespective of the language the poets used ... In the vast territory stretching from Asia Minor to Turkestan and to Bengal, poetry employed the same outlook, literary conventions, forms, metres, rhyming patterns and above all the same imagery ... the models for it were and continued to be Persian."[33] In the fifteenth and sixteenth-century

---

[33] Ehsan Yarshater, "Persian Poetry in the Timurid and Safavid Periods," in Jackson and Lockhart, *The Cambridge History of Iran*, VI, 979. Lest this be taken as Iranian chauvinism, see Kemal Silay's comment. "The earliest *divan* poets of Anatolia (thirteenth through fifteenth centuries) were directly influenced by Iranian literary paradigms." *Nedim and the Poetics of the Ottomaan Court* (Bloomington, Ind.: Indiana University Turkish Series 13, 1994), 31–2. Silay gives examples of the pervasive Iranian influence on Ottoman poets in the sixteenth century as well.

Ottoman Empire and sixteenth-century Safavid Iran and Mughal India, poets often imitated both Firdausi's *Shah-nama*, which had instantly achieved a kind of iconic status in the eastern Islamic world, and also Nizami's *Khamsa*: his five romantic epics, whose human dramas exerted a powerful emotional appeal for a broad audience. Many poets also wrote *qasidas* or panegyrics as a way of soliciting or retaining royal or aristocratic patronage. Such poems represented either employment applications or a form of insurance in a brutally uncertain world. Sa'di of Shiraz in Fars wrote them for a series of local and Mongol rulers in the chaotic thirteenth century, and even Jami of Timurid Herat did so in the late fifteenth century, although he criticized other poets who sought rewards in this way. Some poets also wrote *rubai'iyat*, the four-line poems, somewhat similar in quality to the Japanese haiku, which Fitzgerald popularized in the nineteenth-century English-speaking world by his quirky if appealing rendition of 'Umar Khayyam's verses. However, most poets felt they had to write superb *ghazals* if they were to achieve literary fame. Most took the *ghazals* of Hafiz as their model, even while acknowledging the impossibility of equaling the Iranian poet's unique lyrical skills.

Sometimes described as "odes," *ghazals* were usually poems of from four to fourteen couplets, written in a variety of meters with the rhyme scheme aa, ba, ca, etc. The *ghazal* in essence was and is an Islamic variant of the literary genre of courtly or aristocratic love, one which "celebrated" or lamented, with a kind of emotionally delicious suffering, unrequited love. In these poems the authors recounted their infatuations, sometimes described brief encounters with their beloveds, who were more often than not depicted as being indifferent to their emotional angst. They then dwelt on the agony of separation and usually closed with an expression of fatalistic resignation, using the poetic device of the *takallus*, a pen name, or in some cases their actual names, to identify themselves.

Whether such poems addressed men or women is not certain because neither Persian nor Turkish pronouns distinguish gender, although many scholars feel that these authors addressed young men, as did Shakespeare in some of his sonnets. However, the gender of the beloved was often irrelevant, as most *ghazals* were not autobiographical, but, like Japanese courtly verse of the medieval Heian era, simply conventional demonstrations of literary skill. Or even if they were autobiographical, *ghazals* might involve only literary expressions of friendship or at other times an author's commitment to Sufism, in which the language of profane love was commonly used as a metaphor for spiritual infatuation. The language of Sufism ultimately became so popular and broadly influential among all poets that its use was not by itself a revelation of an author's religious or sectarian commitment. Sometimes, as in other societies and eras, poetry was just poetry.

Ottoman verse

The great "classical" Persian poets and many other lesser writers comprise the literary ancestry of Ottoman, Safavid, and Mughal writers – with one exception: the late Timurid contemporary of Jami, the Turki poet Mir 'Ali Shir Neva'i (d. 1501), whose poems were so popular among the Ottomans they were carried by caravans to Bursa and were still widely known among literati in the Empire until the nineteenth century.[34] The direct or indirect influence of these Persian poets is evident throughout the Ottoman, Safavid, and Mughal literary world.[35] In the case of the Ottomans, whose literary history begins as early as the fourteenth century, the importance of the *ghazals* of Sa'di and Hafiz as genres of lyrical expression is evident in the work of three important pre-Süleymanic poets: Nesimi (d. 1404), Ahmet Pasha (d. 1497), and Necati (d. 1509), the latter a writer who is "Ottoman" only to the extent that he wrote in Turkish in the early Ottoman era. Nesimi was probably a Turk, perhaps from Anatolia, who wrote in both Persian and Turkish. An enthusiastic member of the Hurufi Sufi order, Nesimi was tortured to death by order of the *'ulama* of Aleppo sometime in the first decade of the fifteenth century for publicly advocating the Hurufi idea that the secret meaning of the Quran could be understood by interpreting the symbolic meaning of its Arabic letters. He wrote *ghazals*, which in his case served as religious metaphors for the separation of the believer from God, as in the two lines of this *ghazal*:

> The pain of being far from you
>   causes me to bleed
> From deep within me blood pours
>   from my eyes, I burn.

Nesimi concludes by giving his *takhallus* or pen name in the final two lines, saying:

---

[34] Gönül Alpay Tekin, "Classical Ottoman Literature during the Sixteenth Century," *Encyclopaedia of Islam* II, Brill Online.

[35] The value or quality of Ottoman, Safavid, and Mughal era verse is a matter of considerable dispute, which often reflects the cultural chauvinism or nationalism or, more recently, the academic partisanship of critics. Even Iranians, who are nearly unanimous in their admiration for the classics – Firdausi through Jami – find most Safavid verse uninspiring, but they are more contemptuous of Indo-Persian poetry, known as *sabk-i Hindi*, the Indian style, even when it was written by Iranian émigrés in India. Iranians are less concerned with early Ottoman verse, which even many Ottoman literary scholars have described as being crudely derivative from the Persian-language classics.

> Those who speak ill say Nesimi is burning with grief, it's true
> For he who burns with grief, the beloved loves him deeply – so
>   deeply I burn.[36]

Ahmet Pasha or Ahmet Pasha Bursalı (Ahmet Pasha from Bursa) and Necati are regarded as true Ottoman poets in the sense that both wrote for Mehmet II or members of the imperial family.[37] Ahmet Pasha, who also wrote poems in Arabic and Persian, was born into an Ottoman official's family in the former Ottoman capital and held a series of official appointments there and in Istanbul, where Mehmet II eventually appointed him his companion, tutor, and finally vizier. Writing in the dominant Ottoman dialect, he produced *qasidas* and *ghazals*, but unlike Nesimi's, his *ghazals* celebrated earthly love, especially his passion for a young page – which caused Mehmet first to imprison the poet and then exile him to his native Bursa. His verses are typical of the *ghazal* genre, as shown by these four lines from one poem:

> I have wept so much blood longing for your rubied lips
> Every door and wall of your town are made coral from your
>   tears…
> At dawn Ahmed catches the scent of the rose, and in his
>   anguish sighs, ahhh!
> There is not a nightingale in the garden whose heart is not
>   burned by love.

Necati, regarded by many as the "first great Turkish lyric poet of the pre-classical period," was the son of a Christian prisoner of war and then a slave, who was raised by a Muslim lady of Edirne. He exemplifies the process by which non-Muslims and non-Turks could become Ottomans through conversion and education. Gaining a reputation as a poet at an early age, Necati arrived in Istanbul in 1481 and caught the attention of Mehmet II and then his successor Bayezid II with his inventive *qasidas*. Appointed as a secretary to the *Diwan* or finance ministry, he eventually joined the households, first of Bayezid's eldest son, 'Abd Allah, and later of his younger son, Mahmud. He is widely regarded as the true founder of Ottoman poetry for his adaptation of Turkish to the Perso-Arabic metrical system, his domestication of Arabic and Persian vocabulary, and his use of Turkish proverbs in

---

[36] Walter G. Andrews, Najaat Black and Mehmet Kalpaklı, *Ottoman Lyric Poetry* (Austin: University of Texas Press, 1997), 27.

[37] In the name Bursalı, the Turkish letter ı – in Arabic or Persian *i* – is the *nisba*, the indication of a native place or long-time residence. Thus "Amir Khusrau Dihlavi" is Amir Khusrau from Delhi.

his poems.[38] In certain aspects his verse is characterized by innovations Iranians would describe as *sabk-i Hindi*.[39]

Necati's *diwan*, or collection of poems, was regarded as a model for subsequent Ottoman poets, and Idris Bitlisi in his *Hasht bihisht* or "Eight Paradises" praises him in the highest terms as the Firdausi of Anatolia – high praise throughout all three empires.[40] It is difficult to convey his originality or literary skill in translations of his *ghazals*, which for him as other poets constituted the true test of poetic skill. The freshness of his images – and his sense of himself as a great writer – are, however, partly evident even in translation, as in the following two passages from a *ghazal* which also alludes to the *majlis*, the symposia of wine, dance, poetry and music enjoyed by the royal and aristocratic elite of all three empires in walled gardens:

> Does the one hanging
>   by the noose of your curl
>   touch his feet to the ground?
> With delight he surrenders his life,
>   twisting
>   twirling....
> Oh Nejâtî
>   at this royal party [majlis]
>   it would be pleasing
>   for the musician to dance,
>   before the sultan,
>   before the beloved, turning
>   reciting this fresh new verse.[41]

Safavid verse

Necati died just before Shah Isma'il consolidated his conquest of Iran with a victory over Shibani Khan Uzbek in 1510. Shah Isma'il's own *diwan* of Turki verse contained *ghazals* as well as his extraordinary group of religious poems. Early Safavid Persian-language poets in Iran wrote in a difficult environment as far as patronage was concerned, as Turkish was widely used at the Safavid court; it was the native tongue of the Safavids' principal military supporters, the Qizilbash, Oghuz Turks from Anatolia and northwestern Iran. Safavid verse was distinguished, first of all, by elegies or laments written to commemorate the death of Husain, 'Ali's

---

[38] Andrews *et al.*, *Ottoman Lyric Poetry*, 218 and Th. Menzel, "Nedjati Bey," *Encyclopaedia of Islam* II, Brill Online.

[39] See below p. 156.

[40] Menzel, "Nedjî Bey," p. 1. The term *diwan* has two distinct meanings: a finance ministry, and a poet's collected works.

[41] Andrews *et al.*, *Ottoman Lyric Poetry*, 43–4.

son, on *ashura*, the tenth day of the lunar month of Muharram in 680 AD, which is the principal annual Shi'i religious ceremony. Husain Va'iz Kashifi (d. 1505) wrote one of the earliest such poems, the *Rauzat al-shuhadâ'* ("The Garden of Martyrs"), and Muhtasham of Kashan (d. 1588) composed one of the most widely recited of these laments for Shah Tahmasp.[42] The latter poem describes Husain as "Sun of the sky and land, Light of the east and west; Nourished in the bosom of the Prophet of God, Husain." Like most other such Shi'i verses it emotionally recounts Husain's death on the Iraqi battlefield, describing him as a "Vessel swallowed in the storm of Karbala," and this poem is still used as one of the texts for Shi'i passion plays in modern Iran.[43] Apart from this religious literature, Iranian scholars are nearly unanimous in their dismissal of the work of most Safavid poets as being either uninspired or – worse – characterized by deviation from classical models and the use of far-fetched or novel imagery and opaque allusions.

Known as *sabk-i Hindi*, literally "the Indian style" because of the great number of Indo-Persian poets who wrote Persian verse at this time, this new style had developed over several centuries, not in India but in Iran and Mawarannahr, reaching its pre-Safavid height in the late Timurid period. Eventually the style influenced verse across the entire territory where Persian literary norms prevailed, i.e. Iran, the Ottoman Empire, Central Asia, and India. It is difficult to evaluate fairly the quality of this verse, because until recently subsequent changes in taste led most Iranians to condemn it in their wish to return (*bazgasht*) to verse composed according to classical models. One of the most prominent individuals associated with the style misnamed as *sabk-i Hindi* by modern writers, but known in Iran and India at the time as *shîvah-i tâzah*, "the fresh style," was the Shirazi poet Fighânî (d. 1519). Fighani is widely regarded as the creative originator of the Safavid and Mughal verse that has now begun to attract new scholarship and appreciation.[44]

Like other poets of this period in the Ottoman Empire, Central Asia, and Mughal India, Fighani has been evaluated primarily on the basis of his *ghazals*. In the accepted tradition of all Islamic verse in pre-modern times, he practiced the art of creative imitation, playing off from classical Persian poets such as Hafiz or Amir Khusrau Dihlavi, but creating original or

---

[42] See Yitzhak Nakash, "An Attempt to Trace the Origin of the Rituals of Âshûrâ," *Die Welt des Islams*, new series 33, No. 2 (1993), 170, n. 32. Wheeler M. Thackston gives part of the Persian text in *A Millennium of Classical Persian Poetry* (Bethesda, Md.: Iran Books, 1994), 79–82.

[43] Ibid., 80.

[44] Paul E. Losensky, *Welcoming Fighânî: Imitation and Poetic Individuality in the Safavid – Mughal Ghazal* (Costa Mesa, Ca: Mazda, 1989).

innovative variants on their verse. Fighani especially responded to Amir Khusrau Dihlavi and then also to the late Timurid poet Jami, who himself had written responses to Amir Khusrau's verses. However, while Jami's responses are more conventional – or classical – Fighani developed a distinctively new "tone and voice," which was responded to in turn by Mughal and Iranian poets of the late sixteenth and seventeenth centuries. One Fighani poem in particular reveals a radically different tone and imagery, a kind of existential despair concluded with a gentle self-mocking resignation, in which the indifference of the beloved pales before the poisonous hostility of the universe:

> Poison drips steadily
> from heaven's vial.
> No one ever saw
> any wine in this flask ...
> For the sake of union,
> I've had my fortune told a thousand times,
> but no one has made
> a propitious reading yet.
> Don't seek relief, Fighani,
> and put up with your headache.
> No one has seen rosewater
> in heaven's vial.[45]

Mughal verse

By the late sixteenth century Fighani's "fresh style" had won converts among Persian-language poets in both Iran and India, although this does not mean that all chose to write in this way. Persian had long become established as the administrative and literary language of the north Indian Muslim elite, and with the accession of Humayun in 1530, its hold over Muslims there increased. Humayun himself seems to have preferred Persian to his native Turki – he is known to have composed only a few Turki verses and letters – and apparently even preferred to speak Persian. His poetical *diwan* includes mostly *ghazals* and *rubâ'is* written in a fairly simple, unadorned Persian. One interesting *rubâ'i* is devoted to 'Ali: perhaps a concession to Shah Tahmasp, who demanded his conversion to Shi'i Islam in exchange for military aid, but the poem might also represent no more than a Sunni Muslim's typical praise for the *Ahl-i bait*, the family of Muhammad.

---

[45] Ibid., 233–4.

> We are from our hearts slaves to the sons of 'Ali
> We are ever happy in the memory of 'Ali
> Since the mystic's secret is revealed through 'Ali
> We always recalled the memory of 'Ali.[46]

Not only did Humayun's son, Akbar, encourage the emigration of Persian speakers to India, but the wealth of the Mughal and the central Indian or Deccan courts attracted a constant stream of Iranian émigrés.[47] As a result more Persian verse was produced in Mughal India than in Safavid Iran. The man whom Akbar designated as *Malik al-shu'ara*, the poet-laureate, in 1587, and who was known by his pen name Faizi (d. 1595/96), was not one of these émigrés but a descendant of a Yemeni family that had settled in Sind. The younger brother of Akbar's historian and companion Abu'l Fazl 'Allami, Faizi became one of Fighani's most important literary disciples and was praised by the greatest of the seventeenth-century Iranian poets, Sa'ib, himself a devotee of Fighani's verse. Faizi, who, along with his contemporary 'Urfi, is thought to have influenced Ottoman verse, explicitly advocated the "fresh style" that had become accepted by this time in Iran and India:[48]

> So that poetry might be adorned by you,
> there must be new meanings and old words.
> Advance on the path of your heart and don't turn back –
> don't go circling around someone else's poetry...
> How long will you hoard others' ideas,
> throwing parties with others' candles?
> How long will you hoard others' ideas,
> sewing purses to collect others' cash?[49]

Faizi composed a *diwan* in Persian, works in Arabic, and translations from Sanskrit. He also lectured on the *al-Qanun* of Ibn Sina and evidently practiced Unani or Greek medicine, as he was known to some as Hakim or "doctor" Faizi. His verse does not contain images or ideas as riveting as Fighani's, but he introduces new words into old verse forms, as when in a *ruba'i* he mentions eyeglasses:

---

[46] Muhammad 'Abdul Ghani, *A History of Persian Language and Literature at the Mughal Court* (Allahabad: Indian Press, 1929), I, 15.

[47] See Aziz Ahmad, "Safawid Poets and India," *Iran* 14 (1976), 117–32 and Muzaffar Alam, "The Pursuit of Persian: Language in Mughal Politics," *Modern Asian Studies* 32, No. 2 (May 1998), 317–49.

[48] E. J. W. Gibb, the great British Ottoman scholar, suggested that Faizi and 'Urfi influenced Ottoman writers: *Ottoman Poetry* (London: Luzac, 1902–58), I, 5, 127, and 129.

[49] Losensky, *Welcoming Fighani*, 195. Losensky suggests that Faizi's idea of creativity is Neoplatonic, as he speaks of "the primeval emanation," an idea described by philosophical writers as "divine emanation" (pp. 197–8).

> Faizi, it is the breath of old age, look before thou steppest out,
> Thou art putting thy eyelash-like foot, put it on chosen ground;
> Through the spectacles of glass nothing is visible,
> Thou shouldst cut a slice from thy heart, and put it over
>   thy eye.[50]

Two other late sixteenth-century Mughal poets are associated with this *tazah-gu*, this "fresh speech" or "fresh style." Both were Iranian émigrés: Naziri, a native of 'Umar Khayyam's native city of Nishapur, and 'Urfi, a well-known poet of Shiraz. Naziri came to India because, evidently, he learned of the patronage of the Mughal official Khan-i Khanan (d. 1627), the son of Akbar's guardian, Bairam Khan, who had assembled a literary circle whose members cultivated the fresh style.[51] In fact an Iranian poet, Rasmi Qalandar, in a remarkable poem containing an allusion to Aristotelian logic in its comment on "essence" and "accident," explicitly praised Khan-i Khanan for his support of Iranian émigré poets who wrote in what he called the "new fashion":

> Through the boon of thy praise that weigher of subtle points –
>   native of Shiraz ['Urfi],
> The fame of his poetry reached to Rum [Anatolia] from the
>   East;
> He became acquainted with a new style [*tarz-i tazah*] through
>   praising thee,
> As a handsome face gains ornament from the tire-woman;
> From the bounty of thy name Faizi captured like Khusrau
> The seven climes with the Indian sword;
> Through eating crumbs at thy table, Naziri the poet
> Has attained a position that other poets
> Write each in praise of him a *qasida* so beautiful
> That blood of envy drips from the heart of an eloquent poet;
> The ink of the verse of Shakibi, like the collyrium of Isfahan,
> The people of sight carry as a present towards Khurasan,
> From thy praise Hayati got a second life,
> Ay, the essence is the strengthener of the accident,
> What should I narrate the tale of Nau'i and Kufwi;
> Since they live through thy praise till
>   the morn of Resurrection...[52]

Naziri, known especially for his *ghazals*, nonetheless wrote verses known for their novel images and inventive compounds that enriched the language of the genre, even though he felt constrained by the inimitable

---

[50] Ghani, *A History of Persian Language and Literature*, II, 55–6.
[51] Losensky, *Welcoming Fighani*, 200.
[52] Ghani, *A History of Persian Language and Literature*, III, 221–4.

beauty of Hafiz's lyrical verse.[53] Even the *ghazal* in which he laments the absence of a new Hafiz – a new "falcon" – contains striking images, as in the following verses:

> The kingdom's frontier and plains
> are full of fat game
> Where is the falcon
> that will sink its claws into the partridge ...
> Naziri, the thoroughfare of his imagination
> has been shut down
> The street has filled with lustful men.
> Where is the glance that kills?[54]

The last of these notable early Indian poets was 'Urfi, who was welcomed to the Mughal court by Faizi in 1584–5 and eventually joined Khan-i Khanan's literary circle. A talented, arrogant, argumentative man, he wrote verse that was popular throughout the Persian-speaking world and, apparently, also in Ottoman territories. A writer of *ghazals* and *ruba'is*, he is most famous for his *qasidas*, although in one fragment he, like Jami in Herat, denounced panegyric verse in favor of the *ghazal*:

> Qasida is the composition of people having greed for their
>   profession, O 'Urfi,
> Thou art from the tribe of love, thy recitation is ghazal.[55]

Nonetheless, his *qasidas*, his panegyric poems, seem far more inventive than his other verse, as in his extended poem dedicated to Akbar's son Jahangir, which is an exceptionally attractive example of an art so seemingly dissonant to the ears of those in contemporary Western societies. Having been asked, so 'Urfi reports early in the poem, to write a poem for Jahangir (Salim), he considered what type of verse to write:

> I was taken aback and knew not what sort of *qasida* to compose,
> In tune which may infuse life into the dilapidated bones of the
>   dead;
> I resorted to the complete rejection of the old methods,
> In writing the praise of the age of Prince Salim;
> His birth did the same to the disposition of the wicked of
>   the age,
> As did the appearance of Abraham to the disposition of fire.[56]

And consistent with reports of his self-regard, 'Urfi praises himself:

[53] Ibid., III, 102; Losensky, *Welcoming Fighani*, 207.
[54] Losensky, *Welcoming Fighani*, 208.
[55] Ghani, *A History of Persian Language and Literature*, III, 107.
[56] Ibid., III, 169.

My lord, I say in my own praise just two verses,
Since my worthy disposition cannot avoid it;
If it become aware of the product of my heart and mind,
The precious pearl would revert to its original state through
    shame;

and he concludes with a formulaic bit of self-reproach.

Stop, 'Urfi, thy nonsense talk, it is time for prayer,
Raise thy hand to the court of the All-merciful.[57]

Painting: origins

Just as Ottoman and Mughal poetry derived from the Persian-language
classics, so too the miniature painting that Ottoman sultans and Mughal
padishahs patronized was first an Iranian art. The earliest known paintings
by ethnic Iranians have been found in Mawarannahr, long the eastern
provinces of the Persian cultural sphere. These include, first, Soghdian
wall paintings from Panjikent in modern Tajikistan, dating to the years
between the sixth and eighth centuries CE, which betray Iranian, Greek,
and Indian influences in their depiction of Iranian themes and pre-Islamic
local deities. The other early Iranian pictorial arts were paintings devoted to
Manichaeism, the mixture of Iranian dualistic concepts with Christianity
developed by the third-century Iranian prophet Mani (b. *c.* 216 CE). These
works have been found mainly in Turfan and other western Silk Road cities
in Xinjiang (Chinese Turkistan), where the Manicheans spread their mes-
sage. They also took refuge there after their prophet's execution in Sasanian
Iran, where he offended the sensibilities of orthodox Zoroastrians. Most
Manichean paintings that survive date to the eighth or ninth century CE,
when the Uighur Turks, then Manicheans, had taken over the Turfan oasis
and eastern Silk Road towns. They are remarkable for their stylistic similarity to medieval Iranian painting, such as the examples of the so-called
"Saljuq International Style" found in Iran, Anatolia, and Syria; many of
these Manichean illustrations were done on lavishly decorated, gold-edged
paper and used eastern Turkic Buddhist types for their idealized represen-
tations of human beings.[58]

Iranian painting, therefore, had a continuous tradition in the pre-Islamic
era, and following the Islamic conquests it reemerged, with accompanying
texts written in New Persian. It is known from references in literary sources

---

[57] Ibid., III, 171.
[58] Eleanor Sims with Boris I. Marshak and Ernst J. Grube, *Peerless Images: Persian Painting
and Its Sources* (New Haven and London: Yale University Press, 2002), chapters I, II, and
III and especially p. 38 for the term "Saljuq International Figural Style."

Fig. 3. Turkey, *c.* 1515–35: "Shirin arrives at Khusrau's Palace," from the Persian romance *Khusrau and Shirin* by the Azerbaijani poet Nizami Ganjavi (*c.* 1141–1209). This is a story of romantic love originating in Firdausi's epic poem the *Shah-nama*, which Nizami (a pen name) dedicated to the Saljuq Sultan Tughril II (r. 1131–4). The style of this painting is typical of earlier Persian art and substantially different from contemporary Iranian painting, as can be seen from the Safavid illustration of a different episode of this poem shown on p. 167 below. The text is unusual in that it indicates the pronunciation of both short and long vowels, which is rarely found in illustrated manuscripts and the calligraphy is relatively crude.

that illustrated texts were produced in the eleventh century CE, but none
have survived from then or the Saljuq period, despite Saljuq figural painting
on ceramic wares – especially pottery and tiles. However, it is not really until
the Mongol era, following the capture of Baghdad and murder of the last
'Abbasid Caliph in 1258, that a dynamic tradition of Iranian painting
reemerged under the patronage of the Mongol khans. One reason why
this art form developed so rapidly from the mid-thirteenth century onwards
was the quantum leap in the use of paper, which occurred because of the
"Pax Mongolica" that facilitated sustained contact between China, Central
Asia, and the Islamic world. It was in Tabriz, the Il-Khanid Mongol capital,
that the earliest examples of what later came to be known as works in
classical Iranian style were produced.

Four manuscripts illustrated with miniature paintings are particularly
important examples of Iranian art in the Mongol period. They are significant because of both their subjects and their illustrations. There are three
Iranian texts and one Indian. The Iranian texts are: *al-Athar al-Baqiya* ... or
The Chronology of Ancient Nations by the Greco-Islamic scientist al-Biruni
(1307); *Jami' al-tawarikh*, the "Collection of Chronicles," by the Iranian
minister to the Il-Khanid Mongols, Rashid al-Din' (*c.* 1314), literally a
history of the world written with the aid of informants from Mongol China;
and *Shah-nama* (*c.* 1330–5), Firdausi's Persian-language classic, which was
repeatedly illustrated and its verse forms copied by historians in Safavid
Iran, the Ottoman Empire, and Mughal India. The Indian text is a Persian
translation of the widely popular Indian *Panchatantra*, animal fables known
in Iran as *Kalila va Dimna* (*c.* 1360).[59] These paintings are distinguished by
discernible Chinese influences, particularly in the landscapes. From this
period onward such book illustrations were carefully chosen for their ability
to expressively illumine the printed page.

Following the collapse of the Il-Khanid Mongols of Iran in 1336, successor states continued the patronage of Persian miniature book illustration. Rulers of the Mongol Jalayirid Dynasty of Baghdad and the Timurids
of Samarqand and Herat played pivotal roles in these developments. Late
fourteenth-century Jalayirid rulers in Baghdad – then, as so often before, a
zone within the Persian cultural sphere – patronized exquisitely fine illustrations for the romantic verse of a little-known poet, Khwaju Kirmani:

All the paintings still within the Khwaju Kirmani [manuscript] of 1398
are ... remarkable ... Those showing interiors are among the most lovingly detailed
and beautifully painted of any Iranian book illustrations, anywhere, at any period;
the landscape pictures are equally rich, detailed and complete. Both types of
settings are fully developed examples of these classical genres in the illustration

---

[59] Ibid., 43.

Fig. 4. The *Gur-i amir*, the "tomb of the amir", Temür's tomb, Samarqand.

of classical Persian poetry that are not only remarkable for their appearance... but also for the early date at which they are so perfectly worked out – the very end of the fourteenth century... it is clear that all the significant aspects of the art of manuscript illustration in the "Golden Age" of painting in the Iranian-influenced East, were actually in place at the death of Sultan Ahmad Jalayir in 1410.[60]

---

[60] Sims, *Peerless Images*, 50. Or as another Iranian art historian has put it: "By the mid-1370's... the canon of Persian manuscript painting for the next two centuries was set. Refinements and variations continued, but artists and their patrons had found the balance

This Iranian artistic tradition, which seems to have been nearly fully formed under Jalayirid rulers, was further patronized by the descendants of Temür in Tabriz, Shiraz, and Herat following Temür's death in 1405. Herat in particular became the cultural center of the Timurid-Persian world and remained so until the Uzbek conquest in 1507. In the second half of the century, the rise to power of the Qara Quyunlu and Aq Quyunlu in northwestern Iran also led to a "Turcoman" variant of the Iranian style, characterized by "an intense palette where hues of rocks and hills melt into one another, a disregard for spatial logic, and elongated almost languorous figures."[61]

Most of the paintings completed in the fifteenth century were done to illustrate literary manuscripts. The one remarkable exception to this tradition is the group of atypical individual images of rural or nomadic Central Asian folk, portraits strongly influenced by Chinese painting, which may have been painted in or around Samarqand. Known as *siyah qalam* or "black pen," the images are of people or animals or demons, quite unlike anything found in the urban Iranian tradition of this era. However, the most influential form of Iranian art to emerge from the fifteenth century to fundamentally influence both Safavid and Mughal painting was produced in Herat, initially under the patronage of the Timurid Shah Rukh's son, Baisunghur (1397–1434).

In 1420 Baisunghur was sent to recapture Tabriz from the Aq Quyunlu. Tabriz was then still a Jalayirid center of artistic production, and when Baisunghur returned to Herat he brought with him artists and calligraphers who laid the foundations for the Persian artistic tradition that reached its height at the end of the century with the work of the Herat painter Bihzad.[62] This forced or sometimes voluntary migration of artists explains much about the transmission of styles from one urban center to another in this period. Baisunghur commissioned numerous illustrated texts, and unlike his father, whose preference was for historical works that could be interpreted as demonstrating Timurid legitimacy, he favored illustrated classics of Persian literature.

The geometrical harmony of composition that characterized these paintings became one of the signature characteristics of later Timurid art and of Timurid garden construction. This was also the period when the influence of Chinese designs was at its height, a result of the direct relations between Timurid courts and the Ming emperors and also,

between abstraction and naturalism, color and line, nature and man that best represented the Iranian psyche": Sheila Canby, *Persian Painting* (New York: Thames and Hudson, 1993), 41–2.
[61] Thompson and Canby, *Hunt for Paradise*, 73–4.
[62] Sims, *Peerless Images*, 55.

Fig. 5. Iran, *c.* 1540. Painting of a school scene included in a *muraqqa'* or album. This scene of everyday life is reminiscent of some of Bizhad's Herat works.

Fig. 6. Iran, *c.* 1548. "Khusrau discovers Shirin bathing in a pool," from Nizam's *Khusrau and Shirin*. Compare Fig. 3, an "Ottoman" illustration from this poem. Note Khusrau's distinctive Safavid or Qizilbash-style turban.

perhaps, a consequence of Chinese voyages into the Indian Ocean that the Ming dispatched at this time.[63] What has been called the "formal and theatrical vision" of Timurid art was manifest in Baisunghur's Persian-language edition of the *Shah-nama*:

> It is the most majestic of all the manuscripts created for this most discerning and passionate bibliophile prince. Large, beautifully calligraphed and grandly illuminated, it is illustrated with twenty-one images, a small but carefully chosen pictorial program emphasizing the duties of princes and the responsibilities of rulers toward the people they govern. It is in effect, an "illustrated mirror for princes."[64]

The development of Timurid painting – or Iranian painting of the Timurid era – climaxed with the patronage of Sultan Husain Baiqara (r. 1486–1506) whose artistic patronage "was on a scale to rival that of his contemporary Lorenzo de Medici in Florence."[65] Many rank this painting as the finest Persian art ever produced. Its signature characteristics are brilliant, intense colors, precise modeling, and complex scenes with multiple figures, showing a variety of activities, sometimes from daily life – on building sites, in pastures, in baths and in bazaars, and individualized types – not realism as such, with unique personalities, but differentiated figures.[66] Bihzad is the late Timurid painter who, above all others, is associated with this artistic golden age, and his name was cited and revered by later connoisseurs in Ottoman, Safavid, and Mughal dominions.

Ottoman painting

Timurid art was the principal model for painters in all three Islamic empires, and in the Ottoman and Safavid empires, it was often émigré or refugee Timurid artists who initially maintained Timurid traditions of illuminated manuscript painting. In the Ottoman case only one illustrated manuscript, an *Iskendername* or *Book of Alexander* (1390), produced in the provincial city of Amasya, is extant for the period before the conquest of Constantinople. Mehmet II began the systematic production of illustrated texts by establishing the *nakkaşhane*, literally the "house of painting" or "artistic studio," shortly after taking the Byzantine capital. He began the Ottoman atelier as a subsidiary branch of the army. Painters were the *kadi*

---

[63] Canby, *Persian Painting*, 62.   [64] Sims, *Peerless Images*, 55.
[65] Robert Hillenbrand, *Islamic Art and Architecture* (London: Thames and Hudson, 1999), 174.
[66] Ibid., 225. Hillenbrand's assessment represents the art-historical consensus about late Timurid miniature painting, which is by almost any measure; exquisite.

askers of Ottoman art: another reminder, if one is needed, of the empire's military ethos.[67] Mehmet's paintings were all done outside Istanbul. Artists, calligraphers, bookbinders, and others who were employed in this office, are known to have produced about fifteen illustrated texts in the formative years of Ottoman painting between the conquest and the beginning of Süleyman's reign in 1520.

The earliest imperial manuscripts were written in Persian and sometimes by Iranians. One, the *Dilsizname*, an allegorical work by Badi al-Din al Tabrizi, was finished in Edirne in 1455–6, and contains only five simple paintings. A second illustrated manuscript from Edirne (*c.* 1460–80), the *Kulliyat* or collected works of the writer Katibi, contains similarly simple paintings. However, it is distinguished by images of blue and white ceramics, probably of Chinese origin, which Timurid rulers collected for their *Chini-khanahs* or China-houses, and the first known pictures of Janissaries, wearing their distinctive white hats, the Turkic *börks*, rather than turbans. It was during this period that a distinct genre of portrait painting began in Istanbul when Gentile Bellini, the official Venetian artist, completed a portrait of Mehmet II in November 1481. European stylistic influence can be seen in another famous portrait of Mehmet II, seated cross-legged holding a rose. "Establishing a prototype for Ottoman portraits, the artist has transformed the Renaissance theme into one of local tradition."[68] However, the most important legacy of these portraits is the establishment of an Ottoman tradition of royal portraiture.

During the reign of Mehmet's successor Bayezid II, himself a calligrapher and poet in Persian and Turkish, the *nakkashane* began to produce decorated Qurans and illustrated manuscripts. The first two dated manuscripts are Persian-language texts, one a copy of the Persian translation of Indian animal fables, *Kalila va Dimna* (1495), probably done by a former Aq Quyunlu artist, and the other the *Khamsa* or "Quintet" of the Indo-Persian poet Amir Khusrau Dihlavi, containing Herat-style miniatures which nonetheless include indigenous-style buildings that record the first hint of the Ottomanization of the Persian miniature tradition – in architectural detail, if not yet in subject matter. This trend is even more evident in a third Persian-language text completed in 1498–9 in which Ottoman figures, including Janissaries, decorate a well-known romance by the twelfth-century Iranian poet Nizami, *Khusrau and Shirin*.[69] Bayezid was also responsible for patronizing Melik Ümmi's *Şahname* (*c.* 1500), the first work in what became one of the signature traits of Ottoman miniature

---

[67] The following survey is based on the essay by Esin Atıl, "The Art of the Book," in Esin Atıl, ed., *Turkish Art* (New York: Harry Abrams, 1980), 138–238.
[68] Ibid., 157.   [69] Ibid., 160–1.

painting: the illustration of historical events, predominantly military campaigns, a genre unknown in Safavid Iran but occasionally seen in Mughal art.[70] Overall "The age of Bayezid is important for the development of the Istanbul school of painting. Copying traditional literary works and relying on existing Iranian models, the *nakkaşhane* incorporated the stylistic features of Shiraz and Herat together with the unique attempts of the local painters."[71] Iranian influence only increased during Selim's reign as refugee artists and books arrived from Herat, following the Uzbek conquest of the city in 1507, and Tabriz, after the Ottomans occupied the Safavid capital in 1515, following Bayezid's defeat of Shah Isma'il at Chaldiran a year earlier. However, it was not until Süleyman's reign that Ottoman painting began the dynamic development that was to climax in the works produced under his son and successor, Selim II (1566–74).

Safavid painting

Early Safavid art was also partly indebted to the Uzbek capture of Herat in 1507, for this meant that the Timurid library and many artists and craftsmen eventually were transported to Shah Isma'il's capital, Tabriz, a city that had been a center of Aq Quyunlu art production in the late fifteenth century. The man most immediately responsible for this artistic migration was Sultan Husain Baiqara's son, Badi' al-Zaman Mirza, who fled the Uzbek conquest west into Safavid territories, carrying with him a portion of the Timurid libraries. Then in 1510 Shah Isma'il himself captured Herat, which would have given Safavids access to painters and manuscripts still in the city. In terms of artistic style it was the late Timurid artist Bihzad who served as the "bridge between the traditions of later Timurid painting and the next period of the early Safavids," although it is not certain that he actually took up the post of royal librarian in Tabriz that he was offered by Shah Isma'il.[72]

Safavid appreciation of his art is commemorated in the spectacular album produced under Isma'il's son and successor Shah Tahmasp, which includes a portrait of an aged Bihzad in Safavid costume. It was Tahmasp himself (b. 1514), who succeeded his father in 1524, who formed another link with the Timurid artistic past. As a young child of two, following typical Turkic political tradition, he was sent to nominally govern Herat under the eyes of a

---

[70] Ibid., 164. Mehmet had established the position of *şahnameçi*, adopting the Persian word *shahnama*, but using it to mean the person, indicated by the Turkish suffix -*çi*, who was the imperial historian, chronicling Ottoman conquests. In this way Ottomans adopted the pre-Islamic Iranian imperial tradition for the purposes of Ottoman dynastic glorification.
[71] Atıl, *Turkish Art*, 163.   [72] Sims, *Peerless Images*, 60, 62–3.

guardian, and he is said, without much evidence, to have been taught miniature painting by Bihzad himself. Whether or not the story is apocryphal, there is little doubt that Herat had continued to be an important artistic center, despite the political turmoil of the early sixteenth century, and there is also little doubt that both Shah Tahmasp and his younger brother, Sam Mirza, both studied painting and calligraphy, and learned to appreciate the sophisticated Timurid tradition of the arts of the book that had flourished under several Timurid royal patrons during the fifteenth century.[73]

The artistic interests of Tahmasp, Sam Mirza, and another brother, Bahram Mirza, were manifested in their patronage of illustrated manuscripts during the first half of the sixteenth century. Indeed, Tahmasp commissioned a new *Shah-nama*, which contemporaries and later connoisseurs have regarded as the single most beautiful illustrated manuscript produced under Safavid patronage. Probably begun early in Tahmasp's reign and not completed until about 1540, the now dispersed manuscript was produced by a number of different artists, some of whose paintings represent Safavid versions of Jalayirid and Timurid compositions. Some of the manuscript's approximately 258 illustrations were done hurriedly, but many are exquisite, almost magical, particularly the most famous illustration, the "Court of Gayumars." The calligraphy, paper, ornamentation, and binding of this volume were of comparable quality to the paintings. The political and cultural significance of this particular text, which even contemporary Iranians regarded as a uniquely fine work of art, has, like that of other editions of Firdausi's work, been the subject of varying interpretations.[74]

A second illustrated manuscript of a poetical work produced in 1539–43, the *Khamsa* of Nizami, is an equally accomplished if less ambitious volume with only fourteen illustrations. Nonetheless these paintings are of uniformly high quality, and the album's art summarizes the accomplishments of early Safavid painting, remarkable especially because of the political

---

[73] See Stuart Cary Welch, *The King's Book of Kings: The Shah-Nameh of Shah Tahmasp* (London: Thames and Hudson, 1972), 68–9, for an introduction to Shah Tahmasp's artistic training and enthusiasm for painting.

[74] Ironically, Tahmasp sent this *Shah-nama* as one of a number of gifts to the Ottoman Sultan Süleyman in 1557 in honor of his new imperial mosque. He did so three years after he publicly announced his "sincere repentance," for earlier patronizing the profane arts, rather than concentrating solely on Shi'i Islam. Regarding this particular text and its possible significance see, first of all, Welch, *A King's Book of Kings*, the best introduction to this book; Robert Hillenbrand, "The Iconography of the *Shah-nama-yi Shahi*," in Charles Melville, ed., *Safavid Persia* (London and New York: I. B. Tauris, 1996), 53–7, and Marianna Shreve Simpson, "*Shahnama* as Text and *Shahnama* as Image: A Brief Overview of Recent Studies, 1975–2000," in Robert Hillenbrand, ed., *Shahnama: The Visual Language of the Persian Book of Kings* (Aldershot: Ashgate, 2004), 9–23. The article contains a valuable bibliography of both texts and commentaries.

turmoil caused by Shah Tahmasp's feuding Qizilbash tribesmen, which reduced him to little more than a figurehead early in his reign.

All the components of earlier Safavid painting have merged and matured in these Khamsa paintings: the frenetic, expressive landscapes so unusually colored and peopled by visionaries or other worldly beings that came from Turkmen Tabriz; the limpidly still, coolly colored and perfectly balanced compositional tradition of Bihzad's Herat; the sixteenth century's increasingly naturalistic depiction of human beings in the full range of their daily activities and the contemporary taste for the multiplication of patterns.[75]

Overall the production of these superb manuscripts, and the continued artistic interests of Safavid family members, helped to generate a taste for the pictorial and calligraphic arts in the upper reaches of Safavid society during the sixteenth century. Later workshops in Shiraz and Khurasan helped to disseminate a cultural aesthetic that was shared by a broad range of the literate public: not just the political elite, but prosperous merchants and others who patronized or purchased illustrated Persian poetical classics, reinvigorating a Persianate cultural identity shared by the Persian-speaking elite in Mawarannahr and Mughal India.

Mughal painting

Just as Iranian art, in its Timurid or Turkmen variants, constituted the basis for early Ottoman illustrated manuscripts, so Safavid artists carried the sixteenth-century Iranian variant of those earlier styles to Mughal India. Here again, as in the case of the dispersal of artists to Iran and the Ottoman Empire from Herat and Tabriz, specific and well-known Iranian painters began the Mughal school, which, like the Ottoman, quickly evolved into an idiosyncratic indigenous style. Babur's son Humayun founded the Mughal atelier by inviting two Safavid artists, whom he met while seeking aid from Shah Tahmasp at Qazvin in 1544, to accompany him as he returned to Afghanistan to begin his decade-long campaign to regain his father's Indian conquests. By this time, Shah Tahmasp had begun turning away from his youthful profane indulgences in alcohol and painting, a transformation that was complete a decade later when he ostentatiously proclaimed his newly discovered piety and terminated royal patronage of calligraphy and painting. Even though Humayun was no more than a *qazaq*, a throneless, wandering vagabond, when he visited Qazvin, two outstanding artists, 'Abd al-Samad and Mir Sayyid 'Ali, accompanied him on his return to Afghanistan and worked for years in Kabul. Both Iranians were members of

---

[75] Sins, *Peerless Images*, 64.

Shah Tahmasp's atelier who had worked on the monarch's superb *Shahnama*. Both men had been influenced by the Timurid artist of Husain Baiqara's day, Bihzad: 'Abd al-Samad drew direct inspiration from the Timurid artist and named one of his sons Bihzad; Mir Sayyid 'Ali also painted some of the plates for Nizami's *Khamsa*.

In 1556, following Humayun's accidental death, Akbar, who may have studied with the two Iranian artists, appointed 'Abd al-Samad to head the new Mughal imperial studio.[76] Mir Sayyid 'Ali also became a renowned artist there, more valued than his countryman for his refined precision. Before that 'Abd al- Samad and Mir Sayyid 'Ali had both been active during Humayun's residence in Kabul. During that period 'Abd al-Samad apparently painted the first draft of a famous work of classical Safavid-style miniature art: the brilliantly colorful, lavishly illustrated, precisely drawn "Princes of the House of Temür," one of many such works that Humayun and his successors used to remind themselves of their Timurid legitimacy. 'Abd al-Samad continued to work in the early Safavid style throughout most of his long life, specializing in typical Iranian court and hunting scenes and illustrations of classical Persian poetic works. He died in the last decade of the sixteenth century; his son became an intimate friend of Akbar's son and successor, the artistic aesthete Jahangir. Mir Sayyid 'Ali also remained fundamentally a Safavid artist, although his famous and moving portrait of his father Mir Mussavir, as an old man may reflect Akbar's known preference for lifelike paintings. Despite both men's fidelity to Safavid artistic traditions, they trained Indian artists who helped to create an idiosyncratic Mughal style. 'Abd al-Samad, for example, trained two of Akbar's most important and creative Hindu artists, Basawan and Daswanath.[77]

Basawan was one of several artists who worked on two of the most important early Akbari era manuscripts: the *Tuti-Nama* (*c.* 1560–5) and the monumental *Hamza Nama*, which took nearly fifteen years to complete, from 1562 and 1577. In addition he contributed illustrations to other manuscripts, and organized the design of a history of Akbar's reign, the *Akbar Nama*. While 'Abd al-Samad and Mir Sayyid 'Ali's paintings were "Mughal" miniatures only to the extent that they gave some figures identifiably Indian clothing, not only did Basawan and other Hindu artists, who comprised the majority of painters in Akbar's studio,

---

[76] Amina Okada, *Indian Miniatures at the Mughal Court* (New York: Harry N. Abrams, 1992), 62 and 69. See also Milo Cleveland Beach, *Mughal and Rajput Painting* (Cambridge University Press, 1992) and Som Prakash Verma, *Mughal Painters and Their Work: A Biographical Survey and Comprehensive Catalogue* (Delhi: Oxford University Press, 1994).

[77] I am indebted to Amina Okada and Eleanor Sims for most of this material.

Fig. 7. India, *c.* 1600. Qurachar, a Mongol identified as Chingiz Khan's paternal cousin. A painting suggesting, falsely, that Temür himself was a descendant of Chingiz Khan's family and thus that he possessed Mongol legitimacy. The Mongols' identity is indicated by facial features and their headgear – caps not turbans. From the *Gulshan muraqqaʿ*, now in Tehran.

Fig. 8. India, *c.* 1597: Akbar's son Prince Murad with his wife. This painting, by the renowned Hindu artist in Akbar's atelier, Manohar, probably renders an accurate image of the Mughal prince. Note the distinctive Mughal turbans.

introduce Indian scenes and a greater naturalism, but Basawan in particular was able to combine a mastery of Safavid techniques learned at the
knee of his Persian teachers with an ability to develop an eclectic style that
responded to the techniques of European art, which was just beginning to
arrive at the Mughal court in northern European engravings brought to
the court by Jesuits. One remarkable painting illustrates his exceptional
skill and is unmistakably Indian: "The Battle between Two Groups of
Ascetics," probably a conflict between Vaishnavites and Saivites, the
devotees of the two principal Hindu deities, Vishnu and Shiva, which he
painted around 1590.

Through this powerful work, Basawan demonstrates above all his extraordinary
virtuosity and sense of realism; key details include the fear-and hate-filled faces of
the warring ascetics, and the sagging flesh and belly of dying Shiva chieftan Anant
Kur.... Basawan's interest in psychological portraits was undoubtedly nourished
by his thorough study of European engravings, with their stress on modeling and
volume to enhance naturalistic effects...the originality of Basawan's contribution
becomes evident when such robust realism is compared to the aestheticized,
mannered grace of Persian-style portraits.[78]

In using their traditional Iranian artistic training in this way, Basawan and
his fellow Hindu artists show how they, like their Ottoman counterparts,
began developing regional variants of their shared Iranian artistic legacy.
Mughal art was to become even more distinctive later in the century.

---

[78] Okada, *Indian Images at the Mughal Court*, 84, 90–1.

6   Golden ages: profane and sacred empires

Introduction

In Greek mythology a golden age may have been conceived of as a utopia of social harmony, political stability, prosperity, and peace, a kind of Arcadia, but when it comes to dynastic politics, golden ages tend to be defined as periods of imperial domination and cultural florescence. Often the idea of a golden age consists of little more than nostalgia for an imagined and imaginary past; but in some cases the elite members of a society, who share an intoxicated sense of their power, privilege, and prestige, acclaim their own age as a climactic moment in the history of their civilization. In the case of the Muslim empires, the Ottoman Sultan Süleyman and the Mughal Padishah Shah Jahan presided over what they and also many of their descendants believed to be an apogee in the history of their own dynasty and, in the Ottoman case, its place in the broader Islamic world. While their respective reigns were as different as the geographic and cultural context and political character of the states they inherited, both men made new claims for their legitimacy, and patronized spectacular architectural projects that seem to ratify their imperious self-images and ensure the favorable verdicts of posterity. The most notable of these structures were the sixteenth-century mosque complexes of the Ottoman imperial architect Sinan, and the seventeenth-century Taj Mahal and Shah Jahan's new imperial city in Delhi.

The absence of comparable monumental architecture in Safavid Iran after the death of Shah 'Abbas I reflects the lack of seventeenth-century Safavid rulers who were interested in, much less capable of, carrying the dynasty to new heights of territorial expansion, financial prosperity, and cultural florescence. In the Safavid case also, the original religious basis of the dynasty's legitimacy was sometimes challenged by members of the Shi'i 'ulama, who felt that only the Imam could be recognized as a ruler in a Shi'i society. The most memorable and consequential Iranians in this period were, in fact, Shi'i theologians and philosophers. They collectively produced an intellectual golden age for Shi'i Islam, and bequeathed a legacy more profoundly important to twenty-first century Iran than were the achievements of Süleyman and Shah Jahan for Republican Turkey and independent India.

The Ottoman Empire

The military victories and conquests of Süleyman's immediate predecessor, Sultan Selim, constituted the necessary preface to Süleyman's "magnificence." Following the family bloodletting that typically sealed a new sultan's triumph, Selim moved quickly to nullify the Safavid threat in eastern Anatolia by imprisoning and/or massacring an estimated 40,000 partisans of Shah Isma'il. While all such figures should be regarded skeptically, the report at least reflects the ferocity of Selim's response to the Safavid problem, which he climaxed with a march against Shah Isma'il himself. Just as Mehmet had used Ottoman firearms to defeat Uzun Hasan's tribal cavalry in 1483, Selim in 1514 decisively defeated Isma'il's spiritually intoxicated force of Qizilbash tribesmen at Chaldiran in Azerbaijan, using his artillery and formidable Janissary force of matchlock men arrayed behind the same linked-cart defenses that Babur employed on the advice of his Ottoman counselor, twelve years later in India. While Shah Isma'il had earlier sought artillery from Venice and may have had some firearms at Chaldiran, he had not, evidently, begun to integrate cannon or other firearms into his military, and the Safavids never really used heavy artillery to great effect in their later campaigns.[1]

After securing Ottoman control of eastern Anatolia by forming an alliance with Kurdish chiefs in that region, Selim in 1516 moved south against the Mamluks, the Slave sultans of Egypt and Syria, who may earlier have concluded an alliance with Shah Isma'il. Whether or not such a coalition ever existed, Selim's campaign merely resumed a festering Ottoman–Mamluk conflict, and the economic benefits of controlling Syria and (even more so) Egypt must have been a powerful incentive for an aggressive leader of the Ottoman state. Presenting himself as a savior of the Islamic world, Selim fought and won two battles with the Mamluks between August 1516 and July 1517. With the second of these victories in Egypt, he inherited the Mamluk custody of Mecca and Medina, elevating the Ottomans' religious status in the Sunni Muslim world to the pinnacle of prestige. The additional territory and responsibility for the Muslim holy cities also altered the nature of the Ottoman state, making it for the first

---

[1] Rudi Matthee,"Unwalled Cities and Restless Nomads: Firearms and Artillery in Safavid Iran," in Melville, ed., *Safavid Persia*, 391.

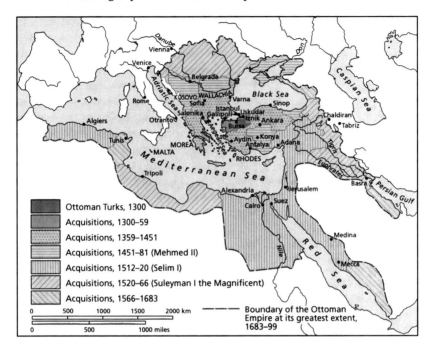

Map 13. The Ottoman Empire in 1566 and 1683

time an unmistakably Muslim empire, in both population and religious prestige. Egypt also gave the Ottomans control of the fertile Nile Delta and the lucrative Indian Ocean–Red Sea transit trade, doubling Ottoman revenues and setting the stage for the reign of Selim's successor, Süleyman.

Süleyman

Known to later Ottoman historians as Süleyman Kanuni and to Europeans as Süleyman the Magnificent, this sultan (r. 1520–66) inherited a confident, dynamic, aggressive state, and as a physically imposing and tirelessly energetic man, he consolidated and systematized the dynasty's centralized control over the empire.[2] He personally commanded a series of successful military campaigns on the Ottomans' eastern and western frontiers, adding substantial new territories to the empire,

---

[2] For a wide-ranging survey of Süleyman's era and achievements see Halil Inalcık and Cemal Kafadar, eds., *Süleyman the Second and His Time* (Istanbul: Isis, 1993).

and lavishly patronized architecture as well as a variety of imperial arts and crafts. Only in his later years did Süleyman adopt a remote, secluded habit, withdraw from public view, become a Muslim ascetic, and thus establish the precedent that dictated sultans no longer took an active role in government. He also, like many past Ottoman rulers, both enjoyed and composed poetry, writing an especially memorable series of Persian and Ottoman Turkish *ghazals* to his favorite wife, the European captive and convert Hürrem Sultan, the mother of three of his four surviving sons.

Süleyman conducted himself as a ruler who exhibited a sense of his unique status in the history of the dynasty and did everything possible to glorify and sanctify his place in the rigidly stratified Ottoman universe. During his lifetime and later, Ottomans themselves recognized Süleyman's special achievements. The contemporary political theorist Kınalzâde Alî Efendi (1510–72) praised Süleyman, in what became a popular text during the next two centuries, by arguing that the Sultan in Istanbul had established an Islamic version of "virtuous city," a Greek concept he took from Nasir al-Tusi's *akhlaq* or treatise on ethics. By the end of the century the historian Mustafa 'Ali and other Ottoman intellectuals – and frustrated bureaucrats – began nostalgically looking back on Süleyman's reign, the longest in Ottoman history, as an Ottoman golden age.[3] It is difficult to disagree with their assessment given this ruler's achievements. Even though the empire was to endure for a further three and a half centuries after his death, it was never again to be so cohesive or powerful, or to produce such a dazzling range of architectural monuments or exquisite art and crafts. None of the later Safavid or Mughal monarchs equaled his achievements – except perhaps Shah Jahan in building the Taj Mahal.

Süleyman's "slave" empire

A man known – in his early private life at least – as modest, generous, and frugal, Süleyman ruled as a monarch devoted to order and justice, the twin principles of Muslim "mirrors for princes" literature. Known as Kanuni, Süleyman was for a long time believed to be responsible for compiling a code of imperial laws. Mehmet II is now known to have been responsible for most of the provisions in these texts, and

---

[3] Baki Tezcan,"Ethics as a Domain to Discuss the Political: Kınalzâde Ali Efendi's *Ahlak-i Alâî,*" in Ali Çaksu, ed., *International Congress on Learning and Education in the Ottoman World* (Istanbul: Research Centre for Islamic History, Art and Culture, 2001), 119. Like Tusi's thirteenth-century Persian work *Akhlâq-i Nâsiri*, Kınsalzade's treatise applies Greek socio-political thought to an Islamic state and is heavily indebted to Galen, who, after Plato and Aristotle, was the third most important Greek thinker for Muslim scholars.

Süleyman's contribution is understood to be limited to the direction or support he gave to his chancelor, Jelalzade Mustafa, in systemizing, adapting, and disseminating the codes. This activity reflected Süleyman's commitment to consolidating the dynasty's centralized control of an empire in which slaves dominated the state as Janissaries and high imperial officials. Of twenty-four viziers who governed during his reign, nineteen were *devshirme* recruits or white eunuchs from the inner palace.[4] The Grand Vizier Ibrahim Pasha (*c.* 1493–1536) was typical of the *devshirme* personnel who now dominated the bureaucracy.

Enslaved as a child, converted and trained within the palace as were so many promising young *devshirme* recruits, Ibrahim first served Prince Süleyman; in 1523 Sultan Süleyman appointed him as his Grand Vizier. In 1524 he married the Sultan's sister (a recurring marriage pattern in the Ottoman system), and for the next twelve years he was a successful military commander. He first commanded victorious armies against Hungary between 1526 and 1532 and then later against Safavid Iran, capturing Tabriz in August 1534 and Baghdad in December of that year. In 1536 the Sultan had him strangled in his bedroom in the Tokapı *haram* for no known reason: a typical form of execution for slave officials who, for whatever reason, had lost favor with the Sultan – perhaps owing to bureaucratic or *haram* intrigue or because they had accumulated victories, fame, and quasi-royal charisma.

Only Ottomans could possess such charisma, and in addition to the prestige generated by his continuous victories, Süleyman had after all inherited the legitimacy of his predecessors, who traced their descent from the mythical founder of the Oghuz tribes, Oghuz Khan. Ottomans also declared they had inherited the legal authority of the Saljuqs, claimed Roman imperial power as descendants of Mehmet II, the conqueror of the Eastern Roman Empire and, after victories in Iran, portrayed themselves as "Chosroes" (Khusrau), the pre-Islamic Iranian ruler of the Persians and Arabs. The new sultan supplemented these declarations of tribal, royal, and imperial legitimacy by asserting, through his chief religious advisor, that God had bestowed the Caliphate upon him, a claim that resonated strongly with Muslims ruled by European colonial states in India and elsewhere in the late nineteenth and early twentieth century. Indeed, Süleyman – who unlike Mehmet II, ruled over a predominantly Muslim empire – did not use Mehmet's secular, imperial title, *Sultan-i Rum*, but a Perso-Islamic one, *Padishah-i Islam*.[5] Süleyman, in fact,

---

[4] Necipoğlu, *The Age of Sinan*, 36.
[5] Bernard Lewis, *Istanbul and the Civilization of the Ottoman Empire* (Norman: University of Oklahoma Press, 1963), 145.

claimed universal sovereignty, "expressed by seven flags of different colours, representing Ottoman rule over the 'seven climes' of the world, and by four [Turco-Mongol] horse-tail standards (*tuğ*) symbolizing dominion over the four corners of the world," also adding to his titles "master of the lands of the Roman Caesars and Alexander the Great."[6]

The degree to which Süleyman exercised centralized power over the broad expanse of the empire was demonstrated by the ability of his officials to carry out land registration in European, Arab, and Anatolian regions, using the example of a survey of the Bursa region under Bayezid II in 1487. Such surveys were probably based on earlier Saljuq examples. This gave him and his immediate successors direct legal and financial control over *timar* holders, the Ottoman equivalent of Mughal *mansabdars*, and the *reaya*, the legally subordinate but imperially protected tax-paying class, most of whom were agriculturalists who were not legally landowners and could not sell their tenures without permission of their *sipahi* superiors, to whom they also owed labor services. In Anatolia at least, these *reaya* were known pejoratively as the *turk*s, whom cosmopolitan Ottomans in Istanbul often ridiculed for their rustic or simple, unsophisticated ways.[7] This was merely one example of the increasingly rigid social hierarchy that Süleyman enforced during his reign, in which he emphasized the distance between the court and *reaya* of all types. Within the palace, for example, a "coded sign language was invented ... to avoid speaking the ordinary language of the people" in the sultan's presence, and "ceremonial representation of imperial grandeur increasingly became elaborated in public parades."[8]

Süleyman also sought to reinforce his control over the *reaya* class by his intensified commitment to Ottoman Sunni Muslim orthodoxy, itself partly a reflection of the Ottoman conquests of the Muslim lands of Egypt and Mesopotamia, but probably more than anything else a response to the ideological challenge of the Shi'i Safavids. He built numerous *madrasas*, ordered the construction of a mosque in every village, and enforced observance of the five daily and Friday prayers; all this stimulated mosque construction. As part of his emphasis on Hanafi Sunni orthodoxy he supported the persecution of heresy, often directed at suspect Sufi *pirs*, but also consolidated imperial control over the *'ulama*, the *'ilmiyye* or clerical class. In doing so he only extended the policy

[6] Necipoğlu, *The Age of Sinan*, 27–8.
[7] Imber, *The Ottoman Empire*, 199–200 and G. Veinstein, "Süleymân (926–74/1520–66)," *Encyclopaedia of Islam* II, Brill Online.
[8] Necipoğlu, *The Age of Sinan*, 33.

inherited from his predecessors, giving Ottoman sultans a degree of control over their *'ulama* which was exceptional in the Islamic world.

Sufism in the Ottoman golden age

Süleyman's policies raise a particular question about the place and role of Sufis in Ottoman society. It was also a contentious issue in Safavid Iran, where non-Safavid Sufis were sometimes aggressively persecuted by Shi'i *'ulama* with the encouragement of the regime. Sufi *khangahs* are noticeably absent as adjunct buildings to some of the great imperial mosques of the Ottoman golden age, and their absence probably reflected these Muslims' *relative* lack of importance for the dynasty, when compared to their religious and social role in the Anatolian countryside in earlier times.[9] While still influential and commonly seen in rural and urban Ottoman society, Sufis were less tolerated and influential during Süleyman's rigid, orthodox reign, despite his personal sympathy for their practices. Nonetheless, Sufi influences pervaded Ottoman Islamic religious piety, and three orders in particular, the Bektashi, the Central Asian-Indian Naqshbandi, and the Anatolian (originally Iranian) Halveti, were popular with Istanbul Muslims and with many sultans.[10] Sufism, however, revived after Süleyman's death, and his successor, Selim II, was an enthusiastic disciple of the most important Halveti *shaikh* of that era.

The degree to which the Halveti and other Sufi orders later prospered in Istanbul is revealed by the seventeenth-century *Kadizadeli* movement's fundamentalist attacks on Sufi practices – singing, dancing, music, reverence for deceased *pir*s, use of coffee, wine, and drugs – between 1630 and 1680. Led by Kadizade Mehmet,[11] who in 1661 was appointed to the Aya Sofia, the movement represented a particularly violent strain of long-standing Muslim critiques of Sufi piety and practices, and Kadizade and his enthusiastic followers violently attacked representatives of the Halveti order in Istanbul. In social terms the Kadizadelis were largely marginal, low-paid members of the *'ulama*, and their movement seemed partly to be motivated by jealousy of and anger toward more privileged members of

---

[9] See also above, Chapter 5.

[10] See again Ocak, *Sufism and Sufis*. For a survey of Naqshbandi influence in the Ottoman empire see Alexandre Papas's review of three books on the order: "Towards a New History of Sufism: The Turkish Case," *History of Religions* 46, No. 1 (2006), 81–90. John Joseph Curry IV discusses the important Ottoman branch of the originally Herati, Halveti order in his dissertation "Transforming Muslim Mystical Thought in the Ottoman Empire: The Case of the Shabaniyye Order in Kastamonu and Beyond," unpublished PhD dissertation, Ohio State University, 2005.

[11] C. Madeline Zilfi, "The Kadizadelis: Discordant Revivalism in Seventeenth Century Istanbul," *Journal of Near Eastern Studies* 45, No. 4 (October 1986), 251–69.

the *ilmiyye* class. Unlike the sporadic but growing Safavid support for persecution of Sufis in late seventeenth-century Iran, Ottoman authorities suppressed the Kadizadeli movement because of the threat to public order – and probably also because of the widespread public and aristo-cratic sympathy for Sufi piety.

Ottoman conquests

Süleyman came to power at a time when Ottoman sultans were still trained in the field as provincial governors and military commanders, unlike the practice he initiated late in his reign, in which rulers remained closeted within the palace and confined their potential heirs to the *haram*, until one would succeed and the others be murdered. He exhibited his training and aggressive instincts as soon as he acceded to the throne, by personally leading a series of military campaigns. Within the first two years of his reign he occupied Belgrade, seized Rhodes from the Knights of St. John, and destroyed an army of Hungarian heavy cavalry with Ottoman artillery before entering Buda, the capital, in September 1528. In 1529 he laid siege to Vienna, the first of two unsuccessful Ottoman attempts to capture the city.

These campaigns were followed by the occupation of the Safavids' northwestern and western territories in 1534, as Shah Tahmasp simply retreated into the interior. In Iraq Süleyman cultivated several sectarian audiences as he pointedly made pilgrimages to the Shi'i centers of Najaf and Karbala, repaired the dome of the Sunni jurist Abu Hanifa, and restored the tomb of one of the most important Sufi *pirs* in the Islamic world, 'Abd al-Qadir al-Jilani. Then three years later, following the exe-cution of Ibrahim Pasha, he began new campaigns, first again in Europe and then later against Iran, and concluded his subsequent victory over Safavid forces by imposing the peace treaty of Amasya in May 1555, giving the Ottomans Iraq, part of Kurdistan, and eastern Armenia, with Tabriz and the surrounding territory left in Safavid hands.

Süleyman only failed militarily in three major naval expeditions that he sent against the Portuguese: in Diu, near Surat, in 1538; against the Persian Gulf port of Ormuz in 1552; and again near the Gulf in 1554. Another expedition at the end of his reign successfully supplied the Atjehnese Muslims in Sumatra, themselves on the front line of Portuguese naval aggression, with guns and military advisors, receiving spices in exchange. The unsuccessful anti-Portuguese expeditions reflected the reasonable Ottoman fear that the lucrative trade through Egypt and the Persian Gulf, which brought in so much wealth to the treasury, would be lost forever to the Portuguese. Nonetheless, whereas in galley naval battles in the Mediterranean the Ottomans could compete with their European foes, they were incapable of defeating heavily armed, sea-going Portuguese ships and had to concede the loss of substantial Indian Ocean commerce, first to the Portuguese and then, in the seventeenth century, to their European competitors, the Dutch and British. In retrospect, these naval defeats represent the beginning of a shift in the power balance between the Ottoman Empire and Europe, which was manifested also in Hungary in the early seventeenth century.

Patronage and poetry

Süleyman's formidable administrative and military achievements would by themselves more than justify his standing in Ottoman and European eyes, but he was also a sophisticated collector and patron of crafts and, above all else, architecture.[12] Like his Timurid predecessors, Shah 'Abbas I Safavi, and Indo-Muslim rulers, he collected Chinese porcelain. Like the Timurids and other Muslim courts, he patronized high-quality book production, including miniature painting, metal working, textiles and ceramics; and like his father Selim and his great predecessor, Mehmet II – and many Safavids and Mughals – he not only patronized poets, but wrote verse himself, compiling a *diwan* of Ottoman and some Persian poems written under the pen-name *Muhibbi*, meaning a lover – both profane and divine. Most of his poems are *ghazals*, modeled on Persian verse.

These poems are unremarkable, utilizing the typical vocabulary of Persian odes that celebrate the bittersweet emotion of unrequited love. However, those that Süleyman addressed to his favorite wife, the European, Christian-born Hürrem Sultan, and to his rebel son Bayezid, are not only a charming, humanistic relief from endless accounts of conquest and autocratic rule, but also demonstrate the many practical uses of a verse form that is often characterized as little more than a literary exercise. One poem to his wife, apart from its passionate but standard vocabulary, is also an exercise in artistic license in which Süleyman claims to possess not only Egypt and Anatolia, but also Khurasan, northeastern Iran, and Badakshan in northern Afghanistan:

> My very own queen, my everything,
>   my beloved, my bright moon;
> My intimate companion, my one and all,
>   sovereign of all beauties, my sultan.
> My life, the gift I own, my be-all,
>   my elixir of Paradise, my Eden,

---

[12] See below, Chapter 7.

My spring, my joy, my glittering day,
    my exquisite one who smiles on and on.
My sheer delight, my revelry, my feast,
    my torch, my sunshine, my sun in heaven;
My orange, my pomegranate,
    the flaming candle that lights up my pavilion.
My plant, my candy, my treasure who gives
    no sorrow but the world's purest pleasure;
Dearest, my turtledove, my all,
    the ruler of my heart's Egyptian dominion.
My Istanbul, my Karaman, and all the
    Anatolian lands that are mine;
My Bedekshan and my Kipchak territories,
    my Baghdad and my Khorasan,
My darling with that lovely hair, brows curved like a
    bow, eyes that ravish, I am ill,
If I die, yours is the guilt. Help I beg you,
    my love from a different religion.
I am at your door to glorify you.
    Singing your praises, I go on and on.
My heart is filled with worry, my eyes with tears.
I am the Lover – this joy is mine.[13]

Like most pre-modern Muslim poets, Süleyman used poetry not only to illustrate his sophisticated literary skills, or to communicate genuine emotion in an artful and culturally acceptable manner, but for a host of other purposes, such as savagely criticizing his son Bayezid, who had lost out to his brother Selim in the complex maneuvering to become Süleyman's favorite and successor. Having received a poem from the defeated Bayezid, in which his son begged for forgiveness – "Dearest one, would you bring on your own Bayezid's destruction, my father?" – Süleyman answered, apparently willing to pardon his son:

Let us say that you have both your hands steeped in blood,
You request our forgiveness and we grant you our pardon
    What can one say?
I should absolve you of crime, my Bayezid, if you stopped
    acting this way:
but at least don't say 'I am without guilt.' Repent my
    dearest one, my son.[14]

---

[13] Talat S. Halman, trans., *Süleyman the Magnificent: Poet* (Istanbul: Dost Yayınları, 1987), 30–1.
[14] Ibid., 76–7.

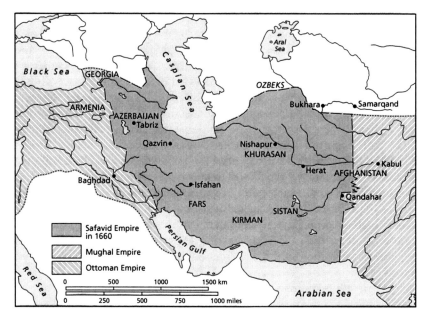

Map 14. The Safavid Empire in 1660

Literary politesse conferred a certain cultured patina on a deadly succession struggle in which no loser could ultimately expect to survive. After Selim defeated him, Bayezid fled in 1560 to take refuge with the Iranian Shah Tahmasp who initially received him warmly. Süleyman and Selim then offered Tahmasp 1,200 ducats and a strategic fortress in exchange for the Ottoman prince. Whether this offer or the subsequent promise of a peace treaty was more persuasive, in 1562 the weak Iranian shah handed Bayezid over to Selim's agent, who immediately murdered him and his four sons. Later the victors killed a fifth infant son, living with his mother in Bursa, leaving the succession clear for Selim.[15]

Safavid Iran

In contrast to the series of dynamic and effective monarchs who ruled the Ottoman and Mughal empires, the Safavid dynasty produced few such individuals and only one following the reign of Shah 'Abbas I. Stasis – "a state where there is neither motion nor development" – seems an appropriate characterization of the political, economic, and military condition

---

[15] Imber, *The Ottoman Empire*, 104–7.

of the Safavids between 1629 and the regime's sudden collapse in 1722. Four Safavid shahs reigned in Iran following the death of 'Abbas, and only one of them, 'Abbas II (r. 1642–66), exhibited impressive military and administrative skills. The other three – Shah Safi (1629–42), Sulaiman (1666–94) and Shah Sultan Husain (1694–1722) – accomplished little of consequence, save some significant architectural and artistic patronage.

The quality of the dynasty during the late seventeenth century may partly be attributed to the same fundamental change in dynastic politics that occurred slightly earlier, after Süleyman's death, in the Ottoman Empire.[16] That is, after 1614 Shah 'Abbas "solved" the problem of impatient, rebellious royal princes by abandoning the earlier practice of appointing young royal sons to provincial governorships under the care of a guardian or tutor, in the Safavid case a Qizilbash chief. Instead princes were confined to the *haram* – which, as in the Ottoman case, did not end the murder of unlucky contenders, but replaced it by the hot-house factional intrigue of these men, their tutors, the *haram* eunuchs, and the princes' different mothers. A "Sultanate of Women" arose in the Safavid realm as a result of these changes, as it did in Istanbul in the late sixteenth century. Shah 'Abbas I himself blinded two of his *haram*-confined sons before his death, thus demonstrating the failure of his own measures to resolve the succession problem. Princes who emerged unscathed from the *haram* to be crowned had no military or administrative experience, and therefore it is not surprising that only one of four seventeenth-century monarchs, 'Abbas II, was an effective ruler, and that may have been partly due to the fact that he was crowned at age ten, without having to spend excessive time in the debilitating environment of the *haram*.[17]

Despite the change in Safavid governance, the history of the dynasty was not one of unrelieved decay, partly because, as in the Ottoman case, several capable ministers assumed effective control of the state at various times. Nonetheless, Iran suffered unmistakable political, military, and economic decline over the course of the seventeenth century.[18] Shah Safi, the first Safavid ruler to have spent his youth in the *haram*, was an alcoholic, a characteristic encouraged by his *haram* upbringing, but hardly a unique trait of its inmates and a common enough characteristic of Mughal rulers, who emulated the drinking habits of their

---

[16] See below, Chapter 8.
[17] Rudi Matthee, *The Pursuit of Pleasure Drugs and Stimulants in Iranian History, 1500–1900* (Princeton University Press, 2005), 25.
[18] See above, Chapter 4.

Turco-Mongol ancestors.[19] Indeed, alcoholism and drug addition so commonly afflicted members of both dynasties that they hardly seem worth mentioning, except for the real effect they often had on governance.

Shah Safi at least was not a sedentary ruler, as were the last two Safavid monarchs; but he possessed little of his predecessor's remarkable personal dynamism, and during his short reign of thirteen years the Safavid army began to deteriorate: without Shah 'Abbas I's leadership, the Ottomans were able to recapture Baghdad and Iraq in 1638, effectively establishing the boundary that still existed in the twentieth century. This represented a serious loss of income as well as territory. A possible contributing factor in the Safavid loss was the massacre, seven years earlier, of most surviving Safavid princes, key administrators, and the governor of Fars province. It was also during Shah Safi's reign that the valuable Safavid state silk monopoly established by Shah 'Abbas I was allowed to lapse, threatening the state's control of the largest single source of badly needed silver currency.

Dying of alcoholism in 1642 at age thirty-one, Safi was succeeded by Shah 'Abbas II, who, before he too died at the young age of thirty-three (and partly also due to alcoholism), established a reputation as an effective and just ruler, although he sanctioned religious persecution of Iran's Jewish community: one sign, evidently, of the increased power of the 'ulama that was also manifested in morality campaigns and the growing hostility to Sufism. These attacks on Sufis intensified during the seventeenth century, although none were as concerted and violent as the Kadizadeli movement in Istanbul. The mentality of the critics in each case was, however, very similar. Some Iranian clerics also invoked the orthodox stereotype of Sufis as disreputable Muslims to smear their ideological or social opponents by identifying them as members of a doctrinally or socially suspect order. Safi's sporadic religious persecution of minorities and Sufis broke with Shah 'Abbas's pragmatic tolerance and heralded the increasing influence of narrow-minded religious orthodoxy that ultimately weakened the regime.

Shah 'Abbas II did succeed in recapturing Qandahar from the Mughals, but otherwise funding and training of the military further declined. His successor, crowned first as Safi II and then a year later as Sulaiman, was another alcoholic product of the *haram* system, and, while he reigned for nearly thirty years, did so almost entirely within the Isfahan's Ali Qapu palace. He presided over a further marked deterioration of the Safavid

---

[19] In fact, a phrase associated with pre-Islamic Iranian rulers, *razm u bazm*, "fighting and feasting," is a helpful reminder of the heavy drinking habits of the Iranian warrior aristocracy.

state. "Drenched in alcohol" during the yearly Nauruz festivals, the Zoroastrian spring celebrations, he nonetheless sanctioned an increasing emphasis on Shi'i orthodoxy. This was accompanied by even more intense denunciations of Sufism and persecutions of Armenians, Hindus, and Zoroastrians, thus further damaging the fragile Safavid economy by attacking members of those non-Muslim mercantile communities.[20] His successor, Shah Sultan Husain, another *haram* product, initially banned alcohol after he was crowned, but this did not reflect his independence as much as his dependence on the *'ulama*, whose influential representative, Muhammad Baqir Majlisi, had become the most powerful figure in the new regime. Yet within a year of his succession the last Safavid Shah repealed his prohibition and began drinking, a change of heart which foreign missionaries attributed to the court eunuchs and the Shah's great-aunt, a Georgian Christian who, like many Georgians then as now, appreciated good wine.[21]

Iran: the intellectual tradition

If the Safavid state evolved from stasis to decline within three-quarters of a century following the death of 'Abbas I, the Shi'i clergy, at least, experienced a golden age of creative intellectual ferment and growing political influence climaxing in Baqir Majlisi's appointment. It is tempting also to ascribe the Iranian intellectual dynamism of this era to Shah 'Abbas I, who is sometimes credited with almost every positive development during the Safavid era; but a reflection on the importance of Iranian intellectuals during the previous 600 years suggests a deeply entrenched intellectual culture that distinguished Iran from its Ottoman and Mughal neighbors. The Italian nobleman Pietro della Valle gained a brief but revealing insight into the intellectual sophistication of even provincial Iranian intellectuals, when he was recuperating from an illness in the southern town of Lar during the first half of 1622. Having lived for the previous eight years in Istanbul and Isfahan, where he learned both Ottoman and Persian, Della Valle observes "that in none of the provinces of Asia that I have been, nor anywhere else, have I ever seen men so learned or so profound as those of Lar," and then identifies a mathematician and astronomer named Mulla Zain al-Din who wanted to visit Europe, as well as a legal scholar, Rukn al-Din, and a writer and philosopher, chemist and astronomer, Qutb al-Din. He also learned

---

[20] Mathee, *The Pursuit of Pleasure*, 56–7.
[21] Ibid., 94. Gene Garthwaite and others have raised pertinent questions about the accuracy of these reports of Safavid alcoholism, particularly in the later years. See, among other sources, Newman, *Safavid Iran*, index entries to "wine" and "alcohol."

about the local persistence of the Nuqtavi sect, and was given information on Hinduism by people in a town connected to India by trade.[22] The presence of learned men in Lar did not reflect an Iranian commitment to broader scientific enquiry during the Safavid period, for Islamic science as a whole, which in medieval times "had a strong Persian element ... was then in decline."[23] These men simply personified an important strain in Perso-Islamic culture that dates back to the early Christian era. Philosophy, metaphysics, theology, and medicine did, however, flourish during the Safavid era, and the dynamism of philosophical and theological schools in Shiraz and Isfahan was the most noticeable and, in the long term, the most important cultural development of the seventeenth century. Coincident and partly related to this was the growth of a politically influential clerical establishment that resulted from the development of an institutionalized, indigenous Twelver Shi'i clergy in Iran during the early seventeenth century and the simultaneous weakness of 'Abbas I's successors.

Shah 'Abbas I established the institutional infrastructure for an indigenous Iranian Shi'i clergy, which had hitherto relied largely on émigrés, but only in 1621 did a native Iranian, Mir Muhammad Baqir-i Damad, become a *Shaikh al-Islam*, although on his mother's side he too was descended from the Karaki family of Lebanese Shi'i scholars.[24] 'Abbas's capital, Isfahan, became the well-funded theological center of a clergy whose intimate court connections helped to persuade many that it was correct to support the political authority of the dynasty for as long as the true twelfth Imam remained in eschatological concealment. The increasing influence and comparable intolerance of many Shi'i *'ulama* was manifested in these men's output of theological tracts, their harassment or persecution of non-Muslims and Sufis, and their growing influence at court. The growth of clerical influence to a degree unimaginable in either the Ottoman or Mughal Empires was manifest by the attitudes of the last Safavid shah, who was nicknamed "Mulla" Husain.

Metaphysics and theology in Safavid Iran

Within the Iranian Shi'i clergy two major groups struggled for prominence. These groups, the Akhbaris and Usulis, differed on fundamental

---

[22] J. D. Gurney, "Pietro della Valle: The Limits of Perception," *Bulletin of the School of Oriental and African Studies* 49, No. 1 (1986), 112.
[23] H. J. J. Winter, "Persian Science in Safavid Times," in Jackson and Lockhart, *The Cambridge History of Iran*, VI, 581.
[24] Devin J. Stewart, "Notes on the Migration of 'Āmili Scholars to Safavid Iran," *Journal of Near Eastern Studies* 55, No. 2 (April 1996), 85.

points of Shi'i theology, and their theological disputes mirrored, to a significant degree, socio-economic and educational distinctions. Akhbaris tended to be clerics from small towns or rural areas and to be less well educated; the most prominent exceptions to this pattern were the members of the Majlisi family who became dominant figures in Isfahan in the mid to late seventeenth century. Akhbaris were often hostile to Sufis or to those Muslims they suspected of mystical piety, although some famous Akhbari clerics in Isfahan were sympathetic to Sufi beliefs and practices. Akhbaris were Shi'i traditionalists or fundamentalists. They mistrusted rationalism and argued that *akhbar*, the reports or traditions of the Shi'i Imams, offered the only true *tafsir* or interpretation of the meaning of the Quran and prophetic *hadith*. Their position was based firmly on the Shi'i assumption that only those descended from the Prophet Muhammad could understand the esoteric meaning of the Quran; they therefore asserted that these *akhbar* represented the final and sacred Shi'i tradition. Many of the most famous Isfahan clerics, such as the father and son of the Majlisi family, Muhammad Taqi al-Majlisi (d. 1659) and Muhammad Baqir al-Majlisi (d. 1699), were moderate Akhbaris; both also wrote numerous tracts on the fundamental tenets of Twelver Shi'ism. Muhammad Baqir al-Majlisi was the dominant cleric in Shah Sultan Husain's time and was appointed by him as the *Shaikh al-Islam*.

In contrast to the Akhbaris, Usulis were concentrated in such cities as Shiraz and Isfahan and were often better educated. They were rationalists, and contended that the *akhbar*s must be interpreted and tested. Clerics had to practice *ijtihad* or interpretation, as the meaning of the texts was not easily understood. The *mujtahid*s, senior *'ulama* who interpreted the texts, therefore occupied a special place in Shi'i society, and wielded far greater power than most *'ulama* in Sunni countries. Moderate Usulis, like moderate Akhbaris, accepted the necessity of cooperating with secular rulers such as the Safavids, but extreme Usulis advocated direct clerical rule, a goal they finally achieved in Iran after the 1979 revolution.

Standing apart from such radical political opinions, a small group of Usulis practiced a sophisticated form of rational philosophy – despite the widespread clerical hostility to such activities, which saw some *'ulama* denounce philosophers as infidels.[25] Several of these rationalists were intimate associates of Shah 'Abbas and probably flourished for that reason. A number of them are still regarded as exceptional scholars, and one man in particular, Sadr al-Din Shirazi, known generally as Mulla Sadra

---

[25] Hamid Dabashi, "Mîr Dâmâd and the Founding of the 'School of Isfahan,'" in Seyyed Hossein Nasr and Oliver Leaman, eds., *History of Islamic Philosophy* (London: Routledge, 2001), 600–1.

(1572–1640), is widely regarded by modern Muslim and Western scholars alike as the most important Muslim philosopher in the last four hundred years.

Mulla Sadra was a member of a group of scholars who are now considered members of the seventeenth-century Isfahan school, perhaps better designated as the Shiraz-Isfahan school of philosophy. They were a very small circle of men, many close friends, dedicated to synthesizing earlier philosophical thinking and integrating it with the accepted truths of Shi'i theology. These men were not also scientists in the mold of their Iranian predecessors, al-Biruni, Ibn Sina, 'Umar Khayyam, or Nasir al-Din Tusi, but they formed the most important philosophical school in all three Muslim empires. They can be regarded as the intellectual heirs of the Iranian philosophical tradition represented by these earlier individuals, especially Ibn Sina and Nasir al-Din Tusi. Some of their distant precursors were contemporaries and students of Tusi. Their most immediate intellectual ancestors were a group of fifteenth-century scholars from Isfahan and nearby Shiraz, who began to unite various aspects of Islamic philosophical and religious thought.

One such was Jalal al-Din Muhammad Dawani (d. 1502–3), a Sunni who had served both the Timurid Abu Sa'id and the Ottoman Bayezid II. Dawani typifies many of the later Usuli philosophers in that he drew on the Greco-Islamic rationalism of Ibn Sina, the ideas of Nasir al-Din Tusi, and the Illuminationist philosophy of the twelfth-century Iranian thinker al-Suhrawardi, whose ideas appealed to Muslim thinkers, especially Sufis, in all three empires.[26] Ultimately he preferred mysticism to philosophy, "because mysticism benefited from divine grace and so was free from doubt and uncertainty and thus nearer to prophethood."[27]

> Like Suhrawardi … Dawani maintained that existence had one reality and no multiplicity. Like Nasir al-Din Tusi (d. 1274), Dawani's cosmology involved the gradual unfolding of intellects, spheres, elements and kingdoms. The active intellect – which he identified with the original essence of the Prophet – bridges the gap between the heaven and the earth.[28]

Unlike Dawani, Mulla Sadra's principal teacher in Isfahan was a committed Shi'i scholar, the octogenarian Mir Muhammad Baqir Damad

---

[26] Hossein Ziai, "Shihâb al-Dîn Suhrawardî: Founder of the Illuminationist School," in Nasr and Leaman, eds., *History of Islamic Philosophy*, 434–64. Al-Suhrawardi's epistemology is the most influential aspect of his thought and in certain respects strongly resembled Sufi mystical doctrines and practices. His ideas strongly influenced "'speculative mysticism' ('irfan-i nazari') in Persia as well as in Persian poetry," 450.

[27] A. J. Newman, "Philosophy in the Safavid Period," *Encyclopaedia of Islam* II, Brill Online.

[28] Ibid.

(1543–1631), whose father was a son-in-law of the major Amili Shi'i of the sixteenth century. Mir Damad, like his Sunni predecessor, brought together the philosophical – the Greek Peripatetic philosophy of Ibn Sina – and the mystical – the Neoplatonic Illuminationist or *ishraqi* ideas – of al-Suhrawardi, with the Gnostic thought of Ibn 'Arabi (d. 1240) and the dialectical theology or *kalam* of earlier Sunni theologians within a framework of Twelver Shi'ism. Regarded – by himself and others – as the "third teacher" after Aristotle and al-Farabi, he nonetheless wrote in such an obscure style that he escaped the censure of most clerical critics.[29] In contrast, his student, Mulla Sadra (d. 1640), wrote clearly enough to antagonize both the *'ulama* and even some Sufis, so much so he had to flee Isfahan for the relative safety of a remote village near the theological center of Qum. In his principal philosophical work *al-Qabasat*, Mir Damad discusses one of the persistent questions of Islamic philosophy, the priority of essence versus the priority of existence and offers an answer – that essence is prior – rooted in both Ibn Sina (or Aristotle) and al-Suhrawardi's Neoplatonic emanation:

Mir Damad proceeds to distinguish between three kinds of "world." First is the "Everlasting World" (*al-'âlam al-sarmâdi*), which is the space for the Divine Presence, His Essence, and Attributes; second is the "atemporal World" (*al-'âlam al-dahri*), which is the space for pure archetypes (*al-mujarradât*); and third is the "Temporal World" (*al-'âlam al-zamânî*), which is the space for daily events, created beings, and generation and corruption.[30]

In terms of the creation, Mir Damad believed that the material world emanated from the Divine presence by the agency of the Light of Lights (*nûr al-anwâr*), which eventually produced the universal intellect, beginning the entire process of creation through a series of emanations.

A well-connected scholar from a wealthy Isfahani family, Mulla Sadra studied Shi'i Islam with the important theologian and legist Baha' al-Din Muhammad al-'Amili (d. 1622) and the rational sciences with Mir Damad. He became an acknowledged "master of the two branches of Shi'i learning – the transmitted and the intellectual – and asserted that

---

[29] Al-Farabi (*c.* 870–950) was one of the most important early Muslim philosophers, who studied Aristotle's works with Christian scholars in Baghdad. For a summary of his career and thought see Deborah L. Black, "Al-Farabi," in Nasr and Leaman, *History of Islamic Philosophy*, 178–97.

[30] Hamid Dabashi, "Mîr Dâmâd and the Founding of the "School of Isfahan," in Nasr and Leaman, *History of Islamic Philosophy*, 611–12. Mir Damad was raised in Mashhad, the Shi'i shrine city in Khurasan, and studied Ibn Sina's works there before arriving in Isfahan via Qazvin and Kashan.

there is harmony between revelation and reason."[31] He knew both Sunni theology, especially the works of al-Ghazali and Fakhr al-Din Razi, and the dialectical theology of Shi'i Islam.[32] In terms of his philosophical training, he was intimately acquainted with Greco-Islamic Peripatetic thought, especially the works of Ibn Sina, which his teacher had earlier studied in Mashhad. He had also read Nasir al-Din Tusi, the formidable scientist, intellectual, and Shi'i theologian, as well as the Illuminationist writings of al-Suhrawardi. He had also studied Sufism, particularly the Gnostic ideas of Ibn 'Arabi, whom he quotes extensively in the last volume of his four-volume magnum opus the *Afsâr*, and had a special love for the Persian Sufi poetry of 'Attar and Rumi.

Mulla Sadra derived his primary assertion from his belief in Ibn 'Arabi's idea of the "unity of being" or *wahdat al-wujud*, which he perceived by intuition. He believed intuition to be the primary form of thought, illustrating his indebtedness to al-Suhrawardi's Illuminationist ideas. Thus he wrote:

In the earlier days I used to be a passionate defender of the thesis that the quiddities are extramentally real while existence is but a mental construct [but] ... all of a sudden my spiritual eyes were opened and I saw with utmost clarity that the truth was just the contrary of what philosophers in general had held. Praise be to God who, by the light of intuition, led me out of the darkness ... As a result [I now hold that] the individual existences of things are primary realities while the quiddities [the real nature of things] are the "permanent archetypes ... that have never smelt even the fragrance of existence." The individual existences are nothing but beams of light radiated by the true light, which is the absolutely self-subsistent Existence. The absolute existence in each of its individualized forms is characterized by a number of essential properties and intelligible qualities. And each of these properties and qualities is what is usually known as quiddity.[33]

Mulla Sadra's quiddities are easily recognizable as Platonic forms, absorbed into Islamic philosophy from Neoplatonism, and for him they have an objective reality superior to the physical world, and exist in a world above and in a sense parallel to the physical world that "seers can experience."[34]

---

[31] Hossein Ziai, "Mullâ Sadrâ: His Life and Works," in Nasr and Leaman, *History of Islamic Philosophy*, 637; Seyyid Hossein Nasr, "Mulla Sadra, His Teachings," ibid., 656.

[32] Majid Fakhry briefly discusses Razi's thought, which was infused with Platonism and Neoplatonism, ibid., 97–106.

[33] Dabashi, "Mîr Dâmâd and the Founding of the School of Isfahan," 615–16.

[34] Seyyid Hossein Nasr, "Mullâ Sadrâ: His Teachings," in Nasr and Leaman, *History of Islamic Philosophy*, 652.

Persian thought in Mughal India

Thinkers who were closely connected with the theological and philosophical scholars in Safavid Iran represent one important strand of Mughal thought, although in India they lacked the intensity and philosophical sophistication of the Shiraz and Isfahan schools. Yet Iranian philosophy and Islamic metaphysics had a discernible and important influence in Mughal India, in contrast with the Ottoman Empire, where the state-enforced dominance of Hanafi Sunni orthodoxy apparently discouraged creative logical and metaphysical speculation. Safavid scholars not only stimulated the growth of Muslim philosophical thinking in India, which had been nearly dormant prior to the late sixteenth century, but also had a long-term influence on Indo-Muslim theology.[35]

Mir Fath Allah Shirazi (d. 1590) was one individual who exemplified the Safavid philosophical connection. He had studied with important scholars in his native Shiraz before, like so many poets, migrating to India, first to the Shi'i sultanate of Bijapur and later in 1583 to Akbar's court. Shirazi was influential in Mughal India, because Akbar appointed him to reform the educational curriculum, which he used to introduce the works of such important Iranian scholars as Sayyid al-Sharif al-Jurjani (d. 1413) and 'Allamah Jalal al-Din Dawani, the reviver of Illuminationist thought, who had himself studied with Jurjani's students in Shiraz. Shirazi is also significant because his students began an intellectual lineage in India, one of whose members helped establish the important late seventeenth-century Lucknow *madrasa* known as the Firingi Mahal.[36]

A second influential Indian-born scholar was Mulla Mahmud Jaunpuri Faruqi (d. 1652). Born in 1603, Mulla Mahmud traveled to Isfahan, where he attended the lectures of Mulla Sadra's teacher, Mir Damad. Mulla Faruqi, who later joined the Qadiriyya Sufi order, wrote a series of works on theology, logic, metaphysics, and speculative philosophy, composing, among other treatises, *Shams al-bazigah*, a work on traditional Islamic philosophy that long continued to be studied in Indian *madrasa*s, along with Mulla Sadra's *Shar-i hidayat al-hikmat*.

A third important thinker was Mirza Muhammad Zahid Harawi, who is particularly important for his impact on later Indian Islam, as he was the teacher of the father of Shah Waliullah, the single most important eighteenth-century north Indian Muslim intellectual. He studied in Afghanistan and Central Asia before joining Aurangzib's court, first as a

---

[35] Francis Robinson emphasizes these cross-border intellectual connections in his essay "Ottomans–Safavids–Mughals: Shared Knowledge and Connective Systems."

[36] Ibid., 13. Robinson discusses the Lucknow *madrasa* in his book *The 'Ulama of the Firingi Mahal and Islamic Culture in South Asia* (London: Hurst & Co., 2001).

mutahsib (an inspector) and later as governor of Kabul. He was a scholar of Sunni theology, Peripatetic philosophy, and Illuminationist thought, and his intellectual interests can partly be understood through a study of the glossaries he prepared on some of the works of Jurjani, Dawani, and Nasir al-Din Tusi.[37]

A fourth significant intellectual and philosopher and religious scholar was Mir Abu'l Qasim b. Mirza Husaini Astarabadi, known as Mir Findariski (d. 1640–1), a man respected both in Isfahan, where he was born, and in India, where he spent time in the 1620s and 1630s. In Isfahan Mir Findiriski taught the works of Ibn Sina – and is known for having criticized Plato using Aristotelian physics – but he was also a Sufi, a poet and, as a result of his Indian sojourns, an important scholar of Hinduism, as is exemplified in his commentary on the Persian translation of the *Yoga Vasistha*.[38]

Religious innovations in Mughal India

Mughal India also witnessed significant indigenous religious evolution in the seventeenth century, as Akbar's religious experiments ended and the latitudinarian attitudes of his son Jahangir (r. 1605–27) gave way to the imperial orthodoxy of Shah Jahan (1628–58) and the pious asceticism of the last great emperor, Aurangzib (r. 1658–1707). Yet the religious situation in Agra and Delhi differed from that in both Safavid Iran and also the Ottoman Empire. Unlike in Iran, members of the *'ulama* in India never denied the legitimacy of the dynasty or attained political power, and unlike in Iran and the Ottoman Empire, some Indian Muslims, most notably Shah Jahan's son Dara Shukuh, searched for religious truth beyond the boundaries of the *shari'a* and even of Sufi thought, as far as Hindu mysticism.

Dara Shukuh's own sophisticated knowledge of Islamic thought and Hindu philosophy, and sensitive response to the unique circumstances of Muslim rule in a predominantly non-Muslim environment, led him to translate the *Upanishads* into Persian and to write *Majma' al-bahrain*, "The Confluence of the Two Oceans," a work stressing the essential identity of Islamic and Hindu metaphysics.[39] The later Latin translation

---

[37] This material is largely taken from Hafiz A. Ghaffar Khan's survey of Indian philosophical thought, "India," in Nasr and Leaman, *History of Islamic Philosophy*, 1051–75.

[38] Marshall, *Mughals in India*, p. 88, No. 112 and Seyyed Hossein Nasr, "Findiriski, Mir Abu'l Kâsim b. Mirza Husaynî Astarâbâdî," *Encyclopaedia of Islam* II, Brill Online.

[39] It is difficult and probably impossible to reconstruct the evolution of Dara Shukuh's thought, which is often attributed to Sufi influences alone. Yet nearly all Mughals were Sufi *murids* or disciples of one order or another and apart from Akbar's initial example, none except Dara Shukuh is known to have publicly asserted the essential identity of Islam and Hinduism.

of this Persian translation of the *Upanishads* strongly influenced German idealists and American Transcendentalists. Yet Dara Shukuh, who like many Mughals preferred Sufism over public orthodoxy, was an ephemeral figure, a fascinating but anomalous personality whose ideas did not exert a discernible influence among Hindus or Muslims then or later. He is principally important in later Indian history as a symbol of Hindu–Muslim amity, which many Indians felt was lost when Dara Shukuh was defeated and then executed by his brother Aurangzib, the victor in the war of succession after the illness of Shah Jahan.

Other Indians shared Dara Shukuh's syncretic instincts, both before and during the Mughal era. Such a man was Dara Shukuh's contemporary, Shaikh 'Abd al-Rahman Chishti (d. *c.* 1683), whose *Risala-yi Taswiya* or *Treatise on Equality* stressed the similarity between Islamic monotheism and the pantheism of the *Upanishads*.[40] In the case of the Sikhs the search for a *via media* between Muslims and Hindus nourished a new religion, the single most significant indigenous spiritual innovation that occurred in India during this period. Founded by a Punjabi later known as Guru Nanak (1469–1539), Sikhism developed as a reaction to formal rigidities or orthodoxies in both Brahmanical Hinduism and Islam, although its final goal was the traditional Hindu and Buddhist desire to escape from the cycle of rebirth. In the Sikh scripture, the *Adi Granth*, proud Brahmans are denounced, as are ascetics whose bodies are "smeared with renunciant ashes, yet darkness prevails within."[41] Muslims are told to pursue an individual faith instead of traditional worship and observance of the *shari'a*, and to reject even reliance on a Sufi *pir* and recitation of the attributes of God on prayer beads:

Make mercy your mosque and devotion your prayer mat, righteousness your Qur'an; Meekness your circumcising, goodness your fasting ... Make good works your Ka'bah, take truth as your *pir*, compassion your creed and your prayer. Let service to God be the beads which you tell and God will exalt you to Glory.[42]

Guru Nanak denied he was either a Hindu or a Muslim: he was a *sikh*, a student or disciple. He preached a strict monotheism, and in social terms, supported communal dining, an implicit critique of the pollution restrictions of upper-caste Hindus.

Sikhism had already begun to attract followers when Babur entered the country. Many of Nanak's original followers came from ritually

---

[40] Cited in Muzaffar Alam, *The Languages of Political Islam, India 1200–1800* (Chicago: University of Chicago Press, 2004), 96–7.
[41] W. H. McLeod, ed. and trans., *Textual Sources for the Study of Sikhism* (Chicago: University of Chicago Press, 1984), 49.
[42] Ibid., 43.

lower-level commercial and agricultural Hindu castes, Khatris and Jats. The movement began and has always been closely associated with the Punjab; the *Adi Granth* is written in a form of Punjabi. It attracted Akbar's sympathetic attention: he gave Guru Nanak's successor the city of Amritsar as a religious site and visited the second Guru, or teacher, there in 1598. Subsequently, however, the growth of the Sikh community as a socially autonomous entity, and the participation of the third Sikh Guru, Arjun, in Mughal succession politics, provoked Akbar's successor, Jahangir (r. 1605–27) to execute Arjun, which, in turn, stimulated the early militarization of the Sikh community. Already in the early seventeenth century the "socio-religious community of Guru Nanak's followers had become 'a state within a state.'"[43]

India's dynastic golden age

When Akbar's son Jahangir ascended the Mughal throne in 1605 he began a half-century in the dynasty's history during which he and his successor, Shah Jahan, expressed in their writing, actions, and patronage a seemingly untroubled sense of imperial power, wealth, and grandeur. Both of them appreciated that their Timurid Empire constituted a splendid achievement. Shah Jahan unmistakably regarded his reign as a golden age. He presented himself to the world as the second Temür and commissioned architecture to demonstrate a historical moment that was also trumpeted in court histories and miniature painting. Jahangir's and Shah Jahan's reigns bear a resemblance to the Ottoman Empire in the era between Mehmet II's death and that of Süleyman the Magnificent in the sense that they, like the sixteenth-century Ottoman sultans, inherited a securely established, dynamic, aggressive empire that was far more wealthy and powerful than any state on its periphery; and they continued to expand their territory, even while presiding over a florescence of elite or court culture.

Nur al-Din Jahangir Padishah Ghazi, as he titled himself after his coronation, was enthroned after suppressing a coup by his oldest son, Prince Khusrau. Years earlier Jahangir himself had rebelled against his father and connived at the assassination of his father's oldest confidant and court historian, Abu'l Fazl 'Allami. Jahangir, like his two successors, Shah Jahan and Aurangzib, had been given independent commands and allowed, in the Mughal tradition, to develop a separate household and nurse imperial ambitions well before his illustrious father's death. Mughal rulers never developed a *haram* system for male children, such as evolved in Istanbul

---

[43] J. S. Grewal, *The Sikhs of the Punjab* (New Delhi: Cambridge University Press, repr. 2005), 42.

after Süleyman or was instituted by Shah 'Abbas in Iran, although Shah Jahan and Aurangzib both practiced fratricide after they came to power.

In personal terms Jahangir was a study in contrasts and psychological complexity, traits that he displays in his revealing autobiography. He probably modeled this work on the memoir of his ancestor, Zahir al-Din Muhammad Babur; he mentions reading Babur's Turki text once while visiting Kabul. Thus, while styling himself, as his father had done after defeating Rajputs in 1527, "Padishah Ghazi," Jahangir never commanded armies in the field during his reign, although "the empire continued to be a war state attuned to aggressive conquest and territorial expansion."[44] Jahangir was also known for impetuous, gratuitous cruelty; yet he carefully cultivated, and in his autobiography advertised, his idealized role as a Just Sultan, perpetually and emotionally concerned for the welfare of his subjects. At the same time he displayed the vulnerable personality of a man who revered his father, but was unable to emulate him. He was also a ruler who for a period, virtually ceded control of the empire to his beloved Iranian wife and her uncle after he himself had descended into alcoholism and drug addiction.

In his autobiography, Jahangir humanizes himself in a way that was, apart from his own ancestor's work, unique among rulers in the Ottoman, Safavid, and Mughal empires. Near the beginning of this naturally self-serving work, he also provides the single most explicit statement of imperial principles made by rulers of any of these dynasties, and in so doing, implicitly testifies to the prosperity and security of the empire in its core provinces. After first noting that he began his rule by ordering a Chain of Justice hung from the walls of the Agra fort for any petitioner to pull, he continues by saying: "I also gave twelve orders to be observed as rules of conduct (Dastur-i-'amal) in all my dominions."[45] The idea for this Dastûr may come from his father's issue of a similarly titled document, but one more concerned with general, ethical norms than Jahangir's proclamation, which is both more specific and, typical for Jahangir, more personal. Whether they were actually enforced or not, these rules at least reflect imperial interests or biases.[46]

Five of the twelve are directly or indirectly concerned with the fundamental imperial goals of stimulating commerce and insuring economic and

[44] Richards, The Mughal Empire, 105.
[45] Tûzuk-i-Jahângîrî, I, 7.
[46] See above, Chapter 3. The difference in these documents may reflect the contrasting personality and intellects of the two men, with Akbar being far more reflective than his son.

social stability. These rules outlawed unusual local tolls, forbade officials to open merchants' bales, instructed locally resident imperial officers[47] to build *caravansarais*, *masjids*, and wells to stimulate trade and settlement, guaranteed that property of both Muslims and non-Muslims would not be confiscated on their deaths but be secured for their heirs, and forbade the seizure of anyone's house. A related regulation stipulates that the officers should not seize peasant lands. A second group of rules deals with politics. One shows Jahangir trying to secure the loyalty of the military and religious classes by confirming his father's appointments, increasing their salaries by anywhere from 20 to 400 percent, increasing the allowance of the *haram* ladies by anywhere from 20 to 100 percent, and confirming the charitable property holdings of "the army of prayer." Another seemingly aimed to prevent officers who held lands as military fiefs from becoming local potentates by outlawing marriages between them and members of the local population without royal permission.

A third category included three rules that reflect personal aspects of Jahangir's reign. One outlaws the manufacture of any intoxicating drinks or drugs, although, as he observes, "I myself drink wine, and from the age of 18 years up till now, when I am 38, have persisted in it."[48] A second outlawed punishment by cutting off nose or ears – with no apparent sense of the inconsistency between this order and Jahangir's frequent acts of cruelty – and a third "in accordance with the regulations of my revered father," outlaws the killing of animals for food for two days each week and for a certain number of days after the emperor's birthday each year.[49] Finally, one rule is consistent with the same Islamic charitable impulse seen in all these empires, for it urges local officials to establish hospitals in large cities, using imperial revenues.

The reigns of Jahangir and his son, Shah Jahan, constitute a distinct period of Mughal rule, an era of almost unchallenged military supremacy and prosperity founded on Akbar's monumental achievements: his military victories, effective administrative measures, and sensitive cultural policies. Neither man substantially altered the structure of Akbar's empire, although both kept imperial armies in nearly constant motion suppressing internal revolts or expanding frontiers, while they conscientiously administered the state.[50] Jahangir even proudly illustrates his own responsible dedication to personally engaged rule by describing how he

---

[47] These officers were the men who held imperial appointments or *mansabs*; in their local landholding capacity they were known as *jagirdars*. See above, Chapter 3.

[48] *Tûzuk-i Jahângîrî*, I, 8.   [49] Ibid., I, 7–10.

[50] For a summary of military campaigns during these two reigns see Richards, *The Mughal Empire*, Chapters 5–6.

once dispensed justice even while suffering from a hangover. His auto-biography and Shah Jahan's histories record their ceaseless preoccupation with the minutiae of campaigns and imperial administration. Yet neither possessed the seemingly tireless military energies of Akbar or of the Ottoman emperors Mehmet II or Süleyman, although Shah Jahan was more ambitious than his father. They little resembled their relentless, ferocious ancestor Temür, and indeed treated their own nobility mildly, when compared with either Temür or Ottoman and Safavid rulers. Shah Jahan, who is unfortunately known opaquely only through the panegyric histories of his reign, is favorably described by one royal historian, Lahuri, who says that "in matters of punishment, His majesty does not regard the nobles as different from ordinary human beings. If per chance mention is made in his presence of the cruelty of the Emperors of Constantinople, Iran and Uzbeks, and of their ferocity in awarding punishment, his maj-esty gets so perturbed that signs of sadness are apparent from his illus-trious forehead."[51]

As emperors neither Jahangir nor Shah Jahan personally led troops into battle, even though Shah Jahan had regularly and successfully done so prior to his accession. Instead they relied on their imperial appointees, their *mansabdar*s – Timurid princes, Rajput chiefs, or Muslim officers. Both were active outside their palaces. They regularly traveled to major cities, including Kabul where they visited Babur's simple gravesite, ordered additions to the complex, and meditated on their ancestor's life. Jahangir lived an exceptionally peripatetic life, once traveling around his dominions for five years before returning to Agra, then still the capital. These trips served to project imperial power and gather intelligence, as well as to provide the imperial family with hunting opportunities and aesthetic experiences in such delightful, well-watered places as Mandu in the Narbada River valley or Kashmir –"that country," in the words of another of Shah Jahan's historians,"resembling paradise."[52]

Aesthetic sophistication, the signature trait of the Mughal golden age, distinguished this empire from Ottoman centralization, military innova-tion, and conquest, and the theological and philosophical ferment of Safavid Iran. Jahangir may have wished to be recognized as an archetypical "Just Sultan," but primarily he was an aesthete. Especially in the early part of his reign, when he was generally sober and not

---

[51] Quoted by M. Athar Ali, "Towards an Interpretation of the Mughal Empire," in M. Athar Ali, *Mughal India* (New Delhi: Oxford University Press, 2006), 139–40. Highly placed Ottoman victims are too numerous to count.

[52] W. E. Begley and Z. A. Desai, eds., *The Shah Jahan Nama of 'Inayat Khan* (New Delhi: Oxford University Press, 1990), 124.

incapacitated by opium, Jahangir continued the Timurid tradition of garden creation by constructing the Shalimar Bagh and other gardens in the vale of Kashmir. Exquisite mountainside creations of symmetrical fountains connected by watercourses descending to Lake Dal and flanked by shade trees, and planted with flowers and aromatic herbs, the gardens have lived on in really bad but somehow endearing twentieth-century English verse which even makes some of Sultan Süleyman's overheated *ghazals* shine by comparison. Thus the opening verse of the"Kashmiri Song" by Adela Florence Nicolson:

> Pale hands I loved beside the Shalimar,
> Where are you now, Who lies beneath your spell?
> Whom do you lead on Rapture's roadway, far,
> Before you agonise them in farewell?[53]

The Shalimar gardens represent the climactic moment of Mughal garden design. Gardens, especially the well known quadrilateral *chahar baghs*, had been one of the single most attractive aspects of fifteenth-century Timurid culture, and they were still the focal point of Timurid political and social life, including the poetic *majlises* and drinking sessions of Babur's time.

Jahangir also became a demanding connoisseur of miniature painting, presiding over an expansion of Akbar's atelier and stimulating stylistic innovations during a time in which this art became even more naturalistic. His interest in fine design extended to coinage, and at his direction artisans produced finely minted coins with elegant astrological designs. Jahangir did not extend his aesthetic sensibilities to architecture; Akbar's tomb is the least attractive Mughal mausoleum. His influential wife, Nur Jahan, commissioned a far more appealing building, an exquisite white marble tomb set in a riverfront *chahar bagh* for her father, Itimad al-Daulah, the chief minister, who died in 1622.[54]

Shah Jahan, who seized the throne after a typical bloody Mughal succession struggle in 1628, followed by the murder of close Timurid relatives, was an emperor who took his title, King of the World, seriously. He revived the title of the Sahib-i Qiran-i Sani or "Second Temür," which Jahangir had also claimed but never justified, as well as proclaiming himself Padishah Ghazi; and, like the Ottoman sultan, he portrayed himself as a latter-day personification of the biblical Solomon, in his phrase, the *Sulaiman makani*, "He who occupied Solomon's throne."[55]

---

[53] Laurence Hope (Adela Florence Nicolson), *The Garden of Kama and Other Love Lyrics from India*, 3rd edn. (London, William Heinemann, 1927).
[54] See Koch, *Mughal Architecture*, 70–90, for buildings of Jahangir's reign.
[55] 'Inayat Khan usefully explains Mughal titles: Begley and Desai, eds., *Shah Jahan Nama*, 3–4.

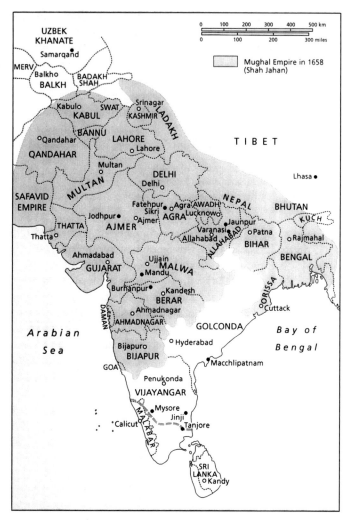

Map 15. The Mughal Empire in 1658

These titles ennobled a man who throughout his entire reign acted as one who saw himself as the personification of the Mughal golden age. His individuality is obscured behind the formal magnificence of what became an increasingly imperious and explicitly Sunni Muslim reign, thus repeating, to a limited degree, the splendor and orthodoxy of the Ottoman Süleyman a century earlier.

The court histories and foreign reports of his rule are consistent in their portrait of a supremely confident man who showed no traces of the conflicted, self-conscious personality of his father. Shah Jahan inherited, after all, an extensive empire whose wealth and population rivaled those of Ming China prior to the Manchu conquest, and he reinvigorated the state both financially and militarily. After his succession he both restored imperial finances that Jahangir had drained, by ordering a greater collection for the central treasury, and rejuvenated Mughal aggressive instincts. By the end of his reign the revenue collections were twice Akbar's totals, and this paid for the campaigns Shah Jahan dispatched to all of the empire's frontiers, cowing its border states, even when his armies did not actually occupy new territory.

Shah Jahan's most notable success was in the Deccan, where he had commanded imperial armies as a prince. His armies completed the conquest of the sultanate of Ahmednagar and coerced Bijapur and Golconda into accepting Mughal suzerainty. By 1657 Mughal armies under the command of Prince Aurangzib were poised to conquer both Deccan sultanates when Shah Jahan fell ill. Yet, apart from the relatively prosperous Deccan, many of Shah Jahan's campaigns were directed against territories of marginal strategic and economic significance. This was particularly true of his 1634 assault on Baltistan or Little Tibet in the mountains north of Kashmir. His ability to sustain these expeditions demonstrates the effectiveness of Mughal revenue extraction from fertile central Mughal lands: the Punjab, the Ganges-Jumna Duab, Gujerat, the Gangetic Valley, and Bengal.

One campaign above all others fits this category of marginal benefits and demonstrates the intensity of Shah Jahan's grandiose self-image as the Second Temür: his attempt between 1645 and 1647 to recover the Timurid homelands in Mawarannahr from the Uzbeks. While a large imperial army initially commanded by Prince Murad occupied the northern Afghan city of Balkh in 1646, he, and after him his brother Aurangzib, found it difficult to supply a large force in the bleak northern Afghan environment and impossible to maneuver a large, cumbersome army effectively against the highly mobile and elusive Uzbeks. Mughal armies never crossed the Amu Darya into Mawarannahr, where they sought to occupy Temür's capital, Samarqand, and after the imperial army retreated back to Kabul (with thousands of men dying in snow-bound passes during the retreat), Samarqand reverted to being an object of revanchist nostalgia in the Mughal imagination. This campaign, and Shah Jahan's failure to retake the south-central Afghan city of Qandahar from the Safavids, also illustrate the outer geographic limits of Mughal power.

Despite the expense of constant military campaigns, the increased Mughal budget was also sufficient to pay for the building projects that constitute the most enduring legacy of Shah Jahan's reign. In the typically baroque Persian of one of his historians, 'Abd al-Hamid Lahuri, the emperor directly oversees the construction of buildings that would demonstrate the splendor of his reign as well as his own aesthetic sophistication, as indeed they did:

The royal mind, which is illustrious like the sun, pays meticulous attention to the planning and construction of these lofty and imposing buildings, which, in accordance with the saying "*Verily our relics tell of us*," speak with mute eloquence of His Majesty's God-given aspiration and sublime fortune – and for ages to come will serve as memorials to his abiding love of constructiveness, ornamentation and beauty.[56]

Among these were his own new peacock throne embedded with precious stones, a ten-million-rupee project completed over seven years, from which Shah Jahan first held court in Agra fort in 1635. Its loss to the marauding Iranian or Qizilbash Iranian invader Nadir Shah in 1739 symbolized the effective end of the Mughal Empire as an empire. In 1632 Shah Jahan had begun the white marble tomb of his favorite wife, Nur Jahan's niece Arjuman Banu Begam, known to posterity as Mumtaz Mahal, the "Ornament of the Palace." Constructed on a high platform at the edge of the Jumna river, it is set in a typical Timurid *chahar bagh*, a four-part garden bisected with waterways, with a mosque and a rest house constructed of red sandstone with marble inlays and domes situated on either side of the mausoleum behind the tomb. Even though the Taj Mahal was constructed in the capital, Agra, in 1639 Shah Jahan began the construction of an entirely new capital city at Delhi.

Delhi was doubly sanctified, as the earliest site of both Indo-Muslim power and of important Sufi tombs, such as that of the Chishti, Nizam al-Din Awliya. Completed in 1648, the new imperial city with its seventy-five-foot high walls two miles in circumference housed the palace, living quarters, *haram*, and mansions of the imperial family and the nobility. Later supplemented by Shah Jahan's daughter Jahanara, who built a commercial complex of shops and *caravansarais* known still as Chandni Chawk, and private imperial gardens, Shahjahanabad, the *abad* or city of Shah Jahan, was also the center of a typical Islamic urban complex, a Mughal *kulliye* completed in 1656, which included the Jama' Masjid, then the largest mosque in India, an open-air building holding at least 2,000

---

[56] Quoted in Begley and Desai, eds., *Shah Jahan Nama*, xxxvii.

worshipers, a *madrasa*, and a hospital.[57] As late as 1836, after a century of invasions, plundering, and imperial neglect, an English visitor still described the city in lyrical terms:

The wide streets, ample bazaars, the shops with every kind of elegant wares, the prodigious elephants used for all purposes, the numerous native carriages drawn by noble oxen, the children bedizened with finery, the vast elevation of the mosque, fountains and caravansarais for travelers, the canals full of running water in the middle.[58]

Shah Jahan fell seriously ill in 1657, an event that triggered another typical but unusually destructive and bloody war of succession among his four mature sons that lasted for nearly two years. It culminated in 1659 with the victory of Aurangzib, the death of one brother, and the judicial murder of two others, including Shah Jahan's chosen successor, the Sufi and scholar of Hinduism Dara Shukuh. Shah Jahan himself, who had recovered his health even as his sons' armies began moving on Agra, was imprisoned by Aurangzib in Agra fort, in rooms that looked out on the Taj Mahal down river. He lived on for a further eight years, accompanied by his daughter Jahanara Begum, meanwhile exchanging angry letters with his son. Despite the death of princes and their sons and the pathos of Shah Jahan's last years, Aurangzib's success promised a continuation of Mughal military success and imperial grandeur. However destructive, the Mughal war of succession once again produced the most capable general as the new emperor, and Aurangzib proved himself to be a tireless campaigner, personally commanding armies right up to the moment of his death in 1707.

---

[57] An interesting study with exceptionally useful maps is Ehlers and Krafft, *Shâhjahânâbâd/ Old Delhi Tradition and Colonial Change.*
[58] Ibid., quoting Bishop Wilson in Society for the Propagation of the Gospel, Historical Sketches, Missionary series, No. 1, "Delhi" (London 1891), p. 4.

7   Imperial culture in the golden age

Introduction

Süleyman the Magnificent and Shah Jahan both thought of themselves as epochal figures, each in his own mind a Solomon, each in his own mind a unique dynastic individual: Süleyman the Padishah-i Islam, the "Monarch of Islam"; Shah Jahan, the Sahib-i Qiran-i Sani, the "Second Lord of the Auspicious Conjunction," the Second Temür. Each man constructed monumental buildings to glorify and legitimize his reign. In the Ottoman Empire Süleyman employed the architect Sinan to erect magnificent imperial *masjids* in Istanbul and Edirne, proclaiming both Süleyman's majesty and his Sunni orthodoxy, while in India Shah Jahan closely supervised costly building projects ranging from the marble enclosure for Babur's Kabul tomb to the construction of a new royal city in Delhi, all of these overshadowed by the Taj Mahal. In Iran after Shah 'Abbas I no Persian Solomon emulated Süleyman or Shah Jahan – or even claimed to be the agent or precursor of the Twelfth Imam. The most important building of the impoverished, politically quiescent late Safavid era was, appropriately enough, Shah Sultan Husain's new *masjid* and *madrasa* complex in Isfahan, a modest place of quiet beauty built near Shah 'Abbas's great *Maidan*. Poetry and painting continued to evolve in Süleyman's and Shah Jahan's empires, as they did in Iran, but it is the seventeenth-century Iranian poet Sa'ib whose work constitutes what is probably the most important literary achievement of this era. He produced a voluminous collection of verse that represents what many critics now believe to be the mature culmination of the influential *sabk-i* Hindi literary style.

Architecture

The Ottomans: Sinan and the imperial architectural norm

The great buildings of the Ottoman golden age are the imperial *masjids*, recognizably Ottoman-style buildings that retain the domed square

208

structural core first seen in the simple 1333 Iznik mosque, a feature which has been called "the spinal cord running through the body of Ottoman architecture."[1] As in early Ottoman history, mosques continued to represent the major imperial buildings, unlike the situation in India, where mosques were less significant than mausoleums and monumental tombs. Sinan (*c.* 1490/91–1588) was the single most important architect in the sixteenth-century Ottoman world and, due to his longevity, stature, and autobiographical writings, he is the most recognized architect in the pre-industrial Islamic world. An Anatolian Christian convert to Islam as one of the *devshirme* draftees, he was, like so many other young men, initially trained as a Janissary. His most important buildings, the Süleymaniye mosque in Istanbul and the Selimiye mosque in the former Ottoman European capital, Edirne, are but two of more than one hundred structures he designed during his tenure as the Master of Works for Süleyman (1520–66), and the plans generated in his office, a specialized government department, were distributed throughout the empire.[2]

Sinan designed triumphant buildings, triumphant in both the architectural and political sense. Architecturally they succeeded not because he broke with the Ottoman past, but because he elaborated earlier features in such a creative way. The exteriors of his mosques, which have been "regarded as a triumphal reversal of the standard Islamic preference of mosque architecture for stressing the interior," are unusually significant because of how they dominate the city's skyline.[3] Externally they are distinguished most of all by two features: their domes and their minarets. The undecorated domes include the great central dome symmetrically surrounded by semi-domes and smaller domes placed in descending elevations, producing from a distance a cascade of massive masonry. Sinan's minarets, four in the case of the Süleymaniye, are exceptionally tall, pencil-thin renditions of earlier designs. In 1614 the Italian traveler Pietro della Valle praised the vision of Istanbul's mosques, ranged along the height of the city, as the most impressive buildings in an otherwise squalid urban landscape. Then as now they dominated Istanbul's skyline, an elevated spectacle of stunning domes and minarets:

What are remarkable are the mosques, and among them four or five in particular, put up by the emperors of Turkey. They are all built high up on the hills so that on both sides they can be seen from the sea, and arranged in line, each one so distant

---

[1] Hillenbrand, *Islamic Art and Architecture*, 257.
[2] J. M. Rogers introduces the architect in *Sinan* (London and New Delhi: I. B. Tauris and Oxford University Press, 2006), but for a substantial, beautifully illustrated study of the cultural history of Sinan's architecture see Necipoğlu, *The Age of Sinan.*
[3] Ibid., 21.

Fig. 9. Süleymaniye Masjid, Ablution Terrace, Istanbul, constructed between 1551 and 1558, designed by Sinan.

from the next that they are spread more or less over the whole length of the city. They are well built in stone. Architecturally they are little different from each other, each one being in the form of a temple, both squared and rounded, like the design of St. Peter's in Rome by Michelangelo; and I believe the model they used was that of St. Sophia.[4]

---

[4] Della Valle, *The Pilgrim*, 8.

Inside the formidable, unmistakably imperial exteriors Sinan designed vast open spaces with warmer interiors than many earlier buildings. His structures were enlivened by colorful tiles with floral designs, tiles now produced at Iznik rather than in Iran. Sinan's tiles, however, occupied a subordinate place compared to their profusion in earlier Timurid buildings. In Sinan's mosques calligraphy took pride of place, and instead of the mixture of Quranic and Persian verse inscriptions common earlier, his contained almost exclusively Quranic passages, religious instruction reinforcing Süleyman's self-image as the *Padishah-i Islam*.[5] The calligraphy intentionally used a monumental script that was legible for literate worshipers, who may have constituted the majority of the usually upper-class males who participated in the Friday prayers at the imperial mosques. Added later perhaps, and a feature that also distinguishes Ottoman from Safavid and Mughal *masjids*, are the enormous roundels hung on the walls of the interior, celebrating Sunni Islam with the names of the Prophet Muhammad and the first four, "rightly guided" caliphs, calligraphic shorthand for Sunni Islam.[6]

Apart from their visual effect, these buildings functioned as statements of Ottoman grandeur in relation to the Byzantine past, and as emblems of Sunni Muslim orthodoxy in service of the Ottoman dynasty. As Ibn Khaldun observed in the fourteenth century, architecture manifested a dynasty's power, and Muslim architects, like earlier non-Muslim builders, consciously sought to surpass the achievements of previous rulers. In the case of Istanbul, the Aya Sofia set a standard of monumental magnificence that Sinan explicitly strove to overshadow, and he claimed, in his autobiographical essays, that he had succeeded:

It is clear and obvious to the engineers of the age and to the overseers of auspicious monuments that buildings constructed in the style/mode of the Hagia Sophia (*Ayasofya tarzında*) did not carry refinement ... until this servant of yours completed the honorable mosque of Şehzade Sultan Mehmed – may God Enlighten His Tomb – which served as a model for the honorable complex of Sultan Suleyman Han – May His Grave Be Pure.[7]

The Süleymaniye was the "new temple of Solomon commissioned by the second Solomon," and Süleyman's octagonal tomb, which stands immediately before the entrance to the mosque, echoed the octagonal design of

---

[5] Necipoğlu, *The Age of Sinan*, 103–8.
[6] Many if not all of these roundels were evidently added to the interior at a later date.
[7] Quoted by Gülrü Necipoğlu in "Challenging the Past: Sinan and the Competitive Discourse of Early Modern Islamic Architecture," *Muqarnas* 10 (1993), 172.

Dome of the Rock, restored by Süleyman, situated on what Muslims believed to be the foundations of Solomon's temple.[8]

In explaining his architectural achievements Sinan ritually cites God's help and the "auspicious sovereignty and lofty aspiration of the country-conquering Ottoman family," but he does not dwell at length on the religious significance of the Süleymaniye complex, which comprised a typical *kulliye* ensemble of buildings.[9] Apart from the mosque itself the complex included a hospital, public kitchen, hospice, medical school, *hammam*, fountain, four *madrasas*, a Quran school, a special school for *hadith* studies, latrines, and eventually the octagonal tombs of Süleyman, his wife Hürrem Sultan, and, tucked away in an inconspicuous corner, Sinan's own simple tomb. Noticeable by their absence were the Sufi hostels that were a prominent feature of pre-conquest Ottoman religious architecture.[10] In this *kulliye* complex, Süleyman's institutional commitment to Sunni Islam is expressed in the special *hadith* institution and four adjacent *madrasas*, each devoted to one of the four orthodox Sunni legal schools.

The specifically imperial function of these *madrasas* is stated clearly in the founding *waqf* endowment deed, where they are described as institutions designed "to elevate matters of religion and religious sciences in order to strengthen the mechanisms of worldly sovereignty and to reach happiness in the afterworld."[11] *Waqf* income from surrounding bazaars supported religious teachers and students and mosque functionaries, such as the Quran readers who prayed for the Sultan every morning, and a preacher, who was charged with giving sermons and praying "for the souls of the Prophet, his companions, earlier Ottoman sultans, and the continuation of the present sultan's caliphate."[12]

A Persian "Indian summer"; an Indian golden age

In architecture as well as in politics and military affairs, Shah 'Abbas I's reign represents the apex of Safavid achievement, even if the Shah did not present himself as an Iranian Solomon; pre-Islamic Sasanian references were sufficient for most Iranian monarchs. 'Abbas's new square and avenues in Isfahan represent his great achievement, and for those Pietro della Valle offers a unique comparative assessment of Ottoman Istanbul and Safavid Isfahan. The architectural differences he highlights reflect Italian biases, as well as fundamental and distinct aspects of Ottoman and Iranian culture: imperial mosques in Istanbul and a garden city in Isfahan.

---

[8] Ibid., 173.   [9] Ibid., 172.   [10] See above, Chapter 6.

[11] Necipoğlu, "The Süleymaniye Complex in Istanbul: An Interpretation," 96.

[12] The fascinating details of this particular *waqf* have been preserved. See Kemâl Edîb Kürkçüoğlu, *Süleymaniye Vakfiyesi* (Istanbul: Vakiflar Umum Müdürlüğü, 1962).

Fig. 10. The Sultan Ahmet or Blue Mosque, Istanbul, constructed between 1606 and 1616, exterior and interior photographs.

Fig. 11. 'Ali Qapı or 'Ali Qâpû ("Sublime Gate") Palace, Isfahan, completed in the mid-seventeenth century.

Della Valle expressed his feelings about what he saw when he arrived in Isfahan on 22 February 1617, responding, as an Italian familiar with piazzas, especially to the *Maidan-i Shah* and the bazaar that surrounded it, and pointedly remarking on the less imposing Safavid *masjids*. The symmetry, water channels, and gardens he describes are symptomatic of Iranian material, literary, and artistic culture:

As for the buildings, in general they are better than those of Constantinople, though they are not so high ... In sum, for the East they are very good; and the bazaars, above all, could not be better, being very well built, large, vaulted, even and architecturally sound ... In detail, then, there are no mosques here, like the five or six made by the Turks in Constantinople; but yet there are two things which, in my opinion, cannot bear comparison with, but which are, of their kind, without doubt superior to everything in Constantinople or wheresoever in Christendom.[13]

One of these is the Maidan or main square ...[14] It is completely surrounded by finely designed symmetrical buildings, uninterrupted either by streets or anything

---

[13] As della Valle notes, the Masjid-i Shah, now the Masjid-i Imam, was under construction when he visited Isfahan, which partly explains his comments about mosques. He describes the Shaikh Lutfullah Mosque opposite the 'Ali Qapu palace. This building was dedicated to one of the émigré Lebanese Shi'i *'ulama* discussed above in Chapter 3.

[14] The *Maidan-i Shah* is approximately seven times the size of St. Mark's in Venice. Note by the editor George Bull in della Valle, *The Pilgrim*, 123.

Fig. 12. Shaikh Lutfullah Masjid, Isfahan, constructed between 1601 and 1617.

else, made with large porticoes, and floors underneath for shops ... This harmony of architecture on so large a scale is so agreeable to the eye that, though the houses of the Piazza Navona [in Rome] are higher and more richly decorated in our way, through their lack of regularity ... I dare to place it before the Piazza Navona. Around the Maidan, on all four sides, not far from the porticoes, flows a big channel of water, beautifully straight, lined with parapets ... And beyond the flowing water,

Fig. 13. Shaikh Lutfullah Masjid, Isfahan.

towards the porticoes, extends a very dense and even row of green trees, which, when they put forth their foliage in a few days' time, will, I believe, be the most beautiful sight in the world.

The "other notable feature" della Valle describes was the adjacent tree-lined Chahar Bagh Avenue, lined with public gardens and pavilions: an elongated version of the typical Iranian four-part garden, featuring a stone channel with a stream and fountains down the middle of the two- to three-mile-long road, which is today, as it was in his time, a public space for evening promenades.[15]

Isfahan after 'Abbas I

Following the death of Shah 'Abbas I in 1629, Safavid Iran did not experience a spectacular golden age of conquests or exceptional architecture, although in terms of government the reigns of Shah Safi I (r. 1629–42) and Shah 'Abbas II (r. 1642–66) did represent a kind of "Indian summer." Even though both rulers emerged from the *haram*, Shah Safi's reign was initially

[15] Della Valle, *The Pilgrim*, 124.

Fig. 14. Masjid-i Shah, Isfahan (after the 1979 revolution, the Masjid-i Imam), interior, constructed between 1612 and 1617.

well managed by an exceptionally capable and honest minister, while Shah 'Abbas II seems to have been in virtually every respect a remarkably decent, responsible individual, who abstained from foreign wars (apart from recapturing Qandahar from his Indian neighbors), while capably and justly administering the state. He was also religiously tolerant, especially toward Christians. He increased the money flowing into the royal treasury by establishing direct control over additional provinces, and personally saw to the administration of his own estates. Like other Safavids and many Mughals, he indulged in alcohol and drugs and the *haram*, and may have died of syphilis, when he was only thirty-nine. Apart from these common addictions, his one conspicuous administrative failing was to allow the Safavid military to atrophy, the continuation of a slow process culminating in the Afghan defeat of the Safavids in 1722.

'Abbas II's two most memorable monuments are the Chihil Sutun palace and the Khadju bridge. The palace, completed in 1647 not far from the *maidan*, is described in a poem by the poet laureate of the time, Sa'ib Tabrizi. It is a large rectangular structure with a high columned porch or *tâlâr* that echoes the Achaemenid audience halls of Darius and Xerxes, and it was used for coronations, diplomatic receptions, and entertainments.[16] Shah 'Abbas II also built the *tâlâr*, the similarly columned section of the 'Âlî Qâpû palace on the *maidan* earlier in his reign in 1643–44 (see Fig. 11, p. 000).[17] The Chihil Sutun features eighteen columns on the porch, and a further two just behind are reflected in a pool, thus giving the name *chihil sutun* or "forty columns" to the building. Surrounded by gardens, it features historical wall paintings as well as traditional Persian scenes of feasting and drinking that combine both traditional Persian and European styles. The historical paintings concern Safavid relations with its eastern neighbors, and one depicts Humayun's reception in Iran by Shah Tahmasp. These paintings may reflect Shah 'Abbas II's preoccupation with reconquering Qandahar from the Mughals, which he accomplished in 1649.[18] The Chihil Sutun might be interpreted as 'Abbas II's own perception of his reign as a kind of Safavid golden age.[19] As for the beautifully conceived Khadju bridge, it is built on the site of a former structure, and serves both wheeled vehicles and, on a series of roofed, arcaded passageways on either side of the roadway, pedestrian traffic.[20] Like its predecessor, the Sih u Sih Pul bridge linking Isfahan with the Armenian suburb of Julfa, built by 'Ali Verdi Khan in Shah 'Abbas I's day, the Khadju bridge also serves as an imaginative urban gathering place because of the stone steps that lead from the covered pedestrian walkways down to the river, stimulating contemplation, smoking, and family picnics.

---

[16] Ingeborg Luschey-Schmeisser, "Cehel Sotûn, Isfahan," *Encyclopaedia Iranica*, Brill Online, 113.

[17] Priscilla Soucek, " 'Âlî Qâpû," *Encyclopaedia Iranica* online, 871.

[18] Sussan Babaie, "Shah 'Abbas II, the Conquest of Qandahar, the Chihil Sutun, and its Wall Paintings," *Muqarnas* 11 (1994), 134–6.

[19] Ibid., 139.

[20] See Della Valle's appreciative description of the bridge he saw in Shah 'Abbas I's time: "at least as wide as any in Rome." *The Pilgrim*, 127.

Apart from the bridge, the other memorable building erected in the latter half of the Safavid era is the *masjid* and *madrasa* complex popularly known as the Mader-i Shah, the Mother of the Shah. After it was built in the early eighteenth century during the reign of the pious and ineffectual Shah Sultan Husain,[21] it was more commonly known as the Sultani or Chahar Bagh *madrasa*, after the nearby street. It too seems emblematic of a reign, in that this lovely, typically enclosed theological college was constructed at a time when the Iranian Shi'i clergy had become exceptionally influential, overshadowing both the Shah as an individual and the Safavids' earlier dual Shi'i and Sufi charisma. By this period the charismatic religious authority of the dynasty seems to have all but evaporated. As the last important Safavid building complex, this *masjid* and *madrasa* seems almost to symbolize the Shi'i *'ulama's* clerical golden age.

India under the "Second Temür," Shah Jahan

In contrast to the modest ambitions and declining fortunes of the later Safavids, Shah Jahan built continuously and splendidly throughout the empire. His lofty self-regard, refined taste and substantial income allowed him to produce a number of secular and religious buildings of surpassing beauty, a Mughal classicism of symmetrical marble architecture.[22] The Taj Mahal is only one of many of Shah Jahan's buildings that have survived intact, but it is the one that deservedly continues to be regarded as among the pre-industrial world's perfectly realized designs. A Timurid-style tomb built over twelve years at a cost of five million rupees, the Taj is also the last great Muslim imperial structure in the Ottoman, Safavid, and Mughal empires. As the contemporary historian 'Abd al-Hamid Lahauri put it, "In this peaceful reign the work of building has reached such a point that it astonishes even the world traveler who is hard to please and the magical masters of this incomparable art."[23] Even the "magical master" Sinan might have been impressed.

---

[21] Stephen Blake discusses this and other Safavid buildings in Isfahan and locates them on useful maps. See *Half the World: The Social Architecture of Safavid Isfahan, 1590–1722* (Costa Mesa, Cal.: Mazda, 1999), 159–63.

[22] See Ebba Koch's articulate discussion of Shah Jahan's major buildings in her *Mughal Architecture*, 93–124 and the rigidly observed principles of this classicism that she discusses in *The Complete Taj Mahal* (London: Thames and Hudson, 2006), 104–13. It is difficult to convey the number and variety of mid seventeenth-century Mughal buildings, which also included the impressive *madrasa* at Thanesar, just under 100 miles northwest of Delhi, that features an octagonal tomb. See Suhbash Parihar, "A Little-Known Mughal College in India: The Madrasa of Shaykh Chillie at Thanesar," *Muqarnas* 9 (1992), 175–85.

[23] Quoted in Koch, *The Complete Taj Mahal*, 84.

Fig. 15. Taj Mahal, Agra, seen from Agra fort, completed between 1632 and 1643.

Fundamentally similar in design to Humayun's octagonal tomb but differently proportioned, the Taj is distinguished by a number of features that combine to make the building unique. Sheathed in luminous white marble and constructed on an imposing marble platform decorated with relief carvings of plants, it features a bulbous dome that may have been derived from Deccani architecture. The four *chatris* on the roof are similar to Humayun's tomb, but the four minarets that flank the building are not typical of earlier Indo-Muslim architecture and may possibly have been inspired by Ottoman examples.[24] The Mughals did not use the colored tiles that characterize Safavid buildings and earlier Timurid structures. Instead the exterior of the Taj is decorated at the entrance by finely rendered Quranic verses, also commonly found in Ottoman and Safavid religious buildings, but it is distinguished by delicate floral designs composed of semi-precious stones set into the marble around the entire structure. Indian craftsmen learnt this Italian *pietra dura* technique – visible in Florentine buildings as early as the fourteenth century – from European craftsmen and also applied it to Shah Jahan's later throne room in Delhi. Flanking the Taj are a small mosque and guest house, each

[24] Ibid., 180

Fig. 16. Jama Masjid, Delhi, constructed between 1650 and 1656.

constructed of red sandstone with marble inlays and three white marble, onion domes. All three buildings sit at the end of a typical *chahar bagh* or four-part garden, which is entered through a monumental gatehouse decorated with its own *chatris*, Quranic inscriptions, and *pietra dura* inlays in white marble.[25]

Outside the Taj the planners laid out a square divided into four parts by two intersecting bazaar streets where four *caravansarais* were built. The *caravansarais* and shops built along the streets were integral to the maintenance of the Taj complex, as they constituted part of the *waqf* endowment, which paid for the upkeep of the buildings and the salaries of the staff. Supplementing these rents were the land revenue collections from thirty nearby villages. In this financial respect the Taj complex was similar to Ottoman Istanbul and Safavid Isfahan in that mosques, tombs, and bazaars – and palaces – formed a standard architectural ensemble in Muslim imperial cities, with shops and villages providing income for the public foundations. Similar too was the economic impact of this

---

[25] Directly across the river from the Taj Shah Jahan had a pleasure garden built known as the Mahtab Bagh, which, perhaps because it was so regularly flooded, was apparently forgotten until the Archeological Survey of India excavated it in the 1990s. See Moynihan, *The Moonlight Garden*.

commercial complex that helped to turn an already prosperous imperial capital into a major commercial center. 'Abd al-Hamid Lahuri described the scene:

And in these sarais they buy and sell merchandise from every land, varied goods from every country, all kinds of luxuries of the day, and things that are essential to a civilized and comfortable life, brought from all quarters of the world. Behind the caravansarais, merchants have built many substantial houses (*manazil-i pukhta*) and caravansarais. And this thriving dwelling–place founded for all eternity, which has become a large city, is called Mumtazabad.[26]

If not "for all eternity," Shah Jahan at least presided over a brief historical moment where the goal of Babur's original Indian conquest was fully realized in his descendant's "civilized and comfortable life."

Poetry

Ottomans: Baki's "civilized and comfortable life" and Naili's sabk-i Hindi

Well before Shah Jahan's reign and by the time of Süleyman, many Ottoman bureaucrats and bureaucratic intellectuals were enjoying a "civilized and comfortable life." This was particularly true for those fortunate enough to be born in Istanbul, where they had access to outstanding *madrasa* education and imperial patronage. One such was Mahmud 'Abd al-Baki (b. 1526), whose life spanned the Ottoman golden age and whose poetry reflects it in many respects. Born of a relatively poor family but in the *ilmiye* class, the son of a *muezzin* at the important Fatih mosque, Baki eventually studied at a *madrasa* where he met a number of poets and scholars, who encouraged his literary talents. By his mid-twenties he had evidently become a skilled poet, for when Süleyman returned from his Iranian campaign in 1555, Baki submitted a *qasida*, a panegyric verse, to the sultan, whose appreciation gave Baki access to the court and the aristocracy of the empire. He became Süleyman's literary boon companion, exchanging verse with and even being asked to correct the sultan's poetry. Baki's political agility matched his literary skill, for he was able successfully to navigate the treacherous shoals of Ottoman court life and enjoy the patronage of Süleyman's two successors. Following Süleyman's death, he was appointed *qadi* in Mecca and Istanbul, before being promoted to the posts of *kadiasker* of Anatolia and Rumeli. Mehmet III

---

[26] Koch, *The Complete Taj Mahal*, 257.

recognized him as the *Sultan al-shu'ara*, the "sultan of poets," and when he died in 1600 he was given a state funeral.[27]

Baki, like his contemporary, the historian and poet Mustafa 'Ali, was a true Ottoman of the *ilmiye* class. He undoubtedly spoke a Turkic dialect as his native language, but would have studied Arabic, the Muslim religious language, and Persian, the pre-eminent literary and courtly language, after he began his formal education around age six.[28] His poetry was written in the complex, highly Persianized form of court language known as Ottoman, a Turkic dialect hardly intelligible to the peasants and nomads of the Anatolian countryside. He, like Ali, may also have enjoyed the "debauchery in the taverns" where young men could indulge adolescent urges "now to pretty girls, now to handsome boys."[29] Baki, like aspiring poets in Isfahan or Delhi, attended the literary *majlises* in Istanbul, where he met other writers and scholars. Throughout his life, even following his important appointment as a religious judge, he was known to be a sociable, engaging man who delighted in the society of learned and witty friends. Like many other members of the Ottoman elite, and their contemporaries in Iran and India, he does not seem to have been either rigidly orthodox or fervently pious, as is suggested by one of his *ghazals* which, along with many panegyric *qasidas*, comprised the bulk of his *diwan*, his collected verse:

> If I were to obey the advice
>   of the holy man of the town
> then what of spring, the beloved,
>   and the pleasant wine?[30]

These sentiments and vocabulary had been staples of Persian poetry for centuries before Baki wrote in Ottoman, and they would be reprised again in Urdu as it replaced Persian among Indian Muslims in the eighteenth century. Poets wrote such verse whatever their personal inclinations, and with another poet these lines might be dismissed as no more than a literary trope. In Baki's case they can be taken seriously – and with his own good humor – for they seem to have accurately reflected his social inclinations.

The poet Na'ili, born about three-quarters of a century after Baki, some time around 1610 (d. 1666), well after Mustafa 'Ali and others had begun lamenting Ottoman decline, offers a contrasting example of an *ilmiye* poet, with a very different career, outlook, and style. Na'ili's father was a minor bureaucrat in the bureau of mines, where his son evidently worked

---

[27] Fahir İz, "Bâkî, Mahmûd 'Abd al-," *Encyclopaedia of Islam* II, Brill Online.
[28] See Fleischer's fine account of Mustafa Âli's education "The Making of an Ottoman," in *Bureaucrat and Intellectual in the Ottoman Empire*, 13–40.
[29] Ibid., 23.   [30] Andrews *et al.*, *Ottoman Lyric Poetry*, 96.

throughout his career after completing his *madrasa* education. A prolific poet and member of the important Halveti Sufi order, he, like Baki, wrote *qasidas* for the Ottoman elite, but unlike his politically successful predecessor, Na'ili never attracted imperial favor or the patronage of secular or religious officials. His lack of success probably resulted from the starkly different quality of his *ghazals*, which cannot simplistically be attributed to declining Ottoman political fortunes, but may have been due to Na'ili's own introverted personality, his failure to attract patronage, and the influence of *sabk-i Hindi* writers in Iran and India. The metaphorical language of Safavid and Mughal poets "enabled him to create a counter-poetics that must be understood on its own terms, and which proved influential among later Ottoman poets of the 17th and 18th centuries."[31] However the personal, professional, and literary influences combined to influence Na'ili's verse, these "counter-poetics" are evident in one poem in which he exploited the perennial association of the garden and the beloved – whether an actual lover or God – to bitterly deride his own fortune:

> Oh Na'ili, from the sapling of the black
>   garden of fortune
> Sprouts neither the bud of desire nor the
>   rose of longing.

Given this contrary imagery in a literary culture in which gardens had always served lovers hoping for union or Sufis seeking God, it is easy to understand why Na'ili was not popular. "His entire poetic strategy was profoundly subversive."[32]

It is impossible adequately to convey the diverse world of Ottoman literary culture – or that of any society – with a brief account of two poets, however influential at the time or subsequently. Baki's contemporary Fuzuli (d. 1556), for example, though considered an Ottoman poet, was a Shi'a from Iraq. He not only composed verse in an eastern Turkic dialect but also wrote in Arabic and Persian and provided verse for the Safavids as well as the Ottomans, depending on who controlled his homeland. Beyond this complication, poetry served many diverse purposes for the Ottoman literati. It was a common means of friendly communication, as among their Chinese contemporaries.

---

[31] Walter Feldman, "The Celestial Sphere, the Wheel of Fortune, and Fate in the Gazels of Naili and Baki," *International Journal of Middle East Studies* 28, No. 2 (May 1996), 199 and n. 21, where the author cites a study by the Turkish scholar Ipekten of the influence of *sabk-i Hindi* on Na'ili's poetry.

[32] Ibid., 212.

Ottomans, like their Persian-language literary compatriots, also expressed sacred and profane love in verse, satirized their enemies, praised their potential or actual patrons, and wrote poems as a memorable way to convey important ideas or information. Many poems, *ghazals* especially, were sung, and written to be sung with instrumental accompaniment; and the most popular were, as has been seen, the inspiration for artful calligraphy and the subject of illustrated manuscripts. Most literate men were poets, and some women as well. The images and subjects of golden age poetry retained their popularity even as Na'ili and others experimented with *sabk-i Hindi* or, like Na'ili, began including popular Istanbul songs in their verse.[33]

Iran: Sa'ib of Tabriz and the triumph of sabk-i Hindi

The Persian poetry of Safavid Iran was just as diverse. Even after Tahmasp's "sincere repentance" led him officially to repudiate traditional court culture in the 1550s, governors of provincial courts in such major Iranian cities as Herat and Shiraz patronized musicians, artists, and poets. Nonetheless many poets from these and other cities eventually migrated to India. Leaving their homeland for a variety of personal, social, religious, or economic reasons, they were nearly all drawn by the wealth and eclecticism of Deccan and Mughal courts. That trend continued even under the more favorable conditions of Shah 'Abbas I's enlightened rule, for he used Iran's limited resources to solve the country's staggering economic, political, and military problems. Kausari, one of Shah 'Abbas' favorite writers, explained the economic reason for many Iranian poets' discontent when he wrote:

> In this country there is no buyer of speech,
> No one attends to the market of speech.[34]

Ashraf Mazandarani, the mid seventeenth-century émigré poet, whose father had married into the Majlisi family in Isfahan, described the financial attraction of India in his lines:

> Whoever comes from Iran to India imagines
> That in India gold is scattered like stars in the evening sky.[35]

The stream of literary émigrés was so great it has been characterized as the "Caravan of India," but Iran was not emptied of its poets. Iranian verse flourished again during the more placid reigns of Shah Safi I and Shah

---

[33] Ibid., 198.   [34] Cited in Ghani, *A History of Persian Language and Literature*, II, 168.
[35] Guchin-i Ma'ani, *Karvan-i Hind* (Tehran: Intisharat-i quds-razavi 1369/1970), I, 71.

Abbas II, when a number of well-known writers lived in Isfahan. Mirza Muhammad Sa'ib of Tabriz (1592–1676) was the most influential figure among these writers and is now widely recognized as the single greatest poet in Safavid history. He too migrated to India – in 1624/25 – even though he came from a wealthy mercantile family; but after seven years, after his aged father came to Delhi to ask him to return home, he agreed and spent the remainder of his life in Isfahan. Yet, although Shah 'Abbas II appointed Sa'ib as *Malik al-shu'ara*, the poet laureate, he was never exactly a court poet. His wealth made him independent of royal or aristocratic support, although he too wrote panegyric verse for both his Indian and his Iranian patrons. The numerous and prosperous Isfahani merchants and bureaucrats probably also offered him many appreciative audiences, apart from literary friends who might have smoked tobacco and drunk coffee or wine with him in one of Isfahan's many coffee houses or taverns.[36]

Sa'ib's long, comfortable life left him free to produce an enormous body of verse. Most of his 75, 000 lines of poetry were included in his *ghazals*, then still the most important verse form for Persian and Turkish poets. During his lifetime, and for at least a century after his death, Iranians praised Sa'ib's verse. Later, and especially in the nineteenth century, it was severely criticized and finally ignored owing to the novel traits that distinguished it from the "classical" verse of Hafiz and Sa'di. It was then that the phrase *sabk-i Hindi* was invented to deride the new-style poetry that many Iranian critics either associated with or blamed on Indian writers, who, from the point of many Iranian intellectuals, represented a soi-disant or debased form of "pure" Iranian culture. In fact, as has been seen, writers such as Fighani originated this style, but in the mid to late seventeenth century Sa'ib was its most prestigious representative and "The popularity of Sa'ib as a poet, in Persia, India, Central Asia and Turkey was unsurpassed by any other poet of Persian language of his day."[37]

Sa'ib was familiar with, and lavishly praised, the Persian verse of the earlier *sabk-i Hindi* poets of Akbar's day, Faizi, Naziri and others:

> O Sa'ib, thinkest thou that thou shouldst
> rival Naziri!
> 'Urfi did not approach Naziri in discourse.[38]

---

[36] Rudi Matthee, *The Pursuit of Pleasure: Drugs and Stimulants in Iranian History 1500–1900* (Princeton University Press, 2005), 165–72.

[37] Ghani, *A History of Persian Language and Literature*, 290. See also M. F. Köprülü, "Literature, the Eighteenth Century," in "Othmânli," *Encyclopaedia of Islam* II, Brill Online.

[38] Ibid., 73.

He referred to the "fresh style" of his own verse, reveled in its new themes and "unfamiliar or alien conceit," and he also introduced popular colloquialisms into the language of the *ghazal*.[39] He alluded to his innovations, as in the following stanza:

> Sa'ib, one who gains the acquaintance
> Of strange and alien themes
> Withdraws himself entirely from
> Worldly acquaintances.[40]

In another poem he expressed his delight in the kind of subtle themes that have discouraged many later readers:

> The moment of luxury for us is to bring
> A fine and subtle theme within our grasp;
> For nothing else is the crescent moon
> That signals the 'Id for us
> Who think subtle and delicate thoughts.[41]

His thoughts are so subtle, he argues, that the reader cannot divine them. After all, he writes:

> The painting, in silent wonder
> Knows nothing of the painter's state
> Don't ask the figure painted on the cloth
> To reveal the meanings that are hidden.[42]

Sabk-i Hindi *in Hind: the enigmatic Bedil*

As in the Ottoman Empire and Safavid Iran, the literary scene in India is too diverse to be satisfactorily personified by a single individual. Even if the coffee shop culture of Istanbul and Isfahan never seems to have materialized in Agra or Delhi to the degree it did in those two imperial cities, the multitude of Indian courts, and the wealth of the Mughal nobility that attracted so may Iranians, guaranteed the continuity of the dynamic literary tradition that was so noticeable in Akbar's later years. The migratory flow of Iranian poets to India was undiminished until it began drying up under the ascetic eye of the last great Mughal ruler,

---

[39] Paul Losensky, "Sa'eb of Tabriz," *Encyclopaedia Iranica* online, 6, 7.
[40] Shamsur Rahman Faruqi, "A Stranger in the City: the Poetics of *Sabk-e-Hindi*," PDF file, Google Scholar, online.
[41] Ibid., 32. 'Id, otherwise known as 'Id al-fitr or 'Id al-saghir, the "lesser festival" or in Turkish *küçük bayram*, marks the end of the Ramadan fast and its beginning is determined by the position of the moon. The other festival of sacrifice is 'Id al-adha, the Feast of the Sacrifice – of Abraham or Ibrahim.
[42] Ibid., 36.

Aurangzib, and the poet laureates of both Jahangir and Shah Jahan were Iranian émigrés.

Mirza Muhammad Talib of Amul (d. 1626/27) became Jahangir's *Malik al-shu'ara* in 1618. A native of Amul in Mazandaran and probably a Shi'a, he wrote panegyric verse in honor of Shah 'Abbas I, but a lack of success in Iran evidently drove him, like so many others, to India. Like so many other writers of these times, he principally composed *ghazals*, and in these poems he experimented with novel similes and metaphors, which led the eighteenth-century Iranian critic 'Ali Beg Azar, in his well-known work *Atashkada*, to disapprove of his writing.[43] 'Ali Beg was similarly dismissive of Mirza Abu Talib Kalim (1582–1651), who was Shah Jahan's *Malik al-shu'ara*. Another Iranian émigré, Kalim came to India from Kashan, going to the Deccan before joining Shah Jahan's court. As is true of earlier court poets, he wrote panegyric poems to celebrate his patron's victories, but he also composed a wide range of other verse, which was widely praised by his contemporaries.[44] However, he too wrote in the "new style," and 'Ali Beg said of him, "For a time he was in Hamadan. At last he went over to India, and lived there for years in the service of Shah Jahan. He possesses all sorts of verses, but in *masnawi, qasida, ruba'i* he does not possess a single voice which is worthy."[45]

However, the later Iranian revulsion for these writers pales in comparison to their reaction to the Indian-born poet Bidil, who to them personifies the *sabk-i Hindi* style at its most extreme – and opaque.[46] It is difficult, though, to categorize Bidil's verse or trace its antecedents precisely because, in his early life at least, he wrote as an ecstatic mystic, a *qalandar* or wandering spiritual vagabond, a man who adamantly rejected court appointments and refused to write panegyric verse.[47] A descendant of Temür's Barlas tribe, Bidil was born in Patna, India, in 1644 as Mirza 'Abd al-Qadir ibn 'Abd al-Khalik; he died in 1724. In his teens he began his spiritual quests in Bengal and Orissa, and eventually traveled to Delhi, where he became the disciple of a *majzub*, a man who renounced all

---

[43] Munibur Rahman, "Talib Amuli," *Encyclopaedia of Islam* II, Brill Online.
[44] See the example of one such verse, written in 1631 to celebrate the arrival in Agra of the severed heads of thirty or more Afghan enemies of the Mughals, in Begley and Desai, eds., *Shah Jahan Nama*, 57.
[45] Ghani, *a History of Persian Language and Literature*, I, 295.
[46] Recently Iranians seem to have relented somewhat, as they held an International Congress on Bidil in Tehran in 2006. See BBC Persian.com. 03/30/2008 for a description of the meeting.
[47] For a list of his works see D. N. Marshall, "Bidil, Mîrzâ 'Abd al-Qâdir," in *Mughals in India: A Bibliographical Survey* (Bombay: Asia Publishing House, 1967), 114–15.

worldly attachments in search of divine grace. Bidil wrote thousands of verses, many still unedited or unpublished, which have a broad popular audience in twenty-first-century Afghanistan, Uzbekistan, and Tajikistan. The titles of some of his works – *'Irfân* ("Gnosticism"), *Nikât* ("Subtleties"), *Tilisim-i hayrat* ("Talisman of Enchantment") – hint at the mystical complexities that characterize much of his verse. While Bidil, like some of his literary predecessors, wrote about "new meanings" and the problems of communication, he was preoccupied with the Sufi quest for spiritual union. Many of his enigmatic poems seem to convey his frustrated attempts to describe his inexpressible spiritual states. Thus:

> An intellect that knew black from white,
> Don't believe that it knew God's mystery
> As it needed to be known. I spoke a word
> But only after I attained perfection;
> You will comprehend when you don't comprehend.[48]

Or again in the following verse:

> Oh, what a multitude of meanings
> Discouraged by unintimate, alien language
> Remained hidden, for all their bold beauty
> Behind secret veils of mystery.[49]

Painting

The Ottomans: realistic battles, stereotypical portraits

The classical or golden age of Ottoman painting is unanimously dated to the reigns of Süleyman and his immediate successors in the late sixteenth century, but like many periods of artistic florescence elsewhere, the art of Süleyman's day was the fruit of earlier developments. By establishing the *nakkaşhane* and appointing the first *şahnameci*, the writer of a "book of kings," Mehmet II had laid the institutional basis for Ottoman miniature art, but Selim I's conquest of Tabriz also gave a powerful initial impetus to Ottoman artistic development – in ceramic tiles as well as painting – because it led to the migration of Iranians to Istanbul. They provided the initial producers of sixteenth-century Ottoman art.[50]

---

[48] Faruqi, "The Poetics of Sabk-i Hindi," 36. See also A. S. Bazmee Ansari, "Bîdil, Mîrzâ 'Abd al-Kâdir b. 'Abd al-Khâlik Arlâs (or Barlâs)," *Encyclopaedia of Islam* II, Brill Online.
[49] Faruqi, "The Poetics of Sabk-i Hindi," 39.
[50] Not until the mid-sixteenth century did Iznik replace Timurid designs on Ottoman decorative tiles. See Gülrü Necipoğlu, "From International Timurid to Ottoman: A Change in Taste in Sixteenth Century Ceramic Tiles," *Muqarnas* 7 (1990), 136–70.

Fig. 17. Turkey, *c.* 1570. An Ottoman Pasha (from the Persian *padishah*): a high official, accompanied by other officials, serenaded above by musicians, and dressed in animal skins, perhaps a *qalandar* or itinerant Sufi. Note the distinctive Ottoman turbans.

The abundance of Iranian artists coming to the *nakkaşhane* from Herat by way of Tabriz, from Tabriz proper, and from Shiraz – together with the private libraries of the last Akkoyunlu and Timurid rulers, and those of the Safavids brought in by Selim I – resulted in the tremendous burst of creative energy observed in the ensuing period.[51]

[51] Atıl, "The Art of the Book," 164.

During Süleyman's reign, *nakkaşhane* artists produced more than fifty manuscripts, three-quarters of them devoted to classic Persian literary works, while most of the remainder consisted of contemporary historic events, the signature genre of Ottoman historiography – and yet another reflection of the overwhelming military ethos of the early and classical Ottoman state.[52] Later genres also included illustrations for poetic anthologies, first known from mid fifteenth-century Shiraz. One late sixteenth-century Ottoman anthology of *ghazals* included works from such well-known Ottoman poets as Baki, Hayreti, the female writer Mihri Hatun, and the Indo-Persian writer Zuhuri.[53]

Stylistically, many and perhaps most early manuscripts were executed in Tabriz style, a combination of Timurid and Aq Quyunlu influences. They include illustrated *diwans* of the late Timurid-era Herat compatriots Nava'i and Jami, who wrote poetry in Turki and Persian as well as Nizami's *Khamsa*, and Firdausi's *Shah-nama*. Ottoman Turks were sensitive to charges that they merely reproduced Iranian verses, paintings, and calligraphy with no creativity of their own, even to the extent that some defended their versions. Thus the sixteenth-century literary historian Sehi Beğ (d. 1548), wrote of the poet Şheyi's rendition of Nizami's *Khusrau and Shirin*:

> Disrobing the beloved [the poem]
>   of Persian attire
> He dressed her at once in
>   Rumi [Anatolian] style.
> Removing from her/his shoulder
>   the shabby cloth,
> He replaced it with the satin cloth of Rum.[54]

As early as 1530, however, an artist produced illustrations for Nizami's *Khamsa* featuring local architectural styles against the backdrop of Iranian landscapes. Painters increasingly produced works that were identifiably Ottoman, not only because they were populated by figures in Ottoman

---

[52] Ottomans and their elites collected illustrated Persian manuscripts, and during the sixteenth century many possessed works produced in Shiraz. See Lâle Uluç, "Selling to the Court: Late Sixteenth-Century Manuscript Production in Shiraz," *Muqarnas* 17 (2000), 73–96.

[53] J. M. Rogers, *Empire of the Sultans* (London: Nour Foundation, 2000), 242. Zuhuri (d. 1616), who was praised by Sa'ib, first wrote for Shah 'Abbas and then, like so many other Iranians, migrated to India, where he spent the remainder of his life in the Deccan at the Bijapur Sultanate. His verse also featured new images that deviated from classical norms, thus placing him within the general category of a *sabk-i Hindi* poet.

[54] Quoted in Serpil Bagci, "From Translated Word to Translated Image: The Illustrated Şehnâme-i Türki Copies," *Muqarnas* 17 (2000), 162.

dress among Ottoman buildings, but also due to the greater realism with which they rendered classic Persian tales.[55]

Realism is also the distinguishing feature of the historic painting genre, in which painters not only depicted military campaigns, but also produced detailed, accurate city and fortress plans and geographies of the Ottoman world. Realism characterizes the *Süleymanname* of 1558, a history of the reign from 1520 to 1558, "the first great Ottoman historical manuscript," which began "the process of blending Shiraz decorative details, Türkmen figural style, and Ottoman narrative traditions."[56] This work, which defined the norms of historical painting for the second half of the century, featured court and battle scenes – with Europeans accurately rendered by a resident European artist. Included among the sixty-nine paintings done by five separate artists is one that depicts the *devşhirme* draft of young Christian children destined for conversion and state service.[57] Later such *şahnameçis* as Lokman, who held the post between 1569 and 1595, produced a number of these histories. Lokman also produced, in 1592–3, the earliest known example of another type of realistic painting, the *Surname*: works that celebrated imperial births, weddings, and circumcisions, ceremonial events that proclaimed Ottoman grandeur publicly in the streets of Istanbul.[58] In addition, Lokman wrote the text for a famous illustrated genealogy of Ottoman sultans, the *Kifayet al-İnsaniye fi Şemail-i Osmaniye*. The paintings in this genealogy, the first of their type, belong, however, to a separate category of individualized royal portraiture that cannot be described either as realistic or as, in contrast to Mughal art, psychologically complex.

The artist Nakkaş Osman painted twelve portraits for this genealogy, the four earliest completely fabricated while the others were based upon Venetian portraits obtained for him by the vizier, Sokollu Mehmet Pasha (d. 1579). He depicted the later sultans with distinct facial features, mimicking the Venetian originals but in exactly the same pose, and in progressively more elegant dress that reflects the increasing grandeur of the empire. Even though Nakkaş Osman adopted his portraits from Venetian originals, he did not employ Italian artistic conventions that had been acceptable during Mehmet II's reign, when the Ottoman court was more cosmopolitan, in contrast to the increasingly rigid orthodox Hanafi Sunni ethos of Süleyman and his successors. The portraits are meant to reflect Lokman's text, which invokes the Islamic science of physiognomy to identify facial

---

[55] Ibid., 171.

[56] Denny, "Dating Ottoman Turkish Works in the Saz Style," *Muqarnas* 1 (1983), 106.

[57] Ibid., 174.

[58] Esin Atıl, "Levni and the Surname: The Story of an Eighteenth Century Ottoman Festival," *Muqarnas* 10 (1993), 181–2.

and other physical features as reflections of intrinsic character. Each Ottoman sultan was in his words a "storehouse of divine inspiration distinguished by innate talents."[59] The purpose of the paintings and the accompanying text was the glorification of the dynastic line, which was legitimized by its very dynastic longevity. In contrast, Akbar and his successors produced royal portrait groups that illustrated their impeccable genealogies, either from Temür or from the mythical Mongol ancestress Alanqua, who was impregnated by a shaft of light.[60]

The noticeable exception to the Ottomanization of the Iranian miniature tradition was the contemporary but fantastic style of *Saz*, so named because it consisted of drawings done with the *saz qalami*, the reed pen. Two Iranian émigrés – Iranian artists once again – are associated with fostering this style in Istanbul: Shâh Qûlî/Şahkuli (d. 1555/56), who was one of Selim's artistic trophies from Tabriz, and Wâlî Jân/Velican, who arrived later in the century, perhaps in 1599. *Saz* paintings represented a form of chinoiserie, known to Timurids, Safavids, and Ottomans by the term *hatayi/khatâ'i* or "Chinese." The drawings feature Chinese-inspired lush foliage of leaves, vines, and flowers, *peris* (fairies) and other mythical creatures, and, most of all, dragons. Ottoman painters' use of this style represents a westward extension of Chinese artistic influence that flourished during the Mongol era and revived again in the Timurid century. A mature example of the style is found on the binding of the *Süleymanname*. *Saz*-style drawings continued to appear in Ottoman art until the late sixteenth century, were revived in the 1630s, and were produced until the eighteenth century. Not only did the style survive in drawings, but "derived from these paper images ... [were] virtually all Ottoman decorative art forms from book binding through textiles, carpets, metalwork, stone carving and ceramics."[61]

One feature missing from Ottoman painting of the classical age – and found in both Iran and India in the sixteenth and seventeenth centuries – is a substantial influence from European art. This is so despite the close contact between the Ottoman and European states.[62] Only in the 1720s, the so-called Tulip Period, did European influence appear or reappear, when the revival of the *nakkaşhane* led to a second classical era in Ottoman art.[63] It is particularly noticeable that the Ottomans, who earlier had

[59] Quoted by Gülrü Necipoğlu, "The Serial Portraits of Ottoman Sultans in Comparative Perspective," in Julian Raby *et al.*, *The Sultan's Portrait* (Istanbul: Iş Bank, 2000), 33–4.
[60] See Sheila Canby, ed., *Humayun's Garden Party* (Bombay: Marg, 1994), where various aspects of the Mughals' dynastic preoccupations are discussed.
[61] Denny, "Dating Works in the Saz Style," 103.
[62] Oleg Grabar, "An Exhibition of High Ottoman Art," *Muqarnas* 6 (1989), 3–4.
[63] Atıl, "The Art of the Book," 223.

Fig. 18. Turkey, *c.* 1600. Sultan Mehmet II (r. 1595–1603), with Janisssary attendants.

sought to employ Italian Renaissance artists, were so slow to interest themselves in Western artistic conventions. Perhaps this was a function of both the perennial hostility between Ottomans and eastern European powers and the Ottomans' intense Sunni orthodoxy – in contrast with the latitudinarian religious attitudes of the early Mughals. In any case, just as Nakkaş Osman was producing his Ottoman portraits, Akbar's painters were beginning to enthusiastically copy Flemish and German secular and religious art brought to Agra by the Jesuits.

Safavids

Just as Ottoman painting was attaining its mature, classical style, Iranian art was fundamentally changing. By 1556 Shah Tahmasp had completely rejected any further royal patronage for painting or any other secular art. No royal illustrated manuscripts were produced on the scale and quality of the earlier *Shah-nama* or Nizami's *Khamsa*, although in regional centers such as Mashhad, ruled by Tahmasp's nephew Ibrahim Mirza, and in Shiraz artists continued to produce less ambitious illustrated manuscripts. Ibrahim Mirza, a dedicated bibliophile, commissioned a beautifully illustrated edition of Jami's poem the *Haft Aurang* before losing his position. Shiraz in particular became a center of production, and some painters who left the now austere Qazvin court settled in the southern city, where they produced many of the texts that Ottoman rulers and bureaucrats acquired. Shiraz painters produced a distinct genre of Iranian art characterized by the prevalence of pastel colors and the rigid adherence to a set of proportions, "a set of numerical relationships, essentially 2 (and #): 5. The ratio controls the size of a folio ... it controls the size of the written surface laid down upon a folio, together with the breadth of the columns of text (in case of poetry), and the width of its colored rulings."[64]

Following Tahmasp's ban, some painters went to India – or more precisely, in the case of Mir Mussavir and Mir Sayyid 'Ali, they accompanied Humayun after he left Tahmasp's court and eventually reached India, where they helped found the Mughal school of painting. Others migrated to Ottoman dominions. A number of those who remained in Iran began concentrating on producing individual pages: portraits, landscapes, samples of calligraphy, or other subjects rather than entire albums. Earlier painters had occasionally produced individual portraits of contemporaries even while they worked on the great royal manuscripts, but when royal patronage suddenly evaporated they produced many more such works, although some painters in small Khurasan towns such as Sabzawar continued to produce less ambitious illustrated versions of verses by Firdausi, Nizami, Hafiz, Amir Khusrau Dihlavi, and others. One aspect of Safavid art that is sometimes associated with the prevalence of so many single-sheet drawings is the *muraqqa'* or album, a

---

[64] Sims, *Peerless Images*, 69.

Fig. 19. Iran, *c.* 1590. An imagined young couple. Typical of many later separate paintings found in albums or produced for individual patrons.

carefully assembled but disparate collection of paintings that included individuals, court and country scenes, flowers and plants, wildlife, and calligraphy. Timurid princes had commissioned *muraqqa's* in the fifteenth century, and the Safavids produced others both well before and after Tahmasp's sudden renunciation of his earlier artistic enthusiasms; one was produced for Shah Tahmasp himself.[65] Yet even if these albums

---

[65] David J. Roxburgh, *The Persian Album, 1400–1600* (New Haven and London: Yale University Press, 2005), 184.

cannot be tied to Tahmasp's rejection of court patronage of the profane arts, they represent an important aspect of Iranian painting that was later copied in Mughal India. The albums consist of a carefully assembled group of individual pages that preserve and display fragile works of art that collectively reflected many aspects of high Perso-Islamic culture and confirmed the elite status of the patron, nearly always a member of the royal family or the aristocracy. The first page of the 1544–5 *muraqqa'* of Shah Tahmasp's brother Bahram Mirza, for example, features a *suhbat* or *majlis* common to the aristocratic culture of all three Muslim empires and to their Timurid predecessors:

The painting portrays a convivial gathering of courtiers, each named in a caption at the top. The event is a *suhbat*, a feat of conversation, singing, music and wine drinking. Presiding over this alfresco assembly is Qarpuz Sultan ('Watermelon Sultan'), the master of ceremonies, decked out in fine clothes.... Tuhfda Jan ('the gift of life'), the cup bearer ('*saqi*'), offers Qarpuz wine ... In the foreground, the red-faced Master Nu'man plays the flute as the rotund Turfa Raqass ('the dancing oddity'), with legs lifted and arms held out, dances to the music. A fifth figure, Mawlana Ahmad Fashsh ('Ahmad the belcher'), drinks from a cup.[66]

Majlis, a term for an assembly or convivial meeting, is particularly associated with royal or aristocratic gatherings, partly because these are the occasions which are occasionally alluded to in the sources devoted to the histories of the dynasties. The term, or its near-synonym *suhbat* or conversation, could also be applied to social sessions among artists, scholars, and aspiring poets in Istanbul, Isfahan, or Delhi – or smaller cities. Babur, the Mughal founder, provides some of the most vivid descriptions of the aristocratic *majlis* in his remarkably informative auto-biography. In October 1519, for example, he reports riding out of Kabul, where he ruled before invading India in 1525–6, to view the fall foliage in a famous village called Istalif, a wine-producing area north of the Afghan capital. He reports that the next day he and his men drank all day long, slept until the midday prayer, traveled slowly to another nearby village to view the autumn leaves, and along the way consumed some *ma'jun*, a drugged confection favored by many Timurids. Then they drank again until the evening prayer. In some of his other descriptions poets compose and/or sing their verses, dancers perform, music is played, young boys or slaves are sometimes pursued, and, if the men are sober enough, military strategy is discussed. This was the Muslim equivalent of the ancient Greek *symposium* where "a state of delight produced by wine and by the pleasure of the occasion ... [generated] the appropriate mood for constructive dialogue and the appreciation of poetry."[67]

---

[66] Ibid., 245.   [67] Dale, *The Garden of the Eight Paradises*, 179–83.

Shah 'Abbas I, who like most Iranian aristocrats, appreciated these sessions (which are so frequently the subject of paintings), appears to have had relatively little interest in art, or at least the art of the book. Nor did he seem even slightly interested in the type of formal, hagiographic portraiture the contemporary Ottomans favored. Most of the art that survives from his pivotal era consists of single-page paintings and large-scale murals. The pre-eminent court artist of Shah 'Abbas's reign, and a man who had a formative influence on Safavid painting during the entire seventeenth century, was 'Aqa Riza or Riza-yi 'Abbasi (b. c. 1565, d. 1635), who joined Shah 'Abbas's court around 1587. He specialized in portraits of youthful courtiers, including sensuously drawn women, as well as other individuals, such as his fine portrait of a scribe.[68]

For a period of about seven years, between 1603 and 1610, he left the court to enjoy a bohemian life in the capital, when he produced a series of emotive drawings of men in wilderness settings. The court historian Iskander Beg Munshi described him in this period as one "who avoided the society of men of talent and gave himself up to association with ... low persons. At the present time he has a little repented of such idle frivolity but pays little attention to his art and ... he has become ill-tempered, peevish, and unsociable."[69] After rejoining the court 'Aqa Riza altered his earlier style, replacing bright primary colors with dark half-tones and painting ponderous figures instead of the delightful, lithe youths of his earlier years. He also sought inspiration in the Timurid past, and did a series of drawings imitating the great Bihzad of Sultan Husain Baiqara's late fifteenth-century Timurid court at Herat. While other artists contributed to illustrated manuscripts he continued to focus on single-page works, as in the painting his most famous pupil, Mu'in Musavvir, did of him as an old man with gray hair and spectacles engaged in painting a portrait of a European man.[70]

Mu'in Musavvir's painting, which he began in 1635 but completed only in 1673, is important for other reasons than as a representation of his influential, irascible teacher. First of all, Mu'in Musavvir's taste for specific, lifelike portraiture, combined with his informative habit of making notes on his paintings to make it possible to date and relate them to specific places and events, provide an example of "fundamental changes in Iranian attitudes towards pictorial art."[71] Second, his portrait of 'Aqa Riza painting a European reminds observers that Iranian artists began

---

[68] Canby, *Persian Painting* (London: Thames and Hudson, 1993), 100.
[69] Quoted in Sims, *Peerless Images*, 72.
[70] Canby, *Persian Painting*, 98–101 and Sims, *Peerless Images*, 274–5.
[71] Sims, *Peerless Images*, 274.

Fig. 20. Iran, *c.* 1650. A formerly pious and abstinent Sufi *shaikh* is satirized for taking wine.

paying attention to Europeans and European art in the early decades of the sixteenth century. Europe now replaced China as the principal source of foreign inspiration, which China had been during the Mongol era. 'Aqa Riza himself seems to have painted Europeans as curiosities – a kind of

Occidentalism – as an exotic but not yet threatening people, at least in Iran. His successors, however, echoed their Indian counterparts in both copying European paintings and absorbing Western artistic techniques, such as shading and the illusion of depth.

Iranian artists began using European techniques in the mid seventeenth century, and by the end of the Safavid era they commonly and unobtrusively integrated Western elements with traditional Iranian settings. The late seventeenth-century artist Muhammad Zaman was the foremost practitioner of this dynamic new eclectic style, which, "Reduced to its essentials ... [was] comprised of a realism in the depiction of persons and events; cast shadows, perspectively rendered trees or sharply angled buildings to suggest spatial recession."[72] One of the most stunningly effective examples of Muhammad Zaman's technique was his 1675 painting alluding to a *Shah-nama* episode, "Bahram Gur slays the Dragon."[73]

In addition, Muhammad Zaman and other painters from this era also began to be influenced by Mughal art, or at least to portray Indian Muslims wearing typical Mughal aristocratic dress in their paintings.[74] In this they were not innovators, for years earlier an Iranian artist had indulged in a bit of his own Orientalism by depicting an Indian scene on one of the walls inside the Chihil Sutun palace: an idea taken from a Persian poem written for Akbar's son Daniyal sometime before 1604. Titled *Suz u gudaz*, "Burning and Melting," the poem depicted the immanent *sati* (immolation) of a young Indian bride, whose husband had accidentally died just after his marriage, and who now chose to sacrifice herself on the funeral pyre of her husband. However, the poem on which the painting was based was meant as a Sufi metaphor, rather than describing an actual immolation.

India

Indian painting itself continued to evolve during the reigns of Jahangir and Shah Jahan, stimulated by the emperors' sophisticated tastes and lavish patronage as well as by the creative eclecticism of Muslim and Hindu artists in the imperial atelier. The Mughals collected illustrated texts and albums in the palace library for three demonstrable reasons, which probably held for Ottomans and Safavids as well: aesthetics, the prestige of possessing works by famous authors and artists, and the monetary value of

---

[72] Ibid., 77.   [73] Ibid., 310–11.
[74] See Muhammad Zaman's "A Prince on Horseback with a Courtier and Servants," in Canby, *Persian Painting*, 112.

each text, which their librarians carefully noted in the margins of each work.[75]

Akbar is known to have personally examined and approved his artists' work, and his son Jahangir boasted of his artistic knowledge to the readers of his memoirs. In a passage from 1618 he wrote:

As regards myself, my liking for painting and my practice in judging it have arrived at such a point that when any work is brought before me, either of deceased artists or those of the present day, without the names being told me, I say on the spur of the moment that it is the work of such and such a man. And if there be a picture containing many portraits, and each face be the work of a different master, I can discover which face is the work of each of them.[76]

In the same passage Jahangir favorably compares one of his favorite painters, Abu'l Hasan, to the Iranian, Ottoman, and Mughal non-pareil of great artists, Bihzad of Sultan Husain Baiqara's Herat. He also mentions that Abu'l Hasan's father was, in fact, a Herati painter named Aqa Riza'i who had joined Jahangir's service while he was still a prince. Jahangir names Abu'l Hasan and another man, Ustad Mansur, as the supremely gifted artists of his and his father Akbar's day. Jahangir had been so confident of his own aesthetic sense and preferences that after his coronation he dismissed many individuals from the imperial atelier because he felt they were inferior artists.

In assessing the volume and quality of Mughal art it is difficult to limit its florescence to one reign, as in the Ottoman case of Süleyman the Magnificent. The art of Akbar's reign is different in certain respects from that of his son and grandson, but not significantly less accomplished. Indeed, Akbar's atelier produced the widest range of art among the three rulers. It would be more accurate to say that Mughal painting flourished over a seventy-five-year period from the last two decades of Akbar's reign until the deposition of Shah Jahan by his son Aurangzib in 1658. As in Iran, later painters produced fewer illuminated manuscripts of literary works. Instead they concentrated on single-page depictions of individuals, couples, social gatherings, and court scenes. Given the voluminous output of the imperial atelier it is difficult to give an adequate impression of painting during Jahangir's and Shah Jahan's reigns. Several trends, however, distinguish seventeenth-century Mughal art from that produced in Istanbul and Isfahan in the late sixteenth and early seventeenth centuries,

---

[75] John Seyller offers a fascinating insight into the emperors' acquisitive motives in his translation and discussion of the marginal notes on imperial manuscripts: "The Inspection and Valuation of Manuscripts in the Imperial Mughal Library," *Artibus Asiae* 57, No. 3/4 (1997), 243–9.

[76] *Tūzuk-i Jāhangīri*, II, 20.

Fig. 21. India, 1615–18. Jahangir, with halo, ostentatiously preferring a Sufi to an Ottoman or an English ambassador, with the painter shown at the bottom left. Cupids reflect Jahangir's eclectic artistic tastes and the presence of Jesuits and other Europeans, who introduced Christian imagery to the Mughals.

Fig. 22. India, seventeenth century. A Hindu village scene, probably from a *muraqqa'*.

and these examples demonstrate again how much the Iranian miniature tradition varied in its distinct Ottoman and Mughal environments.

Jahangir particularly appreciated realistic, psychologically complex por-traiture, and both the Muslim artist Hashim and the Hindus Bishan Das and Govardhan excelled in such work. Mughal painting generally "rec-ognizes, acknowledges, and investigates the individuality and personal uniqueness of the people it portrays; and it becomes more exclusively an art of portraiture" – but not the Ottoman imperial kind.[77] Hashim, a Deccani native, produced many beautifully rendered individualized portraits, such as his painting of Ibrahim Adil Shah II of Bijapur, done sometime in the 1620s when the painter was working in Agra. About the same time he painted two small pictures of Jahangir, one accompanied by the portrayal of an Ottoman and a second a reproduction of a Christian painting, showing a woman with a cross. He produced elegant imperial portraits for Jahangir and Shah Jahan that glorified members of the dynasty.

Bishan Das, in contrast, a nephew of a painter in Akbar's atelier, was a specialist in painting portraits of individuals at social gatherings or historic events, and was chosen to accompany the 1613 Mughal mission to Shah 'Abbas in Isfahan. This mission had two goals: to lessen tensions between the neighboring states and to remind the Safavids of Mughal wealth, with its thousands of servants, hundreds of falconers, and lavishly caparisoned elephants. During the six years the embassy remained in Iran, Bishan Das painted a portrait of Shah 'Abbas which Jahangir praised in his memoirs: "He had taken [the likeness] of my brother the Shah exceedingly well, so that when I showed it to my servants, they said it was exceedingly well-drawn."[78] Govardhan, a "spiritual heir and disciple" of Basawan, began painting in Akbar's atelier and, like his colleagues, produced many splendid imperial portraits as well as renditions of sumptuous court scenes. More than any other Mughal artist, he internalized the lessons of European art, giving his portraits a unique naturalism and expressiveness. His paintings of "A Young Prince and His Wife on a Terrace," and "Jahangir Playing Holi" are examples of his technique, but he is probably best known for his paintings of Sufis and ascetics.[79] Perhaps his most stunning work, however, is his portrait of the dying, drug-addicted, emaciated courtier 'Inayat Khan.[80]

One other signature artistic feature of Jahangir's patronage was the Christian imagery that regularly appeared in paintings produced during his reign. These were not public declarations of Christian sympathy (as many Jesuits devoutly wished or believed), and in interpreting their significance Jahangir's fascination with exotic Western art, Christian or not,

---

[77] Beach, *Mughal and Rajput Painting*, 82.

[78] *Tûzuk-i Jâhangîri*, 116–17. See also the painting reproduced by Amina Okada in *Indian Miniatures of the Mughal Court*, 158.

[79] Holi is the popular Indian spring festival, a fertility rite whose rustic origins are now usually politely disguised with good-humored spraying of colored water.

[80] This discussion is taken entirely from Okada's superb work *Indian Miniatures at the Mughal Court*, 185–206.

has to be taken into account. Christian symbols did not appear in public places but in albums and audience halls, where they would have been seen by a relatively few members of the royal family or the Mughal aristocracy. Pictures of Jesus and Mary are relatively common – perhaps not so surprising as they were revered by Muslims and often mentioned in texts, including the memoirs of Babur's daughter Gulbadan Begim. The cherubs that decorate some of the portraits of Jahangir are, in some cases, quite obviously meant to emphasize his divine status, as in the famous image, dated to about 1620, showing him eradicating poverty with a bow and arrow, while cherubs fly above with a crown.[81] The latitudinarian religious attitudes of Akbar and to a lesser extent Jahangir, the noticeably different atmosphere at the Mughal court during their reigns, and Jahangir's own particular life as an aesthete may explain why such images are found in Mughal art and not, apart from a few exceptions, in Ottoman or Safavid painting.

Mughal art continued to flourish through Shah Jahan's reign, with artists still producing elegant individualized portraits of the emperor and his nobles. Artists also illustrated dynastic histories that had been a stock item in the Mughal atelier since its painters completed illustrations for the *Babur-nama*, and subsequently Abu'l Fazl's *Akbar-nama*, in the late sixteenth century. The lavishly illustrated, finely painted, exceptionally large *Padishah-nama* offers an artistic counterpoint to Shah Jahan's splendid architectural projects: the visual glorification of the Second Temür. Like Ottoman historical texts, its paintings portray actual court events, such as the reception of the Iranian envoy in 1631, weddings and other dynastic celebrations, royal acts of bravery, hunts, battles, and their gruesome aftermath, such as the decapitation of the Afghan Khan Jahan Ludi. With these illustrations, however, the splendid century of Mughal art abruptly ceases, to be revived only in an impoverished form in the eighteenth century.

Aurangzib, who seized his father's throne in 1658, took an orthodox Islamic view of painting and like Shah Tahmasp in Iran in later life, largely eliminated court patronage of the arts. Ironically, however, considering Aurangzib's view of himself as a Muslim ruler, one of the few paintings that date to his reign was done around the time he deposed his father; it features portraits of all the Mughal emperors and their Timurid ancestor

[81] Pratapaditya Pal, *Indian Painting* (Los Angeles: Los Angeles County Museum of Art, 1993), I, 262–5. See also Gawin Alexander Bailey, "The Indian Conquest of Catholic Art: The Mughals, the Jesuits, and Imperial Painting," *Art Journal* 57, No. 1, *The Reception of Christian Devotional Art* (Spring 1998), 24–30.

seated in a semi-circle.[82] It is appropriate that Aurangzib did not bequeath to posterity any great buildings, paintings, or works of literature, but left instead a Hanafi Sunni legal text, the *Fatawa-yi 'Alamgiri*, that subsequently became popular in that hotbed of Sunni legalism, the Ottoman Empire.

---

[82] See the painting by Bhawani Das, "A Dynastic Line from Timür to Aurangzeb," in Linda Leach, "The Timurids as a Symbol for the Emperor Jahangir," in Canby, ed., *Humayun's Garden Party*, 82–96.

8 Quests for a phoenix

Introduction

In 1600 the Ottomans, Safavids, and Mughals constituted three of the world's four most successful dynasties. Only the Ming in China ruled over a larger population, possessed greater territory, and controlled more wealth. Monarchs in each Muslim empire faced many difficulties, but European visitors to Istanbul, Isfahan, and Agra and Delhi were nearly all impressed with the vitality of these capital cities and the empires they represented. A century later, however, the Safavids had become afflicted with terminal lethargy, the Mughals' territorial control of Hindustan was atrophying even as their armies reached India's southeast coast, and the Ottomans, having recently failed catastrophically in their second siege of Vienna, were about to enter the Tulip Period, an engaging label for an era of self-indulgence that symbolized the loss of imperial dynamism. In 1722 the Safavid dynasty collapsed; seventeen years later the Mughal emperors degenerated into rulers of a small north Indian state; and in 1774, following a Russian victory, the Ottomans signed the Treaty of Küçük Kainarji, an event that marked the beginning of a century and a half during which Europeans and Ottoman subjects picked apart the empire.

If the fourteenth-century Muslim philosophical historian Ibn Khaldun had been alive to witness the rise and collapse of these empires, he might have commented, philosophically, that dynastic decline was inevitable, because, as he saw in North African tribal kingdoms, the original dynamism of conquerors and social cohesion of their followers inevitably atrophied due to the social, political, and military environment of their newly established states and the changing psychology of members of the dynasty and the ruling elite. In sociology this phenomenon is known as the Buddenbrooks theory of family lineages, positing that the situation and attitudes of successful families evolve from one generation to the next, inexorably leading to their decline.[1] Apart from the fact that Ibn Khaldun

---

[1] An allusion to the sociological maxim of business families, "From shirtsleeves to shirtsleeves in three generations," taken from Thomas Mann's novel of a North German commercial family, *Buddenbrooks*.

intended his model to explain the cyclical nature of a tribal dynasties, such theories are inevitably simplistic when considering actual states, and Ibn Khaldun in particular, despite the brilliance of his insights, had little to say about anomalous personalities or individual brilliance.

In studying dynastic empires it is natural to look first to members of the dynasties to find causes of their original success and ultimate failure. Individuals such as Mehmet II and Süleyman, Shah Isma'il and Shah 'Abbas, Babur and Akbar, illustrate the importance of fully engaged, dynamic and ruthless individuals in establishing a state, while it is also possible to see that personal flaws of these men's successors often contributed to or were directly responsible for the deterioration in a state's institutions, finances, and territorial control. Beyond these commonplace observations, the factors that led to the final demise of the Osmanlı, Safavi, and Timuri or Mughal empires were distinctly different in each case: structural factors, such as the poverty of resources, were particularly acute in Safavid Iran; profound social, religious or changes in society were especially noticeable in late-Mughal India; external trends, such as the rise and new aggressive expansion of eastern European monarchies and western European commercial states, profoundly affected the Ottomans. These factors contributed in different ways to the demise of the once imposing empires.

The single most fundamental difference among these states was the fact that the Safavids and Mughals declined almost entirely for internal reasons, internal to their territories and societies. These two dynasties had not been fundamentally weakened by European expansion before they collapsed or declined, and their rulers and regimes were fundamentally unchanged in political structure, military organization, and *mentalité* from what they had been a century earlier. The later Safavids were never attacked by a European power, and Iran did not suffer from European expansion until Russians moved into the Caucasus in the early nineteenth century. In India, by the time British forces intervened in Mughal territory (in Bengal, 1757), the empire had become little more than a minor kingdom, hostage to Hindu or Afghan powers and incapable of resisting either internal or external enemies.

The Ottomans, in contrast, battled on, having first undergone a transformation from a dynastic to a ministerial state in the seventeenth century, before, in the late eighteenth century, initiating a radical restructuring of the Ottoman military, the Ottoman state, and even Ottoman society in the image of the European states that threatened the empire's existence. Ottoman attempts to modernize while fending off European expansion, ambitious provincial notables, and nationalism ultimately fell victim to the First World War, which also claimed two European multi-national empires with long dynastic histories.

Safavid Iran

It is not difficult to identify the factors that precipitated the sudden collapse
of the Safavid dynasty in 1722. The immediate, unmistakable cause was the
deterioration of the Safavid military, which had been allowed to atrophy
during the seventeenth century. This was a matter that an individual, strong
ruler or a confident, secure minister could have solved. Shah 'Abbas I had
been able to defeat formidable Ottoman forces with his reconstituted
Safavid army, and even Shah 'Abbas I's first two successors had mobilized
successful military campaigns against the Ottomans and Mughals respectively. The last two *haram*-reared shahs, however, proved to be uninterested
in and/or incapable of reviving Shah 'Abbas I's modernized military, and
during their reigns there was a noticeable decline in administrative efficiency and security in the countryside.

Shah Sultan Husain's Qizilbash-led forces proved incapable of repulsing a poorly armed Afghan tribal force that marched on Isfahan in 1722,
following an Afghan revolt against the Safavid governor of Qandahar. In a
battle near the capital, Isfahan, Afghans defeated a much larger and better
armed but poorly led Safavid army commanded by a Qizilbash tribesman,
and following a devastating seven-month siege, Mahmud Ghilzai entered
the city. Sultan Husain abdicated and proclaimed his Afghan conqueror
the new Shah. Even though one of the Safavid princes escaped and was
proclaimed Tahmasp II, the Safavid state ceased to exist – a political
reality punctuated by the Afghan destruction of the Safavid archives,
which were reportedly dumped into the Zayandih River in Isfahan.

Within seven years, rough-hewn, perennially fractious Afghan tribesmen
proved themselves incapable of ruling the country, and were eventually
displaced by Nadir Quli Khan, the leader of one of the original Qizilbash
tribes, the Afshar, whose clans were then concentrated in Khurasan. A tribal
leader in the mold of earlier ruthless Central Asian conquerors, Nadir Shah
campaigned relentlessly in Iran and Afghanistan and, in 1739, successfully
invaded India to give the coup de grâce to the already weakened Mughal
dynasty. He also expressed an unpopular interest in reviving Sunni Islam in
Iran. Nadir Shah, as he came to be crowned in 1736 after briefly ruling
through two impotent Safavid princes, reigned only briefly before in 1747
his brutality and irrational cruelty prompted members of the Afshar and
Qajar tribes to assassinate him. During the remaining years of the century,
until the Qajar tribe gained supremacy in 1796, Iran dissolved into tribally
dominated territorial factions. Over the course of the eighteenth century
five different tribal dynasties ruled different regions of Iran.

In addition to the demonstrable weakness of the Safavid military, other
factors contributed to the dynasty's collapse. Natural disasters plagued

Safavid Iran in the second half of the seventeenth century, a series of shocks that compounded the deficiencies of the structurally weak Iranian economy.[2] These disasters accentuated the need for dynamic leadership, which was little in evidence during the period. *Haram* upbringing did not necessarily produce incompetent rulers, but the last two Safavid shahs were noticeably ineffectual monarchs. Shah Safi II, later recrowned as Sulaiman (r. 1666–94), was an alcoholic, and while that was not unusual in the Safavid house, he also seems to have had little appetite for active governance over his long, twenty-eight-year reign.[3] Fortunate not to have to face catastrophic crises, as years passed he spent increasing amounts of time in the *haram*, and decreasing amounts dealing with state affairs. During this period Iran's fragile finances deteriorated, despite the efforts of some capable ministers, some of whom performed remarkably well, given their challenges. None of them, however, attained power equivalent to the Ottoman Köprülü Grand Viziers who ruled the Ottoman Empire during the second half of the seventeenth century.[4] Still, the contrast between Sulaiman's indolence and Shah 'Abbas I's boundless energy could not have been greater. Yet when Sulaiman's son Shah Sultan Husain (r. 1694–1722) emerged from the *haram* to be crowned, he was even more ineffectual and disengaged than his father had been. The principal difference between the two was the degree to which the Shi'i *'ulama* dominated the ostentatiously pious, passive, and retiring Husain.

Shi'i Islam in late Safavid Iran

The influence of the Shi'i *'ulama* as an institution, and Muhammad Baqir Majlisi as an individual, substantially influenced later Safavid – and

---

[2] Andrew J. Newman identifies natural disasters, regional and world-wide economic developments beyond the dynasty's control, rather than personal incompetence of rulers, as the underlying cause of Safavid economic and political problems. See his *Safavid Iran*, 94–5. He vigorously criticizes the standard interpretation of the late Safavid era as one of unrelieved decline, but he does not discuss the organization of the military or quality of its leadership.

[3] Regarding late Safavid ministers, and responding to Newman's arguments about the general competence of Safavid rule in the late seventeenth century, Rudi Matthee in two important articles offers a sophisticated analysis of Safavid administration at this period. See first his discussion of the administrative system in which ministers acquired power in direct relation to the weakness of the Shah, "Administrative Stability and Change in Late-17th Century Iran: the case of Shaykh 'Ali Khan Zanganah (1669–1689)," *International Journal of Middle East Studies* 26 (1994), 77–98, and secondly his analysis of Sulaiman Shah's peaceful relations with the Ottomans, which, Professor Matthee suggests, were not solely the result of his indolence but reflected more complex considerations, one of which was, however, the poor condition of the Safavid military: "Iran's Ottoman Diplomacy during the Reign of Shāh Sulaymān I (1077–1105/1666–94)," in Kambiz Eslami, ed., *Iran and Iranian Studies* (Princeton: Zagros, 1998), 148–77.

[4] See below, p. 273.

Iranian – history. Originally created almost out of whole cloth by Safavid monarchs, the Iranian Shiʻi ʻulama institution had steadily grown in influence, especially during the reigns of Tahmasp I and Shah ʻAbbas I. In Iran, the combination of weak rulers who had lost much of their charismatic religious aura and a well-organized clergy, some of whose members recognized the Twelfth Imam as the only legitimate leader of the Shiʻi Muslim community, produced a unique imperial situation at the end of the seventeenth century. Unlike the Ottoman Empire, where the Sultans had subordinated and institutionalized the Sunni clergy as an arm of the state, and the Mughal Empire, whose rulers adopted a traditional Muslim ruler's attitude to clerical patronage while pursuing their own dynastic interests, in Iran the clergy achieved a unique level of autonomy and political influence.

Even before the pliant Shah Sultan Husain was crowned, some members of the ʻulama had advocated the creation of a purer Shiʻi state in Iran. They had frequently persuaded his predecessors to persecute Sufis and religious minorities, and a few Shiʻi clerics even publicly denied the legitimacy of the regime. Baqir Majlisi, the Shaikh al-Islam since 1687 and now installed as mulla bashi, the supreme religious official, represented the steadily increasing power of the Shiʻi ʻulama within the Safavid state, and he also strongly advocated the idea that only senior clerics could act as the Hidden Imam's delegates in interpreting doctrine and ruling on matters of ritual, including religious taxation. In essence he claimed for the Shiʻi ʻulama the authority ʻAli Karaki had exercised in the sixteenth century. Majlisi did not, however, question Safavid legitimacy, but supported the dynasty. Nonetheless, in popular tracts and in hadith studies he worked steadily to further inculcate the popular acceptance of Shiʻi orthodoxy throughout the country.

Majlisi was a complex man, whose religious training exposed him to the divergent doctrinal currents that had swirled through mid seventeenth-century Isfahan. He studied both with intolerant Shiʻi clerics, who persecuted Sufis and hated philosophers, and also with ʻulama who were more liberal and philosophically inclined. Unlike some earlier clerics and ministers, Majlisi did not actively persecute Armenians, Jews, or Sufis, which had been a staple of the vizier Muhammad Bek in the late 1650s and was also a popular policy with one of Majlisi's ministerial contemporaries; but he did harass Hindu merchants and financiers, who became favorite targets of Iranian economic resentment in the late seventeenth century.[5]

---

[5] Newman, Safavid Iran, Chapters 6 and 7.

Without government records it is impossible to quantify the overall state of Safavid government finances during Shah Sultan Husain's reign. The sporadic persecution of religious minorities, which preceded his reign and continued afterwards to some degree, exacerbated the problem of the dynasty's fragile finances. Just by taking Majlisi's advice and eliminating wine shops and other non-Islamic activities, Shah Sultan Husain's regime reduced tax revenues on these lucrative businesses by an estimated 50 kg. of gold per day.[6] More seriously, the harassment of Hindus, one of the two largest, wealthiest, and most influential mercantile communities, inevitably threatened trade and the availability of capital, and further lessened tax revenues, as the earlier attacks on Armenians and Jews had already done. Accurately quantifying the exact extent to which persecution of religious minorities damaged the economy is, however, impossible.

Given the fundamental weaknesses of the Iranian economy, only the kind of careful attention that Shah 'Abbas I gave to stimulating indigenous production and commerce could insure the financial stability of the dynasty. This attention included 'Abbas I's concern for the security of traveling merchants, shown by constructing *caravansarais* and appointing *rahdars* to patrol the main trade routes – a system, which like most other aspects of Safavid government, fell into decay in the late seventeenth century. The production and export of Iran's two major export commodities, silk and carpets, probably declined during the reign of the last two shahs. Bengal silk sold to the British East India Company may also have eaten into Iran's silk market, and carpet manufacturing certainly declined as it was dependent on royal patronage.[7] Without the income from export of these commodities money continued flowing out of the country to India to pay for spices and cloth. By 1722, therefore, even had a new Shah 'Abbas I come to the throne, little money would have been available to rebuild the army and restore order in the state. It was not until oil was discovered and then nationalized in the twentieth century that Iran regained a measure of prosperity, for as Iranians have sometimes told visitors traveling across their country in recent times, "Look around you: without oil, we have nothing!"[8] In Safavid times, the equivalent economic cry would have been, "Without silk we have nothing."

---

[6] Matthee, *The Pursuit of Pleasure*, 93.

[7] R. M. Savory, "Economic and Commercial History: Trade Relations with Europe," in *Safawids*, *Encyclopaedia of Islam* II, Brill Online.

[8] An Iranian's comment to the author during a bus trip from Tehran to Shiraz in November 1976.

Map 16. Qajar Iran in 1798

Post-Safavid Iran: the Qizilbash dynasties

The resuscitation of an Iranian state, or a state in Iran, was left to the Qajars (1796–1925), another Qizilbash tribe, which in 1796 established a new dynasty with a capital at Tehran, near their tribal homelands.[9] The Qajars, a dynasty whose rule in some ways represents a continuation of the Safavids, derived their legitimacy solely from tribal leadership; they did not possess or claim religious sanctity. In terms of legitimacy they performed a balancing act. They supported the Shi'i clergy, but also tried to persuade the Iranian public they represented a reincarnation of pre-Islamic Iranian imperial traditions. Thus they patronized pre-Islamic literature, painting, and sculpture that proclaimed their links with the imperial past.[10] The second Qajar ruler, Fath 'Ali Shah (r. 1798–1834), commissioned a *Shahanshah-nama* illustrated by court artists, in which Fath 'Ali Shah is identified with heroes of Firdausi's *Shah-nama*. In addition he ordered rock-cut relief carvings showing himself hunting

[9] Gene Garthwaite concisely summarizes the Qajar period in *The Persians*, Chapter 7.
[10] See Layla S. Diba, ed., *Royal Persian Paintings: The Qajar Epoch* 1785–1925 (London: I. B. Tauris for the Brooklyn Museum of Art, 1998) for an excellent introduction to Qajar history, ideology, and painting.

and at court, which were purposely located near reliefs of Achaemenid (550–331 BCE) and Sasanian (221–642 CE) monarchs in order to reinforce the shah's imperial image.

Yet during the eighteenth century the Iranian Shi'i *'ulama* had gained increased power and independence, and among them the Usuli faction came to dominate their Akhbari compatriots. Their *mujtahids*, or interpreters of Shi'i doctrine, consolidated their authority in the Shi'i shrines in Iraq, and subsequently became activist clerics in Iran.[11] They steadily increased their influence during the Qajar period. Consequently the Qajars were extremely vulnerable when, in the latter half of the nineteenth century, both Shi'i clergy and nationalist intellectuals openly challenged their legitimacy.

Qajar shahs did restore a measure of centralized control in Iran's major provinces and cities, even while tolerating tribal autonomy in many rural areas of the Iranian plateau. Like their contemporaries in the Ottoman Empire, Qajar rulers were faced with the problem of governing while fending off European incursions, which began with Russian expansion into and conquest of the Caucasus, previously a region of Iranian suzerainty. The Russo-Iranian treaties of Gulistan (1813) and Turkomanchi (1828) that concluded the conquest also gave the Russians "Capitulations," the extra-territorial powers that had by this time become a bane of the Ottomans. This began a century of direct or indirect European involvement in Iran in which Russians and British sought to gain territorial and economic advantage in the country.

European challenges stimulated Iran's first, hesitant steps towards modernization since Shah 'Abbas I's reign, and in 1810 the reigning Qajar monarch, Fath 'Ali Shah, briefly turned his attention from the procreation of hundreds of descendants and sent a group of Iranian students to Europe. As Russian and British Indian governments increased their intervention in Iran, a later Qajar monarch, Nasir al-Din Shah (r. 1848–96), took additional steps to strengthen the Qajar state by appointing a reforming minister.[12] This man, Amir Kabir, began modernizing Iran along the lines of the reforms that were then being instituted for similar reasons by Ottoman ministers, and with which he was familiar from his diplomatic service in Istanbul. Amir Kabir began a systematic reorganization of the military, the state, and educational institutions, but

---

[11] See Gene Garthwaite's Chapter 21 in the forthcoming *New Cambridge History of Islam* for a discussion of eighteenth-century Iran, and Said Amir Arjomand's concise analysis of eighteenth- and nineteenth-century Iranian history in *The Turban for the Crown: The Islamic Revolution in Iran* (Oxford University Press, 1988).

[12] Abbas Amanat, *Pivot of the Universe: Nasir al-Din Shah Qajar and the Iranian Monarchy 1831–1896* (Berkeley: University of California Press, 1997).

before these could take hold, he was murdered by orders of the apprehensive, insecure Nasir al-Din. Afterwards Nasir al-Din largely abandoned attempts to effect structural reforms in his traditional patrimonial dynasty, and instead allowed Iran to become an informal colony of Russia, Britain, and lesser European states, which in the late nineteenth century gained control over many aspects of the economy and military.

In 1872, for example, Baron de Reuter was awarded commercial and industrial concessions. These were later canceled, but in 1889 he received permission to form the first Imperial Bank of Iran, including the right to issue bank notes. The Russians, on their part, were granted the authority to train a Russian-style Cossack brigade, in an attempt to expand the shah's military authority beyond unreliable tribal levies. Other concessions followed, such as Belgian control over the customs. The most contentious of all, a British concession in 1890 to market tobacco throughout the country, triggered a visceral reaction and significant popular protests directed at both the regime and foreign powers. The protests, rightly seen as a proto-nationalist uprising, involved 'ulama, merchants, urban proletariat, and liberal, European-influenced intellectuals.[13]

In 1905–6, during the reign of Nasir al-Din's successor Muzaffar al-Din Shah (r. 1896–1907), anger at increasing European dominance and the corruption of the regime provoked a complex coalition of Western-educated intellectuals, members of the Shi'i 'ulama, and leaders of the Iranian Bakhtiyari tribe of pastoral nomads to revolt and force a constitution on the seriously ill ruler. The coalition was, however, a curious and unstable one. European-educated intellectuals sought liberal parliamentary democracy with a European-style constitutional monarch. The Shi'i 'ulama acted primarily out of their hostility to what they saw as a corrupt and illegitimate political leadership, harking back to some Safavid clerics' criticism of the later Safavids.[14] Bakhtiyaris, led by liberal tribal leaders, were also motivated by traditional tribal hostility to any centralized state.[15]

Riza Shah and the imperial interregnum

This coalition governed fitfully during the next two decades, beset by attempted royalist coups, acute financial problems, and further Russian

---

[13] For a study of one such intellectual, the founder of the first Iranian newspaper, *Qanun*, see Hamid Algar, *Mirzâ Malkum Khan: A Study in the History of Iranian Modernism* (Berkeley: University of California Press, 1973).

[14] Hamid Algar, *Religion and State in Iran, 1785–1906* (Berkeley: University of California Press, 1969).

[15] See among other works the classic study of the British Persianist E. G. Browne: *The Persian Revolution of 1905–1909* (New York: Barnes and Noble, repr. 1966).

and British intervention, highlighted by these powers' division of the country into spheres of influence in 1907.[16] The First World War accentuated all the difficulties of a fragile, divided constitutional regime. In 1926 Riza Khan, an officer in the Russian-trained Cossack Brigade, was crowned as Shah of the new Pahlavi dynasty, named for the *pahlavan*s, the warrior-heroes of ancient Iran, a dynastic name that intentionally recalled the glories of pre-Islamic Iranian monarchies. Pahlavi ideology celebrated Persepolis, the Achaemenid ceremonial capital near Shiraz, rather than Shi'i shrines in Mashhad, Iran, or Karbala and Najaf in Iraq. Riza Khan, a modernizing, centralizing military nationalist in the mold of his contemporary Mustafa Kemal Atatürk, was fundamentally hostile to both the *ulama* and the pastoral nomads, as the two groups which obstructed modernization. Riza Khan began a series of secular modernizing reforms based on the example of Atatürk, who had constructed a Turkish nation-state from the ashes of the Ottoman Empire three years earlier.

Riza Shah and his son never succeeded, however, in creating a legitimizing charisma for themselves, and fifty years of secular modernization and political suppression were insufficient to eliminate the power of the clergy, the only "national" institution apart from the army. In 1979 it was the *ulama* who displaced the Pahlavis and attained power after centuries of grumbling about the illegitimacy of secular authorities in a Shi'i state.[17] The establishment of an Iranian clerical state was a unique event in the history of the Islamic world.

Mughals

If the sudden collapse of the Safavids in 1722 can be fairly easily understood and explained, the same is not true of Nadir Shah Afshar's defeat of the Mughals in 1739, an event that marked the end of the empire *qua* empire and the beginning of the prolonged but unmistakable death rattle of the dynasty. The obvious question to be asked about the Mughals is how the wealthy, powerful empire of Shah Jahan could, eighty years after his deposition, deteriorate to such an extent that the reigning emperor in 1739 could not defend his territory against an Iranian tribal chief and

---

[16] Jennifer Siegel, *Britain, Russia and the Final Struggle for Central Asia* (London and New York: I. B. Tauris, 2002). See also the fascinating account by the American Morgan Shuster, who was appointed as "Treasurer-General" to try to stabilize Iranian finances amid the countervailing internal and external pressures: *The Strangling of Persia* (New York: The Century Company, 1912).

[17] For insight into the ideology, organization, and personalities of the Iranian *ulama* see Michael Fischer, *Iran: From Religious Dispute to Revolution* (Cambridge, Mass.: Harvard University Press, 1980).

prevent the sack of Delhi, the looting of the treasury, and the plundering of the Red Fort, including the symbol of Mughal sovereignty, Shah Jahan's peacock throne. There is no simple answer to this question, nor is there even a generally agreed upon analysis of the factors that precipitated this ignominious Mughal defeat. Most scholars believe the Mughal Empire began to fail during the reign of Shah Jahan's son and successor, Aurangzib, although they rarely agree on the exact nature of the problems or the inevitability of the empire's subsequent collapse.[18]

If the effectiveness of the rulers is the first question to be raised when examining the demise of dynastic empires, in the Mughal case Shah Jahan was succeeded – and imprisoned – by his son Aurangzib, who was an aggressive, proven commander when he came to the throne in 1658. In contrast with Safavid Iran, where the last two monarchs rarely left their palaces, their alcohol, or their prayers, and the Ottoman Empire, whose sultans had long since withdrawn from sight and from day-to-day administration, Aurangzib personally led Mughal armies until the end of his forty-nine-year reign, never succumbing to the dissolute *haram* life of the Safavids or to the wine and drugs that had incapacitated Jahangir and so many Mughal princes in the past. In some respects he resembled Akbar. Like his ancestor he possessed enormous energy, personally led successful campaigns, conquered substantial territories and reigned for nearly half a century. He obeyed Akbar's reported dictum that rulers should be constantly engaged in conquest. In other respects, however, Aurangzib could not have been more different.

Aurangzib had the personality of a religious ascetic, with an ascetic's religious discipline, austere personality, and spiritual egotism. While he denounced intolerance and invoked the religious liberality of his ancestors to win over Rajputs during the war of succession, once in power he often acted as an intolerant orthodox Muslim.[19] He condemned his brother's, Dara Shukuh's, Sufism and latitudinarianism so as to justify his execution, and during the course of his reign he supported orthodox Hanafi Sunni Islam, eliminated practices not sanctioned by Islamic law, and tried to coerce non-Muslims to convert to Islam. Among other suggestive acts, he eliminated the use of the Iranian solar calendar in favor of Islamic *hijra*

---

[18] For a summary of theories explaining the Mughal collapse see especially Alam, *The Crises of Empire*, 2–10; M. N. Pearson, "Shivaji and the Decline of the Mughal Empire," in "Symposium: Decline of the Mughal Empire," *Journal of Asian Studies* 35, No. 2 (February 1976), 221–35; M. Athar Ali, "The Passing of Empire: The Mughal Case," *Modern Asian Studies* 9, No. 3 (1975), 385–96.

[19] Khan, "State in Mughal India," 31–2.

dating.[20] He was a disciple of the restrained, orthodox Naqshbandi Sufi order in the Indian or *mujaddidi* variant developed by Shaikh Ahmad Sirhindi in the early sixteenth century, and he commissioned the monumental Arabic-language collection of Hanafi legal rulings known as the *Fatâwa-yi 'Alamgîrî*, which subsequently became popular among Ottoman clerics.[21] Aurangzib's Hanafi Sunni orthodoxy might seem to echo the Ottoman Süleyman's, but the Ottoman sultan ruled more as a statist who, in typical Ottoman dynastic tradition, was motivated by his concern to stabilize Ottoman rule rather than by pious intolerance. The difference between the two is partly illustrated by Aurangzib's puritanical attitudes and harassment of Hindus.

Somewhat in the mold of the Safavid Shah Tahmasp after his "Sincere Repentance," Aurangzib ended court patronage of most music, poetry, and painting, forbade the use of alcohol and drugs, the writing of new dynastic histories, and the celebration of *nauruz*, the popular Zoroastrian Persian New Year festival.[22] He re-imposed the pilgrimage tax on Hindus and in 1679 the *jizya*, ordered recently built temples demolished, encouraged conversion, and punished apostasy. In brief, over the course of his reign Aurangzib gradually came to govern almost as Zia al-Din Barani wished Indo-Muslim rulers to act in the fourteenth century, or as Aurangzib's contemporary Shah Sultan Husain Safavi sought to rule. While some nobles and local officials objected to his policies, a number of *'ulama* took their cue and terrorized non-Muslims, particularly prosperous Hindus in the towns.[23] Aurangzib not only alienated numbers of Hindus, but by abandoning the traditional aristocratic socializing in the court *majlis*, he also severed close personal relationships with many Muslim and Hindu aristocrats, loosening the critical ties that Babur in the early sixteenth century had advised his son, Humayun, to cultivate if he wished to be a successful monarch. "Solitude," Babur wrote, "is not consistent with kingship."[24]

---

[20] Aziz Ahmad, "Dara Shikoh and Aurangzeb," in his *Islamic Culture in the Indian Environment* (Oxford: Clarendon Press, 1964), 197.

[21] Alan M. Guenther, "Hanafi Fiqf in Mughal India: The Fatâwa-i 'Âlamgîrî," in Richard M. Eaton, ed., *India's Islamic Traditions* (New Delhi: Oxford University Press, 2003), 209–33. See also Mu'in al-Dîn b. Sirâj al-Dîn Khwând Shâh's work *Ganj-i sa'adat*, a 1663 Naqshbandi treatise dedicated to Aurangzib. Cited by D. N. Marshall, *Mughals in India: A Bibliographical Survey*, Vol. I (Bombay, Asia Publishing House, 1967), No. 1297a, and for Sirhindi, Friedman, *Shaykh Ahmad Sirhindi*.

[22] Regarding music see the careful revisionist article by K. Butler Brown, "Did Aurangzeb Ban Music?" *Modern Asian Studies* 41, Part I (January 2007), 77–120.

[23] Satish Chandra, "Jizya and the State in India during the Seventeenth Century," in Eaton, ed., *India's Islamic Traditions*, 133–49.

[24] Richards, *The Mughal Empire*, 173, and Dale, *The Garden of the Eight Paradises*, 45.

Aurangzib's religious puritanism and intolerance are often blamed for the major conflicts that occurred during his reign, and blamed also for the ultimate loss of Mughal control over certain regions within the empire in the latter half of the seventeenth century. Nonetheless it is not a simple matter to demonstrate such causation. Like his predecessors, Aurangzib had to contend constantly with willful or rebellious local lineages or *zamindars* throughout his reign. Akbar's historian, Abu'l Fazl, observed in the late sixteenth century that "The custom of the majority of the zamindars of Hindustan is to leave the path of single-mindedness and to look to every side and to join anyone who is powerful or who is making an increasing stir."[25] Hundreds if not thousands of such men, Afghan Muslims and Hindus, had never accepted the legitimacy or permanence of Mughal rule. Aurangzib, however, had to contend with three serious problems that posed far more of a threat to Mughal sovereignty than revolts of minor provincial notables: the expansion of Sikh influence in the Punjab; a revolt of an important Rajput lineage; and, most of all, the rise of a new, formidable power in the Deccan, the non-Muslim Maratha Confederacy.

The Sikhs in late Mughal India

Aurangzib's dealings with the Sikhs are an instructive example of a problem he did not create, but exacerbated. Sikhism, as has been seen, represented a complex socio-religious movement centered in the Punjab. It began as an attempt to build a bridge between Islam and Hinduism and gradually led to the formation of a distinct social order in one of the Mughals' wealthiest and most strategically important provinces. Jahangir had already helped to radicalize the Sikhs when in 1605 he executed the fifth Sikh *guru* Arjun, who had, Jahangir accurately noted in his memoirs, "captivated many of the simple-hearted of the Hindus, and even of the ignorant and foolish followers of Islam."[26] Jahangir seems to have been far more concerned about social order than religion, but he was right to be concerned about the spread of such a movement. He imprisoned Guru Arjun's son in the same Gwalior fortress where he later sent the Naqshbandi Shaikh Ahmad Sirhindi, also evidently for disturbing social calm, but this did nothing to slow the progress of the movement.

In 1664 the Sikhs chose a new leader, Tegh Bahadur, who during the next decade traveled throughout the Punjab to spread the new faith, and succeeded in converting many more of the Jats, members of the most

---

[25] Quoted by Pearson in "Shivaji and the Decline of the Mughal Empire," 226.
[26] *Tûzuk-i Jahângîrî*, I, 72.

important Hindu agrarian castes in the region. When in the 1670s Aurangzib heard that Sikhs were, as Jahangir earlier observed, converting Muslims to the new faith, he arrested the Guru, tried him before a Muslim religious court for blasphemy, and had him executed. This left the growing Sikh community with an undying hatred for the Mughals and prompted the next Guru, Gobind Singh, to institute a form of baptism that ritually sanctified distinctive Sikh identity. He also organized the militant defense of the new socio-religious community. His teachings intensified the Sikhs' consciousness of their separateness and further diminished imperial control over the province, ultimately leading to the formation of a Sikh state in the Punjab in the late eighteenth century. The Sikh movement was, therefore, not simply a *zamindars'* revolt but a religious movement that evolved into a sectarian community, whose expansion and evolution Mughal rulers could not control. The dynasty did not create the Sikh community, which Akbar had solicitously patronized; Aurangzib only intensified a Sikh hostility to the Mughals that dated from Jahangir's reign.[27]

The Rajput revolt

Shortly after he executed the Sikh Guru, Aurangzib triggered a revolt among a section of the Rajput nobility, the class of privileged Hindu chiefs whom Akbar had defeated, integrated, and promoted within the imperial service, while leaving them in place as administrators of their historic homelands in the desert regions west of Agra and Delhi. Under Akbar, Jahangir, and Shah Jahan, Rajputs developed into the most effective and loyal members of the Mughal imperial system, and the highest-ranked noble in the empire in 1658–59 was the Rajput Maharaja of Jaipur, who supported Aurangzib in the War of Succession.[28] During his reign, however, Aurangzib reduced the number of Rajputs in his service and limited their opportunities and income outside their homeland. Then in 1679, following the death of the Maharaja of Jodhpur, Aurangzib used the now accepted imperial right formally to recognize a new raja to alienate this important family by ignoring their will and designating an unpopular successor – and by offering eventually to crown the family's designated heir, but only after the newly born infant had been raised as a Muslim in the imperial *haram*.

[27] Khushwant Singh, *A History of the Sikhs* (Princeton University Press, 1984), and Grewal, *The Sikhs of the Punjab*.
[28] Richards, *The Mughal Empire*, 179.

When the Jodhpur Rajputs refused this proposal, open conflict erupted and Aurangzib sent troops to occupy Jodhpur who desecrated and destroyed a number of temples in the Rajput kingdom, prompting the neighboring Rajput ruler of Mewar to join the struggle. This occurred in the same year when Aurangzib reimposed the *jizya* tax on Hindus, and while Aurangzib explicitly exempted Rajput nobles from this tax, the emperor's religious intolerance was one of the grievances that his son Akbar cited when he responded to Rajput entreaties, rebelled against his father in 1680, and proclaimed himself emperor in January 1681. Aurangzib defeated his son and the Rajputs of Mewar, who were forced to accept the *jizya* tax, but the Rajputs of Jodhpur fought on for another generation. Other Rajput chiefs did not defect from Mughal service, but by changing the succession process into a religious issue and then forcibly imposing *jizya* on Mewar, Aurangzib transformed imperial relations with this crucial class, many of whose chiefs had by this time enthusiastically embraced Mughal imperial culture.

Knowledge of the Rajput rebellion is important for those who try to understand how Mughal rule atrophied so quickly in the eighteenth century, for imperial territories contained hundreds if not thousands of locally entrenched Hindu and also Afghan lineages, men classified as *zamindars* in imperial parlance or *ayyan*, provincial notables, by the Ottomans. In the Indian case, though, many of the most powerful local notables were non-Muslims. Rajputs stood at one privileged end of the spectrum of men whose loyalty to the empire was conditional on the continued demonstration of coercive imperial power and benefits from their participation in the Mughal system. The Rajputs, for example, had used their imperial connections to consolidate and enrich themselves in their homelands.

When Mughal power decayed in the eighteenth century, hundreds of these lineages, whether former rajas, ambitious peasants, or Afghan adventurers, could and did gradually reestablish their earlier autonomy or create new states in the power vacuum that followed the imperial collapse and preceded the British conquest. A group of cohesive Jat lineages or caste groups, who farmed in the area along the Delhi–Agra road, were one such group, whose corporate identity and difficult homeland terrain enabled them, even in the late seventeenth century, openly to contest taxation, raid imperial caravans, fight pitched battles, and sometimes defeat Mughal commanders.[29]

---

[29] Mahesh Chandra Pradhan, *The Political System of the Jats of Northen India* (Bombay: Oxford University Press, 1966) and R. P. Rana, *Rebels to Rulers: The Rise of Jat Power in Medieval India, c. 1665–1735* (New Delhi: Manohar, 2006).

The Maratha challenge

Aurangzib's difficulties with Sikhs and Rajputs paled, however, in comparison with his struggle to solve the challenge posed by the rising power of the Marathas, a Hindu caste group concentrated in the mountainous regions of Maharashtra, east-southeast of the later British commercial settlement of Bombay. They posed as great an internal threat to Mughal domination as Muhammad 'Ali, the Ottoman governor of Egypt, did to the Ottoman sultans during the first half of the nineteenth century, although the legitimacy of the two was entirely different. Aurangzib's inability to solve the Maratha challenge is generally regarded as his single greatest failure.

He first came into contact with Marathas when Shah Jahan sent him to central India in 1636 as part of persistent Mughal attempts to expand southwards that Akbar had begun nearly a century earlier. Under Shah Jahan, Aurangzib had reduced the last two Muslim-ruled Deccan sultanates to tributary status. These two were Bijapur in the Marathi-speaking west and Golconda in the Telegu-speaking eastern districts. Aurangzib had just negotiated peace terms with the Sultan of Bijapur when his father fell ill in September 1657, the war of succession began, and Aurangzib withdrew north to contest the throne.

In 1681 he returned to the region personally and in force with three princes, the bulk of the imperial army, the *haram*, the household, and most of the imperial administrative staff. He never returned to Agra or Delhi, but spent the remainder of his life campaigning in the Deccan. The contrast with his Ottoman and Safavid palace-reared contemporaries could not have been greater. Ibn Khaldun might have said that Aurangzib was the exception that proved his rule – of inevitable dynastic decline. In any case, Aurangzib's immediate reason for going south at that time was the renewed rebellion of his son Akbar, who after his defeat in 1681 had fled south and taken refuge at the Maratha court, located at a fortress in the rugged mountainous country about 100 kilometers south-southeast of Bombay.

Akbar had framed his rebellion as a response to Aurangzib's intolerant iconoclasm and reimposition of the deeply resented *jizya* tax on Hindus, and the leader of the Marathas, who had crowned himself in 1674, publicly criticized Aurangzib for repudiating Akbar's tolerant policies. By appealing to formidable Rajput and Maratha leaders as well as to Muslim members of the nobility who disagreed with Aurangzib's religious policies, Akbar revealed that substantial members of the Indian elite resented his father's intolerant policies. His rebellion, as a potential Mughal ruler, also represented a formidable threat, all the more so for his new Maratha alliance.

Aurangzib's twenty-six years of campaigning in the Deccan shifted the focus of the Mughal Empire away from its historic center in Agra and Delhi, and his decision to remain in the south was one turning-point in the history of the dynasty. During these years Aurangzib was able to complete the Mughal goal of conquering and then assimilating the Muslim powers in the region, and between 1685 and 1687 he defeated both Bijapur and also Golconda, and began the process of integrating the territories into the empire. By the end of his life his armies had reached the southeast coast near the British settlement of Madras. The Maratha problem was, however, never solved; it had its roots in the 1640s and 1650s with the remarkable achievements of the founder of the Maratha kingdom, Shivaji Bhonsla.

Shivaji was the son of a Marathi-speaking landholder who had spent most of his career in the service of the Muslim Sultanate of Ahmadnagar. After the Mughals swallowed Ahmadnagar, Shivaji's father took service with Bijapur, while retaining his large estates near Pune, east of Bombay, as an independent fief. Shivaji's family belonged to a ritually low agrarian subcaste, many of whose members had also taken military service with one or another of the Muslim Deccan sultanates. Their military service and training distinguished them from other Hindu subcastes in mountainous regions south-southwest of the future British port of Bombay.

Shivaji inherited his father's estates and profession at eighteen and quickly demonstrated that he had broader political ambitions and skills than his father or any of his Maratha contemporaries. By his daring, successful plundering, military victories, extortion, diplomacy, and careful organization, he carved out a substantial new state centered in the Marathi-speaking regions of the jungle-covered mountain range that runs along India's west coast. First seizing territory that was actually or nominally part of the decaying Bijapur Sultanate, by the time of the Mughal War of Succession he had begun to threaten imperial territories. In the 1660s he successfully led two daring raids that generated the charisma of success among his Maratha followers.

In 1663 he attacked the Maratha town of Pune, recently occupied by imperial troops, and even wounded the Aurangzib's Deccan viceroy. Then in 1664 he led a cavalry raid on Surat, the pre-eminent Mughal port in Gujerat, the principal emporium for European and Indian Ocean trade. In retrospect the latter raid stands out as a pivotal moment in the history of the Mughal Empire. It revealed both Shivaji's audacity and the lethargy and indiscipline of the Mughal commanders, who barricaded themselves inside the Surat fortress on the news of the Maratha approach, and did nothing to prevent Shivaji from plundering the city's wealthy merchants, from whom he took an estimated ten million rupees' worth of cash and jewels. This was the most spectacular of a series of swift, predatory cavalry raids, *ghazi*-like incursions, that became the Marathas' signature tactic against Bijapur and Mughal territories, culminating more than a century later in the Maratha occupation of the pitiful remnants of the Mughal Empire in 1760.

On several occasions Aurangzib seemed to have "solved" the Maratha problem. In 1665 one of his Rajput generals, Jai Singh, besieged and eventually captured Shivaji, who in 1666 was brought before the emperor at Agra. The emperor, however, not only failed to win over the Maratha leader and integrate him into the empire as Akbar had earlier done with the Rajputs, but even allowed him to escape. Shivaji returned to his homeland, eventually resumed campaigning against both Bijapur and Mughal territories, and in 1670 again raided Surat against token imperial resistance. In most cases the Marathas were able to out-maneuver Mughal heavy cavalry and cumbersome artillery trains sent after them, in confrontations that shared some characteristics with the relentless Oghuz raids on the Byzantine frontiers of western Anatolia.

This first period of Mughal and Maratha conflict climaxed in Shivaji's coronation as a fully independent Hindu raja in 1674, an event that has been characterized as "one of the most important political acts of the seventeenth century" in India. Shivaji enthroned himself with Hindu rituals, in which a prestigious Brahmin priest declared that he was not actually a low-caste farmer, but a descendant of the same warrior-caste lineage as the prestigious Rajput house of Mewar.[30] His recognition as *Shiva Chatrapati*, the all-conquering incarnation of the god Shiva, resonated not only in contemporary Maharashtra, but also among late nineteenth-century anti-British Marathi Brahmans, who created a Shivaji festival as a ritual expression of their hostility to non-Hindu rule. Mahatma Gandhi's assassin, critical of Gandhi's sympathy for Indian Muslims, emerged from this milieu.

Shivaji's coronation was not a Hindu nationalist event, although some Marathas in the colonial era interpreted his campaigns (and later Maratha conquests) as a Hindu protest against Muslim imperialism. Most Rajput lineages still continued to serve Aurangzib, who was seemingly successful in solving the Maratha problem a second time in 1689, when he captured and executed Shivaji's successor. Yet, instead of being able to pacify the Marathas and/or integrate them into the imperial system, Aurangzib found himself fighting a continuous war with various members of Shivaji's family or their commanders, first in the far southeast and then in Maharashtra.

---

[30] Richards, *The Mughal Empire*, 213.

Aurangzib remained in the Deccan from 1689 until his death in 1707, fighting what had become a hydra-headed coalition of independent Maratha commanders, who profitably raided imperial territories, weakening Mughal resolve and the imperial economy throughout the Deccan. Aurangzib's armies, some still commanded by important Rajput chiefs, continued to win victories in a seemingly neverending series of campaigns between 1689 and 1707, but the emperor was never able to destroy Maratha power or to negotiate a peace that might have stabilized the Mughal frontier. In the Deccan after 1689 "public order, political authority, political stability, and agricultural and industrial production were in descending spiral."[31]

The Mughal collapse

Was this deteriorating situation a personal failure of Aurangzib and directly attributable to his religious attitudes? It may partly have been due to his intolerant personality, but that should not completely overshadow his remarkable energy or tactical military abilities. The Maratha problem resembled the Sikh situation in that both arose independently of Mughal rulers, and presented challenges that Akbar might conceivably have solved, but which they could not. Aurangzib seemed to exude a profound sense of failure before his death, but whether that reflected more his exhausted frustration or his pious regret over slaughtering his brothers and imprisoning his father is not clear. After his death the Marathas evolved into a new, more cohesive political structure led by Brahmin ministers of Shivaji's family, and in 1719 a Maratha force rode to Delhi to join in Mughal dynastic politics. By 1739, when the Iranian Nadir Shah Afshar invaded India and sacked Delhi, Marathas had occupied and were administering much of imperial territory south and west of Agra, and in 1752 they became the "protectors" of an eviscerated Mughal dynasty.[32]

Despite the deteriorating political situation Aurangzib left behind at his death, his successor, Bahadur Shah, was an experienced, battle-tested individual, who had defeated his brothers in a typical Mughal war of succession and inherited an imperial treasury worth 240 million rupees, more funds than Akbar left when he died in 1605.[33] Thus he had sufficient resources to buy the loyalty of old nobles and the experience and

---

[31] Ibid., 252.
[32] For a narrative and analysis of Maratha conquests see Stewart Gordon, *The Marathas 1600–1818* (Cambridge University Press, 1993), 91–153.
[33] John F. Richards, "Mughal State finance and the Premodern World Economy," *Comparative Studies in Society and History* 23, No. 2 (1981), 293.

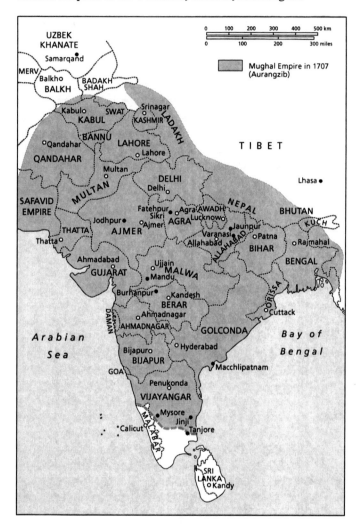

Map 17. The Mughal Empire in 1707

willingness actively to campaign. Bahadur Shah was, in fact, the last capable and effective Mughal ruler, and almost before drawing a breath as emperor, he faced rebellions of the Rajput ruler of Jodhpur, followed by a popular insurrection of Sikhs in the Punjab and continued Maratha depredations in the Deccan, now penetrating into imperial north India.

Bahadur Shah's ultimate failure to restore Mughal authority and arrest the decline of its power relative to the Sikhs, Rajputs, and Marathas stemmed partly from his policies and partly from his age. Following a revolt of Jodhpur Rajputs in 1708, he imposed intolerant Muslim rule in the Jodhpur kingdom, and compromised the loyalty of all Rajput chiefs when he tightened imperial control over Rajasthan, rejecting the old *watan jagirs* or homeland estates, and thus essentially abrogating Akbar's Rajput settlement. Bahadur Shah was not responsible for the Sikh uprising that followed a year later in 1709, but a poorly armed Sikh–Jat peasantry fueled by anti-imperial hatred and religious zeal ravaged much of the vital Punjab plain for more than a year before the emperor himself forced the Sikhs back into the hills, whence however, they organized new assaults in 1711 that the emperor was not able to quell before he died in 1712. Nor was he responsible for the fact that by the time he came to power, Maratha descendants of Shivaji and independent commanders had shredded Mughal authority in the Deccan. Nor was he responsible for his own advanced age; he was crowned at age sixty-four, and therefore, scarcely had time to consolidate his authority when he died, in 1712, aged seventy. His was the shortest reign in the dynasty's history, and his death provoked yet another expensive and disruptive succession struggle, which proved the proximate cause of the dynasty's disintegration.

The years from 1712 to 1739 constitute the last years of the Mughal Empire as an empire. After 1739 Timurids still reigned, but no longer ruled more than a north Indian city-state. The new emperor, Jahandar Shah (r. 1712–13) was largely the creature of a powerful minister, the first time this had occurred in dynastic history since Akbar's youth. Perhaps because of his powerlessness, Jahandar Shah reigned for only a year, as a frequently drunken, frivolous self-indulgent pleasure seeker, dissolutely and publicly enjoying himself with his former concubine, the daughter of a court musician now elevated as his principal wife. The financial and administrative system slowly disintegrated, and while substantial revenues continued to flow into Delhi from a well-administered Bengal province, it was not enough even to repay the troops who had brought the new emperor to the throne. Unlike the Ottoman situation in the mid seventeenth century, when the Köprülüs, a family of viziers, rescued the Ottoman state, no comparable officials became ascendant in Mughal India, perhaps because the activist leadership of the rulers had never allowed for the development of a similarly powerful ministerial class.

Jahandar Shah's disreputable life and inability to buy the loyalty of the imperial nobility left him vulnerable to a coup led by a son of one his brothers killed in the war of succession. The new emperor, Farruksiyar, slaughtered his opponents and blinded three Timurid princes, including his own younger brother. Farruksiyar then struggled for a subsequent six years to secure his rule, and, distracted by his personal struggle for survival, allowed the disintegrating empire to deteriorate still further, until in 1719 he was deposed and blinded by his nominal allies, two Muslim brothers, Sayyids, from families long settled in north India and loyal supporters of the Mughal dynasty. They ruled for one year before a group of nobles tried to resurrect the Timurid house by freeing a captive Mughal emperor, Muhammad Shah, and allowing him to govern. By that time, however, it was too late. Marathas and Rajputs had become independent, Sikhs were increasing their influence in the Punjab and many provincial Mughal governors were gradually turning away from an impotent central government and evolving into local rulers. When Nadir Shah entered the country in 1739, the once powerful Mughal army was incapable of defending the heartland of the Empire. The Iranian seized what remained of the once lavish treasury, took Shah Jahan's Peacock throne and returned with his treasures to fund several years more of brutal campaigns in Iran.

Indian Muslims without a Muslim empire

Unlike the situation in the Ottoman Empire, where scholars began writing about the decline of the empire in the late sixteenth century, few officials or scholars in either Iran or India are known to have developed theories of decline, even as their empires were coming to pieces. Despite their impeccable Turco-Mongol lineage, the Mughals never created the kind of imperial ethos that inspired Ottoman bureaucrats, even (or especially) their "slave" ministers, to feel a kind of state loyalty. One of the few individuals known to react publicly to the disintegration of the Mughal regime was the religious scholar Shah Wali-Ullah (1703–62), who also produced one of the few extant collections of advice writings on the decline of Mughal India.[34]

The son of Shah 'Abd al-Rahim, one of the compilers of Aurangzib's massive Arabic collection of Hanafi Sunni legal rulings, Shah Wali-Ullah was a follower of the orthodox Indian branch of the Naqshbandi Sufi order that Shaikh Ahmad Sirhindi developed in the early seventeenth century and which later spread to Ottoman territories in this form. He was a profoundly serious and influential religious scholar, who had spent years in the Hijaz studying *hadith* and Islamic law at the same time as the important fundamentalist scholar Muhammad Ibn 'Abd al-Wahhab was also studying in Mecca and Medina.

Shah Wali-Ullah returned to India in 1732 and wrote extensively in letters and elsewhere about the political chaos and economic collapse of

---

[34] See among many other sources Aziz Ahmad, "The Walî-Ullâhî Movement," in *Islamic Culture in the Indian Environment*, 201–9.

the Mughals. As was typical of *'ulama* throughout the Islamic world when responding to political crises, Shah Wali-Ullah's solutions were traditional political and religious ones: the reestablishment of Muslim power and the revitalization of Islamic thought and practice. In his case, he invited Afghans to invade India and reestablish Muslim sovereignty, and advocated the consolidation of Sufi practice and the use of *ijtihad* or rational interpretation to reconcile Islam to the evolution of human society. In this latter emphasis Shah Wali-Ullah reflected the radically altered environment that distinguished his time from that of his early seventeenth-century intellectual precursor, the Naqshbandi Sufi Shaikh Ahmad Sirhindi. "The time has come," he wrote in the introduction to *Hujjat Allâh al-bâligha,* "that the religious law of Islam should be brought into the open fully dressed in reason and argument."[35]

Shah Wali-Ullah initiated a series of attempts by Indian Muslims to resuscitate the Indo-Muslim community. In comparison with the Ottoman Empire, whose *'ulama* was subordinate to the regime, Indian Muslims enjoyed a far higher degree of autonomy. In Istanbul no *ilmiye* scholar is known to have produced a major treatise on the decline of Ottoman Muslims in the nineteenth century or to have taken any independent action to reform the community. By contrast Indian Muslims, who had no empire to turn to, developed a variety of responses to the depressed state of a community ruled in the nineteenth and twentieth century by Christians and economically subordinate to Hindus. One of these, an institutionalized religious revival, represented the spiritual continuation of Shah Wali-Ullah's mission. His sons began this work, which was continued by some members of the British-founded Delhi College.[36] It culminated in 1868 with the founding of the Deoband Madrasa, a religious institution opposed to partition but institutionally dedicated to Muslim revival at the local level, based on the authenticity and guidance of the Quran and Hadith and the legitimacy of Sufi piety.[37] This *madrasa* spawned satellite institutions, some of which have been instrumental in training conservative Muslim theologians and students in Pakistan, including members of the Afghan Taliban.[38]

A second strain was closer to some of the nineteenth-century Ottoman Westernizing reform efforts, in that it was led by Sayyid Ahmad Khan, the

---

[35] Ibid., 205.
[36] Peter Hardy provides a survey of British Muslim history in his book, *The Muslims of British India* (Cambridge University Press, 1973).
[37] Barbara Daly Metcalf, *Islamic Revival in British India: Deoband 1860–1900* (Princeton University Press, 1982).
[38] *Taliban* is the Persian-language plural of the Arabic *talib*, a "seeker of knowledge" or a student.

descendant of a family of Mughal officials who ultimately looked to Western rationalism and modern education – but in the aristocratic British Oxford–Cambridge mold, to create a new, devout but Western educated elite. His Aligarh Muslim University trained new Muslims of the same type as emerged from contemporary, late nineteenth-century Ottoman schools, except that the language of instruction was English and the ethos was an Indo-Muslim version of muscular Christianity, with sports and games part of male undergraduate education.[39] Several graduates of this university participated in the Khilafat Movement of 1919–24, the Indo-Muslim political movement aimed at saving the Ottoman Caliphate and ultimately the Ottoman state. Muhammad 'Ali Jinnah, trained as a lawyer, came from this Westernized tradition, although educated in London rather than India, and he hoped to protect Indian Muslims from submergence in a Hindu sea by giving them a new state: not an Islamic one but, like the Mughal Empire, a state ruled by and for Muslims. In 1947 he led north Indian Muslims to form Pakistan, a political refuge for Indian Muslims, but, curiously, a secular state based on British institutions and emphatically not an Islamic theocracy. Most Indian Muslims remained in India, some enthusiastically, others uneasily.

The Ottomans: decline or resurrection?

Following Süleyman's death in 1566 his successors, Selim II (1566–74) and Murad II (1574–95), continued to add territory to the empire, with the conquests of Cyprus and Tunis in 1573 and 1574 and a prolonged successful war against the Safavids after the death of Shah Tahmasp in 1576. The Ottomans occupied parts of the Caucasus and Tabriz in 1583 and 1585 and made Georgia an Ottoman vassal state in 1587. In 1590 the new Safavid ruler, Shah 'Abbas, was forced to sue for peace. Yet despite this continued expansion, in the 1590s the historian and bureaucrat Mustafa Âli (1541–1600) wrote an encyclopedic history in which he bitterly lamented the decline of the empire caused by deviation from the norms of Süleyman's reign: rising corruption, disruption of the military, the declining power of viziers, the loss of authority of the *madrasa*-trained intellectual elite, the *ilmiye* class, to which he belonged, economic problems, and the pernicious influence of the *haram* – all due to the laxity, the irresponsibility of the reigning sultan.[40] In Mustafa Âli's eyes, then, as for many other writers, Ottoman decline was a matter of personal

[39] David Lelyveld, *Aligarh's First Generation* (Princeton University Press, 1978).
[40] This discussion is based on Fleischer's *Bureaucrat and Intellectual in the Ottoman Empire*, Chapter I.

responsibility. He wrote, of course, before the empire was threatened by the expansion of European powers, a phenomenon outside the control of any Ottoman official.

Mustafa Âli was a sophisticated Ottoman whose father was not a member of the elite, non-tax-paying *askeri* class of warriors and bureaucrats, but a prosperous well-educated merchant, and thus a tax-paying *reaya*. His grandfather may have been a Bosnian household slave. Mustafa Âli was educated in elite Istanbul *madrasas* that produced representatives of Ottoman high culture who, with this education, could shed *reaya* status and join the imperial elite. Beginning his monumental work in 1591 at the outset of the Muslim millennium – and during the reigns of 'Abbas I in Iran and Akbar in India – he voiced what was later to grow into a requiem chorus of *ilmiye* intellectuals, as the pace of Ottoman conquests and victories slowed and was reversed in the late sixteenth and seventeenth centuries.

Frustrated by his inability to obtain the imperial appointments he coveted, Mustafa Âli nonetheless identified many of the real and growing problems of the Ottoman state. First, though he could not have known it, the Ottoman–Safavid treaty of 1590 marked the maximum growth of the empire. While the Ottomans were to fight and win many important battles after this time – even laying siege to Vienna for a second time in 1683 – the empire's phenomenal growth had ended. Secondly, the prolonged late sixteenth-century campaigns in the Caucasus and Iran had not produced territory (as had the Egyptian conquest of 1517) that yielded a major revenue increase at comparatively little cost; in 1585–6 the *akçe* was radically devalued to half of its former value in response to the costs of continuous campaigns. It was devalued again at the turn of the century, and from the 1580s to the 1690s the Ottoman government ran a deficit.[41] Thirdly, the system of succession was radically altered after the murder of Bayezid and his sons in 1562. By the end of the century Ottoman succession was no longer decided by wars of succession between princes and the fratricide that inevitably followed.

Selim and Murat both came to power unopposed as the only surviving adult sons, and this pattern continued with the accession in 1595 of Mehmed III, the eldest son of Murat and the only one to serve as a provincial governor – his other sons were too young to do so. These three successions established a precedent or custom of royal primogeniture, and from this time forward also Ottoman princes were not appointed to provincial governorships with their mothers and advisors at a young

---

[41] See references to the *akçe* in Darling, *Revenue-Raising and Legitimacy*.

age – the Timurid tradition that the Mughals in India continued to follow. Instead princes were henceforth raised in the *haram*, and succession was not decided on the battlefield, but by factional maneuvering within the palace. This new pattern took shape contemporaneously with Shah 'Abbas's institutionalization of a *haram* system, and during the century-long era when Ottoman *haram* women exerted unusual power. The period was known as the *kadınlar sultanat*, the "sultanate of women": that began with the prominence of Hürrem, who died in 1568, and continued until the death of the mother of Sultan Murad IV in 1651. During the seventeenth century, sultans lost power to the *haram*, although some rulers asserted their authority more effectively than others.

There were seven sultans between 1595–6 and 1687, and when the last of them, Sultan Mehmet IV (r. 1648–87), became sultan as a child in 1648, he reigned but did not rule. The overlapping periods between the devaluation of the Ottoman currency in 1585–6 and the end of the Sultanate of Women was an exceptionally turbulent, not to say chaotic, era that featured profoundly serious internal and external problems, many of them exacerbated by the empire's acute financial difficulties. First, there were the complex, multiple Celali rebellions of disaffected Ottoman officers and others in Anatolia, which began in 1596 and continued as a crisis until 1610, and fitfully thereafter. Second, the new Iranian ruler, Shah 'Abbas I, led a series of campaigns with his new army and by 1605 recaptured all the Iranian territory lost in the earlier Ottoman–Safavid conflict, including Baghdad. Then in 1622 Janissaries, the previously loyal, disciplined slave troops, rebelled, an uprising which culminated in the murder of the reigning sultan, Osman, his replacement with the mentally incompetent previous ruler, Mustafa, and later the same year, the deposition of Mustafa by the Istanbul *'ulama*. Finally, throughout the first half of the seventeenth century factional conflicts plagued the inner palace, diminishing only with the murder of Kösem Sultan, Mehmed IV's grandmother and the dominant figure in the state at the time of the seven-year-old boy's accession in 1648.

It is no wonder that in 1640 a *devshirme* slave from Macedonia, Gördidjeli Kodja Mustafa Beğ, presented his *Risale* treatise on Ottoman decline to Murad IV: in it he argued that only by a return to the "imagined perfection" of the era before Süleyman I could Ottoman decline be arrested.[42] His treatise was characteristic of early Ottoman decline literature in its essentially conservative or backward-looking perspective, in contrast to the modernization and/or Westernization ideas that

---

[42] C. H. Imber, "Koçi Beg/Gördidjeli Kodja Mustafa Beg," *Encyclopaedia of Islam* II, Brill Online.

characterized most nineteenth-century reform programs. Yet what is remarkable about the Ottoman case is that the seventeenth-century Ottoman state survived, perhaps just because it was changed to such a degree that Kınalzade, Mustapha 'Ali, and Mustapha Beğ would hardly have recognized it. After the Sultanate of Women ended, it was replaced by a Sultanate of Viziers, a bureaucratically administered state.

From sultanate to vizierate

It was a family of ministers, the Köprülüs, who reenergized the empire from 1656 until 1691. They began their work in the same year as the Venetians shattered an Ottoman fleet in the Dardanelles and threatened Istanbul itself. In that year the first Köprülü vizier, Köprülü Mehmed Pasha (r. 1656–61), brutally but effectively began restoring order in an empire that seemed to be coming to pieces owing to Venetian threats, unrest in the Balkans, sectarian conflicts in Istanbul, and revolts in Anatolia. He also sought to restore a social and religious order that distinguished *askeri* from *reaya* – and *saiyid*s, descendants of the Prophet, from non-*saiyid*s, a far more complex and unrewarding task. His descendants also proved to be capable and enlightened administrators, like Nizam al-Mulk under the Saljuqs, rulers in every sense except in name. Ottoman sultans, who were now little more than ciphers, still retained their legitimacy.

This recitation of seventeenth-century problems tends to suggest a kind of pervasive chaos and sense of imminent disintegration that misrepresents the state of an empire that was, for many of its elite members at least, still a viable and rewarding enterprise. In the narrative of the tireless Ottoman traveler Evliya Çelebi, for example, the Ottoman Empire seems an altogether engaging place. The problems of corrupt and oppressive officials and ruthless sultans, which he mentions from time to time in his massive memoir, are far overshadowed by his tour of the Ottoman horizon between 1640 and 1680. The Ottoman Empire seems just as viable, and for him enjoyable, as Mughal India under Shah Jahan.

As someone born into the palace because of his father's occupation as an imperial goldsmith, Evliya, a witty, well-educated and evidently cocky young man, describes many different aspects of Ottoman life, beginning with his adolescent years within the Ottoman palace. In one passage he relates how in 1636 he persuaded Murat IV (r. 1623–40) to appoint him a "boon companion," a recognized post in Muslim courts:

My Padishah, if a man consorts well with everyone in the company he is called a 'companion,' and if it is a drinking party, then he is called a boon-companion. The word *nedim* derives from *münadim* which is a metathesis of *müdamin*, and *müdam* signifies 'wine'. So boon-companionship (*nedamet*) means wine-drinking, that is to say, being drunk with wine (*mest-i müdam*). Such a one in short is deemed the royal friend (*musahib*) or imperial boon-companion (*nedim-i şeriyari*). May God grant my Padishah long life.

"Bravo," cried the sultan.[43]

Two years later, just before the campaign to retake Baghdad from Iran, Evliya "received his [the sultan's] blessings and graduated from the *haram* into the *sipahi* corps with a daily allowance of forty *akçe.*"[44] His appointment highlights how the term *sipahi* itself had evolved to include not just traditional Oghuz cavalry, but any imperial appointee, even a goldsmith's liberally educated son. Contemporary Indians could be appointed as *mansabdars* in a similar way. And Evliya did serve in battle, although primarily as a Quran reciter. Speaking of a 1650 battle against Celali rebels in Anatolia, he writes: "While the others were carrying on their butchery, this humble slave was standing at the foot of Abdullah Pasha's banner, reciting the noble surah of Victory (Koran, Surah 48)."[45]

Structural changes in Ottoman administration

Two fundamental structural changes accompanied this change in Ottoman rule: the rise of provincial notables and the abolition of the *devshirme* system. The rise of provincial notables occurred as the power of Ottoman sultans declined, and it may have been partly caused by at least two changes in Ottoman governance: the decline in the authority and active rule of the sultans, and the financial problems that led to the establishment of the *malilkhane* tax-farming system in 1695, which ceded financial and administrative power to local authorities. It was, in any case, a process that seems reminiscent of and closely analogous to the drastic shift of Mughal fortunes in the late seventeenth and early eighteenth centuries.

As in the Indian case, Ottoman notables represented both indigenous elites, who had remained in place after the Ottoman conquest – like the Rajputs in India – and now reasserted themselves, and officials, who managed to entrench themselves locally through intermarriage and alliances with local elites – exactly the process visible in Mughal Bengal during the first half of the eighteenth century.[46] Indeed, in the eighteenth and

---

[43] Dankoff, *An Ottoman Mentality*, 36.   [44] Ibid., 45.   [45] Ibid., 137.

[46] Philip Calkins vividly describes the process – from imperial governor to provincial ruler – in his article "The Formation of a Regionally Oriented ruling Group in Bengal, 1700–1740," *The Journal of Asian Studies* 29, No. 4 (August 1970), 799–806.

nineteenth-century Ottoman Empire there was a distinction between the so-called *ayyan*, provincial notables with deep roots in the countryside, known in Anatolia as *derebeys* or "valley-lords" – families such as the Çapan-oğlu, descendants of long-settled Turkic tribes in Central Anatolia – and officials with no such links who had become semi-autonomous as the authority of Istanbul waned, such as the family of Süleyman the Great which ruled Baghdad throughout the eighteenth and early nineteenth centuries.[47] The rotation of officials slowed noticeably during the eighteenth century – as it also did in India – allowing this to happen.[48]

From the late seventeenth century the notables also became important as providers of troops for the central government, a development made necessary by a second major structural change: the decline of the Janissaries as an effective fighting force and the deterioration of the *devşirme* system, which was finally abandoned in 1703. Well before that the system had been "corrupted" through increasing recruitment of free Muslims, who saw service in the regiments as a rewarding career path. These men had a very different training from their slave predecessors – if they were trained at all – and different relations with ruling sultans. By the late seventeenth century Janissaries, now poorly trained and badly paid because of inflation, had evolved into privileged urban garrisons of men who made their living as tradesmen, businessmen, and even coffee-shop owners: in fact, a parasitical armed class able to make and unmake sultans, but no longer the feared striking force of Ottoman armies. Like other slave military systems in the Islamic world, the units originally formed to provide loyal, disciplined troops had become semi-autonomous kingmakers.

The background and policies of two eighteenth-century Ottoman officials illustrate how profoundly the empire had changed from its earlier incarnation under Mehmet II and Süleyman. Both born in the 1660s, these men are Ibrahim Pasha Nevshehirli (*c.* 1662–1730) and Ibrahim Mütaferrika (*c.* 1670–1745). Ibrahim, who became Ahmet II's grand vizier in 1718, was not a slave but a free-born Muslim who entered imperial service through family connections. Married to the sultan's favorite daughter (following an earlier pattern), Ibrahim was, initially at

---

[47] For a case study of *ayyan* see Gabriel Piterberg, "The Formation of an Ottoman–Egyptian Elite in the 18th Century," *International Journal of Middle East Studies* 22, No. 3 (August 1990), 275–89.

[48] Donald Quataert, *The Ottoman Empire 1700–1922* (Cambridge University Press, 2nd edn. 2005), 46. See also J. H. Mordtmann, "Derebey," *Encyclopaedia of Islam* II, Brill Online. In the Ottoman case there were also descendants of the Mamluks who were especially powerful in Egypt and the adjoining Arab provinces. For eighteenth-century Ottoman-Egyptian history see Jane Hathaway, *The Politics of Households in Ottoman Egypt: The Rise of the Qazdağlis* (Cambridge University Press, repr. 2002).

least, committed to peace, which would allow for economic development and stabilization of the empire.

A poet, calligrapher, and, like the unengaged sultan, a hedonist, Ibrahim was the first vizier who openly looked to Europe, and France in particular, for models to reform the Ottoman state. He either patronized or directed a whole series of progressive measures, including the establishment of a fire department, a textile mill, a translation society, and numerous libraries, presided over by the poet Nedim, whose innovative verse is associated with this era.[49] He also presided over one of the most charming artistic and social eras in Ottoman history, the "Tulip Period" during which tulips, exported back to Istanbul from Holland, stimulated a new architectural style, realized in the Lale Cami or Tulip Mosque, and associated artistic and literary trends. During the years of his appointment he and the sultan also constructed some of the lovely *köşk*s or kiosks on the hillsides along the Bosphorus, which became centers for aristocratic *majlises* of wine, music, and verse. In 1730 he finally lost his life in a popular uprising against Ottoman aristocratic indulgence. The uprising was led by an Albanian Janissary, a former second-hand clothes dealer. The poet Nedim also lost his life in this violence. Ahmed III was forced to abdicate a short time later.

Ibrahim Mütaferrika (*c.* 1670/74–1745), one of Ibrahim's ministers, was a Unitarian Christian from Transylvania who, escaping Hapsburg religious persecution, converted to Islam and wrote a treatise condemning Roman Catholicism. After joining Ottoman service he became an envoy to several European states, but is best known as one of the early advocates of modernizing reform. He personifies the new type of Ottoman reform advocate: not like Mustapha Âli, who looked back to a golden age, or like clerics who wished to purify and strengthen Islam, such as the Indian Shah Wali-Ullah, but someone like the nineteenth-century Indian Sayyid Ahmad Khan, who saw adoption of elements of European administrative structures, technology, and culture as a means of preserving the empire. Ibrahim may have helped to compose a memorandum presented to Ahmed III which advocated the adoption of European military technology and the employment of European officers, but he is best known for his establishment of an Ottoman Turkish printing press in 1727.

In doing so he was supported by the Grand Vizier, Ibrahim Pasha, and, importantly, by the *Shaikh al-Islam*, the supreme Muslim religious authority, whose office had long since overshadowed the early Ottoman office of

---

[49] Silay, *Nedim and the Poetics of Ottoman Culture.* Nedim questioned old forms, introduced new colloquial vocabulary, and, especially in his Persian poems, explicitly reveled in his homosexual desire, even praising the erotic appeal of beards over eyes, lips, and tresses (p. 100).

kadi asker. Ibrahim Mütaferrika evidently won over this religious official by arguing that Islamic learning would profit from printing, but his press published only works on secular humanistic and scientific subjects. One of the books it printed, for example, was a study and critique of mid seventeenth-century Ottoman naval affairs by the outstanding seventeenth-century Ottoman scholar Katib Çelebi.[50] In a 1731 publication, Ibrahim Mütaferrika himself analyzed the causes of Ottoman decline by comparing the empire with European countries, explicitly warning about the threat of Peter the Great's radical reforms. In this treatise he stressed the need to introduce modern sciences that had been developed in Europe.[51]

The Ottomans and Europe

The Grand Vizier's attempt to modernize Istanbul and the Ottoman state, in which he emphasized close relations with France, and his support for his Transylvanian colleague and other reform-minded individuals highlight the contrasts between the geographical, military, and cultural world inhabited by Ottoman officials and intellectuals from that experienced by the Iranian or Mughal elite in the early eighteenth century. In 1718, when Ahmed III appointed Ibrahim Pasha as Grand Vizier, no Safavid or Mughal ruler or minister felt particularly attracted to or threatened by European powers. Europeans had long been present in both empires, but as marginal individuals: Jesuit priests, European adventurers, and merchants. Portuguese high-seas piracy and armed uprisings by small groups of English East India Company merchants were insufficient stimuli and paled in comparison with indigenous threats. The contrast between the Ottoman and the Safavid and Mughal situations was partly due to the presence in Istanbul of men such as Ibrahim Mütaferrika: knowledgeable European defectors or captives who became loyal servants of Ottoman sultans. No comparable official ever served in Isfahan, Agra, or Delhi during the rule of the Safavids and Mughals.

In geographic terms, the Ottomans had been a Mediterranean and European power since the late fourteenth century, perpetually in conflict with one European state or another, which stimulated the evolution of their military armaments and tactics. Yet despite frequent conflicts, close commercial relations with states such as Venice also fostered artistic and intellectual exchange. Ottoman expansion had, from the time of the dynasty's

---

[50] Orhon Şai'k Gökyay, "Kâtib Çelebi," *Encyclopaedia of Islam* II, Brill Online.

[51] Nizazi Berkes, "Ibrâhîm Mütaferrika," *Encyclopaedia Islamica* II, Brill Online. For a discussion of the historiography of this era see Jane Hathaway, "Rewriting Eighteenth-Century Ottoman History," *Mediterranean Historical Review* 19, No. 1 (June 2004), 29–51.

first intervention in Byzantine succession disputes, also led sultans to form convenient alliances with other, more distant European states, such as Süleyman's alliance with France in 1536, leading to many later diplomatic, commercial, and cultural contacts with the French monarchy.[52] The French sent ambassadors to Istanbul in the sixteenth century and maintained permanent missions there during the first half of the seventeenth century. They sent Islamic books and art to Europe and arranged for European texts to be delivered to the Istanbul court.[53] Conflict, commerce, and cultural and intellectual exchanges between Istanbul and Europe also stimulated Ottoman scholarship on subjects virtually unheard of in Safavid Iran or Mughal India. It is impossible to find any seventeenth- or even eighteenth-century Iranian or Indian – Muslim or Hindu, Jew, Christian or Zoroastrian – with the same range of knowledge of and interest in European affairs as the truly remarkable seventeenth-century intellectual, reformer, and follower of the Illuminationist doctrines of al-Suhrawardi, Katib Çelebi (1609–57), who wrote treatises on astronomy, geography, and the religions and political systems of European governments, and attributed the Europeans' military successes, such as the Venetian victory in 1656, to their scientific and geographical knowledge.[54]

The advice literature and reform plans that Katib Çelebi, Ibrahim Pasha, Ibrahim Mütaferrika, and later Ottoman scholars and officials produced were stimulated by a genuine decline in Ottoman fortunes. During the course of the eighteenth century, or the period between the failure of the second siege of Vienna in 1683 and Napoleon's invasion of Egypt in 1798, as the sultans' or their ministers' authority continued to decline relative to the influence of *ayyan*s, the balance of power between the Ottoman Empire and Europe was reversed. Ottoman armies, even without disciplined Janissary units, sometimes won significant engagements during these years: against Russia in 1711 and Venice in 1715. They lost critical major campaigns, however, and beginning with the Treaty of Karlowitz in 1699, the empire ceded major territorial conquests:

---

[52] Prior to the early sixteenth century Ottoman–French relations often shifted, sometimes influenced by Christian ideals, at other times by changing state relations. In the 1490s, for example, Charles VIII of France, having captured Rome, threatened to lead a crusade against Istanbul. However, by the late sixteenth century the consolidation of European states produced more consistently friendly Ottoman–French relations, and French influence strengthened over time to become the dominant foreign cultural strain in the nineteenth century.

[53] See Avner Ben-Zaken's summary of these exchanges in his article on Ottoman astronomy, "The Heavens of the Sky and the Heavens of the Heart: The Ottoman Cultural Context for the Introduction of Post-Copernican Astronomy," *British Journal for the History of Science* 37, No. 1 (March 2004), 6–10.

[54] Dankoff, *An Ottoman Mentality*, 231.

in this case Hungary, Slovenia, Transylvania, and Croatia were lost to the Hapsburgs. Seventy-five years later Ottomans were defeated in a six-year conflict with another resurgent European monarchy, the Romanovs, resuscitated earlier in the century by Peter the Great and now ruled by Catherine, an equally formidable monarch. In course of their victory the Russians even sent their Baltic fleet into the Mediterranean to destroy an Ottoman fleet in the Aegean Sea. With the 1774 Treaty of Küçük Kainarjı the Ottomans lost control of the Crimea, whose Khan had supplied the most important military units that filled the gap left by the deterioration of Janissary regiments. The treaty also granted the Tsarist regime the rights to construct an orthodox cathedral in Istanbul and to act as protectors of Ottoman orthodox Christians.

These latter, extraterritorial privileges over orthodox Christians represented Catherine's claim to rights that other European powers had earlier gained in their so-called "capitulation" agreements with various Ottoman sultans. These agreements, known generally by their Arabic term *imtiyazat*, "separation" or "distinction," originated as imperial concessions to European merchants, offering them legal security and trading privileges within the Empire. Based on well-established Saljuq practice and a common commercial device of many pre-modern states, the earliest such concessions were made to the Venetians, but from the middle of the sixteenth century other, ultimately more formidable European states also sought these privileges. The French were the first Europeans to secure such concessions, which Ottomans often awarded in response to shifting European alliances. French privileges were renewed again in 1597 and 1602, when the Ottomans also granted them the right to protect Christian pilgrims to Jerusalem: a return to the Crusades, but in diplomatic form. In 1690 the French won additional privileges: a reduction in Egyptian customs and Ottoman agreement to grant some Christian sites in Jerusalem to the Catholic Church.

By that time the English were fast expanding their own interests in the Mediterranean, having been granted concessions in 1580 and again in 1601; the latter, which exempted gold and silver imports from customs duty, reflected pressing Ottoman needs for more currency imports in this period.[55] If these early capitulations were mutually beneficial, by the late seventeenth century Europeans began to exploit them to free themselves from customs duties and establish extraterritorial bases in Ottoman

---

[55] Seventeenth-century English capitulations are summarized in Paul Ricaut, *The capitvlations and articles of peace between the Maiestie of the King of England, Scotland, France and Ireland &c. and the Svltan of the Ottoman Empire: as they haue been augmented, & altered in the times of euery embassadour....* [microform] (Constantinople: Abraham Gabai, 1663).

territory, ultimately gaining the subversive right to offer Ottoman Christian subjects who worked for the French or British – or who could buy a false certificate from them – equal legal protection with Europeans. Capitulations both reflected and intensified Ottoman decline relative to European states, so much so that in 1788 the French ambassador described the Ottomans as "une des plus riches colonies de la France."[56]

Ottoman modernization/Westernization

The Ottoman Empire's semi-colonial status prompted eighteenth-century Ottoman sultans to "modernize," that is "Europeanize," the military. During the eighteenth century they began by employing French military advisors and in 1793 Selim III (r. 1789–1807) created the *Nizam-i Jedid* or "New Force," as part of his comprehensive attempt to revitalize the old order.[57] He not only wished to fend off more European advances but also hoped to reestablish central control over the provincial notables. The desirability of this goal was demonstrated when, in 1799, he ordered – or pleaded ineffectually – with *ayyans* in Palestine to resist Napoleon's advance into Syria.

Creating a new military force was but one of a series of measures he took to resuscitate the Ottoman state. These included the revival of old institutions and social controls as well as innovative reforms of the educational system and the administrative apparatus. Thus, he tried to reform the *timar* system, as well as attempting to mandate that Ottoman subjects classes should resume wearing the traditionally sanctioned costumes that indicated their social status.[58] In contrast to these essentially backward-looking acts, Selim opened embassies in Europe, established the first "modern," that is secular, schools with European instructors in Istanbul to train a new officer class, and began creating a new administrative infrastructure to support the *Nizam-i Jedid* military units.

Selim's military and associated educational and administrative reforms echoed advice given earlier in the century, and created the nucleus of a new class of Ottomans who knew French and appreciated European sciences. The Janissaries, however, rebelled in 1807 with the help of prominent members of the *'ulama*, leading to the intervention of a

[56] Halil Inalcık, "Imtiyâzât," *Encyclopaedia of Islam* II, Brill Online.
[57] Stanford Shaw, "The Origins of Ottoman Military Reform: The *Nizam-i Cedid* Army of Sultan Selim III (1709–1807)," *Journal of Modern History* 37 (1965), 291–306.
[58] Among many studies of Ottoman modernizing reforms see Bernard Lewis's early work *The Emergence of Modern Turkey* (Oxford University Press, 2nd edn. 1961) and Carter V. Findley, *Bureaucratic Reform in the Ottoman Empire: The Sublime Porte 1789–1922* (Princeton University Press, 1980).

powerful notable who placed a new sultan on the throne in 1808. This led to an agreement which on the surface had something of an air of an Ottoman Magna Carta. The new sultan, Mahmud II, under threat from provincial armies, agreed to recognize provincial notables' lands as inheritable property in exchange for their recognition of the legitimacy of the sultan and his agent, the Grand Vizier.[59]

Ottoman notables, however, constituted a much more fragile class than the thirteenth-century English landed aristocracy, and they never really questioned the legitimacy of the Ottoman dynasty, which was, after all far more prestigious and long-lived than the Angevin monarchy.[60] Indeed, it is suggestive of the Sultan's latent legitimacy that this "constitutional" crises ultimately led to the reemergence of the Ottoman sultan as an autocratic ruler over an increasingly centralized "modern" bureaucratic state, more centralized, in fact, than at any time since the early seventeenth century. During the next quarter of a century Mahmud II was able to use the new *Nizam-i Jedid* army to finally rid the regime of the Janissary menace by slaughtering the Istanbul Janissaries in 1826 and persecuting their Bektashi Sufi associates. Afterwards he eliminated the by now archaic *timar* system, integrating the remaining *sipahi* cavalry into the new military organization, and was even able to seize some of the lands of the notables and distribute them to his own supporters. He also established a new *waqf* administration to assert central control over the tens of thousands of "charitable" holdings that represented valuable agrarian and mercantile resources, an imperial echo of Mehmet II's seizure of many *waqf* lands in the fifteenth century. The *Shaikh al-Islam* was also incorporated as a religious advisor in this emerging state system, which now included a number of "modern" ministries – civil affairs, foreign affairs, agriculture – and schools to train bureaucrats, perhaps on the model of the French *écoles*.[61]

Mahmud II restructured the Ottoman system even as the empire continued to contract, mainly owing to events beyond his control or that of even modernized ministries. During Selim II's reign, the already tenuous Ottoman hold on Hijaz and Egypt evaporated. First, followers of the ascetic, fundamentalist 'Abd al-Wahhab took control of the Hijaz in 1803; two years later, following Napoleon's invasion of Egypt and Syria, an Ottoman officer of Albanian origin, Muhammad 'Ali, seized power in Egypt. Muhammad 'Ali controlled Egypt and later Syria until his death in

---

[59] Kemal H. Karpat, "The Transformation of the Ottoman State, 1789–1908," *International Journal of Middle East Studies* 3, No. 3 (July 1972), 251–4.
[60] See Karen Barkay's sensible comments on this event in *Empire of Difference*, 223.
[61] Ibid., 254–5.

1848, nominally still an imperial servant, but in reality an independent ruler with a formidable army. In 1824 he suppressed a Greek revolt on behalf of the sultan, but in 1832 the Egyptians overwhelmed the new Ottoman army near Konya, and would probably have taken Istanbul itself had not the Russians intervened to prevent the establishment of a powerful new state in the capital. This was an anomalous incident, for throughout the nineteenth century it was usually the British and French who limited Russian territorial expansion in Ottoman territories. The Crimean War was one unhappy example of Anglo-French cooperation in this cause. Nonetheless, it is indicative of the reality of the relative weakness of the Ottoman regime, even after the successful modernizing efforts of Selim II and Mahmud II. During the century the Ottoman Empire continued to exist at the pleasure of European states, and after that pleasure evaporated during the First World War, Europeans and Arabs presided over its demise. Its longevity was a function of European rivalries.

Over the course of the nineteenth century down to the end of the First World War the Ottoman Empire continued to shrink, through a combination of Russian expansion and indigenous independence movements, such as the Greek Revolt that by 1830 finally produced the Greek nation-state. Apart from demonstrating the difficulty of revitalizing and modernizing an empire under siege from disparate forces, the effect of this

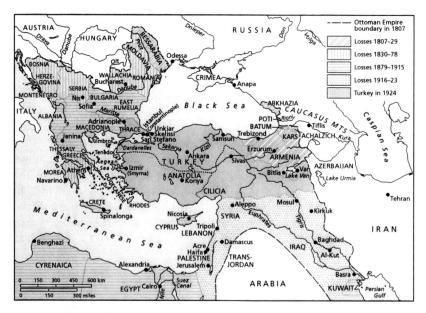

Map 18. Ottoman territorial losses, 1807–1923

contraction was to transform the empire into a more Turkic Muslim state, albeit with substantial Jewish, Greek Orthodox, and Armenian Christian minorities.

Nineteenth-century Ottoman reforms

Mahmud II's successors continued struggling to reconstitute the Ottoman state in ways that would strengthen it against its European opponents and critics, partly motivated by a simple desire to be rid of the capitulations that so compromised Ottoman sovereignty. After Mahmud II's death Reşit Pasha, the former Ottoman ambassador to London and minister of the new sultan Abd al-Mecid, announced in 1839 a new series of measures meant both to strengthen the state and to curry favor with European powers. Known as the *Tanzimat* or "Ordering," the proclamation promised security of life and property, equal treatment of all citizens, Muslim and non-Muslim alike, and a system of fixed taxes to replace tax farming, and promised a number of other measures such as a new penal code. Changes in taxation were designed to improve imperial finances, while equal citizenship served at least two purposes: placating European criticism and articulating a new imperial ideology of Ottoman citizenship – even as the numbers of Christian subjects were being reduced by conquest and revolt.

The *Tanzimat* proclamation initiated a period of reforms that climaxed with the announcement of a written constitution in 1876 and the two-year parliamentary period that followed. The earlier emphasis on military modernization declined somewhat in favor of administrative and political reform which, among other effects, exponentially expanded the bureaucracy to oversee functions such as education that had previously been in private hands, and in the case of education, largely the responsibility of the *'ulama*.[62] Part of the *Tanzimat* reforming energy was directed to the establishment of a national, secular education system, and between the 1850s and 1880s a number of schools and faculties were opened, including law, medicine, and political science. The *Dar al-Funun* or University, which was opened in 1869, was forced to close two years later because of pressure from members of the *'ulama*. Nonetheless, gradually a new educated class was trained outside the old *'ilmiye* religious system, and students in state schools received Western European secular and scientific training, much of it based on French models and often mediated through the French language.

Of all the new schools founded during the *Tanzimat* era, however, the *Harbiye* or War College established in 1846 probably had the greatest

---

[62] Quataert, *The Ottoman Empire*, 168–72.

influence. The college represented the culmination of a series of earlier military reform measures and it emphasized the teaching of math and foreign languages, initially French and later German. It produced a number of politically engaged graduates, who were not only active in the late nineteenth century – many students were tried for "subversion" in 1897 – but in the post-Second-World War era as well – some were involved in the 1960 military coup.[63]

It was typical of countries not directly colonized by Europeans that the military was the first institution to be reformed as a matter of self-defense, and typical also that many of the early leaders of indirectly colonized states such as the Ottoman Empire and Iran, were officers who commanded the most "modern" institutions. Atatürk and Atatürk's contemporary in Iran, Riza Khan, later Riza Shah Pahlavi (r. 1925–1941), were two such. In contrast, the eventual leader of Indian Muslims, Muhammad Ali Jinnah, the founder of Pakistan, was trained as a lawyer in Britain, as was his Hindu contemporary Gandhi. In British colonies military commands were reserved for the British, while law, as in the eighteenth-century United States and in nineteenth- and twentieth-century British India, offered advancement and sometimes wealth for ambitious colonial subjects.

The modernization of culture

Overall, the establishment of French schools and the training of Ottomans in France produced a class of intellectuals that somewhat resembled the colonial elite of British India or Francophone Africa. One of the cultural consequences of the powerful influence of French culture was the transmission of European, and particularly French, literary and artistic styles to Istanbul. In literature, French-educated intellectuals such as Shinasi and Namık Kemal turned away from traditional Persianate verse models that had retained their currency, but not their vitality, throughout the eighteenth century. Eighteenth- and nineteenth-century French literature, now translated into Ottoman Turkish, became the model and standard for a new European-influenced bourgeoisie.

Namık Kemal was the outstanding figure in this new literary movement during the second half of the nineteenth century, whose representatives tentatively began articulating an incipient middle class Ottoman nationalism that the *Tanzimat* reforms had catalyzed. A poet, journalist, dramatist, novelist, critic, and political activist, Kemal had a traditional Ottoman religious and literary upbringing, schooled in Ibn 'Arabi's

---

[63] See, among many other general sources for this period, the references in Lewis, *The Emergence of Modern Turkey* and Barkay, *Empire of Difference*.

Sufism, and Persian and Ottoman Turkish poetry. Beginning his career as an Ottoman official, he was influenced by the rise of an independent press and literary journals that began to be published after the reforms of 1860. After expressing Ottoman nationalist sentiments that offended the government, he left for Paris with members of the Young Ottoman Society, which, among other "progressive" ideals, worked for the establishment of a constitutional assembly.[64]

After returning to Istanbul under an amnesty in 1870, Kemal spread his ideas through the newspaper *Ibret* and began writing and staging patriotic dramas. The most famous is generally known simply as *Watan* or "Homeland," a play extolling Ottoman "national" virtues, which in 1873 led to his being imprisoned and exiled to Cyprus, where he spent three productive years writing. During these years he wrote his first novel; he completed a second, expressing Pan-Islamic ideals, years later in 1881. Returning to take office as a member of the State Council under the new sultan, 'Abdühamit II, in 1876, he was exiled again in 1877 to Mytilene for careless remarks about deposing the sultan and because he was apparently seen as a political threat in the newly formed Ottoman parliament, which opened in 1877. Nonetheless, his important connections eventually helped him to a government appointment on the island and later on Rhodes, where he worked to improve the position of Muslims, a minority in a largely Christian population. He was given Ottoman awards for his work, and wrote many patriotic poems during his years in the Aegean – poems in a European mode – but the Ottoman history he completed shortly before he died in 1887 was banned. Kemal, in fact, personified the contradictory situation of Young Ottomans who, while supporting the Ottoman state against European intervention, spread European political, social, and intellectual ideals that threatened the despotic regime of Abdülhamit II (r. 1876–1909).

With Abdülhamit II Ottoman history entered its final phase, due to both continued territorial losses and internal political developments. A paranoid monarch with brutal propensities, Abdülhamit came to the throne at the high tide of European imperial power, marked by Ottoman losses in the Ottoman–Russian War of 1877–8 and the peace treaty brokered by the German chancellor Bismarck. The treaty took away most Russian conquests, but still essentially stripped the Empire of its valuable Balkan possessions, the last of its European territory, in the Balkan Wars of 1912–13. One of Abdülhamit's responses to Ottoman territorial losses, which increasingly changed the multi-cultural Eurasian

---

[64] F. A. Tansel, "Kemâl, Mehmet, Nâmik," *Encyclopaedia of Islam* II, Brill Online. The overwhelming majority of scholarship on Namık Kemal is only available in Turkish.

Empire into a largely Anatolian Turkish Muslim state, was to exploit the Pan-Islamic feelings that Kemal and others had begun articulating and which after all appealed to the now overwhelmingly Muslim population.

In his role, however dubious, as Caliph, Abdülhamit II played on Islamic sensitivities, Muslims' increasing feeling of being overwhelmed by European imperialism. He invited the international Muslim revolutionary Jamal al-Din al-Afghani to reside in Istanbul, along with other individuals who responded to this appeal, such as the far less well-known Hadhrami cleric Sayyid Fadl, from Kerala, India's southwest coast, the home of its oldest Muslim community.[65] The Ottoman Sultan's role as Caliph, the guardian of the sanctity of Mecca and Medina, appealed particularly to Muslims living under colonial regimes in India and Southeast Asia, for whom the last, lingering Muslim power served an important psychological need. In India, where the British had eradicated the pitiful remnants of the Mughals when they retook Delhi in an orgy of destruction and indiscriminate slaughter during the Indian Mutiny in 1857, the Pan-Islamic Ottoman appeal stimulated the development of the Khilafat Movement among Indian Muslims following the First World War.[66] Indian Muslims held demonstrations in support of Ottoman territorial integrity, and to this day, Ottoman uniforms and medals are displayed in obscure Kerala villages during yearly harvest festivals, although their original significance has been lost.[67]

Abdülhamit's Pan-Islamic venture may have been a natural response of an autocratic monarch who needed an ideology to legitimize his own reign and unify Ottoman and foreign Muslims in defense of the Ottoman Empire. Nonetheless his invocation of religion flew directly in the face of the scientific officers and secular intellectuals who had graduated from military and secular schools in Istanbul and elsewhere since the mid-century. And it was these latter groups who increasingly seized the political initiative as the Young Ottomans gradually lost influence. Still they had helped to give birth to the nationalist ideals that motivated their successors, the Young Turks, a movement fueled by the new intellectual class and led by a staff officer trained in the same mold as one of their own fellows:

---

[65] Stephen F. Dale, *Islamic Society on the South Asian Frontier: The Mappilas of Malabar* 1498–1922 (Oxford: Clarendon Press, 1980), 157.

[66] William Dalrymple movingly describes the fate of the last Mughal and the destruction of late Mughal literati in *The Last Mughal* (New York: Vintage Books, repr. 2006). For the Khilafat Movement see Gail Minault, *The Khilafat Movement: Religious Symbolism and Political Mobilization in India* (New York: Columbia University Press, 1982).

[67] Stephen F. Dale and M. Gangadhara Menon, "Nerccas: Saint-Martyr Worship Among the Muslims of Kerala," *Bulletin of the School of Oriental and African Studies* 51, No. 3 (1978), 523–38.

Mustafa Kemal, later known as Atatürk. The secret nationalist association of Young Turks, seeking political salvation in a secular Turkish state, first met in 1889 as the "Committee for Union and Progress."

Between that year and 1908, when they successfully staged the first revolution in Ottoman history, many members lived abroad, where they published newspapers and essays articulating their new ethnic nationalism. Nonetheless it was middle-level Ottoman officers, stationed in Salonica and supported by Muslim notables in the Balkan towns, who carried out the successful Young Turk Revolution of 1908.[68] It represented the denouement of Ottoman history, as these officers laid the ground for a secular Turkish multi-party republic which, by its very nature, defined itself territorially as the Turkish-majority area. Unlike the Young Ottomans, with their ideal of a multi-national or multi-ethnic empire, the Young Turks turned their back on the Arab provinces and the religious centers of Mecca and Medina in the Hijaz.

It was, however, the First World War which sealed the fate of the Ottoman Empire. The war and the Ottoman alliance with Germany had two fundamental consequences. First, they allowed the British, either directly or indirectly through their Arab allies, to strip non-Turkish provinces in Mesopotamia, Syria, and Saudi Arabia from Ottoman control. This meant that the empire reverted to its fourteenth-century incarnation as an almost entirely Turkish state. Secondly, the war gave exceptional power to the Turkish officer class, which represented the most cohesive and modern Ottoman institution and which included among its number some of the most radical Turkish nationalists.

Following his success in the 1915 Gallipoli campaign against British and Commonwealth troops, Mustafa Kemal emerged as a leading officer, a reputation that he cemented in campaigns during the remainder of the war. Then, after the armistice, when the French and British occupied Istanbul and encouraged or permitted the Greeks to pursue their revanchist dreams by occupying Smyrna or Izmir, Atatürk in 1919 rallied Ottoman units in Anatolia and led the campaign to expel the Greeks and create a new Turkish national state. By 1923 the man who became Atatürk in 1935 was successful: he and fellow officers abolished the Ottoman Empire and the Caliphate, and promulgated a republican constitution in Ankara, the heart of Turkish Anatolia.[69]

---

[68] Karpat, "Transformation of the Ottoman State," 279–81 and M. Şükrü Hanioğlu, *The Young Turks in Opposition* (Oxford University Press, 1995).

[69] An accessible biography is by Patrick Balfour (Lord) Kinross, *Atatürk: A Biography of Mustafa Kemal, Father of Modern Turkey* (New York: Morrow, 1965).

Conclusion

The world that was lost

During the two centuries between 1722 and 1923 the Safavid, Mughal, and Ottoman empires withered and collapsed. The charisma and dynamism of these dynasties' early rulers had atrophied and largely evaporated by the time Afghans entered Isfahan, Nader Shah sacked Delhi, and the British and French landed troops in Istanbul at the end of the First World War. Apart from their architectural monuments, exquisite painting, and memorable poetry, dynastic collapse left markedly different legacies in the territories of these empires.

Iran

In Iran, the Safavids, the weakest of all three dynasties, left the most profound and enduring legacies: the resurrection of Iranian political identity by the establishment of a state, called Iran, in the historic heartlands of the Achaemenid and Sasanian empires; the patronage of an identifiably Persian literary and artistic culture; the equation of the Iranian state with Shi'i Islam and the conversion of the formerly majority Sunni population to Twelver Shi'ism; and the institutionalization of a powerful, semi-autonomous, Shi'i clergy. The institutionalization of an Iranian Shi'i *ulama* had unintended consequences, as many clerics dismissed the legitimacy of monarchs or political leaders apart from the Twelfth Imam or his earthly representatives, the *Ayatollahs*, the senior Shi'i clerics or *mujtahids* who were, like the seventeenth-century Lebanese scholar al-Karaki, competent to engage in *ijtihad* or interpretation of Shi'i theology. Yet, despite the increase in the power of the Shi'i *ulama* that occurred during the Qajar period, imperial Iranian political and cultural traditions also endured, to be revived by Riza Shah in 1926, and they have easily survived the Islamic revolution and subsequent rule of the Shi'i clergy in the late twentieth and early twenty-first century.

288

India

The Mughal legacy was far more muted, and the collapse of the empire far more traumatic for Indian Muslims than was the disappearance of the Safavids for Muslims in Iran. Iranians, after all, continued to be ruled by Persian-speaking, Shi'i Muslim shahs who spoke in the same religious and imperial idiom as the Safavids. As Mughal rulers devolved from emperors to kings of Delhi to Maratha puppets, and finally British pensioners, they left behind them the political detritus of empire in the persons of such regional rulers as the Nawabs of Oudh in the Gangetic Valley and the Nizams of Hyderabad in the Deccan. These and other, lesser figures sustained regional variants of Mughal court culture, including the patronage of dynastic histories, literature, and art. Miniature painting declined along with their incomes, but poetry, long the distinctive hallmark of Persianate culture, survived. In the eighteenth and nineteenth centuries, however, Persian gave way to Urdu, the highly Persianized form of Hindi that is written in the Arabic script. Men such as the eighteenth-century writer Mir Muhammad Taqi 'Mir' exemplify the evolution of Mughal literary culture from Persian to Urdu, in that he wrote his autobiography in Persian but became famous as an author of Urdu *ghazals*.[1] North Indian Muslim literati have maintained the literary traditions of Persian verse down to the present day.

While elements of Mughal culture survived in South Asia, the collapse of the Delhi court and the eventual British occupation of the subcontinent deprived north Indian Muslims of cultural and religious patronage, employment and, most of all, sovereignty. Mughal India was, after all, a Muslim empire that directly or indirectly supported a large number of *'ulama* and Muslim literati, bureaucrats, and soldiers, and most of these men's prosperity and prestige declined, just as Anglo-Indian associates of the British Raj were marginalized in independent India. The Indian Khilafat Movement of 1919–23 was one manifestation of Indian Muslims' sense of displacement in a British India that was about to become a theoretically secular but Hindu-dominated democracy. Elements of the British Indian population responded to this situation differently, but, as has been seen, two groups were especially important and were preoccupied with a loss of Muslim sovereignty. These were members of the *'ulama* and British-educated professionals.

The Indo-Muslim *'ulama*, as has already been shown, responded most of all in traditional religious terms, seeking to resuscitate the Muslim community by reforming its religious beliefs and practices, but having

---

[1] See C. M. Naim, ed. and trans., *Zikr-i Mir* (New Delhi: Oxford University Press, 1999).

no united position on the question of Partition. Many British-educated bureaucrats and professionals, such as graduates of Aligarh, sought both to modernize the community and to seek a political solution to their problems. Initially this meant, for many of them, protected status within an Indian democratic state. Members of both groups contributed to the realization of Pakistan, but it was the unquestionably secular Muslim and British-trained lawyer Muhammad 'Ali Jinnah who compelled the British authorities to accept Partition of their empire into two states, an avowedly secular Indian democracy and Pakistan, a refuge for Indian Muslims.

Jinnah's Pakistan demand was, however, more than anything else, a quest simply for sovereignty in the traditional mold. Pakistan was founded as a state for Muslims, but it was based on British, that is secular, constitutional and democratic political norms; it was certainly not a theocratic state in the Iranian Shi'i mold. In Pakistan, as in Iran, questions, tensions, and conflicts endure over the preferred nature of the state. In these debates the Mughal Empire is rarely mentioned, and the contrasting symbolisms of the liberal Akbar and the conservative, ascetic Aurangzib have little resonance. During the second half of the twentieth century some politicians, as well as many 'ulama and conservative Muslims, increasingly advocated turning Pakistan into an Islamic state, but the Western-educated middle and upper classes, men and women in Jinnah's mold, generally oppose this goal.

Turkey

The legacy of the Ottoman Empire is as idiosyncratic as that of the Safavids and as complex as that of the Mughals. The First World War left the empire with a Turkish heartland, an antiquated political structure, a traditionally subordinate and quiescent Sunni 'ulama, and a fiercely nationalistic officer class. A representative of this officer class, Mustafa Kemal (1881–1938), acquired an unmatched charisma of military success in leading the reconquest of Anatolia from the Europeans and Greeks. He used his unequaled authority to impose his vision of a Turkish nation-state that would be modernized on Western European models. In 1935 Kemal formally proclaimed his commitment to a Turkish, not an Islamic, political identity when he assumed the title Atatürk, "Father of the Turks," and simultaneously renounced the titles Pasha and Ghazi. He was not to be a *Padishah-i Islam*, for Kemal Atatürk, as he was henceforth known, had a visceral contempt for the clergy as a class and for Islam as a religion. In his eyes, the phrase "Islamic civilization" was an oxymoron. "If only," he once said of the Turks, with a flash of cynicism, "we could make them Christians."[2] Even if this was little more than a passing remark, it reflected his goal. "His was not to be the reformed Islamic state for which the faithful were waiting: it was to be a strictly lay state, with a centralized government as strong as the Sultan's, backed by the army and run by his own intellectual bureaucracy."[3]

Between the founding of the Turkish Republic in 1923 and his death in 1938, Atatürk did everything in his power to transform Turkey into a Western European state. Turks were compelled to remove their by that time common headgear, the fez, and replace it with European-style hats: a significant change in a traditional society, in which sultans had passed sumptuary regulations that proclaimed Turkish Muslim superiority, as well as discouraging social presumption among the non-Muslim population. Turks were also ordered to adopt surnames, rather than the single names they normally used, causing a sometimes comic panic to find suitable names. The alphabet was changed to the Latin script, a change that honestly reflected the unsuitability of the Arabic script to represent Turkic sounds, but which cut off Turks of the Republic from their Ottoman cultural heritage, so that in the twenty-first century most Turks cannot read the inscriptions on mosques or other buildings, whether they are in Arabic, Persian, or Turkish. Even more profoundly radical, beginning in the mid-1920s women were emancipated – except Atatürk's own wife – invited to dances and dinners with their husbands, given the vote, and encouraged to enter the professions. A secular, Swiss-inspired legal code was also adopted, and law schools were opened to train members of what became a genuinely independent judiciary. Law schools were just one manifestation of an educational system which now became completely secular, building on some of the models of the nineteenth century.

The obverse of all these reforms was the complete legal subjugation of the *'ulama* to the status of an institution overseen by a government department, still no doubt supporting Hanafi Sunni Islam, but not permitting any clerical influence in social or political life. The department, known as the *Diyanet Isleri Bashkanlığı*, the Presidency of Religious Affairs, was established to ensure that the *'ulama* confined their activities to spiritual life and refrained from any attempt to impose religious norms in social life or politics. The *Diyanet*, as it is commonly known, paid for religious teaching, including publications, using funds from the state budget, for the Republican government had abolished the traditional religious

---

[2] Balfour, *Atatürk: A Biography of Mustafa Kemal*, 497.   [3] Ibid., 497.

institutions, *waqfs* and *madrasas*, that funded *ilmiye* education in the empire.[4] Yet in spite of the juggernaut of Kemalist secularism, not only did Islam survive but some Turkish Muslims dedicated themselves to its revitalization. One of the most influential of those who sought to revivify Turkish Islam was Bediuzzaman Said Nursi, a precocious Muslim autodidact from Turkish Kurdistan. Nursi established an organization known as the *Risale-i Nur* (The Prophecy of Light), dedicated to renewing Islamic piety and individual spiritual perfection at the grassroots level, avoiding religious political activism in an era of state secularism.[5]

Nursi's program had a certain general resemblance to the Deoband Madrasa in late nineteenth-century India, to the extent that both movements operated within secular environments, emphasized individual spiritual revival, and abstained from political activism. In the early twenty-first century the democratic election of a religious political party demonstrates that in Turkey, as well as in Pakistan, the question of the relationship between religion and the state is still unresolved, and in fact may never be definitively settled, even to the limited degree it has been in the world's two largest secular democracies, India and the United States.

---

[4] Seyfettin Erşahin, "The Ottoman Foundation of the Turkish Republic's *Diyanet*: Ziya Golkalp's *Diyanet Ishları Nazâratı,*" *The Muslim World* 98, Nos. 2–3 (April 2008), 182–98. This entire double issue of *Muslim World* is devoted to the policies and practices of the *Diyanet*.

[5] Şükran Vahide, *Islam in Modern Turkey: An Intellectual Biography of Bediuzzaman Said Nursi* (Albany: State University of New York Press, 2005).

Glossary

adab (Ar.) belles-lettres, polite learning, including literature and history; knowledge of *adab* was usually an attribute of "boon companions"

ahl-i kitab (Ar./Per.) "People of the Book," i.e. Jews and Christians

akçe (T.) Ottoman silver coin used until the seventeenth century

Akhbaris (Ar.) Shi'i *'ulama* (q.v.), traditionalists or fundamentalists, who reject *ijtihad*, the interpretation of texts

akhlaq (Ar.) a common name for ethical or political theory treatises, often derived from Greek sources

'Ashura (Ar.) the tenth day of Muharram in the Muslim religious or lunar calendar. It is a day of mourning for Shi'as and commemorates the death of Husain, son of 'Ali and grandson of the Prophet Muhammad, at the Battle of Karbala in Iraq in 680 CE

askeri (Ar.) literally "soldiers": the Ottoman governing classes, including the military, *sipahis*, and Janissaries and the *'ulama*, the clergy

atabeğ (T.) a guardian or "tutor," literally "father of a *beğ*," q.v.

beğ (T.) Turkic aristocrat or officer, later a term of respect

beğlik (T.) One of a number of small Oghuz chiefdoms or principalities in Anatolia

Bhakti (Sanskrit) devotional Hinduism, similar in spirit to Sufism in Islam

Caliph (Khalifa) (Ar.) "successor": in Islam, political successor to Muhammad

caravansarai (Per.) rest house, usually fortified, for merchants traveling in caravans

Chaghatai (M.) name of the second son of Chinggis Qan who inherited the territory of Mawarannahr, q.v.

chahar bagh (Per.) a four-part garden, featuring running water, fruit trees, and aromatic plants; frequent location for the aristocratic *majlis* (q.v.)

Chinggis Qan (T./M.) founder of the Mongol empire; "Chingiz Khan" in Persian

dar al-Islam (Ar.) the "world of Islam," i.e. where Muslims are sovereign

293

Deccan (Sanskrit) "the South," a general term for territories south of
Hind, such as the Indo-Muslim city of Hyderabad

devshirme (T.) Ottoman draft (*devşir*) of Christian boys for imperial service

dhimmi (Ar.), *Zimmi* (Per.) a person tolerated or protected in a Muslim
state, usually Jews and Christians, otherwise known as *ahl-i kitab*,
people who have received a prophetic revelation in the Mosaic
tradition

diwan (Per.) a royal court; the finance ministry; a collection of one writer's
poetry

farr (Per.) the divine essence of pre-Islamic Iranian kings, invoked by both
Safavid and Mughal rulers

ghaza (Ar.) war or raid, especially on Muslim–non-Muslim frontiers

ghazal (Ar.) an ode or sonnet in Persian or Turkish with from four to
fourteen lines

ghazi (Ar.) one who conducts a *ghaza*, q.v.

ghulam (Ar.) a military slave, legally a slave, but in political and military
contexts an enslaved and converted individual who might wield
great influence and power

guru (Sanskrit) religious teacher

hadith (Ar.) authenticated reports of the actions or sayings of
Muhammad: with the Quran, one of the two most important
sources of Islamic law

hajj (Ar.) pilgrimage to Mecca

hammam (Ar.) public bath, often built near a *masjid*, q.v.

Hind (Per./Ar.) north India, the territory east of the River Indus

'id or *'Id al-fitr* (Ar.) festival that celebrates the end of the Ramadan fast

ijtihad (Ar.) rational theological interpretation

Il-Khans (Ar./T./M.) Mongol rulers of Iran

ilmiyye (Ar.) Ottoman term for the official *'ulama*, q.v.

Imam (Ar.) a leader of a Shi'i community; also a prayer leader in a *masjid*,
q.v.

iqta' (Ar.) a grant of land, or an entire province, in exchange for military
support

Iran (Per.) pre-Islamic name for territory on the Iranian plateau and
neighboring regions; revived during the Mongol era

Iranians (Per.) Indo-European population of Iran; an ethnic and cultural
term

ishraqi (Ar.) "Illumination," the Neoplatonic doctrine associated with al-
Suhrawardi; stresses intuition over logic

Isma'ilis (Ar.) Shi'i Muslims who believed that there were seven, not
twelve, legitimate Imams. *See* Shi'as

iwan (Per.), *eyvan* (T.) a portico or open gallery; a common architectural feature in *masjids* and *madrasas*, q.v.

jagir (Per.) military land grant to support troops in Mughal India.

jihad (Ar.) effort or striving: *jihad al-akbar*, the greater or spiritual striving; *jihad al-saghir*, the lesser striving or military campaign against non-Muslims or heretics

jizya (Ar.) canonical tax levied on non-Muslims

kadi asker (Ar/T.) "army judges," the leading *qadis* or judges of Islamic law in the early Ottoman period. Later overshadowed by the *Shaikh al-Islam*

kalam (Ar.) Muslim scholastic theology

kanun/Qanun (Ar.) administrative regulation or imperial order or law, not part of the *Shari'a* (Muslim canonical law)

khan or qan (T.) – Central Asian ruler, usually Turk or Mongol

khangah (Per.) a hospice or meeting house for Sufis; synonym for *tekke*

khutba (Ar.) the Friday prayer; a ruler's name given in this prayer was, with coinage, one of two symbols of sovereignty in Islamic societies

kulliye (Ar.) Ottoman mosque complex, usually including a *madrasa* (q.v.), a *hammam* (q.v.), and often other public facilities such as a kitchen or library

laqab (Ar.) honorific Muslim name, e.g. Qutb al-Din or "Pillar of the Faith"

madhhab (Ar.) (Per. *mazhab*) doctrine, sect, or legal school, such as the Hanafi Madhab or the Shafi'i Madhab. Four schools in Sunni Islam

madrasa (Ar.) Muslim religious college, often built next to a *masjid*, q.v.

Mahdi (Ar.) the "Guided One," or future redeemer in Islam, sometimes associated in Shi'i Islam with the Hidden Imam

maidan (Per.) an open field, an arena, a square

majlis (Ar.) a gathering for camaraderie, conversation, drink, and/or poetry and music; also known as *suhbat*

maktab (Ar.) Muslim primary school

malikhane (Ar/Per.) Ottoman tax-farming system that began in the late seventeenth century

mamluk (Ar.) military slave; see also *ghulam*

mansabdars (Ar./Per.) Mughal military and bureaucratic elite, most of whom held temporary land grants known as *jagirs*. Similar to Ottoman *sipahis*

masjid (Ar.) a mosque

Mawarannahr (Ar.) Transoxiana or western Central Asia

mihrab (Ar.) niche in the wall of a *masjid* that indicates the direction of Mecca and, therefore, the proper focus of prayer *millat* (Ar.) religious community: term applied by Ottomans to Jews and Christians

mirza (Ar.) a Mughal prince, e.g. Babur Mirza

muezzin (Ar.) mosque official who announces the call to prayer

muhtasib (Ar.) a market superintendent; a police official who maintains urban social order

mujtahid (Ar.) one who interprets Muslim theology, especially in Iran

muqarnas (Ar.) geometric niches, located where columns meet a dome

murid (Ar.) a religious student, especially of a Sufi

murshid (Ar.) a teacher, especially a Sufi

mutawalli (Ar.) the legal executive of a *waqf* (q.v.)

nama (Per.) book, text, or treatise, e.g. *Shah-nama*, the "Book of Kings"

nasihat (Ar.) advice, as in *nasihat-nama*, an advice treatise or "mirror for princes"

nauruz (Per.) New Year, the spring or vernal equinox; a popular pre-Islamic festival of Persianate societies

nedim (Ar.) "boon companion," counselor; a specific post in Muslim courts

nisba (Ar.) personal name that indicates native place or long-time residence, e.g. Isfahani, from Isfahan

Oghuz (T.) Turkic peoples originating in Mawarannahr, q.v.

ortaqs (T.-M.) a merchant; a commercial agreement between the Turco-Mongol elite and merchants

Peripatetic Philosophy: the philosophical school of Aristotle and his contemporaries, who "walked about" and lectured in the Athens Lyceum

pir (Per.) Sufi teacher. *See also shaikh*

pishtaq (Ar.) a porch projecting from the façade of a building

qadi (Ar.), *Qazi* (Per.), *Kadi* (T.) a Muslim religious judge

qalandar (Per.) a wandering, itinerant Sufi

qasida (Ar.) an elegy, usually longer than a *ghazal*

qazaq (T./M.) a throneless ruler or political vagabond

raj (Sanskrit) rule; thus *raja*, ruler, and *maharaja*, "great ruler" or emperor

ruba'i (Ar.) a four-line poem resembling the Japanese *haiku*

sahra-nishin (Ar./Per.) a desert or steppe dweller, a pastoral nomad

shah (Per.) a king or ruler; also *padishah*, a great ruler, and *shahanshah*, an emperor, literally "king of kings"

shahid (Ar.) a "witness" for the faith, a religious martyr

shaikh (Ar.) a tribal chief or a Sufi *pir* q.v.; also used generally to show respect

shaikh al-Islam (Ar.) supreme religious authority; in the later Ottoman period more important than the *kadi asker*

shari'a (Ar.) literally "straight road"; the Law of God, based primarily on the Quran, God's revelations to Muhammad, and the *hadith*, reports of the actions and/or sayings of the Prophet

Shi'as (Ar.) Muslims who believe that prophecy and religious legitimacy passed from Muhammad to his son-in-law and cousin, 'Ali and then to blood descendants known as Imams, q.v.

silsila (Ar.) literally a chain or series; a synonym for a political dynasty or a spiritual lineage, e.g. in Sufi orders

sipahi (Per.) cavalryman, soldier; a traditional Ottoman trooper who held a *timar*, q.v. Similar to the Mughal *mansabdar*, q.v.

Sufism (Ar.) system of Muslim religious orders led by *pirs* or *shaikhs* (q.v.) that de-emphasize orthodox practice in favor of the search for individual salvation; often described as "devotional" or "mystical" because of its emphasis on love between man and God and use of music or even dance to induce spiritual states

suhbat (Ar.) see *majlis*

sultan (Ar.) independent ruler, with no claim to religious legitimacy

Sunni (Ar.) "tradition": the majority Muslim tradition that reveres the first four Caliphs (q.v.) as Muhammad's legitimate successors and rejects the idea that anyone after Muhammad, "the Seal of the Prophets," possessed prophetic insight

tafsir (Ar.) interpretation of and commentary on the Quran

Tajik (Per.) an ethnic or cultural Iranian

Tatar (Mongol) member of one of the Mongol tribes at the time of Chinggis Qan/Chingiz Khan, q.v.

tekke (T./Ar.) from *takya*; synonym for *khangah*, q.v.

Temür (T.): Turkic conquerer, (d.1405)

timar (Per.) Ottoman land grant given in exchange for military service; similar to the Mughal *jagir*, q.v.

Timurids: descendants of Temür, otherwise known in Persian as Timür-i leng or in English as "Timür the Lame" (Tamerlane)

türbe (Ar.) Ottoman tomb

Turk (T.) name for a member of any of the Turkic-speaking peoples originating in Mawarannahr (q.v.) or more generally, in Central Asia. Sometimes used as a synonym for "rustic"

Turki (T.) name for the Turkic language spoken by the Timurids; now sometimes identified as "Old Uzbek"

'ulama (Ar.) Muslim clergy, literally the "learned", i.e. in the Islamic sciences

ulucami (T./Ar.) Ottoman Friday; cathedral mosque

umma (Ar.) the world's community of Muslims

Upanishads (Sanskrit) the last and metaphysical group of Sanskrit
texts, part of the corpus of pre-Common Era religious literature
known as the *Vedas*. The pantheism of the Upanishads appealed
broadly to non-Indians, including Muslims and American
Transcendentalists

vizier or *wazir* (Ar.) a minister, especially in the Ottoman Empire ("Grand
Viziers")

wahdat al-wujud (Ar.) the "unity of being," the idea originally associated
with Ibn 'Arabi

waqf (Ar.) a charitable or "pious" endowment of property or even money
used to provide funds for public institutions, such as mosques,
schools, or baths, or established to safeguard family property

yasa, yasak (T/M.) traditional Turkic or Mongol law

zamindar (Per.) in Mughal India, a Hindu or Muslim landowner or chief.
An independent or autonomous individual, sometimes similar to
an Ottoman *ayyan*

zimmi see dhimmi

Dynastic lists[1]

I. OSMANLIS/OTTOMANS: 1260–1923

The Turkish pronunciation is given first, followed, when appropriate, by the Arabic.

LEGENDARY ANCESTOR: OĞUZ KHAN (CENTRAL ASIA)

Osman (Uthman), 1290–1324 (eponymous founder)
Orhan (Orkhon), 1324–62
Murat I (Murad), 1362–89
Bayezit (Bayezid), 1389–1402
Mehmet I (Muhammad), 1413–21
Murat II (Murad), 1421–44 and 1446–51
Mehmet II (Muhammad) Fatih, 1444–46 and 1451–81
Bayezit II (Bayezid), 1481–1512
Selim I Yavuz, "the Grim," 1512–20
Süleyman I, Kanuni, 1520–66
Selim II, 1566–74
Murat III (Murad), 1574–95
Mehmet III (Muhammad), 1595–1603
Ahmet I (Ahmad), 1603–17
Osman II (Uthman), 1618–22
Mustafa II, 1617–18 and 1622–3
Murat IV (Murad), 1623–40
Ibrahim I, 1640–8
Mehmet IV (Muhammad), 1648–87
Süleyman II, 1687–91
Ahmet II (Ahmad), 1691–95
Mustafa II, 1695–1703
Ahmet III (Ahmad), 1703–30

---

[1] See C. E. Bosworth, *The Islamic Dynasties* (Edinburgh University Press, 1967).

Mahmut I (Mahmud), 1730–54
Osman III (Uthman), 1754–57
Mustafa III, 1757–74
Abdülhamit I (Abd al-Hamid), 1774–89
Selim III, 1789–1807
Mustafa IV, 1807–8
Mahmut II (Mahmud), 1808–39
Abdülmecit I ('Abd al-Majid), 1839–61
Abdülaziz ('Abd al-'Aziz), 1861–76
Abdülhamit II ('Abd al-Hamid), 1876–1909
Mehmet V (Muhammad), 1909–18
Mehmet VI (Muhammad), 1918–22

THE SAFAVIDS: 1501–1722 (1732)

SHAIKH SAFI AL-DIN OF ARDEBIL, 1252–1344, FOUNDER OF SAFAVI/ SAFAVID SUFI ORDER

Isma'il I, 1501–24
Tahmasp I, 1524–76
Isma'il II, 1576–78
Muhammad Khudabanda (Sultan Muhammad Shah), 1578–88
Shah 'Abbas I, 1588–1629
Shah Safi I, 1629–42
Shah 'Abbas II, 1642–66
Safi II (Sulaiman I), 1666–94
Shah Sultan Husain I, 1694–1722
Tahmasp II, 1722–32 (powerless figurehead)

MUGHALS: 1526–1858

TEMÜR, 1336–1405 AND CHINGGIS QAN (CHINGIZ KHAN), 1160–1227

TIMÜRIDS OF CENTRAL ASIA, IRAN, AND AFGHANISTAN, 1405–1506

Zahir al-Din Muhammad Babur, 1526–30
Nasir al-Din Humayun, 1530–40 and 1554–5
Jalal al-Din Akbar, 1556–1605
Nur al-Din Jahangir, 1605–28
Shihab al-Din Shah Jahan, 1628–58
Muhyi-al-Din Aurangzib ('Alamgir I), 1658–1707
Shah 'Alam I Bahadur Shah, 1707–12
Mu'izz al-Din Jahandar, 1712–13
Farrukh-siyar, 1713–19

Nasir al-Din Muhammad, 1719–48 (after 1739, kingdom rather
than empire)

Ahmad Shah Bahadur, 1748–54

Aziz al-Din 'Alamgir II, 1754–60

Jalal al-Din 'Ali Jauhar Shah 'Alam II, 1760–88 and 1788–1806
(British control from 1801)

Mu'in al-Din Akbar II, 1806–37

Siraj al-Din Bahadur Shah II, 1837–58 (British terminated
dynasty in 1858)

Bibliography

OTTOMANS

Ágoston, Gabór, *Guns for the Sultan: Military Power and the Weapons Industry in the Ottoman Empire* (Cambridge University Press, 2005).

Andrews, Walter G., Black, Najaat and Kalpaklı, Mehmet, ed. and trans., *Ottoman Lyric Poetry* (Austin: University of Texas Press, 1997).

Antonius, George, *The Arab Awakening* (Philadelphia: J. B. Lippincott, 1939).

Atıl, Esin, "The Art of the Book," in Esin Atıl, ed., *Turkish Art* (New York: Henry Abrams, 1980), 137–239.

"Levni and the Surname: The Story of an Eighteenth-Century Ottoman Festival," *Muqarnas* 10 (1993), 181–200.

Babinger, Franz, *Mehmed the Conqueror and His Time*, ed. William C. Hickman, trans. Ralph Manheim (Princeton: Bollingen Press, 1978).

Bagci, Serpil, "From Translated Word to Translated Image: The Illustrated Şehnâme-i Türki Copies," *Muqarnas* 17 (2000), 162–76.

Balfour, Patrick (Lord Kinross), *Atatürk: A Biography of Mustafa Kemal, Father of Modern Turkey* (New York: Morrow, 1965).

Barkay, Karen, *Empire of Difference: The Ottomans in Comparative Perspective* (Cambridge University Press, 2008).

Ben-Zaken, Avner, "The Heavens of the Sky and the Heavens of the Heart: The Ottoman Cultural Context for Post-Copernican Astronomy," *British Journal for the History of Science* 37, No. 1 (March 2004), 1–28.

Berkes, Niyazi, "Ibrâhîm Mütaferrika," *Encyclopaedia of Islam* II, Brill Online.

Börekçi, Gunhan, "A Contribution to the Military Revolution Debate: The Janisssaries' Use of Volley Fire during The Long Ottoman–Habsburg War of 1593–1606 and the Problem of Origins," *Acta Orientalia* 59, No. 4 (2006), 407–38.

Casale, Giancarlo, "The Ottoman Administration of the Spice Trade in the Sixteenth Century Red Sea and Persian Gulf," *Journal of the Economic and Social History of the Orient* 49, No. 2 (2006), 170–98.

Çizakça, Murat, "A Short History of the Bursa Silk Industry," *Journal of the Economic and Social History of the Orient* 23, Nos. 1–2 (April 1980), 142–52.

"Cash Waqfs of Bursa, 1555–1823," *Journal of the Economic and Social History of the Orient* 38, No. 2, 313–54.

Crane, Howard, *The Garden of Mosques: Hafiz Hüseyin Al-Ayvansarayi's Guide to the Muslim Monuments of Ottoman Istanbul* (Leiden: Brill, 2000).

Curry, John Joseph IV, "Transforming Muslim Mystical Thought in the Ottoman Empire: The Case of the Shabaniyye Order in Kastamonu and Beyond," Unpublished PhD dissertation, Ohio State University, 2005.

Dankoff, Robert, *An Ottoman Mentality: The World of Evliya Çelebi* (Leiden: Brill, 2004).

Darling, Linda, *Revenue-Raising and Legitimacy: Tax Collection and Finance Administration in the Ottoman Empire, 1560–1660* (Leiden: Brill, 1996).

Denny, W. B., "Dating Ottoman Turkish Works in the Saz style," *Muqarnas* 1 (1983), 103–21.

Ergene, Boğac A., "On Ottoman Justice: Interpretations in Conflict (1600–1800)," *Islamic Law and Society* (2001), 52–87.

Erşahin, Seyfettin, "The Ottoman Foundation of the Turkish Republic's *Diyanet*: Ziya Golkalp's *Diyanet Ishları Nazâratı*," *The Muslim World* 98, Nos. 2–3 (April 2008), 82–98.

Faroqhi, Suraiya N., ed., *The Cambridge History of Turkey* (Cambridge University Press, 2006), 3 vols.

The Ottoman Empire and the World Around It (London and New York: I. B. Tauris, 2004).

Pilgrims and Sultans: The Hajj Under the Ottomans 1517–1683 (London and New York: I. B.Tauris, 1994).

Towns and Townsmen in Ottoman Anatolia: Trade, Crafts and Food Production in an Urban Setting, 1520–1650 (Cambridge University Press, 1984).

"*Vakıf* Administration in Sixteenth Century Konya. The Zaviye of Sadreddin-i Konevi," *Journal of the Economic and Social History of The Orient* 17, No. 2 (May 1974), 145–72.

Feldman, Walter, "The Celestial Sphere, the Wheel of Fortune, and Fate in the Gazels of Naili and Baki," *International Journal of Middle East Studies* 28, No. 2 (May 1996), 193–215.

Findley, Carter V., *Bureaucratic Reform in the Ottoman Empire: The Sublime Porte 1789–1922* (Princeton University Press, 1980).

Fleischer, Cornell H., *Bureaucrat and Intellectual in the Ottoman Empire: The Historian Mustafa Âli (1541–1600)* (Princeton University Press, 1986).

"Royal Authority, Dynastic Cyclism and 'Ibn Khaldunism' in Sixteenth Century Ottoman Letters," in Bruce Lawrence, ed., *Ibn Khaldun and Islamic Ideology* (Leiden: Brill, 1984), 198–220.

Gerber, Haim, *Economy and Society in an Ottoman City: Bursa, 1600–1700* (Jerusalem: The Hebrew University, 1988).

Gibb, E. J. W., *A History of Ottoman Poetry* (London: Luzac, 1902–58), 6 vols.

Gökyay, Orhon Şai'k, "Kâtib Çelebi," *Encyclopaedia of Islam* II, Brill Online.

Goodwin, Godfrey, *A History of Ottoman Architecture* (New York: Thames & Hudson, 1987).

Grabar, Oleg, "An Exhibition of High Ottoman Art," *Muqarnas* 6 (1989), 1–11.

Halman, Talat S., trans., *Süleyman The Magnificent: Poet* (Istanbul: Dost Yayınları, 1987).

Halman, Talat S., and Jayne L. Warner, *Nightingales and Pleasure Gardens: Turkish Love Poems* (Syracuse University Press, 1987).

Hanioğlu, M. Şükrü, *The Young Turks in Opposition* (Oxford University Press, 1995).

Hathaway, Jane, *The Chief Eunuch of the Ottoman Imperial Harem* (Oxford: One World Publications, 2005).

The Politics of Households in Ottoman Egypt: The Rise of the Qazdağlis (Cambridge University Press, repr. 2002).

"Rewriting Eighteenth-Century Ottoman History," *Mediterranean Historical Review* 19, No. 1 (June 2004), 29–53.

Hattox, Ralph, *Coffee and Coffeehouses: The Origins of a Social Beverage in the Medieval Near East* (Seattle: University of Washington Press, 1985).

Imber, Colin, "Koçi Beg/Gördidjeli Kodja Mustafa Beg," *Encyclopaedia of Islam* II, Brill Online.

The Ottoman Empire 1300–1650: The Structure of Power (Basingstoke and New York: Palgrave Macmillan, 2002).

Inalcık, Halil, Bursa I: "Asir Sanayi ve Ticaret Tarihine Dair Vesikalar," in *Osmanlı Imperatoruğlu*, 203–58.

"Capital Formation in the Ottoman Empire," *Journal of Economic History* 39, No. 1 (March 1969), 97–140.

Essays in Ottoman History (Istanbul: EREN, 1998).

"Imtiyâzât," *Encyclopaedia of Islam* II, Brill online.

"The India Trade," in Inalcık and Quataert, eds., *An Economic and Social History of the Ottoman Empire*, 315–63.

"Mehemmed II," *Encyclopaedia of Islam* II, Brill Online.

"Osman Ghazi's Seige of Nicea and the Battle of Bapheus," in *Essays in Ottoman History*, 55–84.

Osmanli'da Devlet, Hukuk, Adâlet (Istanbul: EREN, 2000).

Osmanli Imparatoruğlu (Istanbul: EREN, 2nd edn. 1996).

"Osmanli'larda Saltanat Verâseti Usûlû ve Turk Hakimiyet Telakkisiyle Ilgisi," *Siyasal Bilgiler Fakultesi Dergisi* 14 (1959), 69–94.

The Ottoman Empire: The Classical Age 1300–1600, trans. Norman Itzkowitz and Colin Imber (London: Phoenix Press, repr. 1988).

Inalcık, Halil and Kafadar, Cemal, eds., *Süleyman the Second and His Time* (Istanbul: Isis Press, 1993).

Inalcık, Halil and Donald Quataert, eds., *An Economic and Social History of the Ottoman Empire 1300–1914* (Cambridge University Press, 1994).

Isanoğlu, Ekmeleddin, *Science, Technology and Learning in the Ottoman Empire* (Aldershot: Ashgate, 2004.)

Îz, Fahir, "Bâkî, Mahmûd 'Abd al-," *Encyclopaedia of Islam* II, Brill Online.

Kafadar, Cemal, *Between Two Worlds: The Construction of the Ottoman State* (Berkeley: University of California Press, 1995).

Karamustafa, Ahmet T., "Origins of Anatolian Sufism," in Ahmet Yaşar Ocak, ed., *Sufism and Sufis in Ottoman Society* (Ankara: Turkish Historical Society, 2005), 67–95.

Karpat, Kemal, "The Transformation of the Ottoman State, 1789–1908," *International Journal of Middle East Studies* 3, No. 3 (July 1972), 243–81.

Köprülü, Mehmet Fuat, *Islam in Anatolia after the Turkish Invasion*, trans. and ed. Gary Leister (Salt Lake City: University of Utah Press, 1993).

"Literature: The Eighteenth Century," in "'Othmânli," *Encyclopaedia of Islam* II, Brill Online.

The Seljuks of Anatolia: Their History and Culture According to Local Muslim Sources, ed. and trans. Gary Leister (Salt Lake City: University of Utah Press, 1992).

Kuran, Aptullah, *The Mosque in Early Islamic Architecture* (Chicago: The University of Chicago Press, 1968).

Kürkçüoğlu, Kemâl Edîb, *Sülemaniye Vakfiyese* (Istanbul: Vakiflar Umum Müdürlüğu, 1962).

Lewis, Bernard, *The Emergence of Modern Turkey* (Oxford University Press, 2nd edn. 1961).

Istanbul and the Civilization of the Ottoman Empire (Norman: University of Oklahoma Press, 1963).

Lifchez, Raymond, ed., *The Dervish Lodge: Architecture, Art and Sufism in Ottoman Turkey* (Berkeley and London: University of California Press, 1992).

Menzel, Th., "Nedjâtî Bey," *Encyclopaedia of Islam* II, Brill Online.

Mordtmann, J. H., "Derebey," *Encyclopaedia of Islam* II, Brill Online.

Necipoğlu, Gülru, *The Age of Sinan: Architectural Culture in the Ottoman Empire* (Princeton University Press, 2005).

Architecture, Ceremonial and Power: The Topkapi Palace in the Fifteenth and Sixteenth Centuries (Cambridge, Mass: MIT Press, 1991).

"Challenging the Past: Sinan and the Comparative Discourse of Early Modern Islamic Architecture," *Muqarnas* 10 (1993), 169–80.

"Framing the Gaze in Ottoman, Safavid and Mughal Palaces," *Ars Orientalis* 23 (1993), 303–42.

"From International Timurid to Ottoman: A Change in Taste in Sixteenth-Century Ceramic Tiles," *Muqarnas* 7 (1990), 136–70.

"The Serial Portraits of Ottoman Sultans in Comparative Perspective," in Julian Raby et al., *The Sultan's Portrait* (Istanbul: Iş Bank, 2000), 22–61.

"The Süleymaniye Complex in Istanbul: An Interpretation," *Muqarnas* 3 (1985), 92–117.

The Topkapı Scroll: Geometry and Ornament in Islamic Architecture (Santa Monica, Ca.: Getty Center for the History of Art and the Humanities, 1995).

Ocak, Ahmed Yaşar, ed., *Sufism and Sufis in Ottoman Society* (Ankara: Atatürk Kültür, 2005).

Oren, Michael, "The Mass Murder They Still Deny," *New York Review of Books*, 10 May 2007, 37–9.

Özkoçak, Selma Akyazıçı, "Coffeehouses: Rethinking the Public and Private in Early Modern Istanbul," *Journal of Urban History* 33, No. 6 (September 2007), 965–86.

Pamuk, Şevkat, *A Monetary History of the Ottoman Empire* (Cambridge University Press, 2000).

"Money in the Ottoman Empire, 1326–1914," in Inalcık and Quataert, eds., *Economic and Social History of the Ottoman Empire*, 947–81.

"The Price Revolution in the Ottoman Empire Reconsidered," *International Journal of Middle East Studies* 33, No. 1 (February 2001), 69–89.

Papas, Alexandre, "Towards a New History of Sufism: The Turkish Case," *History of Religions* 46, No. 1 (2006), 81–90.

Peirce, Leslie, *The Imperial Harem Women and Sovereignty in the Ottoman Empire* (Oxford University Press, 1993).

"Changing Perceptions of the Ottoman Empire: The Early Centuries," *Mediterranean Historical Review* 19, No. 1 (June 2004), 6–28.

Piterberg, Gabriel, "The Formation of an Ottoman–Egyptian Elite in the 18th Century," *International Journal of Middle East Studies* 22, No. 3 (August 1990), 275–89.

Quataert, Donald, *The Ottoman Empire 1700–1922* (Cambridge University Press, 2nd edn., 2005).

Rogers, S. M., *Empire of the Sultans* (London: Nour Foundation, 2000).

Sinan (London and New Delhi: I. B. Tauris and Oxford University Press, 2006).

Roxburgh, D. J., ed., *The Turks, A Journey of a Thousand Years* (London: Royal Academy of Arts, 2005).

Runciman, Steven, *The Fall of Constantinople 1453* (Cambridge University Press, repr. 1953).

Shaw, Stanford, "The Origins of Ottoman Military Reform: The *Nizam-i Cedid* Army of Sultan Selim III (1709–1807)," *Journal of Modern History* 37 (1965), 291–306.

Silay, Kemal, *Nedim and the Poetics of the Ottoman Court* (Bloomington, Ind.: Indiana University Turkish Studies Series, 1994).

Stavrides, Theoharis, *The Sultan of Vezirs: the Life and Times of the Ottoman Grand Vezir Mahmud Pasha Angelović (1453–1474)* (Leiden: Brill, 2001).

Stierlin, Henri, *Turkey from the Selçuks to the Ottomans* (Cologne: Taschen, 1998).

Stierlin, Henri and Anne Stierlin, *Islamic Art and Architecture* (New York: Thames and Hudson, 2002).

Tanman, M. Baha, "Ottoman Architecture and Sufi Orders," in Ahmed Yaşar Ocak, ed., *Sufism and Sufis in Ottoman Society* (Ankara: Atatürk Kültür, 2005).

Tansel, F. A., "Kemâl, Mehmed Nâmik," *Encyclopaedia of Islam* II, Brill Online.

Tekin, Gönül Alpay, "Classical Ottoman Literature during the Sixteenth Century," *Encyclopaedia of Islam* II, Brill Online.

Tezcan, Baki, "Ethics as a Domain to Discuss the Political: Kınalzâde Ali Efendi's Akhlak-i Alâî," in Ali Çasku, ed., *International Congress on Learning and Education in the Ottoman World* (Istanbul: Research Center for Islamic History, Art and Culture, 2001), 109–20.

Türer, Osman, "General Distribution of Sufi Orders in Ottoman Anatolia," in Ahmet Yaşar Ocak, ed., *Sufism and Sufis in Ottoman Society* (Ankara: Turkish Historical Society, 2005), 220–56.

Uluç, Lâle, "Selling to the Court: Late Sixteenth-Century Manuscript Production in Shiraz," *Muqarnas* 17 (2000), 73–96.

Ünsal, Behçet, *Turkish Islamic Architecture in Seljuk and Ottoman Times 1071–1923* (London and New York: St Martin's Press, 1973).

Vahide, Şükran, *Islam in Modern Turkey: An Intellectual Biography of Bediuzzaman Said Nursi* (Albany: State University of New York Press, 2005).

Veinstein, G., "Süleymân (926-74/1520-66)," *Encyclopaedia of Islam* II, Brill Online.

Wittek, Paul, *The Rise of the Ottoman Empire* (London: School of Oriental And African Studies, 1938).

Wolper, Ethel Sara. *Cities and Saints: Sufism and the Transformation of Urban Space in Anatolia* (University Park, PA: Pennsylvania State University Press, 2003).

Zilfi, C. Madeline, "The Kadizadelis: Discordant Revivalism in Seventeenth Century Istanbul," *Journal of Near Eastern Studies* 45, No. 4 (October 1986), 251–69.

SAFAVIDS

Abisaab, Rula Jurdi, "The Ulama of Jabal 'Amil in Safavid Iran, 1501–1736: Marginality, Migration and Social Change," *Iranian Studies* 27, No. 1–4 (1994), 103–22.

Algar, Hamid., *Mîrzâ Malkum Khân: A Study in the History of Iranian Modernism* (Berkeley: University of California Press, 1973).

"Nakshbandiyya," *Encyclopaedia of Islam* II, Brill Online.

"Nuqtawiyya," *Encyclopaedia of Islam* II, Brill Online.

Religion and State in Iran, 1785–1906: The Role of the Ulama in the Qajar Period (Berkeley: University of California Press, 1969).

Amanat, Abbas, *Pivot of the Universe: Nasir al-Din Shah Qajar and the Iranian Monarchy 1831–1896* (Berkeley: University of California Press, 1997).

Arberry, A. J., *Classical Persian Literature* (London: George, Allen & Unwin, 1967).

Arjomand, Said Amir, *The Shadow of God and the Hidden Imam* (Chicago University Press, 1984).

The Turban for the Crown: The Islamic Revolution in Iran (Oxford University Press, 1988).

Babaie, Sussan, "Shah 'Abbas II, the Conquest of Qandahar, the Chihil Sutun, and its Wall Paintings," *Muqarnas* 11 (1994), 125–42.

Babayan, Kathryn, "The Safavid Synthesis: From Qizilbash Islam to Imamite Shi'ism," *Iranian Studies* 27, No. 1/4 (1994), 135–61.

Bashir, Shazad, "After the Messiah: The Nurbakhshiyya in Late Timurid and Early Safavid Times," in Newman, ed., *Society and Culture in The Early Modern Middle East*, 295–314.

"Shah Ismai'il and the Qizilbash: Cannibalism in the Religious History of Early Safavid Iran," *History of Religions* 45, No. 3 (2006), 234–56.

Beaumont, Peter, "Âb," *Encyclopaedia Iranica*, ed. Ehsan Yarshater, I (London: Routledge & Keegan Paul, 1985), 27–39.

Behnan, J., "Population," *The Cambridge History of Iran*, vol. I, *The Land* (Cambridge University Press, 1968), 468–88.

Blair, Sheila, "The Octagonal Pavilion at Natanz: A Reexamination of Early Islamic Architecture in Iran," *Muqarnas* 1 (1983), 69–94.

Blake, Stephen, *Half the World: The Social Architecture of Safavid Isfahan 1590–1722* (Costa Mesa, Ca.: Mazda, 1999).

Boyle, John Andrew, ed., *The Cambridge History of Iran*, vol. V, *The Saljuq and Mongol Periods* (Cambridge University Press, 1968).

Browne, E. G., *The Persian Revolution of 1905–1909* (New York: Barnes and Noble, repr. 1906).

Canby, Sheila, *Persian Painting* (New York: Thames and Hudson, 1993).

Chardin, (Sir) John (Jean), *Travels in Persia 1673–1677* (Mineola, N.Y.: Dover Books, repr. 1988).

Dabashi, Hamid, "Khwâjah Nasîr al-Dîn Tûsî: The Philosopher Vizier and the Intellectual Climate of His Times," in Seyyed Hossein Nasr and Oliver Leaman, eds., *A History of Islamic Philosophy* (London and New York: Routledge, 2001), 527–96.

"Mîr Dâmâd and the Founding of the 'School of Isfahan,'" in Nasr and Leaman, eds., *A History of Islamic Philosophy*, 597–634.

Dale, Stephen Frederic, "A Safavid Poet in the Heart of Darkness: The Indian Poems of Ashraf Mazandarani," *Iranian Studies* 36, No. 2 (2003), 197–212.

Davis, Dick, *Shahnameh: The Persian Book of Kings* (New York: Viking Penguin, 2006).

De Bruijn, J. T. P., *Of Piety and Poetry: The Interaction of Religion and Literature in the Life and Works of Hakîm Sanâ'î of Ghazna* (Leiden: Brill, 1983).

Persian Sufi Poetry (Richmond, Surrey: Curzon Press, 1997).

Della Valle, Pietro, *The Pilgrim: The Journeys of Pietro della Valle*, trans. and abridged George Bull (London: The Folio Society, 1989).

Diba, Layla and Maryam Ekhtiar, eds., *Royal Persian Paintings: The Qajar Period 1785–1925* (London: I. B. Tauris for the Brooklyn Museum of Art, 1998).

Elias, Jamal J., "The Sufi Lords of Bahrabad: Sa'd al-Din and Sadr al-Din Hamuwayi," *Iranian Studies* 27, Nos. 1–4 (1994), 53–75.

Eskander Beg Monshi, *History of Shah 'Abbas the Great (Tarik-e 'Âlamârâ-ye 'Abbâsi)*, trans. Roger Savory (Boulder, CO.: Westview Press, 1978), 3 vols.

Fernea, Elizabeth Warnock, *The Guests of the Sheik: An Ethnography of an Iraqi Village* (New York: Doubleday, repr. 1989).

Ferrier, R. W., "An English View of Persian Trade in 1618: Reports from the Merchants Edward Pettus and Thomas Barker," *Journal of the Economic and Social History of the Orient* 19, No. 2 (May 1976), 182–214.

Fischer, Michael, *Iran: From Religious Dispute to Revolution* (Cambridge, Mass.: Harvard University Press, 1980).

Floor, Willem, *The Economy of Safavid Persia* (Wiesbaden: Reichert Verlag, 2000).

Floor, Willem, and Patrick Clawson, "Safavid Iran's Search for Silver and Gold," *International Journal of Middle East Studies* 32 (2000), 345–68.

Fragner, Bert, "Social and Economic Affairs," in Jackson and Lockhart, eds., *The Cambridge History of Iran*, VI, 491–567.

Garthwaite, Gene R., *The Persians* (Oxford: Blackwell, 2005).

Golombek, Lisa, "The Safavid Ceramic Industry at Kirman," *Iran* 41 (2003), 253–69.

Golombek, Lisa, and Donald Wilber, *The Timurid Architecture of Iran and Turan* (Princeton University Press, 1988), 2 vols.

Gordon, Stewart, *The Marathas* 1600–1818 (Cambridge University Press, 1993).

Grube, Heinz, *Iranian Cities* (New York University Press, 1979).

Gurney, J. D., "Pietro della Valle: The Limits of Perception," *Bulletin of the School of Oriental and African Studies* 49, No. 1 (1986), 103–16.

Hillenbrand, Robert, "The Iconography of the *Shah-nama-yi Shahi*," in Melville, ed., *Safavid Persia*, 53–78.

Hourani, Albert, "From Jabal 'Âmil to Persia," *Bulletin of the School of Oriental and African Studies* 49, No. 1 (1986), 133–40.

Hunahgani, Khusrau Ihtishami, *Dar Kuchih Bagh-i Zulf Isfahan dar Sh'ir-i Sa'ib* (Tehran: Sara, 1368/1989).

Jackson, Peter and Laurence Lockhart, eds., *The Cambridge History of Iran*, vol. VI, *The Timurid and Safavid Periods* (Cambridge University Press, 1986).

Johnson, Rosemary Stanfield, "Sunni Survival in Safavid Iran: Anti-Sunni Activities during the Reign of Shah Tahmasp I," *Iranian Studies* 27, No. 1/4 (1994), 123–33.

Kazemi, Ranin, "Morality and Idealism: Abu'l-Fazl Bahaqi's Historical Thought in Tarikh-i bayhaqi," unpublished MA dissertation, Ohio State University, 2005.

Keyvani, Mehdi, *Artisans and Guild Life in the Later Iranian Period* (Berlin: Klaus Schwartz, 1982).

Khanbaghi, Aptin, *The Fire, the Stone and the Cross: Minority Religions in Early Modern Iran* (London and New York: I. B. Tauris, 2006).

Kheirabadi, Masoud, *Iranian Cities: Formation and Development* (Austin: University of Texas Press, 1991).

Khonsari, Mehdi and Minouch Yavari, *The Persian Bazaar: Veiled Space of Desire* (Washington: Mage, 1993).

Koch, Ebba, *The Complete Taj Mahal* (London: Thames and Hudson, 2006).

Mughal Architecture: An Outline of its History and Development, 1526–1858 (Munich: Prestel, 1991).

Lambton, A. K. S., "Quis Custodiet Custodes? Some Reflections on the Persian Theory of Government," in A. K. S. Lambton, *Theory and Practice in Medieval Persian Government* (London: Variorum Reprints, 1980), II, 126–46.

Lentz, Thomas V., and Glenn D. Lowry, *Timur and the Princely Vision: Persian Art and Culture in the Fifteenth Century* (Los Angeles and Washington: Los Angeles County Museum of Art and the Arthur M. Sackler Gallery, 1989).

Losensky, Paul E., "Sa'eb of Tabriz," *Enclopaedia Iranica* online, 1–13.

Welcoming Fighânî: Imitation and Poetic Individuality in the Safavid–Mughal Ghazal (Costa Mesa, Ca.: Mazda, 1998).

Luschey-Schmeisser, Ingeborg, "Cehel Sotûn, Isfahan," *Encyclopaedia of Islam* II, Brill Online.

McChesney, Robert D., "Four Sources on Shah 'Abbas's Building of Isfahan," *Muqarnas* 5 (1988), 103–34.

"Waqf and Public Policy: The Waqfs of Shah 'Abbas, 1011–1023/1602–1614," *Asian and African Studies* 15 (1981), 165–90.

Manz, Beatrice Forbes, *Power, Politics and Religion in Timurid Iran* (Cambridge University Press, 2007).

"Women in Timurid Dynastic Politics," in Guity Nashat and Lois Beck, eds., *Women in Iran from the Rise of Islam to 1800* (Urbana and Chicago: University of Illinois Press, 2003), 121–39.

Matthee, Rudi, "Administrative Stability and Change in Late-17th Century Iran: The Case of Shaykh 'Ali Khan Zanganah (1669–89)," *International Journal of Middle East Studies* 26 (1994), 77–98.

"Anti-Ottoman Politics and Transit Rights: The Seventeenth Century Trade in Silk between Safavid Iran and Muscovy," *Cahiers du Monde Russe* 35, No. 4 (2003), 739–61.

"The Career of Mohammad Beg, Grand Vizier of Shah 'Abbas II (r. 1642–1666)," *Iranian Studies* 24, No. 1/4 (1991), 17–36.

"Iran's Ottoman Diplomacy during the Reign of Shâh Suleyman I (1077–1105/ 1666–1694)," in Kambiz Eslami, ed. *Iran and Iranian Studies* (Princeton University Press, 1998), 148–77.

"Merchants in Safavid Iran: Participants and Perceptions," *Journal of Early Modern History* 4, Nos. 3–4 (2000), 233–68.

"Mint Consolidation and the Worsening of the Late Safavid Coinage: The Mint of Huwayza," *Journal of the Economic and Social History of the Orient* 44, No. 4 (2001), 506–39.

The Politics of Trade in Safavid Iran: Silk for Silver 1600–1730 (Cambridge University Press, 1999).

The Pursuit of Pleasure: Drugs and Stimulants in Iranian History, 1500–1900 (Princeton University Press, 2005).

"The Safavid, Afshar, and Zand Periods," *Iranian Studies* 31, Nos. 3–4 (Summer/Fall 1998), 483–93.

"Unwalled Cities and Restless Nomads: Firearms and Artillery in Safavid Iran," in Melville, ed., *Safavid Persia*, 389–416.

Meisami, Julie Scott, *Medieval Persian Court Poetry* (Princeton University Press, 1987).

Melville, Charles, ed., *Safavid Persia: The History and Politics of an Islamic Society* (London and New York: I. B. Tauris, 1996).

"New Light on the Reign of Shah 'Abbas: Volume III of the *Avdal al-Tavarikh*," in Newman, ed., *Society and Culture in the Early Modern Middle East*, 63–96.

Minorsky, Vladimir, "The Aq Qoyunlu and Land Reforms," *Bulletin of the School of Oriental and African Studies* 17, No. 3 (1955), 449–62.

La domination des Dailamites, Publications de la Société des Etudes Iraniennes, no. 3 (Paris, 1932).

"The Poetry of Shâh Ismâ'îl I," *Bulletin of the School of Oriental and African Studies* 10, No. 4 (1942), 1006a–1053a.

Minorsky, Vladimir, ed. and trans., *Tadhkirat al-Mulûk: A Manual of Safavid Administration c. 1137/1725* (Cambridge University Press for the E. J. W. Gibb Memorial Series, repr. 1980).

Morgan, David M., "The Grea Yasa of Chingiz Khan and Mongol Law in the Il-Khanate," *Bulletin of the School of Oriental and African Studies* 49 (1986), 163–76.

Medieval Persia 1040–1797 (London: Longman, 1988).

Moussavi, Ahmad Kazemi, "Shi'ite Culture," *Iranian Studies* 31, Nos. 3/4 (Summer/Autumn 1998), 639–59.

Moynihan, Elizabeth B., *The Moonlight Garden* (Washington, DC and Seattle: The Arthur M Sackler Gallery and the University of Washington Press, 1999).

Naim, C. M., ed. and trans., *Zikr-i Mir* (New Delhi: Oxford University Press, 1999).

Nakash, Yitzhak, "An Attempt to Trace the Origin of the Rituals of Âshûrâ," *Die Welt des Islams* 33, No. 2 (1993), 161–81.

Nashat, Guity and Lois Beck, eds., *Women in Iran from the Rise of Islam to 1800* (Urbana: University of Illinois Press, 2003).

Nasr, Seyyid Hossein, "Findriskî, Mîr Abu'l Kâsim b. Mirza Husaynî Astarâbâdî," *Encyclopaedia of Islam* II, Brill Online.

"Mullâ Sadrâ: his teachings," in Nasr and Leaman, eds., *A History of Islamic Philosophy*, 643–62.

Nasr, Seyyid Hossein and Oliver Leaman, eds., *A History of Islamic Philosophy* (London: Routledge, 2001).

Newman, Andrew J., *Safavid Iran* (London and New York: I. B. Tauris, 2006).

"Philosophy in the Safavid Period," *Encyclopaedia of Islam* II, Brill Online.

Newman, Andrew J., ed., *Society and Culture in the Early Modern Middle East* (Leiden: Brill, 2003).

Nizam al-Mulk, *The Book of Government or Rules for Kings: The Siyar al-Muluk or Siyâsat-nâma of Nizâm al-Mulk*, trans. Hubert Drake (London: Routledge and Keegan Paul, 1969).

Planhol, X. de, "Ardebil," in Ehsan Yarshater, ed., *Encyclopaedia Iranica* (London and New York: Routledge and Keegan Paul, 1987), II, 357–61.

Potter, Lawrence G., "Sufis and Sultans in Post-Mongol Iran," *Iranian Studies* 27, No. 1/4 (1994), 77–102.

Quinn, Sholeh, "Notes on Timurid Legitimacy in Three Safavid Chronicles," *Iranian Studies*, 31, No. 2 (Spring 1998), 149–58.

Rahman, Fazlur, *The Philosophy of Mulla Sadr (Sadr al-Din Shirazi)* (Albany: State University of New York Press, 1975).

Rashîd al-Dîn ibn Talib, *The History of the Seljuq Turks from the Jâmi' al-tawârikh: An Il-Khanid Adaptation of the Saljûq-nâma of Zâhir*, trans. Kenneth A. Luther and Clifford Edmund Bosworth (Richmond, Surrey: Curzon, 2001).

The Successors of Genghis Khan (New York: Columbia University Press, 1971).

Rizvi, Kishwar, "Transformations in Early Safavid Architecture: The Shrine of Shaykh Safi al-din Ishaq Ardebili in Iran (1501–1629)," unpublished PhD dissertation, Department of Architecture, Massachusetts Institute of Technology, 2000.

Roxburgh, David J., *The Persian Album 1400–1600* (New Haven and London: Yale University Press, 2005).

Savory, R. M., "Economic and Commercial History: Trade Relations with Europe," in "Safawids," *Encyclopaedia of Islam* II, Brill Online.

Shah Tamasp, *Tazkirah-i Shah Tamasp*, ed. Imralah Safari, (Tehran, 2nd edn., 1363 (1984)).

Shuster, Morgan, *The Strangling of Persia* (New York: The Century Company, 1912).

Siegel, Jennifer, *Britain, Russia and the Final Struggle for Central Asia* (London and New York: I. B. Tauris, 2002).

Simpson, Marianna Shreve, "*Shahnama* as Text and *Shahnahma* as Image: A Brief Overview of Recent Studies, 1975–2000," in Robert Hillenbrand, ed., *Shahnama: The Visual Language of the Persian Book of Kings* (Aldershot: Ashgate, 2004).

Sims, Eleanor, with Boris I. Marshak and Ernst J. Grube, *Peerless Images: Persian Painting and its Sources* (New Haven and London: Yale University Press, 2002).

Smith, John Masson, Jr., *The History of the Sarbadâr Dynasty and Its Sources* (The Hague: Mouton, 1970).

Soucek, Priscilla, "Âlî Qâpû," *Encyclopaedia Iranica* online, 871.

Stewart, Devin J., "The Lost Biography of Baha' al-Din 'Amili and the Reign of Shah Ismai'il II in Safavid Historiography," *Iranian Studies* 31, No. 2 (Spring 1998), 177–205.

"Notes on the Migration of 'Âmilî Scholars to Safavid Iran," *Journal of Near Eastern Studies* 55, No. 2 (April 1996), 81–103.

Subtelny, Maria E., *Timurids in Transition* (Leiden: Brill, 2007).

Szuppe, Maria, "Kinship Ties between the Safavids and the Qizilbash Amirs in Late-Sixteenth Century Iran: A Case Study of the Political Career of Members of the Sharaf al-Din Oghli Tekelu Family," in Melville, ed., *Safavid Persia*, 79–104.

"Status, Knowledge, and Politics: Women in Sixteenth-Century Safavid Iran," in Nashat and Beck, eds., *Women in Iran*, 140–69.

Thackson, Wheeler M., *The Baburnama* (New York: Modern Library, 2002).

A Millennium of Classical Persian Poetry (Bethesda, Md.: Iran Books, 1994).

Thompson, D., "Silk Textiles in Iran," in "Abrîşam, Silk," *Encyclopaedia of Islam* II, Brill Online.

Thompson, Jon and Sheila R. Canby, eds., *Hunt for Paradise: Court Arts of Safavid Iran 1501–1576* (New York: Asia Society, 2003).

Welch, Anthony, *The King's Book of Kings: The Shah-Nameh of Shah Tamasp* (London: Thames and Hudson, 1972).

"Safavi Iran as Seen through Venetian Eyes," in Newman, ed., *Society and Culture in the Early Modern Middle East*, 97–123.

Werner, Christoph, *An Iranian Town in Transition: A Social, and Economic History of the Elites of Tabriz, 1747–1848* (Wiesbaden: Harrassowitz, 2000).

Winter, H. J. J., "Persian Science in Safavid Times," in Jackson and Lockhart, eds., *The Cambridge History of Iran*, VI, 581–609.

Woods, John E., *The Aqquyunlu: Clan, Confederation, Empire* (Minneapolis and Chicago: Biblioteca Islamica, 1976).

Yarshater, Ehsan, "Persian Poetry in the Timurid and Safavid Periods," in Jackson and Lockhart, eds., *The Cambridge History of Iran*, VI, 965–94.

Zarinebaf-Shahr, Fariba, "Economic Activities of Safavid Women in the Shrine City of Ardabil," *Iranian Studies* 31, No. 2 (Spring 1998), 247–61.

Ziai, Hossein, "Mullâ Sadrâ: His Life and Works," in Nasr and Leaman, eds., *A History of Islamic Philosophy*, 635–42.

"Shihâb al-Dîn Suhrawardî: founder of the Illuminationist School," in Nasr and Leaman, eds., *A History of Islamic Philosophy*, 434–64.

MUGHALS

Ahmad, Aziz, *Islamic Culture in the Indian Environment* (Oxford: Clarendon Press, 1964).

"Safawid Poets and India," *Iran* 14 (1976), 117–32.

Alam, Muzaffar, *The Crises of Empire in Mughal North India: Awadh and the Punjab 1707–1748* (Delhi: Oxford University Press, 1986).

A European Experience of the Mughal Orient, translated with an Introduction by Seema Alavi (New Delhi: Oxford University Press, 2001).

The Languages of Political Islam: India 1200–1800 (Chicago: University Of Chicago Press, 2004).

"The Pursuit of Persian: Language in Mughal Politics," *Modern Asian Studies* 32, No. 2 (May 1998), 317–49.

Alam, Muzaffar, François 'Nalini' Delvoye, and Marc Gaborieau, eds., *The Making of Indo-Persian Culture* (New Delhi: Manohar for the Centre des Sciences Humaines, 2000).

Ali, M. Athar, *The Mughal Nobility Under Aurungzeb* (Delhi: Oxford University Press, repr. 1997).

"The Mughal Polity – A Critique of Revisionist Approaches," *Modern Asian Studies* 27, No. 4 (1993), 699–710.

"The Passing of Empire: The Mughal Case," *Modern Asian Studies* 9, No. 3 (1975), 385–96.

"Recent Theories of Eighteenth Century India," *Indian Historical Review* 13, No. 1–2 (1986–1987), 103–10.

"Towards an Interpretation of the Mughal Empire," in Hermann Kulke, ed., *The State in India* (Oxford University Press, 1995), 263–77.

'Allâmî, Abû'l Fazl, *The Â'în-i Akbarî*, trans. H. Blochmann, ed. D. C. Phillott (New Delhi: Crown Publications, repr. 1988), 3 vols.

Alvi, Sajida S., "Religion and State During the Reign of the Mughal Emperor Jahângîr (1605–1627), *Studia Islamica* 69 (1989), 95–119.

Ansasri, A. S. Bazmee, "Bîdil, Mîrzâ 'Abd al Kâdir b. Abd al-Khâlik Arlâs (or Barlâs)," *Encyclopaedia of Islam* II, Brill Online.

Antonova, K. A., *Russko-Indiiskie Otnosheniia v. XVII Veke: Sbornik Dokumentov* (Moscow: Nauka, 1958).

Aquil, Raziuddin, "Conversion in Chishtî Literature: (13th–14th Centuries)," *Indian Historical Review*, 24, Nos. 1–2 (1997-8), 70–94.

"Miracles, Authority and Benevolence: Stories of *Karamat* in Sufi Literature of the Delhi Sultanate," in Anup Taneja, ed., *Sufi Cults and the Evolution of Medieval Indian Culture*, ICHR Monograph Series No. 9 (Delhi: ICHR & Northern Book Centre, 2003), 109–38.

"Sufi Cults, Politics and Conversion: The Chishtîs of the Sultanate Period," *Indian Historical Review* 22, Nos. 1–2 (1995–6), 190–7.

Asher, Catherine B., *Architecture of Mughal India* (Cambridge University Press, 1992).

Asimov, M. S. and C. E. Bosworth, eds., *History of Civilizations of Central Asia: Age of Achievement, 875 A.D. to the End of the 15th Century* (UNESCO, 1998).

Al-Badâonî, 'Abdu-l Qâdir Ibn-i-Mulûk Shâh, *Muntakhabu-T-Tawârîkh*, trans. George S. A. Ranking, Introduction by Brahmadeva Prasad Ambashthya (Patna: Academica Asiatica, repr. 1973), 3 vols.

Bailey, Gavin Alexander, "The Indian Conquest of Catholic Art: The Mughals, the Jesuits, and Imperial Painting," *Art Journal* 57, No. 1 (Spring 1998), 24–30.

Balabanlilar, Lisa, "Lords of the Auspicious Conjunction: Turco-Mongol Imperial Identity on the Subcontinent," *Journal of World History* 18, No. 1 (2007), 1–39.

Beach, Milo Cleveland, *Mughal and Rajput Painting* (Cambridge University Press, 1992).

Begley, W. E. and Z. A. Desai, eds., *The Shah Jahan Nama of 'Inayat Khan* (New Delhi: Oxford University Press, 1990).

Al-Biruni, Muhammad ibn Ahmad, *Tarikh al-Hind*, ed. Ainslee Embree (New York: Norton, 1971).

Blake, Stephen P., "The Patrimonial-Bureaucratic Empire of the Mughals," *Journal of Asian Studies* 39, No. 1 (November 1979), 77–94.

Bosworth, C. E., *The Ghaznavids: Their Empire in Afghanistan and Eastern Iran 994–1040* (Edinburgh University Press, 1963).

The Islamic Dynasties (Edinburgh University Press, 1967).

The Later Ghaznavids. Splendour and Decay: The Dynasty in Afghanistan and Northern India 1040–1166 (Edinburgh University Press, 1977).

Brand, Michael, and Glenn D. Lowry, eds., *Fatehpur-Sikri* (Bombay: Marg, 1987).

Brown, K. Butler, "Did Aurangzeb Ban Music?" *Modern Asian Studies* 41, No. 19 (January 2007), 77–120.

Calkins, Philip B., "The Formation of a Regionally Oriented Ruling Group in Bengal, 1700–1740," *The Journal of Asian Studies* 29, No. 4 (August 1970), 799–806.

Canby, Sheila, ed., *Humayun's Garden Party* (Bombay: Marg, 1994).

Chandra, Satish, "Commercial Activities of the Mughal Emperors during the Seventeenth Century," in Satish Chandra, ed., *Essays in Medieval Indian Economic History* (New Delhi: Munshiram Manoharlal, 1987), 163–9.

"Jizya and the State in India during the Seventeenth Century," in Eaton, ed., *India's Islamic Traditions*, 133–49.

Cole, J. R. I., *Roots of North Indian Shi'ism in Iran and Iraq: Religion and State in Awadh* (Berkeley: University of California Press, 1988).

Currie, P. M., *The Shrine and Cult of Mu'in al-din Chishti of Ajmer* (New Delhi: Oxford University Press, 1989).

Dale, Stephen F., *The Garden of the Eight Paradises: Bâbur and the Culture of Empire in Central Asia, Afghanistan and India (1483–1530)* (Leiden: Brill, 2004).

Indian Merchants and Eurasian Trade 1600–1750 (Cambridge University Press, 1994).

Islamic Society on the South Asian Frontier: The Mappilas of Malabar 1498–1922 (Oxford: Clarendon Press, 1980).

Dale, Stephen F. and M. Gangadhara Menon, "Nerccas: Saint-Martyr Worship Among the Muslims of Kerala," *Bulletin of the School of Oriental and African Studies* 51, No. 3 (1978), 523–38.

Dalrymple, William, *The Last Mughal* (New York: Vintage Books, repr. 2006).

De Bruijn, J. T. P., *Of Piety and Poetry: The Interaction of Religion and Literature in the Life and Works of Hakîm Sana'i of Ghazna* (Leiden: Brill, 1983).

Delvoye, Françoise 'Nalini', in *Confluence of Cultures: French Contributions to Indo-Persian Studies* (New Delhi: Manohar, 1995).

Digby, Simon, "The Naqshbandis in the Deccan in the Late Seventeenth and Early Eighteenth Century A.D.: Bâbâ Palangposh, Bâbâ Musâfir and Their Adherents," in Marc Gaborieau, Alexandre Popovich, and Thierry Zarcone, eds., *Naqshbandis* (ISIS: Istanbul and Paris, 1990), 167–207.

Du Jarric, Father Pierre, *Akbar and the Jesuits: An Account of the Jesuit Missions to the Court of Akbar* (London: Routledge, 1926).

Eaton, Richard M., *India's Islamic Traditions* (New Delhi: Oxford University Press, 2003).

Ehlers, Eckhart and Thomas Krafft, eds., *Shâhjahânâbâd / Old Delhi* (Delhi: Manohar, repr. 2003).

Elias, Jamal J., *Death before Dying: The Sufi Poems of Sultan Bahu* (Berkeley: University of California Press, 1998).

Embree, Ainslee, ed., *Târikh al-Hind* (Muhammad ibn Ahmad Biruni) (New York: Norton, 1971).

Faruqi, Shamsur Rahman, "A Stranger in the City: The Poetics of *Sabk-e-Hindi*," PDF file, Google Scholar, online.

Friedmann, Yohanan, *Shaykh Ahmad Sirhindi: An Outline of his Thought and a study of his Image in the Eyes of Posterity* (Montreal: McGill Institute of Islamic Studies, 1971).

Ghaffar Khan, Hafiz A., "India," in Nasr and Leaman, eds., *A History of Islamic Philosophy*, 1051–75.

Ghani, Muhammad 'Abdul, *A History of Persian Language and Literature at the Mughal Court* (Allahabad: Indian Press, 1929), 3 vols.

Gibb, H. A. R., *The Travels of Ibn Battuta A.D. 1325–1354* (Cambridge University Press for the Hakluyt Society, 1971).

Gopal, Surendra, "The Coffee Trade of Western India in the Seventeenth Century," Institut Français d'Archéologie Orientale, *Cahiers des Annales Islamologiques* 20 (2001), 298–318.

Gordon, Stewart, *The Marathas 1600–1818* (Cambridge University Press, 1993).

Grewal, J. S., *The Sikhs of the Punjab* (New Delhi: Cambridge University Press, 2005).

Guenther, Alan M., "Hanafi Fiqf in Mughal India: the Fatâwa-i Âlamgîrî," in Eaton, ed., *India's Islamic Traditions*, 209–33.

Gulbadan, Begim, *The History of Humâyûn (Humâyûn-Nâma)*, trans and ed. Annette Beveridge (Delhi: Idarah-i Adabiyât-i Delli, repr. 1972).

Habib, Irfan, ed. *Akbar and His India* (New Delhi: Oxford University Press, 1997).

An Atlas of the Mughal Empire (Delhi: Oxford University Press, 1982).

"The Systems of Agricultural Production: Mughal India," *The Cambridge Economic History of India*, I, *c. 1200–c. 1750* (Cambridge University Press, 1982), 214–25.

Habib, Mohammed, *The Political Theory of the Delhi Sultanate* (including a translation of Ziauddin Barani's *Fatawa-i Jahandari* of c. 1358–9 AD) (Allahabad: Kitab Mahal, 1961).

Haider, Najaf, "Precious Metal Flows and Currency Circulation in the Mughal Empire," *Journal of the Economic and Social History of the Orient* 39, No. 3 (1996), 298–364.

Hardy, Peter, *Historians of Medieval India* (London: Luzac, 1966).

Hillenbrand, Robert, "Political Symbolism in Early Indo-Islamic Mosque Architecture: The Case of Ajmir," *Iran* 26 (1988), 105–17.

Hope, Laurence (Adela Florence Nicolson), *The Garden of Kama and Other Love Lyrics from India*, 3rd edn. (London: William Heinemann, 1927).

Jackson, Peter, *The Delhi Sultanate: A Political and Military History* (Cambridge University Press, 1999).

"The Mongols and the Delhi Sultanate in the Reign of Muhammad Tughluq (1325–1351)," *Central Asiatic Journal* 19, Nos. 1–2 (1975), 118–57.

Jahangir [Mughal emperor], *The Tûzuk-i Jahângîrî* or *Memoirs of Jahângîr*, trans. Alexander Rogers, ed. Henry Beveridge (Delhi: Munshiram Manoharlal, repr. 1978).

Kazemi, Ranin, "Morality and Idealism: Abu'l Fazl Baihaqi's Historical Thought in *Tarikh-i Bayhaqi*," unpublished MA dissertation, The Ohio State University, 2005.

Keay, John, *India: A History* (New York: Grove Press, 2001).

Khan, Iqtidar Alam, "State in Mughal India: Re-Examining the Myths of a Counter-Vision," *Social Scientist* 29 No. 1/2 (January–February 2001), 16–45.

Khwaja Nizam al-Din Ahmad, *The Tabaqat-i-Akbari*, trans. Brajendranath De, ed. Baini Prashad (Calcutta: Asiatic Society of Bengal, 1937).

Khwând Shah, Mu'in al-Dîn b. Sirâj al-Dîn, *Ganj-i sa'adat* (a 1663 Naqshbandi treatise dedicated to Aurangzib), cited in D. N. Marshall, *Mughals in India: A Biographical Survey* (New York: Asia Publishing House, 1967), I, No. 1297a.

Koch, Ebba, *The Complete Taj Mahal* (London: Thames and Hudson, 2006).

Mughal Architecture (Munich: Prestel, 1991).

Mughal Art and Imperial Ideology (New Delhi: Oxford University Press, 2001).

Kozlowski, Gregory C., "Imperial Authority, Benefactions and Endowments (Awqaf) in Mughal India," *Journal of the Economic and Social History of the Orient* 38, No. 3 (1995), 355–70.

Lal, Ruby, *Domesticity and Power in the Early Mughal World* (Cambridge University Press, 2006).

Laoust, Henri, "Ibn Taymiyya, Taki al-Din Ahmad Ibn Taymiyya," *Encyclopaedia of Islam* II, Brill Online.

Lawrence, Bruce, trans. and ed., *Nizam al-Din Awliya: Morals for the Heart* (New York: Paulist Press, 1992).

Leach, Linda, "A Dynastic Line from Timur to Aurangzeb," in Canby, ed., *Humayun's Garden Party*, 82–96.

Lelyveld, David, *Aligarh's First Generation: Muslim Solidarity in British India* (Princeton University Press, 1978).

Le Strange, G., *Lands of the Eastern Caliphate* (Cambridge University Press, 1905).

Lowry, Glenn D., "Humayun's Tomb: Form, Function and Meaning in Early Mughal Architecture," *Muqarnas* 4 (1987), 133–48.

Marshall, D. N., "Bidil, Mîrzâ, 'Abd al-Qadir," in *Mughals in India: A Bibliographical Survey* (New York: Asia Publishing House, 1967), I, 114–15.

Mughals in India: A Biographical Survey, Vol. I (New York: Asia Publishing House, 1967).

McLeod, W. H., ed. and trans., *Textual Sources for the Study of Sikhism* (Chicago: University of Chicago Press, 1984).

Metcalf, Barbara Daly, *Islamic Revival in British India: Deoband 1860–1900* (Princeton University Press, 1982).

Minault, Gail, *The Khilafat Movement: Religious Symbolism and Political Mobilization in India* (New York: Columbia University Press, 1982).

Mirza, Muhammad Wazid, *The Life and Works of Amir Khusrau* (Delhi: Idarah-i Adabiyat-i Delli, repr. 1974).

Moosvi, Shireen, "The Silver Influx, Money Supply, Prices and Revenue Extraction in Mughal India," *Journal of the Economic and Social History of the Orient* 30, No. 1 (1987), 47–94.

Moynihan, Elizabeth B., ed., *Paradise as a Garden In Persia and Mughal India* (New York: Braziller, 1979).

O'Hanlon, Rosalind, "Manliness and Imperial Service in Mughal North India," *Journal of the Economic and Social History of the Orient* 42, No. 1 (1999), 47–93.

Okada, Amina, "Kesu Das: The Impact of Western Art on Mughal Painting," in Ashok Kumar Das, ed., *Mughal Masters* (Mumbai: Marg Publications, 1998), 84–95.

Indian Miniatures of the Mughal Court (New York: Harry N. Abrams, 1992).

Pal, Pratapaditya, *Indian Painting* (Los Angeles: Los Angeles County Museum of Art, 1993).

Parihar, Suhbash, "A Little-Known Mughal College in India: The Madrasa of Shaykh Chillie at Thanesar," *Muqarnas* 9 (1992), 175–85.

Pearson, M. N., "Shivaji and the Decline of the Mughal Empire," *Journal of Asian Studies* 35, No. 2 (February 1976), 221–35.

Pinto, Desidero, "The Mystery of the Nizamuddin Dargah: The Accounts of Pilgrims," in Troll, ed., *Muslim Shrines in India* (New Delhi: Oxford University Press, 1989), 112–24.

Pottinger, Henry, *Travels in Beeloochistan and Sinde* (London: Longman, 1816).

Pradhan, Mahesh Chandra, *The Political System of the Jats in Northern India* (Bombay: Oxford University Press, 1966).

Quereshi, Regula Burkhardt, *Sufi Music in India and Pakistan* (Cambridge University Press, 1986).

Rahman, Munibur, "Tâlib Âmulî," *Encyclopaedia of Islam* II, Brill Online.

Rana, R. P., *Rebels to Rulers: The Rise of Jat Power in Medieval India, c. 1665–1735* (New Delhi: Manohar, 2006).

Rashdi, S. Hussamuddin and Muhammad Sabir, eds., *Diwan of Bayram Khan. Introduction by Mahmudul Hasan Siddiqi* (Karachi: The Institute of Central and West Asian Studies, 1971).

Raychaudhuri, Tapan and Irfan Habib, eds., *The Cambridge Economic History of India*, I: *c. 1200–c. 1750* (Cambridge University Press, 1982).

"The State and the Economy: The Mughal Empire," in *The Cambridge Economic History of India*, I, 172–93.

Richards, John F., *The Mughal Empire* (Cambridge University Press, 1994).

"Mughal State Finance and the Premodern World Economy," *Comparative Studies in Society and History* 23, No. 2 (1981), 285–308.

Robinson, Francis, ed., *The Cambridge Illustrated History of the Islamic World* (Cambridge University Press, 1996).

"Ottomans–Safavids–Mughals: Shared Knowledge and Connective Systems," *Journal of Islamic Studies* 8, No. 2 (1997), 151–84.

The ʿUlama of the Farangi Mahall and Islamic Culture in South Asia (London: Hurst & Co., 2001).

Schimmel, Annemarie, *The Empire of the Great Mughals*, trans. Corinne Atwood (London: Reaktion Books, 2004).

Seyller, John, "The Inspection and Valuation of Manuscripts in the Imperial Mughal Library," *Artibus Asiae* 57, No. 3/4 (1997), 243–9.

Sharma, Sunil, *Amir Khusrau: The Poet of Saints and Sufis* (Oxford: Oneworld, 2005).

Persian Poetry at the Indian Frontier: Masʿūd Saʾd Salmân of Lahore (Delhi: Permanent Black, 2000).

Shokoohy, Mehrdad, "Architecture of the Sultanate of Maʿbar in Madura and Other Muslim Monuments in South India," *Journal of the Royal Asiatic Society*, 3rd Series, I, Pt. I (April 1991), 75–92.

Singh, Khushwant, *A History of the Sikhs* (Princeton University Press, 1984).

Steel, Richard, and John Crowther, "Journey of Richard Steel and John Crowther, from Ajmeer in India to Isfahan in Persia, in the Years 1615 and 1616," in Robert Kerr, ed., *A General Collection of Voyages and Travels* (Edinburgh: Blackwood, 1824), 206–19.

Taknet, D. K., *Industrial Entrepreneurship of the Shekawati Marwaris* (Jaipur: Taknet, 1986).

Thackston, Wheeler M. (trans.), *The Baburnama* (New York: Modern Library, 2002).

Thapar, Romila, *Somanatha* (London and New York: Verso, 2005).

Troll, Christian W., *Muslim Shrines in India* (Oxford University Press, 1989).

Verma, Som Prakash, *Mughal Painters and Their Work: A Biographical Survey and Comprehensive Catalogue* (Delhi: Oxford University Press, 1994).

Welch, Anthony, and Howard Crane, "The Tughluqs: Master Builders of the Delhi Sultanate," *Muqarnas* 1 1983), 123–66.

GENERAL

Allsen, Thomas T., *Culture and Conquest in Mongol Eurasia* (Cambridge University Press, 2001).

"Mongolian Princes and their Merchant Partners, 1200–1260," *Asia Major*, 3rd Series II/2 (1989), 83–125.

Baer, Gabriel, "The Waqf as a Prop for the Social System (Sixteenth to Twentieth Centuries)," *Islamic Law and Society* 4, No. 3 (1997), 264–97.

Blair, Sheila S., and Jonathan Bloom, *The Art and Architecture of Islam 1250–1800* (New Haven and London: Yale University Press, 1994).

Chittick, William C., *Sufism* (Oxford: One World Publications, 2000).

Ibn Arabi Heir to the Prophets (Oxford: One World Publications, 2007).

Coulson, Noel J., *A History of Islamic Law* (Edinburgh University Press, repr. 2006).

Daftary, Farhad, *Ismailis in Medieval Muslim Societies* (London and New York: I. B. Tauris, 2005).

Dale, Stephen F., "Ibn Khaldun, the Last Greek and First Annaliste Historian," *International Journal of Middle East Studies* 38 (2006), 431–51.

Ernst, Carl, *Teachings of Sufism* (Boston: Shambala Publications, 1999).

Fakhry, Majid, *A History of Islamic Philosophy* (New York: Columbia University Press, 3rd edn. 2004).

Farooqi, N. R., "Six Ottoman Documents on Mughal–Ottoman Relations during the Reign of Akbar," *Journal of Islamic Studies* 7, No.1 (January 1996), 49–61.

Fletcher, Joseph F., "Integrative History: Parallels and Interconnections in the Early Modern Period 1500–1800," in Beatrice Manz, ed., *Studies on Chinese and Islamic Central Asia: Collected Articles of Joseph Fletcher* (Aldershot: Variorum, 1995), 1–35.

Goldstone, Jack, "The Problem of the Early Modern World," *Journal of the Economic and Social History of the Orient* 41, No. 3 (1998), 249–84.

Gross, Jo-Ann, "Multiple Roles and Perceptions of a Sufi Shaikh: Symbolic Statements of Political and Religious Authority," in Marc Gaborieau, Alexandre Popovich, and Thierry Zarcone, *Naqshbandis* (Istanbul and Paris: ISIS, 1990), 109–21.

Gulchin-i Ma'ani, Ahmad, *Karvan-i Hind* (Tehran: Intisharat-i quds-i razavi 1369/1970), 2 vols.

Halm, Heinz and Angelika Schefter, "The Islamic Law Schools up to the End of the Samanid Dynasty," in *Tübinger Atlas des Vorderen Orients (TAVO)* (Wiesbaden: Dr. Ludwig Reichert Verlag, 1977).

Hillenbrand, Robert, *Islamic Art and Architecture* (London: Thames and Hudson, 1999).

Hitti, Phillip H., trans., *An Arab-Syrian Gentleman and Warrior in the Period of The Crusades: The Memoirs of Usamah Ibn Munqidh* (New York: Columbia University Press, 2000).

Hoexter, Miriam, "Waqf Studies in the *Twentieth* Century: the State of the Art," *Journal of the Economic and Social History of the Orient* 41, No. 4 (1998), 474–95.

Ibn Khaldun, *The Muqaddimah*, trans. and ed. Franz Rosenthal (Princeton University Press, 1980), 3 vols.

Joseph, Suad et al., *Encyclopaedia of Women in Islamic Cultures* (Leiden: Brill, 2003–06), 6 v.

Lapidus, Ira, *A History of Islamic Societies* (Cambridge University Press, 2nd edn. 2002).

Lewis, Franklin, *Rumi Past and Present, East and West* (Oxford: One World Publications, 2005).

McNeill, William H., *The Age of the Gunpowder Empires 1450–1800* (Washington DC: American Historical Association, 1989).

Mahdi, Muhsin, *Ibn Khaldun's Philosophy of History* (London: George Allen and Unwin, 1957).

Nasr, Seyyed Hossein, and Oliver Leaman, eds., *A History of Islamic Philosophy* (London: Routledge, 2001).

Necipoğlu, Gülru, "Framing the Gaze in Ottoman, Safavid, and Mughal Palaces," *Ars Orientalis* 23 (1993), 303–42.

Nicholson, Reynold Alleyne, *The Kashf al-Mahjûb: The Oldest Persian Treatise on Sufism* (London: Luzac, 1976).

Studies in Islamic Mysticism (Cambridge University Press, repr. 1967).

Peters, R. *et al.*, "Wakf (A)," *Encyclopaedia of Islam II*, Brill Online.

Preiss, Reuven Amitai, and David Morgan, *The Mongol Empire and Its Legacy* (Leiden: Brill, 1999).

Rachewiltz, Igor de, "Personnel and Personalities in North China in the Early Mongol Period," *Journal of the Economic and Social History of the Orient* 9, No. 1/2 (November 1966), 88–104.

"Yeh-lü Ch'u-Ts'ai (1189–1243): Buddhist Idealist and Confucian Statesman," in Arthur C. Wright and Denis Twitchett, eds., *Confucian Personalities* (Stanford University Press, 1962), 189–216.

Rashîd al-Dîn ibn Tabîb, *The Successors of Genghis Khan* (New York: Columbia University Press, 1971).

Rosenthal, Erwin J., *Political Thought in Medieval Islam* (Cambridge University Press, 1968).

Saliba, George, *Islamic Science and the Making of the European Renaissance* (Cambridge, Mass. and London: MIT Press, 2007).

Schimmel, Annemarie, *Mystical Dimensions of Islam* (Chapel Hill: University of North Carolina Press, 1975).

Stierlin, Anne, and Henri Stierlin, *Islamic Art and Architecture* (New York: Thames and Hudson, 2002).

Tibi, Amin T., ed. and trans., *The Tibyan* (Leiden: Brill, 1986).

Van Der Veer, Peter, "The Global History of Modernity," *Journal of the Economic and Social History of the Orient* 41, No. 3 (1998), 285–94.

Index

CPSIA information can be obtained at www.ICGtesting.com
Printed in the USA
LVOW07s0714250815

451382LV00016B/257/P

9 780521 691420